The Best of Ascent

THE BEST OF
ASCENT

Twenty-Five Years of the
Mountaineering Experience

edited by
Steve Roper and Allen Steck

Sierra Club Books
SAN FRANCISCO

The Sierra Club, founded in 1892 by John Muir, has devoted itself to the study and protection of the earth's scenic and ecological resources—mountains, wetlands, woodlands, wild shores and rivers, deserts and plains. The publishing program of the Sierra Club offers books to the public as a nonprofit educational service in the hope that they may enlarge the public's understanding of the Club's basic concerns. The point of view expressed in each book, however, does not necessarily represent that of the Club. The Sierra Club has some sixty chapters coast to coast, in Canada, Hawaii, and Alaska. For information about how you may participate in its programs to preserve wilderness and the quality of life, please address inquiries to Sierra Club, 730 Polk Street, San Francisco, CA 94109.

Copyright © 1993 by Sierra Club Books

Library of Congress Cataloging-in-Publication Data

The Best of Ascent : twenty five years of the mountaineering
   experience / edited by Steve Roper and Allen Steck.
     p.   cm.
   ISBN 0–87156–517–X
   1. Mountaineering.   2. Rock climbing.   I. Roper, Steve.
II. Steck, Allen.   III. Ascent (San Francisco, Calif.)
GV200.B516   1993
796.5'22–dc20   92-24722
                                                           CIP

Production by Amy Evans
Cover design by Mark Ong
Book design by Mark Ong

Frontispiece photograph: In the Needles of South Dakota. Steve Roper.

Printed in the United States on acid-free paper containing a minimum of 50% recovered waste paper of which at least 10% of the fiber content is post-consumer waste.

10 9 8 7 6 5 4 3 2 1

Contents

Foreword

I remember clearly the day in 1967 when I held a copy of the first *Ascent* in my hands. I was torn between delight and disapproval. The thing was unmistakably beautiful, and beyond that, impressive: it was a luxury to turn the pages and stare and skim. But there was something scandalous about treating climbing as if it were a fine art worth celebrating with big photographs on glossy stock.

"Slick" was the adjective we eastern-trained climbers immediately slapped on *Ascent*. No wonder that it came out of California, land of Sierra Club Exhibit Format books, of the Beach Boys, of movie-star politicians. Most of us took photos when we climbed, but the impetus was documentary, not artistic. That a mountaineer caught by the lens in midmove might form an arresting image; that a climb recounted in stream-of-consciousness narrative might get at the truth of the deed of ascent—these were radical premises in 1967.

And then there was the price of *Ascent:* by the second issue it had risen to a daunting $2.50. A climber had to think hard before plunking down so much cash for even the most handsome publication. If memory serves, you could buy two Bedayn carabiners for the same sum.

Looking back a quarter-century later at the first issues of *Ascent,* I am smitten by the prescience of the endeavor. To an eye grown jaded with the Lycra narcissists heel-hooking 5.13 that decorate every climbing mag today, the early issues seem not slick at all as much as funky and fresh. It took Allen Steck, Steve Roper, and the other editors a while to figure out what *Ascent* ought to be. They published their share of bad poetry, and it wasn't until the eighth issue that they gave up the odd practice of publishing guidebook notes on recent climbs in the Sierra Nevada.

But from the very start *Ascent* had what you can only call—forgive the much-abused word—a vision. If I had to paraphrase that vision, it would go something like this: "Look, we know that climbing is the greatest thing in the world—maybe the only thing. But it's dangerous too, not because you can get killed, but because it's subversive, useless, wacko. That's what we want to sing about—not the latest international expedition to Everest." *Ascent* had everything to do with the counterculture, which we knew breathed the same ether as wafted around our beloved crags. Before *Ascent* we had no medium—certainly not the pages of the august and taxonomic *American Alpine Journal,* nor those of the homely-hearty *Summit* or *Appalachia*—in which to declare our passion.

Michael Chessler of Chessler Books says that a 1967 *Ascent* goes nowadays for eighty-five dollars. No other mountaineering journal of comparable vintage fetches anything near that price. The closest rival is the first issue of *Vulgarian Digest.* And though in appearance the two publications were at polar opposites (*VD* had shoddy rag paper and muddy snapshots), the same zest and authenticity coursed in the veins of both: through satiric japery and lyric flights, the two magazines celebrated climbing as it really was.

The early issues of *Ascent,* one realizes with mild astonishment today, contained a fair number of the articles and illustrations that have come to be canonic, even legendary, in the genre. I think of Royal Robbins's "Tis-sa-ack," Jeff Long's "The Soloist's Diary," Warren Harding's "Reflections of a Broken-Down Climber," Ed Drummond's "The Incubus Hills," and Roper's "Dresden," among many others. In the superbly printed photos of Ed Cooper and Tom Frost, the mountains for the first time looked as thrilling on the page as we knew they were in the flesh.

One of *Ascent*'s fortes was its portraits of climbers. In its pages I first got to see what some of my heroes—Joe Brown, Dougal Haston, and Tom Patey—actually looked like. The 1971 cover, which featured Yvon Chouinard's great photo of Doug Tompkins soloing a Scottish gully in a storm, was the first picture I ever saw that captured the grim exhilaration of climbing through the worst the weather could throw at you. On the lighter side, the spoofs by Joe Kelsey and the wonderful cartoons of Sheridan Anderson gave voice to the rich whimsy that laces our sport.

Having served as a contributor (and briefly as book-review editor) over the years, I caught glimpses of the heroic and unpaid labors of Steck and Roper to put together their quirky and inimitable "book." (Roper confesses, "Well, we got a few hundred dollars to cover expenses. Wine *is* an expense, after all.") Over the phone Roper was always moaning, "Where are the good writers? We just can't find any." Steck would cajole, "Can you get something for us out of so-and-so. Of course, we can't pay beans." Meanwhile, they took chances: commissioning long works of fiction, going to pricey hardback and once-every-four-years publication, or putting a microphotograph on the cover.

Their care and craft have made *Ascent* what it is: not only the finest mountaineering journal of the last quarter-century, but the most influential. As we pause to salute this phenomenon in 1993, let us reassure Steck and Roper that all their toil and sweat and hangovers were worth it. Climbers will be reading future issues and this anthology long into the twenty-first century.

David Roberts

Introduction

Twenty-five years? Impossible, say our friends, colleagues, contributors. Impossible, we agree. But that's how long *Ascent* has been appearing. As the world of climbing has changed, our magazine-turned-book has evolved in mysterious ways, for, needless to say, we have gone through a few metamorphoses ourselves.

When we began *Ascent* in 1967, only a few thousand oddballs did time on the cliffs and glaciers. Today, 150,000 Americans, mostly "normal" folk, call themselves climbers. This burgeoning population we welcome—with certain mixed feelings. How should we deal with our ever-changing constituency? Should we ride the tides of new fads such as sport climbing? If we don't, are we risking the danger of sinking into the sea bed to become fossils?

This volume of *Ascent* will look and feel different to those who have held previous issues in their hands. Partly because of a budget crunch at the Sierra Club, this is the first of the thirteen issues to appear in a small format. And our once-heralded photographs are now smaller and fewer in number. Is this the end of *Ascent* as we know it? Yes and no.

For our twenty-fifth anniversary issue we have decided to treat our readers to some of our favorite articles from previous issues. Most of these *Ascent*s are extremely hard to find. Of the twelve prior issues, only two remain in print today. We tend to hold a wake when a particular number of *Ascent* goes out of print, an event that happens with regularity: the demise of a work that doesn't sell is as natural as death itself. Young climbers have often approached us, wondering where they could pick up—cheaply, of course—a 1969 issue or a 1971 issue. As David Roberts points out in his foreword, these early issues are not cheap. So we end up photocopying and mailing the particular article our supplicants desire. And mourn once again.

With exceptions explained later, we are reprinting material from the ancient, out-of-print issues. The vast majority of the selections we chose first appeared in the 1960s or 1970s; only a few articles from later issues have been included.

The decision to reprint articles was easy in theory, difficult in practice. Which articles to choose? Since we chose them all in the first place, we obviously like them all. We mourn anew, for several of our favorites have been omitted because of our desire to have chapters that reflect themes or localities. Some of these chapters were so swollen with potential pieces that our list changed weekly.

Although we think we have fielded an excellent selection, it's clear that this book could have been twice the size. We'd like to apologize to the authors we've neglected: we thought about your article, pondered chapter organization, and fretted about redundant subjects. And in the end we decided we just couldn't use it.

For those faithful individuals who have memorized previous issues of *Ascent,* we present eight new pieces. These, mostly appearing in Chapter 8, range from a winter ascent of Denali to a light-show climb of the Petit Dru to adventures in outer space.

Again and again during our selection process we debated a central question: what makes a climbing article memorable enough to consider it worth reprinting? An excellent writer who chooses a compelling subject is off to a good start, obviously. But timing is important also. For instance, Chuck Pratt's "View From Deadhorse Point" came out just as climbers became aware of the potential of the nearly uncharted desert region. And the marvelous literary essays of David Roberts struck a nerve precisely because climbers were just then beginning to contemplate the subject we are discussing here: what constitutes good climbing writing? Pratt's article made us want to leave for Shiprock the next day; Roberts's pieces made us want to read one of his recommended books—or even start writing one of our own.

Another criterion for excellence is, oddly, somewhat the opposite of timely: timeless. The articles mentioned above were timely, yes. When one reads them years later, however, what emerges is the authors' sense of thoughtfulness about climbing. They instinctively homed into the verities of the sport: the fear, the exhilaration, the solitude; and they seemed to convey the feeling that the *essence* of climbing does not—and will not—change.

A great article, then, is both timely and timeless. And we can add yet a third criterion: influential. An article that is remembered years later is an influential one.

We are proud, in turn, to have influenced a few writers who have since become well respected. Doug Robinson may have been the first. He was a shy college kid when we first met him in 1968; now his fluid prose is known to many, and he will soon have a book out for our pleasure. Edwin Drummond, Jeff Long, Ron Matous, David Roberts, and Galen Rowell also appeared in *Ascent* early in their careers. If we can't claim to have "discovered" these craftsmen, then at least we helped them get through those difficult periods—the teenage years, so to speak—known to all writers. Among other authors who enhanced our lives and those of our readers are Geoff Childs, John Daniel, and Joe Fitschen. We regret that we don't have the room here to publish pieces from these three writers—or others.

In 1967 we weren't thinking of nurturing writers; we simply wanted to publish dramatic pictures and soulful articles. And we were certainly thinking of doing this only for a few years, not a few decades. We had lots of help at first: the following editors, unpaid and sometimes unappreciated, came and went during the initial years: Edgar Boyles, Glen Denny, Dave Dornan, Joe Fitschen, Chuck Pratt, David Roberts, Jim Stuart, and Lito Tejada-Flores. These talented people went on to become professors, writers, filmmakers, photographers, and mountain guides, and we hope they remember their halcyon days at *Ascent*.

Over the years we grew from a forty-eight-page magazine to a hardcover book. Along the way we lost our California provinciality—and certainly some of our quirkiness. During the 1980s, with the arrival of a fine new group of climbing magazines, we changed our focus from topical nonfiction to fiction. We deal further with this intriguing subject in the introductions to Chapters 5 and 8.

Our focus has also changed regarding photographs. Magazines nowadays publish so many remarkable color photos that by now readers are surely jaded. Words, if eloquent and sensitive, can convey the nuances of climbing in a way that a photo of an athlete on a 5.13 overhang cannot. We have long been enthralled by the psychological aspects of climbing, and words, we feel, are the most evocative way to describe these. Still, we mourn the loss of the high-quality, full-page, duotone shots we featured in our early issues.

This volume has been arranged into eight chapters, organized, as mentioned, by either theme or location. In each chapter the pieces are arranged chronologically so that readers can follow the progression of techniques and attitudes over the years.

The initial chapter contains stories about Europe, the cradle of mountaineering. In Chapter 2 we head for Yosemite, the site of the renaissance of American rockclimbing. Chapter 3 concerns the high Himalaya: off the hot granite and into the world of frostbite we go. In Chapter 4 we can relax and laugh. Our early fiction occupies Chapter 5, and this is followed by a chapter that contains essays, polemics, reminiscences, and reflections. Chapter 7 brings us home to adventures in North America. In the final chapter we present new fiction, previously unpublished and full of thought-provoking motifs.

At the end of this book we present two appendixes: the first describes the contents of the previous twelve issues; the second catalogs our contributors over the years. We hope these lists bring back memories to our long-term readers—and aid future researchers.

Will there be another *Ascent?* Time will tell. We would like to continue, but we need material. We'd appreciate hearing from poets, artists, and women writers, along with our more traditional writers. We know you're out there. Please contact us early in 1994 for contributors' information at 335 Vermont Avenue, Berkeley, CA, 94707.

Again, we'd like to thank our readers and our contributors for making the past quarter of a century a rewarding time. To the men and women at the Sierra Club, people who recognize what the word "tradition" means, thanks. Dave Brower and Will Siri, geniuses both, were instrumental in getting the first issue started. Later, though *Ascent* rarely made a penny for the Club, the Publications Committee and the editorial staff supported our labors, rarely complaining, rarely interfering.

This particular volume was helped along the way by Jim Cohee and David Spinner, our Club editors. Marcella Friel read all the pieces, old and new, and tried to establish consistent spelling as well as straighten out syntax and grammar, two matters we didn't pay much attention to in the old days.

And finally we must thank Jon Beckmann, the Club's main book man, who, during lunches in San Francisco's delightful restaurants, counseled us, soothed.our feelings, explained our lack of royalties— and, of course, footed the bill.

Steve Roper
Allen Steck

1

TALES FROM THE
OLD WORLD

Editors' Introduction

Over the years *Ascent* has endeavored to include stories and illustrations relating to mountaineering in Europe. Our mountaineering heritage, after all, has its origins in the mountain regions of Western Europe and the crags of the British Isles. The historian Ronald Clark, in *A Picture History of Mountaineering,* suggests that the Golden Age of Mountaineering "begins in the early 1850s and ends with the conquest of the Matterhorn by Edward Whymper in 1865." Whymper's memoirs, titled *Scrambles Amongst the Alps,* appeared in 1871, about the time when the English pioneers of Alpine climbing were showing interest in their own hills.

Many of us associated with *Ascent* began reading the writings of Whymper and his young contemporary, Albert Mummery, early in our climbing careers. Gradually we learned of later ascents that had been made during the 1930s and 1940s on the great limestone cliffs of the Dolomites and the Kaisergebirge, and on the icy ridges and gullies of the Bernese Oberland and Chamonix. We were drawn to these exciting events because the raw action of extreme rock and ice climbing paralleled our ambitions. The climbs of Cassin, Comici, Gervasutti, Heckmair, Kasparek, and Preuss quickly became legendary. We learned of these ascents from friends in Europe and from Giusto Gervasutti directly when his writings were translated into English in 1957.

When the Sierra Club funded *Ascent* in 1967 and we began selecting material for the first volume, Gervasutti naturally came to mind. His book *Gervasutti's Climbs* (published posthumously in 1947 as *Scalate nelle Alpi*) covers his career from his earliest adventures around 1930 through 1942. Some of his climbs are impressive indeed: among them are the second ascent of Pointe Croz on the north face of the Grandes Jorasses in 1935 (just hours after the first-ascent party had completed the route) and the first ascent of the Gervasutti Pillar on the Frêney face of Mont Blanc in 1940. We chose a short excerpt from his book for our first issue—and this volume—not only for its gripping account of a solo climb, but for the author's evaluation of his motives for climbing.

It would be unthinkable to produce a best-of-*Ascent* volume without a contribution from the English writer Edwin Drummond. Many of his stories and poems have landed on our desk over the years, but "The Incubus Hills," the story of an ascent of a seacliff on an island off northern Scotland, remains a dynamic, classic tale. Drummond's prose is rich in imagery, and though occasionally mannered and cryptic, it has a refreshing and vigorous flow to it. *Ascent* editors once argued that Drummond is "the only true successor to Scotland's immortal Robin Smith as a creative climber/author . . . his style and goals have always seemed off-beat, out of the mainstream of British climbing . . . and though his climbs, like his prose, have aroused controversy, several must be recognized as masterpieces."

Back to the mainland we go for our next story. The remarkable sandstone towers of the *Elbsandsteingebirge,* along the Elbe River in what was once the repressive East Germany, are the focus of Steve Roper's "Dresden." Visiting this region in 1973 as a guest of Fritz Wiessner, Roper fears he is being touted to the local tigers as the "Yosemite Star." His humorous account is written in a modest, engaging manner, and one does learn that he indeed was a "Yosemite Star," if not an *Übermensch,* and that he performed his role adequately.

This extensive *Klettergarten* had a decisive role in the early development of a new mountaineering specialty at the turn of the century: pure rockclimbing. The early pioneers were already climbing in the 5.9 range in the early 1900s and making elegant first ascents in the Dolomites as well. Notable among these early climbers was an American, Oliver Perry-Smith, whose climbing exploits are still part of local lore. Later, in the mid-1920s, Wiessner perfected on these vertical cliffs the skills that would assist him in his remarkable mountaineering career. The local masters climb today at a remarkably high standard, often barefoot, and are guided by an ethical system more rigorous than exists in any other climbing area in the world.

Our last selection, "Man Meets Myth," concerns an early American ascent of the north face of the Eiger. Ron Matous describes the route in an introspective, soulful manner as he and his partner struggle past place names that define the locations of all the tragedies played out on this vast wall. Contemplating the definable, visible obstacles on the Eiger's huge face is fearful enough even without climbing into its cold embrace with all the myths as an additional emotional burden.

A Moment of Suspense

Giusto Gervasutti

The little train ambled along; the ascent was too steep for its worn-out pistons, and it gasped and spluttered its way up the valley. Sitting in a corner of the practically empty coach, I turned over in my mind the impulses which had brought me to the hills and I dreamed of climbs to come. I had set out alone, as I often did that year. My aim was modest . . . to lose, on the heights, all those evil humours accumulated during the long monotonous hours of city life; to find serenity . . . in the long silent communion with the sun, the wind, the blue sky, in the nostalgic sweetness of the sunset . . . no softer or more passive view of life could make me change my mind. I reached the little station in darkness, and as I wanted to reach the hut that same night I looked on the list of paths for the distinctive mark to follow. After wandering for a while among the pines and on the higher pastures, taking twice the normal time, I knocked at the door of the hut at two in the morning,

The Vajolet Towers, Catinaccio region, northern Italy. ALLEN STECK.

drank two steaming grogs, and then lay down full dressed on one of the bunks to rest for a couple of hours.

I left the hut at dawn. As the slope grew steeper I made my way up lightly with the cool mountain air giving me that delicious sensation of floating. My body was tingling with a wonderful sense of well-being, and ready to rise to whatever demands I made on it.

The weather had not completely cleared: wisps of mist curled round the yellow towers, alternately masking and revealing them, ghostly, distant, higher and bolder than in real life. I climbed up a grassy ridge, treading on a staircase of tufts, then on scree, slithery and exhausting like all Dolomite scree, but short, and so came to the foot of the climb where I changed my nailed boots for espadrilles. I took the rope from my sack and slung it round me, but I had neither pitons nor hammer, for I knew that on the descent I should find rappel loops already in position. Leaving sack and boots under a boulder, I approached the rock.

It began by a not very difficult vertical crack. I touched the rock with my hand, almost stroking it, as one strokes something one loves but has not seen for some time. It was still cold, but when I looked up the sun—seen through the mist, a yellow disc with a halo round it—had already appeared above a jagged ridge. Everything round me was quiet, with the rather startled silence of high places. I rubbed my foot two or three times on a polished bit of rock, as though to test its adherence, then I raised my arms in search of holds for my hands and, bracing my muscles, began to climb. I moved very slowly, without the least hurry, quietly looking for holds, studying each move so as to economize effort to the full. When a climber is on his own he can't afford to make the slightest mistake, for if he does, there is no friend to encourage him. And if danger suddenly strikes, all he can do is to risk everything; but if he loses, it is his life that is forfeit.

All went well for about four hours, and the higher I climbed, the more impressive appeared the vertical wall beneath me. Down below, very far below, the last scattered fir-trees appeared as minute dots against the grassy ridge.

I had done about three-quarters of the climb, and was in a chimney blocked by an enormous chockstone which I had to get over. I went up with my legs wide apart, arrived beneath the chockstone, got round it by wriggling my body between it and the wall and then, raising my hands, I took hold of it. I now had to swing out under the overhang and mantelshelf up. Kicking off with my feet, I made the effort.

But I had miscalculated. My chin came only on a level with the edge and I looked about for other handholds, but higher up the chockstone was rounded, smooth and polished without the vestige of a crack. So I let myself down slowly, trying to get my feet back onto their holds, but as my face was right up against the rock, I could not see. Beneath the overhang was the chimney, dropping down into space. I tried in every direction; it was no good, although my feet did come in contact with the rock, I couldn't find the holds. I realized then that if I did not get up at once, all was over: the drop to the scree was getting on for 1,000 feet. I gave a spring and pulled up again on my fingers, but I could not get beyond the point I'd already reached. A shiver ran down my spine. Again I made the effort, even using my teeth to get a hold, with no other result than a bloody mouth. I slipped back, still clinging with my finger-tips to the sloping edge, and stayed there, panting, for a few minutes; and while I tried unsuccessfully to find a reasonable way out of this fix, my strength began to ebb. My fingers were gradually slipping from the holds, and I could no longer see or think. Then, in a fury, I succeeded in giving a heave that brought my chest above the upper edge of the chockstone. For a fraction of a second I managed to hold myself in position with the help of my chin while I reversed one hand and got it palm downwards on the rock. I transferred my weight to it, holding on by friction, gradually pushed myself up and, with a final effort, got my body on to the chockstone and lay down, utterly exhausted. When the trembling caused by nervous reaction began to subside, I sat up and looked down into the valley. Everything was just as it had been before. In the stillness of the air there was nothing to give away my presence. The grey mountain was indifferent. The valley floor was green and peaceful. Even the wind had died down. It was I, and I alone, who had sought this moment of suspense, created it, compelled it. Everything round me was motionless and static, had played no active part. And again the question surged up: "Why?"

No answer came—perhaps it never would. But when I reached the sun-flooded summit, with waves of floating mist beneath me, my heart sang for joy. The exaltation of that moment, out of the world, on the glory of the heights, would be justification enough for any rashness.

Reading through these lines, written many years ago about a venture of my younger days, I have often asked myself the same question: "Why?" And I know now how impossibly difficult it would be to give any clear answer.

There are many people more competent than myself, at any rate in the art of writing, who have tried to give an answer, without much result beyond the controversies they have stimulated. I find it entirely natural that such attempts to define mountaineering should have produced no satisfactory result. For there is no such thing as objective mountaineering, there is only a form of activity, generically termed mountaineering, which enables certain people to express themselves, or gives them a means of satisfying an inner need, just as there are other forms of activity and other means by which other people may try to attain the same ends.

Of course, since the need is completely different for each individual, we have many forms of mountaineering. It may take the form of a need to live heroically, or to rebel against restraint and limitation: an escape from the restricting circle of daily life, a protest against being submerged in universal drabness, an affirmation of the freedom of the spirit in dangerous and splendid adventure. Or it may well be the pleasure of physical fitness and moral energy, elegance of style and calculated daring; ordeals gaily faced with friends themselves as firm as rock, the hard life of the high huts, the happy relaxation on remote pastures as one smokes a pipe or sings mountain songs. It may be the search for an intense aesthetic experience, for exquisite sensations, or for man's never satisfied desire for unknown country to explore, new paths to make. Best of all, it should be all these things together.

It follows that, at a certain moment one's personal preference for a particular line is bound to lead to the formation of a set of values. When a man, rising above the banality of his everyday existence, tries in one way or another to create for himself a higher mode of life, there are generally two possibilities open to him: either the way of pure imagination, or some mode which can be transformed into reality through action.

The first is generally considered the superior; but to be able to endow pure thought with a value, one must be a poet and an artist. Only those who have attained to poetry can allow themselves the luxury of giving a universal value to the creations of their imagination, while remaining comfortably in their armchairs. But the others, and among them mountaineers, if they do not wish to limit themselves to the pleasures of imagination, must seek the satisfaction of their spirit's needs in action, and this satisfaction will be greater, and more complete, in proportion to the intensity of the action.

In other words it seems to me that the contemplative side of mountaineering can only have an interpretative value, and that the ecstasy of creation can come from action alone.

1967

The Incubus Hills

The Long Hope route on St. John's Head,
Hoy, Orkney Islands

Ed Ward Drummond

THURSDAY, JULY 23, 1970: THE END

He was furious. His eyes marbled in a big rage like some Beethoven
in heat as he pounded at the pitons I had almost welded into the perfect
fault. The crack diagonaled the wrong way, overhung like drunk and
forced him to use his wrong arm. But all the time he was really laughing. We were nearly there.

The sense of awe was still bossing me as I stood on a cat-thin ledge
and the wind hunted around me under the arches and pillars of rust
sandstone. It was as though the whole wall were slowly toppling over
into the crystal shattering sea. I remembered the time I saw on a television newsreel a helicopter lowering the spire onto a rebuilt church
steeple. The helicopter suddenly stalled, buckled, and dropped the

mere two hundred feet to the ground, killing the pilot and his mate. I was twelve at the time.

A minute would pass while his left arm dripped hammer blows. Now we were limpets on the S.S. *Great Britain,* stuck to the prow of Brunel's great boat in white charge at the world's seas. The boat had recently come home to Bristol, which was where he and I began to climb in 1964.

It became evident to me that one of my strongest reasons for asking him to come on this climb was his inexperience. He seemed to guarantee failure without danger to my fantasy. But he didn't play it that way and I still find it hard to believe that he was that hard, was that mad.

At last. I welcomed him like a long-awaited guest to my belay. He was a long time coming but left no pins I saw as I took a long last look before stepping onto the last pitch. I saw green and nodding cotton grasses, the green grass waving only a hundred feet away at the summit place. At last.

THURSDAY, JULY 16: THE BEGINNING

From leaving Jack Rendel's farm, swaying like camels under our masters, up the incubus hills, it took us two days to set foot on the untrodden beach of St. John's Head. We had logistical piles. And after our minstrel from Afreet Street, Tony Greenbank (Greensleeves), left us, we hung our hammocks for the darkless night, then donned monk-cowled black anoraks for a walk along the beach. Like two unfrocked priests leaving by the back door of St. Peter's, we felt we were being watched as we upped and downed over bus-big boulders to grab a look at the West Wall. This was to take us to the North Face. Up there.

FRIDAY, JULY 17

I have a dream that one day I shall wake from a bivouac feeling like a child. Not this day. Oliver gets out first to brew tea-bag tea with tit-sweet condensed milk, making me feel like I've never been gone. But I have to and on the first pitch from the stonehenged beach in grizzling rain the cold gnaws my fingers to their bones and I nag him for slowness, and as well blame him for a haul caught so tight that the wind blows an organ note on the steel perlon, bringing tears to Quasimodo's eyes. The thought of a week on this wall is intolerable and at the end of the first pitch, begging but he doesn't hear me, I give him the opportunity to call it off, to give me a sanction. But he just blasts me for playing Grand Master chess with nuts, gets there, and I creep off on the second pitch. Which isn't too bad and brings me to Hog Ledge, vast and almost empty of the fowl that foul. And a roof over our heads. While the tomato soup warms I sloth around the edge of the roof smashing brittle plates at the lip, and fix a pitch really lonely once I'm out of his sight. Get back, last light, a dim darkness, lips kissing hot soup in instant pleasure. At night the wind fills my scarlet hammock like a vast kite and my mind rides out.

SATURDAY, JULY 18

Oliver is out first and brews tea like wine. The gull chick whose mother had fled on our arrival has died in the motherless night. Heading north we cannot stop and to keep the heart warm I knit at the rate of twenty-five feet per hour for four hours, through a craze of traverses to land on a lawn, greeted by a hand of fat butterflying puffins, nodding like dons in the afternoon sun. Fifty feet higher we sleep on lush grass, the House of Lords that night. Herring fillets, dried bananas, and a reading from James Baldwin's *Tell Me How Long the Train's Been Gone* and we doze in ermine.

SUNDAY, JULY 19

Above us the wall won't go away. Until one lowers the eyes. Tongue rattling nineteen to the dozen when we see what's looking down at us. On the sea below hangs the shadow of an axe. I saw it last year but with the wuthering we've had since we began this is the first time it's come out to watch us crawl.

Two easy pitches on grassy slabs then I'm off up rock so perfect we call it Tuolumne Wall after a California meadow that we know. While we are in such chorus Greensleeves appears on Lookout Point and we blow kisses across half a mile. Last Thursday, on the beach, as he turned to go he said to me, "Good luck, Marra (a coal miner's term for his pit mate), see you at the top in a week." It sounded like a prison sentence in my ears and my enthusiastic "Sure man" worried me. Later this day I climbed the Vile Crack. The Vile Crack is one hundred feet long and the width of a full-weight boxing glove. Boots skinheading, you have to fight it with slow uppercuts. One could have done without the roller skates on the boots, though boxing gloves would have helped.

Then a leftward traverse on a ledge of windowsill thickness where my never-bending finger enables me to place a protection peg for Oliver. Then, using a box spanner for a bolt holder as the proper one broke when we were trying it out on the beach, I place belay bolts and rappel back to the Commons where vile gulls greet me with spits of hot yellow vomit. Not until the next day do I discover the value of a handful of dirt down their throats as an antiemetic.

During the night it rains and my hammock weeps. A year previous to this I had been at this same bivouac with three rare lads: Jack the Sprat, Leo the Lionheart, and Ben (without Bill). The route (the West Face) was no plum; more of a crab apple and such taste is unusual, though crab grapes were a popular choice during the three days we spent doing the route. The experience gave me a perception of what could be tomorrow; during the night, rain and worry got into the hammock; tomorrow was almost today. Perhaps today will not be like that.

MONDAY, JULY 20

But it is. I wake up in a carriage of the last train to Belsen. Oliver has a cup of wine for me that tastes like tea and the train leaves without me. Then I prusik on a not-quite-empty stomach. Jumars would be easier, somebody says. One is not amused and goes on, knocking sleep from elbows and knees. Then he comes, so you photograph and try to forget. Above us sway weird flakes and horns of rock, a kind of right-left Unconquerable. While I'm arming up it I keep saying "The Wipe-Out Flake" to myself, but like me it does no more than rattle when I put a fist deep inside, making it clear its throat. One of the things that bewildered me about the route was the stability of this apparently insane flake. Perhaps real instability lies in silence and uniformity, in keeping it all quiet. At the top of the flake I blow again. I almost go crazy at this gull, which just keeps shitting at me. Not content with a four-foot deadly puke, rotating like a flywheel it must thrust its feather-fringed arse at the pole of my face and let fly. Then it whips around and pukes, the whole action taking less than three seconds. Christ I went crazy. I mean I was scared. The rock was dust in my hands and my

Oliver following on the Long Hope Route. ED WARD DRUMMOND.

protection below me was, well, below me. I don't remember how I got away. The vomit, dyed into my stockings (which I was, of course, wearing over my face) never will, and the memory is now precious. So we go on to fresh insights and foolishness.

Higher, just before an elbow of overhanging rock, I find myself praying like a miser and I seek charity with a four-inch bong. Pleading, this fourth day ends forty feet higher on Hanging Garden Ledge where we are able to boil water, which we spice with antiseptic to lave our cut, tattered hands.

It was good to be there that night. At sunfall we saw the puffins, tipsying and hurrying, innumerable as bees around the summit of our world. Blackbodied, white-chested, with orange nut-cracking beaks, nibblers of each other. We even talked of finishing, I did.

TUESDAY, JULY 21

This day was bloody awful. Branding-iron winds burnt the cheeks, and mad mists hid the tearing sea as I stumbled out on an easy ledge traverse past frozen birds with their gull-cold looks. In the middle of the ever-narrowing north wall I crept around a decrepit roof while Oliver trembled. Jammed nuts for aid and the wind was banging me about. The wind was gale force that day; we felt it, later we learnt it. It butchered us and I shall never forget Oliver's face, cold-purpled like raw meat, his mouth a kind of wound as he tried to complain. I found it hard to moan that day as the sight of Oliver suffering did something to me. Three pitches and already we were wondering where to sleep to escape the arctic lick. On I go up the three Giant Steps, each eight feet high. Then I have to crawl left forty feet on my stomach inside a two-foot cleft. This was comic relief indeed as my bundle of iron traveling horizontally across Oliver's line of vision was all that could be seen. But once a gargoyle peered down, mouth full of fear. I knew what I had seen and I did not want to sleep there. Surreal it was, oh hell, for real. I was under the thumb that night and I had a bad time. Worrying that the cleft itself might close, that tomorrow would never come, and that when it did I would not be able to face it. We slept in the gutter and I ate a tin of salmon, my last food, and the tin slept by my head. Sure we had water for tea, but the wind blew away the flame and someone turned out the light. Self-pity fanned to seething anger. I tried to use Oliver as some kind of shield from the wind but it didn't seem to make much difference. Hell, we weren't married.

WEDNESDAY, JULY 22

Corpse prostrate, we shared his food. Dark in here, out there the day beamed and we beamed too. If he resented sharing his food he didn't show it. The wind had dropped, the night was over. I felt it had to be the summit today. Nailing up this brittle crack in the wall, only way to go, I placed a bolt in case the insane flake above me would not be trod on. Above me to the right the fifty-foot roof of the northwest arête prowered; altogether elsewhere. Not that way but this and I had no choice but to edge up to what, in my mock mockery of the night before, I had called the Guillotine. A fifteen-foot blade of red dark sandstone, tapering like a knife from five feet to six inches at the end I had to stand on.

The thin crack I am knifing in dies, so I ask for it and climb out of the trench of my aid slings and start running. Oliver is getting smaller; freezing me with a stare that is not nice and I can no longer hear what he is saying as his voice shrinks to mind size. My ropes run under the flake, butter to knives if this breaks. Fall forever, or run forever?

I keep running, the bolt kit is in my hand and I'm smashing at the door crying to be let in when the key breaks in the lock and hands are around my throat and everything goes black very quickly.

I have no choice, have I? There is a limit. That's it, we go down. I shout across to Greensleeves that I cannot go on because . . . he cannot hear me. Oliver finds it difficult to refuse; at least he can hear. But his anger shows he does not realize the vitality of bolts, I mean how vital bolts are, I mean would have been. Anyway.

Then I hear this voice. Some kind of male witch in hot gloat. "At last. So this is what you're really like." I feel like I've been caught masturbating in church. "This is what you are." And it hurts me a lot and I wonder whether my climbing is some kind of suicide; whether I am about to kill myself. Can a man know that he is mad? Perhaps I have gone, and I scream "Who's that? Stop it." And I scream it again and Oliver has come back. He's looking at me like that.

I do not know. I did not know then. How I went on but I went on. The black bag around my head burst and I did murder to get at the crack too far above my head and my fist locked solid. Then I'm away in this fist-thick crack, forgiveness making me sweat. Oliver royaled up, "Those skyhooks are flashing." In fact they winked twice, but I'm married and he isn't and it's easy to confuse a flash with a wink. Perhaps fear is the possibility of ecstasy. Oh we warbled. Then I reached, and prayed, and hooked and pleaded on fingertips, scratching to reach

Thank God Ledge, invisible from below, where, being numbered among the angels I just Enoch-Powelled my head off for a full five minutes. Boy, I was beating my chest.

I hauled our home and Oliver came up for air like he's being born, saying he doesn't know how. We were eatless that night but content, and while the sun hung about on the edge, curious, I walked out in its last light and found a thin thread of a crack in the sheerness. Impregnability perfected by a single perfect flaw.

THURSDAY, JULY 23

We drink scalding hot orange at dawn, sweet like a thin syrup with the last of our sugar in it, while gently we talk hopefully of food and success. I dreamt of her in the night. That hadn't happened for years. Swaying up the final leaning wall I feel the privilege of the lookout in the crow's nest on a whaling ship when he sights the whale first. Oliver scarecrow, below, out to my left on the bivouac ledge; peering, waiting. "Do you think you'll ever come here again?" He doesn't hear me. Tomorrow, next year. "Will you ever come back?" But he doesn't hear.

1971

Dresden

Steve Roper

I had slowed down, no doubt about it. Climbing less than once a month, and nothing very demanding at that, had made my muscles flaccid, my brain porous. Other (read *safer*) interests, coupled with far too much wine, had interfered with a solemn promise made to myself fifteen years previously: *I love climbing, it is the best of all possible activities, and I will climb, climb, climb for the rest of my natural life.* So I had to smile a wry smile when I was asked along on a climbing trip to East Germany by a man who for over fifty years had actually obeyed this credo. Fritz Wiessner, before I was even born, had climbed in Asia (reaching 27,500 feet on K2), made numerous short forays into the Alps, and put up about fifty new routes in North America, among them Waddington and Devil's Tower. But of all the places Fritz had been there was one that he loved above all others: Saxon Switzerland, a hundred-square-mile area along the banks of the Elbe River near Dresden. He was born in this incredibly lovely place in 1900 and by the age of eighteen was already leading some of the hardest climbs of the region.

The name Saxon Switzerland is misleading. It does, in fact, lie in the state of Saxony, but whoever bestowed the rest of the name must never have seen Switzerland, for there is no permanent snow and the highest point fails to attain even two thousand feet. The German name for the area, *Elbsandsteingebirge,* seemed too hard to say, so I began to refer to the region simply as Dresden. It is hilly country and the river makes very lazy turns through forests and fields. Occasionally a ridge of sandstone has been eroded by the Elbe and it is here that the climber pauses. The rock is a dense and noncrumbly variety of sandstone, much more akin to that of El Dorado Canyon in Colorado than to the towers of the American Southwest. About five thousand routes have been established on the nine hundred–odd pinnacles. Though the climbs nowhere exceed eighty meters in length, there is a great exposure and, as I was to find out shortly, great continuity. Steep and continuous. Intimidating. Scary.

Over the years I had known him, Fritz had intimated that the Dresden climbers were equal to the best free climbers in the world. A startling Dresden climbing movie he showed at the annual American Alpine Club dinner in 1967 left the audience wiping palms on pants and me feeling that Fritz might well be right. By this time I was literally off big-wall climbing, preferring short free climbs in new areas. So to me the movie offered a fascinating glimpse into what easily could become my personal mode of climbing: head for a strange area, get into shape on the old classics, swill wine and bullshit with the locals, loaf, then build up to some of the new classics. Then split. No pressures, no aid climbing, no bivouacs. An easy way to climb, you say, but it would be my *own* way.

In the winter of '68–'69 I received a letter from old Fritz: Come with me to Dresden in May. I met him in Interlaken; we gravitated south, climbing in small areas, getting into shape. Then, halfway up a two hundred-meter wall in the south of France, Fritz began striking his chest, cursing in his gentlemanly style, and proclaiming "indigestion." Unfortunately, it was a bit more serious than that: his heart was beginning to crap out. A few months of rest and Fritz was completely recovered, but in the meantime our 1969 expedition to Saxony had met its end on the Riviera.

My next chance came in the spring of '73; Fritz was seventy-three; I felt like fifty-three (a winter of nose-to-the-grindstone hedonism had taken its toll); it seemed an inauspicious time and a team of which no one could have said—as I did in my early Valley days, in mock serious-ness—"This is the finest team ever assembled." A third member was Fritz's daughter Polly, who, during those frequent interludes when Fritz would rattle along in German to his old and new cronies, became a valued friend. Already used to climbing barefooted, Polly would fit into the Dresden climbing scene with ease.

Paranoia is not my usual state, but I had begun to have a nagging fear that on this trip I was to be exhibited as the Yosemite Fanatic, fresh from wild cracks and thousand-meter walls. So as we drove down the deserted *Autobahn* toward our destiny, I began my final harangue: Fritz, old chap, I'm in foul shape, you know; haven't even *been* in the Valley for a year, and I do *not* wish to be portrayed as the American Star, I do *not* want to get hurt, not badly, anyway, a sprained ankle would be quite nice, we could motor over to Prague and sightsee; you realize, Fritz, that I've never been in this part of the world and I'd sure hate to miss Prague, indeed, why don't we spend a few days over there when the weather goes bad as I hope—ah, I mean as it's *sure* to do sometime and there's no point in sticking around in a drizzle, right, Fritz; and by the way there's also no point in jumping right into the tiger climbs; we'll be here sixteen days, after all, and I don't really want to get hurt this far from home, Christ, I don't even speak the language, imagine a hospital stay, Jesus, they're asking me for my identity card and here I am lying here with a—Then Fritz breaks in, saying, don't worry, Steve, we can climb in the rain, it's done all the time, not the sevens of course, but the sixes, he assures me, will be in fine shape. Then I recover, seeking my manhood, saying, boy it's sure nice to be headed for a new climbing area, what are we doing tomorrow?

Tomorrow. Overcast, visibility a mile in rain and fog. I am introduced to two climbers, old types in their thirties. Günther and Friedrich give crushing handshakes while their eyes seek the secrets of Yosemite. But they're not mine to give, fellows, not any more. I'm just here be-cause . . . *because god, Roper, get a grip, quit whining. Calm your brain.*

A few easy climbs lull me into rainy-day torpor. Then, at the base of a giant overhanging pinnacle, I see a confab. I know no German, but I get the idea pretty quick. I follow their looks upward, I watch Fritz making some sort of apology (I'm not paranoid, I reiterate!), and I see an agreement reached. Perhaps this agreement has doomed me, but I have no choice. So must an unwilling bride feel as the dowry is dis-cussed. With downcast eyes I follow Günther to the rock. Then Fritz, my savior, speaks: At first you would like to follow, yes? To get used to the rock, which is much different than in your Valley.

And so the first days go by and I get into a bit of shape. I love the rock, even though Fritz thinks I prefer Valley granite. Actually, I think I climb better on almost all other kinds, and the Dresden rock is a super-rock, solid, with edges, offset cracks, flakes; beautiful. Often just Fritz, Polly, and I climb together. It is often pure joy to watch the septuagenerian climb, a half-century of technique behind him, every move precise and thoughtful, but then I feel sad when I watch once-powerful arms quiver with the strain of a pull-up. But god, if I could climb like that in 2014. . . .

The grading system used in the area is just about as inconsistent, illogical, and provincial as most other systems. Roman numerals from I to VII are used to indicate free-climbing difficulty. At some point they ran into that problem faced in so many areas: when harder climbs are done, what do you call them? Rather than go to VIII, they have subdivided the VII category into a, b, and c. Yet it seemed to me each letter represented a palpable step upward: VIIa is to VIIb as V is to VI. They can no more jump up to an VIII and a IX than the NCCS can head toward a 12. Only the Australians seem to have solved this particular problem: they have an open-ended system with no magic top number. Thus, when a climb recognized as harder than their present hardest (a 21) is done, it becomes, without controversy, a 22.

Late in the first week Fritz tells me that the breaking-in period is over; tomorrow we meet Herbert Richter, an Ex–Master of Sport, and now a physicist. He will climb with us for a week. With trepidation, I shake hands with Herbert. He looks amenable, is a bit of a clown, and speaks English to a degree. Later, Polly teaches him the phrase: 'so-and-so is lewd, crude and socially unacceptable.' He loves this, and soon I hear him muttering, in the midst of a 5.10 move, "this rock is lewd, crude . . . " A fine chap, I liked him immediately. But he *was* an Ex–Master of Sport and he was serious as hell about climbing. To be a Master of Sport (a phrase I like to roll around on my tongue much like Herbert with his lewd, crude . . .) one must climb a set number of fearsome death routes per year. Apparently Herbert hadn't done enough of these or had had a falling out with the people in charge of Sports, for he was an Ex.

Unlike the U.S. State Department, the East German regime recognizes that their hot climbers are an asset and they send them to various places within the Eastern bloc for climbing competitions and expeditions. But unlike their Polish, Czech, or Russian counterparts, they are never allowed to cross into Western Europe, and I sensed that Herbert must mourn this, that he must often have thought, My whole climbing life will be spent on these rocks, no wonder I am an expert here, but what of the Alps? I dream of the Eigerwand, the great Chamonix aiguilles; perhaps I would fail there, but how do I know? I read what I can, but we get few books here, and I have a family and cannot flee. And perhaps it is not that good outside? Herbert, I would gladly have told you of the rotten, insane, and corrupt form of government our democracy provides us with. But I'm not sure I would have liked to tell you this: We're free, man, we can travel thousands of miles with no controls whatsoever; we can climb anyplace on earth.

And so the Ex-Master and I trotted over to one of the new classics, the *Höllenhund* (the Hound of Hell), an eighty-meter wall averaging about ninety degrees. *Sieben C* (VIIc) he told me. 1967. A fine route. It was a different kind of rock from what I had already become accustomed to: it was full of small holes, tiny jugs, stalactites. It didn't look too bad. Polly and Fritz stationed themselves in relaxed positions to watch the debacle. Herbert took off, climbing flawlessly, reminding me instantly of Robbins, not particularly graceful, but super-cool, super-competent, almost arrogant in his control. And very safe. He threaded runners through holes so tiny that a seven-millimeter rope would not fit doubled. He would hover above me, clinging to pinch holds, untie a length of rope, thread it through a hole, then retie and jerk. Yeah, it didn't look too bad. I think one reason I hate to climb with guys like Robbins and Herbert is that they make it look so easy that I relax and lose the fine psychological edge which I have built up to on the approach march.

I think I could have done better if I hadn't had to stop and untie twelve jerked-taut runners. My arms ballooned and I dwelled overly long on Robin Smith's phrase, "Then my fingers turned to butter." Mine went buttery just as I lunged for his hanging belay. Jesus, I told him, good lead dad, what's it like above? The same, eh? Well, Herbert, be a good fellow and lead on, I'm wiped out, you know, jet lag and bad food, no, not bad, Herbert, just different, actually, you Germans sure know how to cook, yes siree, those giant liver dumplings are out of sight, as we say, yes sir. And so Herbert danced on, savoring his role, assuaging my inferiority complex with kind words. God, I thought, we have another week of this and my arms will be horrible tomorrow; how can I talk Fritz into Prague?

Luckily, there were a few rainy days, and Fritz took us around Dresden and reminisced: Here was where our school was, here there was a marvelous square with a fine view toward the museum. It was all *was*, for on my fourth birthday, as I was mindlessly devouring a cake, the

Allies were mindlessly bombing this most beautiful of cities. The war had only eighty days to run; Dresden was an acknowledged nonmilitary target, a cultural landmark. Nevertheless, a hundred thousand people and a city among cities no longer exist. So it goes. The damage has, of course, been swept away, but the reconstructed buildings are cheap and efficient; aesthetics have received a low priority under the present regime.

Fritz had insisted that I buy a pair of EBs for this trip and I had rebelled, of course, for one doesn't like to be ordered about, especially by a father-figure, and anyway I had a beautiful pair of RRs, perfect fit, no complaints, and here I *had* to buy a pair of weird expensive shoes. I bought them as instructed but I hated the idea. From the first day, however, the EBs were magical; it was a case of the shoe fitting the place, or however the cliché goes. I could put my foot anywhere and it would stick. So imagine my anxiety at the base of the Höllenhund when I saw Herbert strip his wretched hiking boots and strap on bizarre gauntlets of leather that covered only half his foot, leaving vulnerable the (to me) crucial part, the toes. Christ, I can't even walk barefooted along a street, and here this dude, strapping on a device best left to a porno flick, was preparing for 5.10. But East Germans have prehensile toes, it seems, and I would slack off belaying to watch entranced as those toes would sensuously seek a hold, and then I would glance down at my beautifully encumbered feet and curse, knowing that once again I'd been had. And sure enough, the magical EBs can't compare with the great toe when it comes down to a one-inch by one-inch hole in the rock.

One day I was informed that a new climber would join us. Herbert, with just the barest trace of envy, said, "It is our Star, Berndt Arnold." Your *Übermensch?* I asked, and Herbert had to laugh. Not quite the exact translation, perhaps, but we laughed a lot and it became a trip phrase. When you're among friends the language barrier is not what it's made out to be. We met Arnold at dawn at the printing shop which he runs, an inconspicuous place in a village twenty miles out of Dresden; and they told me of the Star leaving work at five and trotting a few miles to the rocks and bouldering until he was exhausted, and then the weekend would arrive and with it his comrades from the city, and he would shine and shine and was surely fated for the National Team. I must say that he was an intense climber, a Master, a true *Übermensch.* I watched from below while he and Herbert climbed a fearsome wall, a Master climb. I had begged off, so Fritz and I lay down in classically comfortable postures and watched the drama above, Fritz thinking how a few years ago he would have been first on the rope and poor humbled Roper thinking how glad he had made his feeble mark and was no longer compelled to get up there and prove his worth and, more importantly, risk his balls. But I loved watching the climbers move, and it showed me at last what Fritz had been implying all along: these fellows around Dresden are among the best free climbers on the planet.

I had been worried about the lack of protection ever since I had seen Fritz's movie. I can't say my fears were exactly groundless, but most of the climbs which I did were reasonably safe; even the hard ones I was shown looked no worse than some of the renowned modern climbs in Yosemite. A death route is, after all, a death route. In Dresden pitons are absolutely *verboten* and nuts are unknown. Thus, the only form of protection (outside of infrequent horns and holes) is the bolt. They really go in for the large, safe variety over there, I'll say that for them. Over half an inch in diameter and placed about five inches into the rock, they have huge rings into which a carabiner will barely fit. These bolts, called *Ringen* in German, rings by me, are rarely used for protection.

I must explain this anomaly. Dresden climbing often consists of short but desperate class 4 pitches. Class 4 as in 5.7 through 5.11. (Ortenburger will smile ironically if he reads this.) Each ring is a belay station, often a hanging station, for the rings are installed not so much near ledges as just before hard moves. Therefore, it can be seen that the hard moves are reasonably well protected. Sometimes the pitches are less than thirty feet in length, and rarely are they more than fifty feet.

I recall once approaching a ring, relaxing as it got closer. I became horrified to find that I couldn't let go to clip in. I really couldn't let go. Briefly I thought of continuing, but the moves above definitely appeared to justify the ring. Finally, I balanced and leaned and cavorted about and lunged for the mother. As I sat in my belay seat it came to me that it would have been impossible for anyone to have placed the thing while leading. Fritz was watching from a nearby parapet, so I asked him about this seeming paradox. In fact, I opened my mouth too quickly, as usual, and stated in unequivocal terms that it was pretty low-class to place bolts on rappel. "No, no, no,!" he shouted instantly, "We don't do that, it was placed on the lead." But, Fritz, I couldn't let go to clip in. No one could let go with both hands, for christ's sake, it's vertical. The shouting match didn't resolve itself at the time, but later in the beer parlor it turned out that these amazing chaps really *had* put them in on the lead, drilling the holes by hand—no hammers were used. The rock is fairly soft and a strong person can cling onto pinch holds while the drill is turned with the other hand. Upon getting tired,

Herbert and Berndt on steep, pitted rock. STEVE ROPER.

the driller will climb down to a resting stance. Sometimes the work is so strenuous that he must come back day after day to work on his hole. When the drill gets far enough into the rock he will rest in a seat sling from the drill itself. But after such a rest, which one gathers is not terribly long for these Übermenschen, it's off the seat, back to pinch holds, and more grinding away.

Belaying is another strange story. Pictures of Europeans belaying have always amused me, and once in the Dolomites I saw a man belaying his entire family up a class 4 pitch; he wasn't anchored, he had the rope over his shoulder, he was leaning over the void to give advice, and I fled lest I see blood splashed on limestone. I had, just the day before, watched a blind climber, and I was beginning to think that European climbing was really quite bizarre. Anyway, back to Dresden belaying. Because most of the falls are steep drops with no intervening protection, the locals have developed their own peculiar belay habits. It is difficult to recall the actual technique, let alone describe it here, but somehow the rope is placed around the waist, then twisted a few times to induce friction. It is devilishly hard to learn how to pay out rope quickly, and I was all thumbs at first. Although I was trying to adhere to the old "when in Rome" philosophy, I was a bit put off when I couldn't use my own belaying style. I knew that I would never try to force a foreigner to adopt my own belay habits, feeling that however odd his system might be, it was at least safer to let him have the obvious advantage of familiarity. Sometimes, when Herbert couldn't see me, I reverted to my California belay.

So far I have not mentioned the history of the area, primarily because I am intimidated by J. M. Thorington's excellent article in the 1964 American Alpine Journal. Briefly, though, it seems that by 1914 the hardest rockclimbs in the world were to be found in this area. Curiously, an American, Oliver Perry-Smith, was probably the best climber during the Golden Age of Dresden climbing, 1900–1914. I did only a few of Perry-Smith's routes—a bold 5.7 jamcrack flashes into my mind, but this was by no means his hardest route. My feeling is that there could easily be a 5.9 route somewhere among his thirty-two first ascents. The other great figure of these early days was Rudolf Fehrmann. He was not only a superb climber, but a visionary as well. He realized that by using artificial aids any tower could be overcome, so by means of lectures and articles he soon established the basic ground rule of Dresden climbing, which has persisted to this day: no aid climbing whatsoever. Another stringent rule was developed in those early days: only the first ascent party can place rings; subsequent ascents do it the original way or come back. Or fall. As Thorington comments, " . . . the death rate has always been high, mainly due to rope breakage and because the climber was not equal to the task."

Accidents are a regular occurrence; ropes don't snap much anymore, but arms do give out on strenuous sections and competition for the coveted Master Rating takes its toll. One day while walking along a dirt road we noticed a commotion: first-aid people gesturing effusively, revealing that orgiastic look common to ambulance drivers and rescue freaks the world over—blood, excitement, heroics. A youth had just smashed his spine on a climb we had done the preceding day. It was an unprotected 5.7 overhang with the chance of a thirty-foot drop onto a wide, hard ledge. I had been truly gripped on the thing; it hadn't looked bad, but my arms started to go at the crux move. With no finesse I adrenalined my way through, cursing Fritz, East Germany, and climbing. And the next day we had done a wonderful climb, and on top Fritz casually mentioned that his cousin had taken a one-hundred-fifty-foot groundfall here in the early 1920s. It seems the chap lost his balance on top of the slender pinnacle. You can bet I cowered low on *that* summit.

But I never got hurt; in fact I never even fell while leading. It seems that a lot of my fears are only in my head, as Dylan so sardonically puts it. Except for a few nightmarish armbusters that I *had* to do with Herbert (because they were such fine classics, I suppose), I actually enjoyed the climbing, just like I've heard can be done. It's entirely possible that I got into the best shape of my life. And as the trip came to a close, I almost wished it wouldn't. There was so much left to do. I figure I did only about thirty routes, and out of a total of 5,000 there must be about 1,000 that are really worth doing. So: nine-hundred-seventy left, thirty per trip; jesus, I might make it to the year 2014 yet.

1974

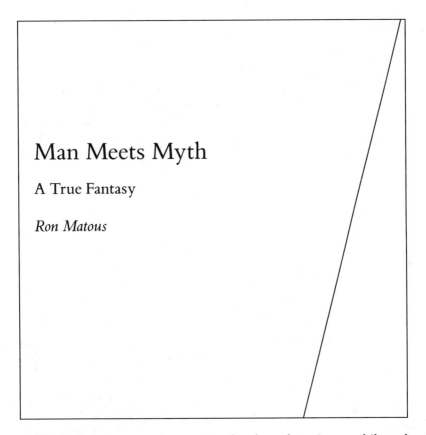

Man Meets Myth

A True Fantasy

Ron Matous

Pilgrimages are not easy to come by these days. In a mobile and iconoclastic society there are few places or objects that retain both the mystery and the historical value necessary to be worthy objects of a pilgrimage. Traveling thousands of miles to stand in awe of some revered relic is no longer considered a socially useful act. Our myths are no longer universal, shared and cherished by entire nations and dealing with themes of creation and ancient history; they have become more modern and secular, focused on shorter periods of time and events of purely provincial significance. Only erudite people now know the story of Prometheus or Ulysses; but who in this country does not know of Abe Lincoln, Mickey Mouse, or the Frankenstein monster? And for climbers, there is the Eiger. . . .

Were it not for all the tales of terror and epic struggles that have emanated from its undesirable flanks, I would never have been drawn

27

to the Eiger. And if it had not been so obscured in the mists of hyperbole and climbing history, I would have known better just what I was getting myself into that spring day when Mike Munger, possessed by a wild lust nurtured by such epics as *The White Spider* and *I Chose to Climb,* asked, "Would you like to do the Eiger?"

I quickly and truthfully answered yes, although the meaning of that affirmation was closer to "I would like to have done the Eiger" than to "I would like to try it." Still, how could a climber in search of his heritage, reared on stories of Edward Whymper and the Creagh Dhu, go to Europe without at least looking at the Eiger? There was some consolation, too, in the knowledge that the weather was usually too poor even to attempt it.

One does not go to the Alps for a wilderness experience. They are the most heavily used mountains on the planet, and have been for centuries; they were the birthplace of this strange activity we love so much, and figure prominently in mountaineering's mythology. By going to the Alps, Mike and I were engaging in a pilgrimage, indulging our curiosity, escaping the rapid flux and competition of the climbing vanguard. We were retreating to dig among our roots. The climbs we had in mind were not the modern technological horrors of the "Seventh Grade," but rather the classics whose names had existed so long in our minds that quite definite (and usually incorrect) pictures of their nature had accreted around the germinal facts.

June and July saw us in the Dolomites and at Chamonix, enjoying ourselves, doing a lot of climbing, not really thinking about the Eiger except as a place we would get to sometime during the summer, when things felt right. Every day revealed the inaccuracy of our preconceptions about Europe, but nothing tarnished the idyllic nature of what we were doing. We were simply having a good time.

As the first days of August approached, then, we were feeling very satisfied with what we had seen and done. It was time to take seriously our promise to ourselves. All that would be required to make the summer perfect was an ascent of the original route on the Eiger's north face. Not much to ask but I was still in the grip of legend, full of thoughts of the Hinterstoisser party, of rockfall, frozen ropes, sudden storms, and irreversible sections. When you go to climb the Eiger, you do not go to climb a mountain but rather to vanquish a myth, to scramble upon the stuff of legend, and to discover firsthand what you know that everyone before you had discovered—that you do not really want to be there except to make that discovery. To learn for yourself. . . .

I will not attempt to unravel the labyrinthine tangle of motivations that lead anyone to climb, least of all myself. Too much inconclusive, turgid prose has been printed on the carcasses of too many majestic trees to justify still another attempt. But what I do want to understand is not *why* but simply *what* I was feeling in the shadow of that mile-high symbol which, from the vantage point of our tent, underwent a constant metamorphosis of size, shape, color, and import, depending on the time of day, weather, and the state of my lower intestine. Because obviously it was the myth, not the reality, that was the living thing here; it was fascinating to watch the slow transformation of the one into the other as we waited, watched, and finally climbed.

After two days of hitchhiking to cover a mere hundred miles, I arrived in Grindelwald in the midst of a rare week of perfect weather. That is, it was perfect everywhere in Europe except at the Eiger, where it was raining. So already the stories were proving true: the Eiger was living up to its reputation of having the worst weather in Europe. The face itself was still hiding; I thought I knew approximately in which direction. My imagination was working overtime trying to peel back the clouds, and all the while fragments of truth gleaned from photos and books were falling together into patterns that made sense, at last, like a revelation.

All summer long the knowledge that I intended to have a go at the Eiger had been festering in the back of my mind, accompanied by the most extreme mixed feelings. There was no question that I wanted to see firsthand the Icefields, the Death Bivouac, the Traverse of the Gods, the Spider, the summit icefield. But I knew myself well enough to realize that this desire would be satisfied only by an honest attempt, and the reports I had heard of the objective dangers on the Eiger made me feel as if I were willfully throwing myself into the whimsical hands of fate. Only two weeks earlier, I learned in Kleine Scheidegg, two Germans who had successfully climbed the face were killed while descending the west flank. What was I committing myself to?

A myth. I was committed to discovering the truth behind the myth, to peeling back the onionlike integuments of human fabrication to see the face in all its stark, raving, immense beauty. I wanted to decipher the myth, undiminished even after forty years' worth of ascents.

Many climbers are in the habit of belittling the achievements of their predecessors with comments that betray a gross misunderstanding of the significance of the first ascent. To climb at the current high standards, it is first necessary to climb on the shoulders of earlier visionaries who, in turn, were accomplishing a precarious balancing act. It is a beneficial exercise in humility, when doing an established climb, to imagine what it was *really* like for the first-ascent party. I had heard plenty of disparaging remarks about the Eiger: that the ice was only fifty-five degrees, the rock only 5.5, the first two thousand feet were third-classable, the face was festooned with pitons and fixed ropes, and so forth. Now, although these comments came from people who had never set foot on the face, I did not doubt the veracity of their second-hand information. But I still suspected that they were missing some-thing, some factor lost in the analysis of the whole into its technical parts, that accounted for the ascendence of the climb into the mytho-logical realm. That factor, as it turned out, was the numinous aura of its history, which hangs palpably over the black face like an eternal storm.

My first view of the *Nordwand* (which, to perpetuate the myth, Ger-man climbers call the *Mordwand*) was by full moonlight, after the first night's rain had cleared away. It was instantly recognizable from the photos I had seen, yet it bore no resemblance to my expectations. They had been blown up out of all proportion to produce a frowning mono-lith four miles high, black as pitch and inhabited by lightning bolts, which overhung its base by three hundred feet and occasionally dis-gorged bits of climbers with a satisfied belch. In reality, however, this looked like an actual mountain, with snowfields, ridges, and a summit; the rumblings emanated solely from the regurgitating cows surround-ing my tent. There was even a light on the lower face, a sight as com-forting as a mother waiting up for her son. No headlamp was that bright, so I concluded it must mark the "railway window" I had heard so much of. (No feature of the north face causes so much perplexity among armchair mountaineers as these so-called railway windows. They have figured in many accounts of attempts, rescues, and at-tempted rescues, but I had always scratched my head and wondered just what the hell a railroad was doing up there, anyway? Certainly there was nothing in my experience to compare to it; for me the windows had been an anomaly best glossed over while I went on to the more comprehensible parts of the Eiger legend. I will not add to the confu-sion—or diminish anyone's imaginative fantasies—by an explanation here. The point I wish to make is that, on location, it was the work of a second to rectify several years' worth of sloppy conjectures.)

On the following day, now that I was aware I was facing reality instead of my preconceived notions, the north face assumed more un-derstandable proportions. It was with great optimism, therefore, that

I strolled the short distance to Kleine Scheidegg to meet Mike, just up on the train. It was difficult to keep a straight face as I passed the time watching the tourists thronging around the legendary telescope outside the hotel. (I kept looking for Clint Eastwood . . . reflecting that only since the advent of cinematography have we been able to enjoy the luxury of modeling the world after our fantasies, rather than vice versa.) Here I was laughing not at the popularized portrayals of Kleine Scheidegg but at how closely the reality resembled them. I was giddy because something was backwards here; there was some kind of cosmic practical joke being played.

During the ensuing two and half weeks there were numerous times when the Eiger briefly shed its Olympian façade and condescended to join the ranks of more mundane geographical features. That long spell of unsettled weather—it rained a little each day, and sometimes for two or three days without a break—gave me an unsurpassed opportunity to oscillate wildly between every conceivable attitude and perspective my subconscious could create. Nor were these thoughts within my conscious control; by the very act of arriving at Kleine Scheidegg I had relinquished any responsibility for the final outcome. We would remain until we could wait no longer, and if the weather and conditions allowed, we would try it, and simply climb to the best of our ability toward success or failure. We did not doubt that when the time came either to leave or to start climbing, the moment would impress itself upon us with an insistent salience that neither rationalization nor argument could alter. In order to sustain any chance at all of doing the climb, we had to relinquish control to the ambiance and symbolism of the place; otherwise, even a moment's rational consideration would have sent us packing, off to go swimming in the sunny south.

If the mountain occasionally forgot its reputation and shone in the rare light of a sunset breaking through the afternoon's accumulation of mist, there were days when the place was as uninviting as we could imagine, and it seemed that no amount of blue sky could entice us to venture into that shadowed, treacherous world from the sunlit meadows where we lay among the blueberries. Looking up at the wall from the warmth of our tent as the first rays of a clear morning burned the night's frost away was like looking at an illustrated article on the moon from the depths of a fireside easy chair.

One day, when returning from a morning's foray into Grindelwald to restock our supply of body fat, we saw the clouds part theatrically to reveal they had not been idle during the night. The entire face was moving in slow motion, as rivers of fresh snow poured down gullies and over cliffs, down icefields and into space, creeping with infinitesimal slowness down the immensity of rock and ice. It was the first demonstration we had actually had of the true scale of things here, to see what we knew were good-sized avalanches moving inexorably downward like a slow drift of dandelion puffs.

In retrospect, the chain of events that finally drove us onto the face was as carefully orchestrated as a Shakespearean comedy, and I wonder just how much of it we could even take responsibility for. On Thursday, August 19, fifteen days after our arrival, the afternoon storm clouds drew aside briefly to show us the most depressing sight our vigil had yet produced: fresh snow down to the level of the talus, a mere hundred meters above our tent. It seemed unlikely that the increasingly shorter days, even without the clouds, could produce enough afternoon sunshine to get the face back into the kind of condition we wanted for the climb. And we had been impressed enough with tales of the difficulty of retreat to be very reluctant to go up in conditions which seemed less than ideal. Unfortunately, the great fallacy in our reasoning was that the Eiger, almost by definition, is never in good condition. With little snow on the face, one is forced to climb on rock that breaks off under one's boots and rains down from above like an aerial bombardment. If there is enough snow to hold the loose rock in place, then there is enough to fill the cracks with ice and make protection and climbing difficult. In cold weather one climbs over verglas; in warm, through waterfalls. Only one thing was obvious that Thursday afternoon: we didn't want to climb while the face looked like *that*. We calculated that even with perfect weather beginning the next day, it would be two or three days before the snow consolidated enough to climb on, after which we would want three good days on the wall to be sure of success (we hoped to climb it in two, but some margin seemed desirable). This meant we were asking for six consecutive days without storms, a seeming impossibility.

So it was with a wide spectrum of emotions that I packed my gear that night in preparation for leaving on the morning train. On the one hand, I was free of the burden of commitment: we had put in our time, and if the opportunity to climb had not presented itself, it was no fault of ours. On the other hand, I was greatly disappointed, for a lot of energy had gone into anticipation, and our long period of waiting was to no avail. But rationally I had known that our chances of climbing the Eiger on this visit had been slim. People as determined as Don

Whillans had been thwarted countless times; another Englishman I spoke with had been on the face eight times, turned back by everything from rockfall to the discovery of a severed human hand. That night I fell asleep to the familiar sound of rain, confident that our decision to leave in the morning was irreproachably correct.

Imagine my dismay, then, to awaken to the clearest morning we had yet seen in Switzerland. The haze that had obscured the horizon each morning, foreboding rain, was gone; not even the wispiest puff of vapor marred the sky. By an amazing display of mental gymnastics, we dismissed within seconds all the careful reasoning of the night before in favor of the argument that, having arrived at the end of one spell of fine weather, we would never forgive ourselves for leaving at the beginning of the next. No other course of action was possible: we had to stay.

The afternoon brought a few clouds, of course, but no rain, and that was novel. We agreed to consider this day as the first of the requisite six and slept that night with renewing hopes and fears. Fortunately, we were quite used to such rapid and massive shifts of attitude, and so slept soundly despite the excitement. I wasn't ready to believe anything until I saw it.

The length to which emotions had been stretched might be measured by an event of the previous night, when we had converted a bottle that had been saved as victory wine into a bottle of consolation wine. We had also tried hard to eat the rest of our food, not wanting too heavy a load while hitchhiking. So on Friday afternoon I once more made the long trek to Grindelwald to stock up again on bivouac food, and to avoid thinking too much.

By the next morning the fact was being pounded into my consciousness: good weather. Another clear day. Our reconnaissance the previous week—we had taken advantage of a fine morning to scramble up the lower fifteen hundred feet of the face to the Difficult Crack and back—had settled us on the strategy of an afternoon approach and subsequent bivouac on a fine ledge at the base of the Difficult Crack as the most logical way of doing the climb. It was the least committing, gave us the greatest head start, and offered the best chance of being beyond the Third Icefield by two o'clock, when the afternoon sun hit the top of the face and the stonefall began. We could use the rest of the afternoon to climb the relatively sheltered Ramp. If we failed to cross the icefield by two o'clock, we would be forced to waste valuable time sheltering in the protection of the Death Bivouac.

The next question was, which afternoon to start? The longer we waited, the more ice and snow would melt out of the Exit Cracks, which we knew from our reading would be very difficult in poor conditions. But the longer we waited, the greater would be the chance of being caught in the inevitable next storm. It became obvious that we might as well begin that afternoon, Saturday. By the time we expected to reach the Exit Cracks on Monday, they would have had three sunny days in which to clear off.

Coming so soon after our unequivocal decision to return to Chamonix, this reversal of our situation was incredible. The decision to climb fell upon a mind already so numbed by two weeks of waiting and gyrating emotions that I could do no more than mechanically pack my gear, then sit down and read a book to pass the time until two o'clock, when we figured on starting. Why sit on a ledge all afternoon when we could lie in a meadow all morning? Besides, it still might rain.

No such luck. That evening found us perched upon what was to be the finest of three bivouac sites, watching the slow decline of a brilliant day. A steady curtain of meltwater pattered off the protective overhang to splash at my feet, maintaining the proper degree of moisture in the mud floor of our little cave, lest it get uncomfortably hard. I was silent and stoic, wondering with detachment just what the following days would bring. They held a magnificent potential for the profoundest ecstasy or despair; but though somehow I felt that the fate of our attempt was already ordained, with only the motions to be gone through, I was vouchsafed no clue as to what it might be either by the events of the day or by the infinitely impersonal and tranquil scene before my eyes.

We had strolled along the meadows to the base of the climb with a funereal gait, not wanting to work up a sweat or get to our ledge too early. Despite the unmatched opportunity for contemplation, I avoided it, instead disappearing into the first phase of an egolessness that my subconscious deemed essential to the success of this climb. To have allowed the face in all its domineering presence full access to my mind would have been to invite demoralization; to succeed, a businesslike attitude was required, dealing with each pitch or problem as it arose because, unlike the monstrous whole, no single one of them seemed insuperable.

A surrealistic note of undivined significance crept into that first afternoon, when we passed the railway window near the Shattered Pillar. A wooden door set into an oval cement frame faced us incongruously like a gateway to some other world. Inside, a short passage revealed the railway tracks slanting steeply upward parallel to the face and a scant ten feet within. On the wall next to the track an electric bulb illuminated a placard reading not "Abandon hope, all ye who enter here," as I half expected, but "Open All Year Round" in four languages. For our benefit, or the passengers'? I'll never be sure. The line dividing fantasy from reality became even thinner.

As we slowly pieced together the climb over the next two days, one pitch at a time, the last traces of our quotidian existence disappeared, and each ropelength occupied our entire consciousness. As we climbed higher and farther from the possibility of retreat we must have become slightly mad, seeing nothing but the next difficult step, knowing nothing but a need to go up as going down became more improbable. At our second bivouac, high on the Ramp, we were at least a day's journey in either direction from safety. Yet sitting there on a small ledge, I could hear the cowbells below us as if they were again just outside our tent.

So far the weather had been excellent, and we had encountered nothing to make us despair of success. At that point, in fact, we had to succeed or die trying, for it seemed it would be equally difficult to reach the summit or the bottom safely; this saved us the trouble of thinking about retreat. Exhaustion and dehydration actually saved us the trouble of thinking at all; we had elected to save weight by not taking a stove, but had been unable to get close enough to any of the afternoon drips to replenish our water supply. Eating snow was not enough to slake our thirst, and a liter bottle of packed snow, slept with, produced a measly third of a liter of liquid for breakfast. We consoled ourselves with optimistic thoughts of being free from suffering in only one more day.

Conditions on the climb turned out to be vastly different from anything we had been led to expect. The preceding two weeks of storms had plastered the wall with ice and hard snow, which made the icefields a romp but the rock pitches extreme. If there were fixed pitons, most of them were buried, and so were the cracks. The Hinterstoisser Traverse was an eighty-degree wall covered by three inches of ice. A nagging fear occupied us: the Exit Cracks might be even more difficult than we were prepared for.

As it happened, they were. A third bivouac was needed only two pitches from the summit icefield, among a discomfiting proliferation of clouds. As the sun set, we found ourselves in a forty-five-degree ice gully capped by overhanging rock. The route above looked dubious at

Mike Munger leading the Ice Hose. RON MATOUS.

best and ridiculous to attempt by headlamp. We set to work chopping a foot-wide ledge in the ice on which to spend the night; in the process the pick of my axe snapped cleanly off, leaving me aghast but not terribly chagrined. I still had my North Wall hammer and knew that no more steep ice lay ahead. But the Eiger had given us a glimpse of its unforgiving nature and it had more to show.

The afternoon clouds had been thicker than usual, but as darkness fell they seemed to disperse, and the stars felt close. Despite my fettered position, I slept for a few hours. A strange vision woke us around midnight: a helicopter flew in slow passes over the meadow far below, using a searchlight beam which must have illuminated a square mile with the brightness of the sun. Had some of the sacred cows escaped? We were at a loss otherwise to explain this bizarre activity at such an absurd hour. After half an hour it disappeared over the horizon, still unexplained.

I dozed for a few more hours, but awakened finally to see, with bitter, deep despair, the thunderless play of lightning on the predawn horizon. Wouldn't it be getting light soon? In a heavy storm I knew it would not matter, for we would not be able to move. I heard Mike shifting position and knew he was also watching.

For a long while neither of us spoke a word, feeling like a couple of kids caught stealing candy. We should have known. How could we have expected to get away with a fifth day of good weather?

Again I had the sensation of being in a movie, so carefully orchestrated was this dramatization. After an hour or so the lightning, which had slowly been drawing closer, simply stopped. I thought I detected the first graying of dawn; there were stars too; a clearing.

Then, unexpectedly, it started to snow. Dense, round pellets of graupel tapped on my parka. Lightly, then it stopped. Lightly again, then heavier. I took out my cagoule and pulled my bivouac extension up to my shoulders. It snowed harder, and after five minutes I began to hear snow slithering down our gully in a dry stream. Piling up against our backs, it began forcing us off our ledge. Quickly I stood up, brushed off my ice ledge, and sat again. After that I had to arise every few minutes if I wanted to retain my perch. The snow kept funneling down, pouring over us. It was getting light enough to see, and across the upper face I could see the snow torrents that we had watched with such smugness from the valley not long before. We were thankful to be so high, near the top of this avalanching face, and glad our gully was topped by an overhang.

I would have been much happier, though, if we had not been there at all. If only we had made it up those last two pitches of the Exit Cracks the day before; if only it was not so obvious that we were stuck, quite indisputably, at least until the end of the storm. The Exit Cracks had produced the most difficult climbing we had yet seen. The rock was coated with ice, the cracks were filled with snow, and fixed pitons (if the tales were true) were buried until spring. Now the last two pitches, which looked harder than anything below, had been converted into snow chutes for the summit icefield to shed its load. Having sat through two weeks of stormy weather in the meadow, we found little reason for optimism about the length of this storm. I sat there, still warm and dry but with the snow pouring around me, thinking only of the struggle ahead.

With the stage so carefully set, with our emotions so precisely manipulated to a perfect tragic pitch, the punchline was delivered. The snowfall stopped, the clouds parted, and our reprieve was granted. Although the day was not clear, it was without immediate threat. Light usurped the place of darkness. We sensed that the storm had been obligatory, but not malevolent. To have climbed the Eiger without encountering a storm would have been close to sacrilege. We gathered the remnants of our wits, shook ourselves off, and slowly undid our elaborate bivouac preparations. This was no easy task: imagine two people on a one-by-four-foot ledge, putting on boots (oh, think of the consequences of dropping one!) and crampons. The rope had been thoroughly soaked by the soggy snow of the preceding afternoon and now it held its shape quite stubbornly. We bent it into a coil of sorts that would fit into Mike's pack and removed the still-dry nine-millimeter rope to use on the remainder of the climb.

One never gets away with anything in the cosmic perspective. Those last two pitches took us as many hours, and even having arrived on the summit icefield Mike couldn't rest his nerves: he was faced with an imaginary belay on two inches of ice while I sweated up the last and hardest pitch with as much tension as he dared give. What comes next, I wondered?

What came next were waves, billows, a veritable tsunami of relief. Emerging from the top of the gully, I saw only the lower-angled snow that curved back toward the summit, five hundred feet above. With the suddenly increasing certainty of success (and, by implication, survival), the consciousness of my life and its joys came flooding back into a numb mind that for three days had repressed all thoughts not essential to the task at hand, pouring the salve of ecstasy over the jagged harshness that had become my world.

We took great care traversing the narrow summit arête and descending the sodden snows of the west flank. Our lives, for so many years taken for granted, had been revealed as fragile things, and like works of glass we guarded them carefully against even the minimal dangers of the descent. Much more awaited us in the meadows now than we had left behind.

There was no sudden revelation, no lightninglike flash that I could point to along the way as the moment at which it happened; nevertheless, the myth and I had each subsumed the other, and both emerged quite changed. The battle had raged not on the face, but in the unknown vortices of my own mind. The mountain, except for a piton or two we had to leave behind, was unchanged. But I had not been climbing on the mountain. I had been climbing on some vast accretion of stories, childhood fantasies, rainy-afternoon daydreams, and photo books. Never again could I see or think of the face in quite the same way or read those accounts with uncorrupted innocence. Lying in the meadow the afternoon after the descent, I tried hard to revive the awe that had dominated me in that very spot just three days earlier. It was not possible. Despite all I had gained, there was also the feeling of something lost.

1980

2

IN THE VERTICAL
PARADISE

Editors' Introduction

During the Golden Age of Yosemite rockclimbing—roughly 1957 to 1972—untouched granite walls loomed everywhere above a mere handful of resident climbers. By and large, Californians plucked the plums, for at the beginning of this era outsiders rarely visited the area. One reason was that few locals wrote about their achievements. Most were either too busy climbing, too antiestablishment to care, or too awed by the Ivy League cliques back east who in the 1950s, because of their historical dominance, still ruled American climbing.

But in 1963 a visionary youth named Yvon Chouinard broke the ice by writing an intriguing account of Yosemite Valley's climbing significance for the *American Alpine Journal,* which at the time was a staid eastern journal. This seminal piece, "Modern Yosemite Climbing," coupled with the appearance of Steve Roper's guidebook the following year, soon attracted climbers. A fresh group of pilgrims meant a fresh group of writers, and within a few years some began to describe the charms and horrors of the incomparable granite gorge.

Naturally, the young, active California climbers who edited *Ascent* followed the events in Yosemite with extreme interest, for it didn't take much foresight to figure that the Valley was playing a pivotal role in the history of rockclimbing. In our first issue we ran a short vignette by Ian Howell, an Englishman who had visited the Valley at a time when foreigners rarely made the long, expensive journey. Impressed with the infamous slippery cracks of Yosemite, Howell called his progress up them "more like swimming than climbing." A statement like this undoubtedly attracted more climbers, eager to prove him wrong.

Of our early Yosemite writers, Royal Robbins was an *Ascent* favorite. A daring and immensely talented climber, he wrote with intimate passion about his achievements. Although Robbins was heckled for baring his soul—sometimes he committed the crime of using Shakespearean imagery—these criticisms usually spewed forth from those who didn't know King Lear from King Kong.

Robbins prided himself on his ruthless honesty about the feelings and motives of climbers who performed at the ragged edge. The two pieces by him featured here exemplify this genre. In "The West Face" he not only portrays a splendid new route on El Capitan, but captures in the process the nuances of Yosemite's most renowned funny man, TM Herbert. In "Tis-sa-ack" Robbins narrates with infinite patience the tale of a partnership turned sour. The background: in 1968, Robbins, Chuck Pratt, and Dennis Hennek attempted a new route on the vertiginous face of Half Dome but failed after a few days. The following year, Robbins and Don Peterson completed the route, but not without personality conflicts. The author, in a typical paroxysm of self-examination, attempts to reconstruct the thoughts of his various companions.

By the mid-1970s climbers from around the world poured into Camp 4, the dusty, boulder-speckled campground favored by the rock jocks. Free-climbing standards rose with astonishing rapidity. But the days of solitude and anonymity diminished quickly as rockclimbing made its way toward acceptance and popularity. We were lucky to have had a perceptive observer on hand during this period of transition. Eric Sanford's "Spring Weekend Love Affair" asked cogent questions about the direction Yosemite climbing was going. These questions and their variations, we hope, are still being discussed around the campfires of old Camp 4, now called Sunnyside.

Ascent, of course, was not alone in relating the wonders of Yosemite. Galen Rowell issued an anthology of Valley articles in his *Vertical World of Yosemite.* Chris Jones's *Climbing in North America* contains an excellent chapter on the Valley and its denizens. But oddly enough, the best in-depth portrayal of Yosemite climbing to date is by a German mountaineer, Reinhard Karl. Perhaps an outsider was needed to put Yosemite and its absorbing history into perspective. Unfortunately, his eloquent and astute book, *Yosemite: Klettern im Senkrechten Paradies (Yosemite: Climbing in the Vertical Paradise)* has not yet been translated from the German, except for a chapter *Ascent* translated and published in 1989.

Our final author in this section, Dick Shockley, came to El Cap's Salathé Wall as a pilgrim; he left as a convert. He would have us believe that he "cruised" the wall, but if you read between the lines you'll find that simply because an ascent is routine doesn't mean it's not ultimately rewarding.

The West Face

Royal Robbins

Live it up, fill your cup, drown your sorrows
And sow your wild oats while ye may,
For the toothless old tykes of tomorrow
Were the tigers of yesterday.
   —*from a song by Tom Patey*

Some people are bothered by thoughts of decay and death. Not me. Rather, I am obsessed. Death . . . decay . . . decay and death. Herbert is similarly obsessed. Which is part of the reason we are friends. I know of no man so aware of human suffering, so conscious of the pitiable absurdity of the human condition. I know of no man more loyal to a friend, no one more quick to be outraged and sickened by human cruelty. But Herbert doesn't dwell on these things as I do. He reacts by laughing. Or rather, by making others laugh. He never tries to be funny. It erupts like a spring gushing from the mountainside. Herbert is a great pop artist, and he was one long before that neologism gained currency. He has an amazing ability to distill the essence of contemporary life and spit it at you, and you roar until your sides ache, all the while crying softly inside. Herbert is like a laxative; he helps you get rid of excrement of the soul.

The first sketch of Yosemite, drawn in 1855. THOMAS AYRES.

When Herbert isn't joking on a climb, you know he is scared. Chouinard has told of one climb where Herbert was astonishingly serious: the eight-day ascent of the John Muir Route on El Capitan, the most adventurous ascent on rock ever accomplished by Americans.

But the west face of El Capitan. "Oh yes, just where *is* it?" "Well, it's sort of hidden up behind the west buttress. You can see it from the tunnel, but it doesn't show its style."

The west face loses dignity being juxtaposed with the west buttress and the majesty of the Salathé Wall. A couloir slicing up its left side robs it of symmetry and never does it strike the eye of the casual observer. But the golden age of Yosemite climbing is past, and the less attractive walls are being sought out and stripped of their virginity, one by one. Finally the siren call of the coquettish face reached the ears of would-be hard men festering on the floor of Eden.

The crabs of our predecessors hang like earrings from the arch above. Wrong way. Dead end. We sally from a ten-ton boulder on the right. White crystalline granite passes beneath me as I swing up to the right on good holds. And then a ladder of nails back left. A knifeblade straight up and then . . . nothing. Except a little ledge too far away. Too far? A wall-clinging claw on a two-foot wire-extension ladder spans too-far distances. Then all it takes is courage. That's what hurts. Rationalization helps—there's a good piton down there somewhere. Slowly ease onto the hook and toes are soon on the ledge and the hook again bites rock. Five more feet. A flake tries to become a nutcracker. Five feet more. A slow way to make two thousand. Pitons, and the rock thunks like a watermelon. Fear, coolness, and caution. Then it gets better and I reach a small ledge—my home for three hours.

Angry jumars bite the cord of life as Herbert comes up. Grim jazz above—an eighty-foot flake that may try to speak as pitons are driven into its mouth. A few gentle nuts help. An hour closer to eternity, Herbert reaches the end of the crust of rock. Nowhere to go I think but he miraculously moves left with nuts, runners, and body English. Then a blank section. Herbert tries vainly to get around it, over it, under it. No go and a bolt's the answer. Brute force focuses on a point as Herbert pricks the skin of El Capitan. Soon he's up and the hour is late. Two quick pitches and then we sleep. Is the hundredth bivouac different from the first? Warmer. But what will tomorrow bring?

A crag, that's what. We're at the base of a three-hundred-foot arch. We must pass it. That means surmounting an overhang beetling with convolutions and jutting corners. In other words, a crag. And we are cragsmen! Much better to be a cragsman than a mere rockclimber. A crag still has the air of adventure about it. A rockclimb is mostly technique nowadays. So we go crag climbing, First it's back and foot, then bridging in a shallow groove. Loose rock is treated gingerly and the key is a slotted nut at the lip of the overhang. The door opens and it's a new world—firm rock, cracks, hollows, spikes, and knobs. Joy comes in a rush as the muscles work swinging upward in balance past an occasional runner. The easy going is interspersed with bits of questioning calling for quirky answers. A hand jammed and the opposite foot set high in a hole and move up in one fluid motion pivoting and changing the jam to a lieback and reaching for the next spike above. When you do it right, it *feels* right.

Herbert leads the next pitch and belays in slings, his first but not last hanging belay on this climb, for there were five altogether and Herbert got every one. Typical Herbertean luck.

Then a long and interesting pitch with three rurps in a row— hatchet-faced little quarriers biting into a thin line barely there. But not biting deeply. I dare not use them one at a time but spread my weight always on two. With great relief I slip a nut in a tiny slot right on the surface of the crack that would take no more rurps. Another door is opened with thirteen nuts, four runners, and twenty-five pitons.

Then Herbert has cake—easy nailing for a hundred feet to a good ledge he can't use for there is no anchor. So long-faced, rubber-faced Herbert swings in slings two feet below. I told you he was lucky.

The next pitch is a bit fussy to begin—not too bad but a fall would be a thirty-footer with nothing between us but a rope and hope. Better not to fall. Instead of falling, I nail right fifty feet, pegs barely nose-nudging in, lots of air, thin air, below. Where does this fifty-foot road lead? Nowhere and everywhere. I turn a corner and belay in a niche. Herbert comes and goes—diagonal and down. A rappel brings us to the El Capitan Arms which seems, considering the tearful aspect of the sky, as good a place as any to stop for bed and breakfast.

That night the sky cried and so did Herbert. Naturally, his cagoule leaked. In the morning the rain continued, and we waited patiently, almost hoping it would not stop so we wouldn't be bothered *trying*.

But about noon the rain turned showery and dribbled off into mere gloomy vapor which closed about us and hid the wall and all. Our excuse for lethargy gone, we bestirred ourselves, and Herbert nailed upward into the mist muttering and wondering where he was going but eventually getting there and so did I joining him in his hanging belay. The deceitful fog now led us astray. I climbed a splendid pitch of aid and free using nine natural runners on chockstones and horns. It's such a great pitch I wish others might do it. Unfortunately, it ends in a blank wall. I had already hit the drill twice when I spied a horn thirty feet away. That's where I should have been. For fifteen minutes I played cowboy, finally looping the knob. Thus another bolt that almost was, wasn't. Herbert cleaned that pitch spic and span and then it was down the elevator to the Arms to sit in the last golden rays and gaze westward. Gaze and think of the beauty of the Incomparable Valley and all the small beauties there: the white granite warmed by the sun, the sweet smell of the pines, the pungent odor of chaparral, the wind blowing through the meadows, and the birds—the boldness of the jay, the hesitancy of the robin, the near-foolish trustfulness of the grosbeak . . . these beauties . . . get them by heart, as the poet said. Ah, Jeffers, had you sung the Sierra you would have sung it as well as your beloved Coast Range. The Sierra too has its hawks. And they too are free and so were we. The beauty of that red sun in the west had set us free. We were as free as children. We forgot to get it by heart.

We were awake and chewing beefstick when the red firs and sugar pines above Ribbon Fall turned golden. And as another day slowly exploded into being we performed the abhorrent ritual of ascending our fixed lines. In Yosemite you go where the cracks go. They slashed up left through minor streams draining the meager and evanescent summit snowfields. We followed and at two P.M. stood on a bush-and-boulder-covered ledge. Creeping around the west buttress, the sun started a meteorologic dance of the elements, and fog was born amorously hugging the wall. Evading the wind, I snuggled amid coarse gravel and manzanita, holding the rope for Herbert who was thirty feet above, swinging into a corner filled with loose blocks where he used nuts because they didn't *pry*. Above, it was pitons, nuts, and *etriers,* for as Herbert said, "This ain't no *free* climbing, Jack," and the only belay spot hanging free in a streamlet. TM, how *do* you do it? Herbert cursed his bad luck, the universe, and me, and explained his misfortune in terms of the loving actions of a deity.

I remove Herbert's ladder by pounding and jerking and use the rungs to make my own. This is fine for a hundred feet, but then the slimy crack overhangs and yawns too big for our pins (three-inchers; no fair taking larger). The face on the left might go . . . some tiny ledges there, but it's wet and mossy. A good one-inch is banged in and, just to make sure, there goes a nut above. Now I can risk it. I climb out and from small holds on the face raise my right foot and place the toe delicately on a slippery nubbin. Quasi-supported, I place the heel of my left hand on a one-inch ledge and mantle. Now what? My cool is blowing fast as I fumble for a bong. It's off the crab and I stretch and seat it and then the hammer and I feel something's about to slip but I just go right ahead thinking I'll be in the air soon, and it's one ringing hit—two-three, and Herbert's yelling "It's good, man, it's good," and me doubting but using and at last my left foot on the mantle and WHOOWEE! Hey, Herbert, boy that was so close, baby! And quickly sink a bombproof three-quarter. But enough of North Wall heroics. I know a lady past ninety who has outlived her son and is just waiting, yet waiting with such spirit and courage that you don't even see she's waiting unless you look twice. That's heroism. How many heroic deeds are being done around us every day that we don't even notice because part of the heroism lies in disguising itself? Climbing is a game in which we play at acquiring the courage necessary to a beautiful life.

We passed the night in a cave on Thanksgiving Ledge, a perfect bivouac—comfortable, sheltered, plenty of firewood. Of course our matches were wet, so Herbert sat in drenched clothing shivering stoically through the night.

The midmorning sun was softening the crust of lenticular snow patches when we strode onto the gently sloping crown of El Capitan. Occupying the summit was a ragged army of sturdy individualists—

long-armed, plated Jeffries and gnarled fibrous Sierra Junipers, trees with the rugged, deeply etched character of the face of an old Italian guide. They were old friends, these trees. But we didn't linger to chat. We were in a hurry. There was red wine waiting, and friends and lovers. Fifty springs are indeed little room. *Tempus fugit.*

1968

Tis-Sa-Ack

Royal Robbins

HENNEK: It was Robbins' idea, mainly. It was on a lot of guys' minds. Had been for a long time. I had thought of it, and when I loaned him my glass I figured he was taking a look. Meant more to him than anyone. He already had two routes on the face and couldn't bear to see anyone else get this one. He wanted to own Half Dome.

ROBBINS: In the afternoon, Marshall—I call him Marshall because Roper started that. Roper likes to call people by their middle names, and such. Like he calls me "Roy," because he hates the pretentiousness of my first name. And I can't help that. Anyway he likes to call Pratt Marshall, so I will try it for a while. Marshall led a nice pitch up into this huge slanting dihedral of white rock streaked with black lichen: the Zebra. Those black streaks, legend tells us, were made by the tears of the Indian girl for whom I named the route.

PRATT: I belayed in slings at the top of this pitch, which wasn't too bad, except at the start where you're thirty feet out with nothing in and then you start aiding with a couple of shitty pins. Royal liked the next pitch because it was loose and gave him an excuse to play around with those damn nuts and feel like they were really doing some good, which I doubt. But I am, it's true, rather conservative. Then we came down on fixed ropes and slept on a big ledge we called the Dormitory.

HENNEK: We would have been all right in the Zebra but we didn't have enough big pitons, even though we were carrying two sets of hardware. We needed about ten two-inch and a dozen inch-and-a-half pitons. The reason we had two sets of hardware is so one guy could be climbing all the time while another was cleaning. I led to the top of the Zebra and Pratt came up and started leading around the overhang at the top while Robbins cleaned the last pitch.

ROBBINS: From Hennek's hanging belay the crack widened to five inches. So Marshall used a four-inch piton, our biggest, endwise. It was weird, driven straight up like that. Then he got in a couple of good pins and used two nuts behind a terrible flake. Pitons would have torn it off. He didn't like it. Marshall hates nuts. He was talking about how it was shifting and then lodging again, just barely. I think he wanted it to come out so he could say, Robbins I told you so. But it held long enough for him to place a bolt but it wasn't very good because he wanted to get off that nut before the nut got off the flake.

HENNEK: We couldn't see Chuck bolting above the overhang, but Glen Denny, who was taking pictures from across the way, got some good shots of us hanging there and Pratt working away. About dusk I lowered Royal out to jumar up and then I started cleaning the pitch.

ROBBINS: When I got up there I saw Marshall had managed to bash three pins into unlikely cracks. There was nothing to stand on. When I pictured the three of us hanging from those pitons I immediately got out the drill. Marshall isn't known as an antibolt fanatic—it's true about that thing on Shiprock, but that was mainly Roper—he isn't known as a fanatic, but there is no one slower on the bolt gun draw than Marshall Pratt. I got in a good solid bolt and we settled down for the night.

HENNEK: Royal says settled down but he didn't get settled very fast. He was screwing around and cursing in the blackness, and then I heard this rip. He had put too much weight on one end of his hammock, and he ought to know better having designed the mothers, and then there was this explosion of screeching and shouting and terrible foul language that would have done credit even to Steve Roper. I thought it was funny. It went on and on. Fulminations in the darkness. I was amazed that he so completely lost control because he always seemed like such an iceberg.

ROBBINS: I had a unique experience the next day: placing sixteen bolts in a row. It was just blank and there was no way around. But it was a route worth bolting for, and after a time I began to take an almost perverse joy in it, or at least in doing a good job. I put them in all the way, so they're good solid reliable bolts, and I put them quite far apart, so I think that it's perhaps the most craftsmanlike ladder of that many bolts in the world. Still, I was really happy to reach with the aid of a skyhook a crack descending from a ledge fifty feet higher. When Marshall came up he was raving. He raved a lot on that wall. He's an outstanding ravist, often shouting at the top of his lungs like Othello in heat. "Why, why, why," he shrieked, "Why didn't I re-up? Christ, I could be a sergeant by now, with security and self-respect. Why did I start climbing in the first place? Shit, I could have been a physicist, with a big desk and a secretary. A secretary!" he repeated, brightening, a leer breaking across his face. "But, no, no, I couldn't do that. I had to drop out of college. Because I . . . I," his voice rising in a crescendo, "I, like Christian Bonington, chose to climb." I was convulsed. We were having a good time. Nobody uptight. No ego trips. But we were low on bolts and low on water. We would have to go down the next day. It was late afternoon and—

HENNEK: I'll take over here to save all of us from another of Royal's glowing descriptions of how the sun goes down. After a night on the ledge—and a rather long October night at that—we rappelled, placing bolts and dropping from one hanging stance to another. We all wanted to return. It was going to be a good route and we left a lot of hardware at the base, to save carrying it up next time.

PRATT: But when next time came in June, the summit snowfield was still draining down the face. It had been a heavy winter. So we put it off until the fall and I went to the Tetons, Robbins went to Alaska to stroke his alpine hang-up, and Dennis went fun-climbing in Tuolumne Meadows and redamaged an old injury so he was out of the running for the year. In October I got a card from Robbins saying he'd be up in a few days for the Dome, and when he didn't arrive it really pissed me off, and when days later he still didn't arrive I said fuck it and made plans to go on El Cap with Tom Bauman. Christ, when Robbins didn't show, people were looking for him on Half Dome, solo. And then when he finally came up several days late his mood really turned me off. He was tense and cold. He said he couldn't wait until Tom and I had done our climb; he was taking the Dome too seriously, so I decided not to go.

ROBBINS: When Chuck said he wouldn't go I was almost relieved. At least now he couldn't make me feel like I was dirtying the pants of

American Mountaineering. I feel guilty with a camera when Pratt is on the rope. It's like asking a Navajo to pose, and I would never do that. Marshall hates cameras as much as he hates my puns and 5.10 psychos. He doesn't want anything to get between him and the climbing experience. He suggested I ask Don Peterson. Peterson had been up the Dihedral Wall and was hot to go on anything as long as it was difficult. Although he had never studied the wall, it didn't take much persuading.

PETERSON: We agreed to go up in the morning. Robbins was like a man possessed. He was totally zeroed in on Half Dome. He had a lecture date soon and he had to squeeze it in. It rained like hell that night and looked bad in the morning but Robbins figured we might as well go up because it might not storm. I didn't like it but I didn't say anything and we started walking up expecting to get bombed on any minute.

ROBBINS: Our loads were murderous. We stopped where the great slabs begin and gazed upward. "Didn't know what you were getting into, did you?" I asked facetiously. "Well," replied Don, "it can't be any harder than things I've already done." I turned absolutely frigid. The tone of the next eight days was set right there.

PETERSON: What I didn't like was his assumption of superiority. Like he figured just because he was Royal Robbins he was the leader. I didn't buy that. Christ, I had done climbs in the Valley as hard as he'd done, and I did the Dihedral faster. Yet when we got up to the base of the wall he sent me to fetch water. I just don't buy that crap.

ROBBINS: On the way up Don asked if there was anything on the North America Wall harder than the third pitch. I told him no—as hard but not really harder. Well then, he said, we shouldn't have any trouble with the rest of it. Mead Hargis and I have been up the third pitch and it wasn't too bad. Oh really, I said. Well, it might be a little easier now because Hennek and Lauria had to place a bolt. Oh no, he said, we chopped it. We went right on by.

In a few hours we were at the Dormitory. It was strange climbing with Don. Like many young climbers he was intensely impatient. He was used to great speed and just going. Speed is where it's at. It's not the noblest thing in climbing, but it moves many. Still, I didn't expect to feel the pressure of Don's impatience running up the rope like a continually goading electric current. And I didn't expect a generation gap, but there it was. For eight days we would be locked in sullen conflict, each too arrogant to understand the other's weaknesses.

PETERSON: On the second day we reached the top of the Zebra. Royal belayed in slings while I led the pitch over the top. Right away there was the wide crack. Robbins told me Pratt had knocked a four-incher

Peterson following an aid pitch halfway up the wall. ROYAL ROBBINS.

endwise into the five-inch crack. I screwed around for a while, wondering why he hadn't brought a bigger bong this time. I couldn't get it to work so I took three bongs and put them one inside the other and that filled the crack okay, but God was it spooky. Still, I thought it was a pretty clever piece of engineering.

ROBBINS: After Don made this strange bong maneuver, he reached the flake where Marshall had had his wild time with those tiny wired nuts. "It's been a long time since I've used nuts," said Don, to cut the power of any criticism I might have of his chocking ability. After he had put his weight on the second one it pulled and he ripped out the other, falling fifteen feet. He didn't like that and this time he nested two pins first. But he still couldn't drive a pin higher as the flake was too loose so he put the nut back in and got on it. It was holding so he started to take in rope and as he was reaching for Pratt's bolt the chock came out and down he came, pulling the pins and falling twenty feet this time. I feared he might be daunted but he swarmed right back up the rope and got the top nut in and got on it and pulled in a lot of rope and got the bolt this time. Fighting spirit, I thought. I reflected how Don was a football player and how he must charge the line the way he charges up those pitches.

PETERSON: Robbins was rather proud of his bolt ladder and bragged about it while he was leading it. I passed his belay in slings and led on up to the previous high point, which Robbins called Twilight Ledge. In the morning he took a long time leading around several lips of rock. I was getting pretty antsy by the time he finished. Christ, was it all going to be like this?

ROBBINS: Above us rose a deceptive five-inch crack. Don went up to look at it and said do you want to try it? It won't hurt to try I replied, but when I got up there I wouldn't do it without a bolt, and we had no bolts to spare. So for about an hour I played with bongs driven lengthwise, and with four-inch bongs enlarged by one-inch angles driven across their spines. It was distasteful as hell, and if anything came out I'd be right in Don's lap. I was trembling with more than exertion when I finally clawed my way to Sunset Ledge. When Don came up I was gratified to hear him say he didn't think he could have done it. Maybe now the tension would be eased between us. He probably wanted me to say, "Sure you could," but I couldn't give up the one point I had won.

PETERSON: It was a good ledge. We were halfway or more. It was my lead but Royal had a lot more bolting experience so he led off, placing a bolt ladder diagonally across a blank section. In the morning I finished the ladder, nailed a big loose flake and put in a bolt, and belayed in slings. When Robbins came up three or four pins just fell out.

ROBBINS: The first thing I did was put in another bolt, for above Don's belay rose another of those vile five-inch cracks, too big for our pins and too small to get inside. I launched an all-out effort, struggling and thrashing desperately in the slightly overhanging crack. Four months later I still bear the scars. The top of the flake was like a big stone fence without mortar, but I got across that and placed a few bolts and then nailed a thin horizontal flake. I placed seven pins there and four fell out before I had finished. With two good bolts for a belay and hanging bivouac I was safe and happy with nothing on my mind but the next eight hundred feet. Don wanted to try the jamcrack because I had said it was probably the hardest free climbing I had done on a big wall, but I told him we don't have time, man, which we didn't. I was very relieved, for I was afraid he would come up easily and go down and tell the fellows I said it was hard but he didn't find it so. What the hell, that would happen in the next ascent anyway. Let the pitch have a reputation for a year.

PETERSON: At about this point I wasn't feeling too happy. Robbins had taken almost a whole day to lead one pitch. I just didn't see how we could make it at this rate. I knew he had to place a lot of bolts, but it about drove me out of my skin waiting for him to finish. I felt I could have gone faster. We were using too many bolts when we still had this big blank section above us. What if we didn't have enough? But the only thing Robbins had to say was "We can always turn back, or else they can pull us off." I didn't think we were going to make it. I had never gone so slowly on a climb in my life.

ROBBINS: I hated drilling those bolts. We had these extra-long drills that were all we could get at the last minute, and we had a long drill holder too, so I was bending over backwards drilling, and drilling is plenty bad enough without that. Here I was working away and always this mumbling and bitching from below, and finally the shocking ejaculation, "This is a lot of shit." From then on I felt I was battling two opponents, the wall and Peterson. I had learned to expect a grumble whenever I made the slightest error, such as not sending up the right pin ("Goddamn it, everything but what I need"), or forgetting the hauling line. I began to feel incompetent. It wasn't really so much what Don said, it was that he said it. It was a new experience climbing with someone who gave his emotions such complete freedom of expression. I was shocked and mildly terrified by Peterson's dark passions bubbling repeatedly to the surface. It probably would have been healthier to have responded in kind, to have shouted "Fuck you, Peterson," every time I felt scorn, real or imagined, coming my way. I didn't lack such feelings. The things I was calling Don were far worse than anything he said, direct or implied. But when I said them I kept my mouth shut.

PETERSON: On the fifth morning I had to use up three more bolts because there was another five-inch overhanging crack. I finally got into it and went free for a hundred feet completely inside a huge flake for half the way. Then we had three straightforward pitches before some bolting brought us to a great ledge, where a ramp led up to a huge blank area below the summit. That night our water froze. In the morning I led up the ramp to a tight little alcove. The blank wall started about thirty feet up. It looked awfully big.

ROBBINS: As I nailed up to the blank area, I thought hard about our remaining thirty bolts. We would place some so they were barely adequate, allowing us to pull and reuse them. We had now traversed too much to descend. Those long drills were murder. I had three Rawl drills and another holder, and I used them to start the holes. They were extremely brittle, but I soon learned that a broken Rawl worked fine, and if they didn't break well, I would rebreak them with the hammer. I was saving three short Star drills for the end. I didn't get far that day. It was slow going. I used one drill seven times before discarding it. Don spent the night scrunched in his cave while I bivouacked in a hammock. The weather, which had been threatening, was holding well. The next day was an ordeal. Sometimes it took nearly an hour for one bolt. Whenever I wasn't drilling I had my head against the rock in despair and self-pity. And always that electricity along the rope, that distracting awareness that Peterson must be going mad. Poor Peterson, but poor mé too. Besides the hard work, there's something mentally oppressive about being in the middle of a large, totally blank piece of rock. I was sorry I had disdained bat-hooks, believing as I had that if you're going to drill a hole you ought to fill it with a good bolt. I was so far gone now that anything went. I just wanted to get up. But there was nothing to do but what we were doing. When Don came up to my hanging belay the first thing he said was, "I was sitting down there for twenty-four hours!" That's energetic youth. Don had suffered as much sitting as I had drilling. That afternoon Don placed a few bolts, more quickly than I had, but with no more enthusiasm. The next day I again took over the bolting, inexorably working toward the barely visible lower corner of the Dihedral leading to the summit overhangs. That edge of rock was our lodestone, drawing us like a magnet.

PETERSON: Robbins had hoped to do the wall in six days, but this was the eighth. We really wanted to get off and thought maybe we could. The bolting was going a little faster now with Robbins using the short drills and not putting the bolts in very far. He would place one fairly well and then two poor ones and then another good one and then come down and take out the two bad ones and re-place them above. He did this about twenty times. Robbins rarely said anything while he was working on a pitch. He was like a beaver working away on a dam, slow and methodical. At times I felt I was going to burst, just sitting in one place doing nothing. I like to climb. This wasn't climbing, it was slogging. But I had to admire Robbins's self-control. He had about as much unmanageable emotion as an IBM machine.

ROBBINS: We reached our lodestone just as the sun was reaching us. Don eagerly grabbed the lead, nailing up from the last bolt. Thin nailing it was, too. By stretching a long way from a rurp, he drove a knifeblade straight up behind the rottenest flake imaginable. It seemed impossible it could have held. I had vowed that I wasn't going to give Peterson an inch, but I weakened. I told him it was a damn good lead. It would have been too flagrant not to have done so. We were now on a ledge beneath the final overhangs. Above, gently pivoting with grotesque finality in the afternoon breeze dangled a gangly form, mostly arms and legs, with a prophet's head of rusty beard and flowing locks. It was the artist Glen Denny. He and the rock around him had already taken on a golden hue as I started up in an all-out effort to reach the top before dark. It didn't look far, but using two rurps just to get started was a bad omen. I went as fast as possible but not fast enough to escape Peterson's urging to greater speed. The summit tiers overlapped one another, building higher and higher like the ninth wave. On several, reaching the crack separating the folds was barely possible. On one, a hook on the wire of a nut saved a bolt. Everything happened at once as I neared the top. The cracks became bad, the light went, pulling the rope was like a tug-of-war, and I was running out of pins. I had just gotten in a piton and clipped in when the one I was on popped. As I got onto the next one the piton below dropped out and then I was off the aid and onto a sloping smooth slab in the blackness, realizing I was really asking for it and picturing the fall and the pulled pins and hanging in space above Don. I backed down and got into my slings and cleaned the top pin with a pull, then began nailing sideways. Glen Denny is watching silently as I start to crack but I realize I am getting melodramatic and find myself looking at it through Glen's eyes, completely objectively and so cool down and feel with fingers the cracks in the darkness and bash away with the hammer smashing my fingers and pins coming out and me complaining in the darkness putting fear into the heart of my companion and asking him to send up his anchors so I can use them but he refusing and me saying to Glen that's the way it's been all the way up.

1970

Spring Weekend
Love Affair

Eric Sanford

Friday afternoon. Cramp four. Smell of creased knickers; tinkle of aluminum money. You can feel a hastiness in the air. What am I doing here? What are *they* doing here?

Berserk repetitive strokes up the burning, stone-cold vertical highway. Fill 'er up and check my water. Thanks. A ten-cent tip and you're on your way. Village spamburgers; A5 traffic.

Just finished a twenty-hour bivy in the snow after four off-route pitches. Four days is just too much—gotta come down. Froze my ass off! Think I'll become an armchair mountaineer, a real boon to my sport. Hell, if you don't climb, you can't hurt the rock. Everybody but Royal hurts it anyway. Why try?

What a great bunch of routes. Dotted lines and rest areas. A tram to the top of the Apron? BHOS Dome? Coonyard. Magic Mushroom. Bet Royal's pissed! Where's Batso now that we need him? Think I'll sneak a route up the back side of Half Dumb: "*Up Yours, VII, 5.2, A6.*

This highly unaesthetic cynical climb starts two hundred feet to the right of the left-most dihedral just before a giant spider web located three hundred inches directly uphill from a large tree. Unenjoyable, dirty climbing then leads to the summit. This horrible route, having been climbed once, will hopefully fade into well-deserved obscurity. Carry hooks, of course. Bashies useful. . . . "

Talk drifts toward my van window . . . incessant chatter by prophetic janglers—hard 5.6 . . . had to come down . . . dropped a jumar . . . it's pronounced "u-mar" . . . see this new rope . . . wow! What is *that?* . . . AHHHHHHH! Shut up! I'm trying to hibernate. Back to my *Ascent.* Let's see . . . 5.10F . . . Where's my *Mad?*

Okay, move all those campsites back a hundred yards. *What???* A blue orange red green yellow brown primusmolybdinummacaronirope ghetto. Who stuffed toilet paper in the sink? Wish all those damn groads would move over to Yellow Pine. "Why don't you take your twenty-four-hour-a-day jam sessions, your groady dogs, *and* your 'hoots,' and *scram!*"

Back to the van. Let's talk about being bummed out. Okay. I'm bummed out. Probably leave . . . last time here. What's it all about, anyway. What is climbing in Yosemite Valley, U.S.A., all about?

Well, it's about *it,* and it's about *us. We* are the flat-footed coeducated blue suede semilocal 5.10 hopeful hot-dogs. It's . . . well, what can you say? It is Yosemite. Too bad it and us can't get together to write the laws. Section 4.3, Article 8: Anyone caught using a piton takes a forty-foot leader fall. Second offense, your belay anchors pull. There's no third time. . . .

So now it's chalk marring the rock, ruining the "natural wilderness experience" for the next guy. What I want to know is this: just what "wilderness experience" am I ruining? You mean to tell me that people actually come here expecting a wilderness experience? You think anyone actually wants it?

Yosemite is no longer any type of wilderness experience. New York is. Miami Beach is. Los Angeles is. Yosemite is not. It is simply a one-by-five-mile vertical gymnasium with car-campers in the bleachers. Period. Sunnyside locker room. Leaning Tower trapeze. Half Dome Bar and Grill. Twenty-two water bubblers and an audience. Score: one to one. You lose. Don't get me wrong! Heavens no! I love it here . . . for what it is. Came here four years ago . . . learned the ropes. Free showers, ice, food, laundry, TV, movies . . . shhhh! . . . don't tell anyone. And tomorrow another first-timer: steel biners, greenline, new set of polyhydrofleximatic nuts. Shit, gotta sell all my

Camp 4 inhabitants Jim Bridwell and Royal Robbins, circa 1966. EDGAR BOYLES.

old ones again. Never even used them. And to him it will be just like it was to me four years ago. If you don't know what to expect, then whatever turns up is okay. On the ground, that is.

Just part of the South-Face-of-the-Columnpinned-out Blues, I guess. Yup. "Supplied with four topos, two guides, seventeen gallons of prune juice, twelve pounds of bologna, ninety-five pins, one hundred and seventy-five nuts (kept at the bottom of the haul bag; 'ya, we took more nuts than pins . . . '), eight ropes, bashies and mashies and smashies and trashies, bolts (thunder), three *Masked Marvel* comic books, and a spare pair of BVDs, we trudgened ever onward." Oh, no! We forgot the ice axes. Any of you guys seen an ice axe around? I've got a modified custom-chrome twin-shafted duplex Brontosaurus. Funny, I knew something was wrong. Had to come down . . . after the crux and all. I thought the crux was leaving the ground? No? Climbed up one pitch, rapped off two. Did some interesting caving. Got "bummed out" by all the fixed pins. What? Ya, had to leave a couple to rap off, you know. A1. A nested rurp#10hexjumarbashietieoffcanopener. Must have pulled. Found it in the bushes next to a rusty sardine can. . . . Just part of the blues.

Made some new friends. Good ones. Much talk. Wish I had some Winnebago stock. Nasal off-key blues pierce the air. Ukulele Larry is at it again. Wish the "mad bolter" would take care of *him!* Think I'll spend next summer on the Oasis. With my luck they'd start the Firefall again.

Think I'll get ready for a climbtapebenzoinchalkcontactcement-epoxyEBkneepadwhitesuit. Let's go. North Buttress of the Chin-Up Bar Direct. Maybe after, the Parallel Bar, Left Side. First free ascent, 1980, by Morton Monkey, on loan from the L.A. Zoo. Think I'll name my new route the Direct Direct Direct on the Direct Direct. I climbed it by rappelling upside down. Should have brought my TV. Why not be comfortable? Isn't that what it's all about?

Perhaps comfort is just one of the things which have combined to ruin Yosemite Valley. That and automobiles, fire, horses, potato chips, Curry Company, communists, vibram, and people. Least of all climbers. How can someone who sleeps like a bat and smells of that from which he came ruin anything? Climbers are simply like everyone else: they take advantage of the ruination. Sunnyside my ass! Where *is* the trail to Yosemite Falls?

Let's all go somewhere else. Tuolumne . . . the Tetons . . . Wind Rivers . . . Alaska . . . Patagonia. . . . Hell, let's all go to the North Pole! Man is certainly no different than any other animal. He just plays his part. The dinosaurs once ruled the earth (or so we are told) only to become extinct by overusing and underreplenishing their environment. And the dodo bird, gone too. And now man must look forward toward his future and his possible extinction. When will "progress" end? Can I live in Site 23 forever?

So now the incumbent climbers must look to the future with introspective eyes and decide if they should fill igneous voids with only nuts, thus limiting their aerial progress, or form their own voids and fill them with bolts; both are so much a part of the technological era which Reinhold Messner despises, yet one carries a bit more risk than the other. But from a purely ethical standpoint perhaps some magical, undisclosed number of nuts constitutes the same rucksack-stuffing courage-load as a ten-pound bag of bolts and an electric drill sharpener. Who will draw the line?

Really! How artificial is a bolt? A guidebook is a bolt. You find a climb that interests you. Get some inside info. How hard? How long? Who did it last? When? Approach? Deproach? What do I need? Pin list. Topo. Off we go to seek our death-defying wilderness experience natural adventure. Now the clincher: it was ruined as a natural experience because there was chalk on some of the holds. Shit! You're lucky you didn't have to stand in line. Real lucky! Try doing El Cap in May. Six parties a day. Hurry, they'll catch us. Hurry, they won't. Don't worry, to hell with 'em. ROOOOOCK!! A can of peaches whistles by my head, earthbound.

Had to nail the headwall in the dark. Slept in slings all night. Ten feet from the ledge; couldn't see it . . . didn't know it was there. Dropped my glasses. Dropped the haul bag cover. Dropped the haul bag. It wasn't so bad. Big walls are a walk-up. Lotta work. Dirty. Lucky parties hit a storm, have some adventure. Forgot my ice axe. Where *is* my ice axe? Too hot. Too cold. What if you can't come down? REEEEEEEEEESCUE! Natural dangers (climbing being one of them). Read the latest *AAJ*. How many accidents are actually attributed to something other than human error?

Yosemite Valley is man-made. Climbing is purely a technical problem. Did you do it all nuts? All free? No rope? No hands? Who is our guiding light, Hot Henry or Joe Sunday over on the Apron having an epic? EB stands for EveryBody. And after all this, how come Every-Body has joined in the cry for ecological climbing? "Oh well, you see . . . I've been telling people for years . . . I've been saying all along. . . . " Face it: Yosemite (pronounced yō-sĕm-ĭt) cannot be saved. Not from me for you, or from you for me. Does it need to be saved? Does it need to be saved just for climbers? Why? If you are following a prescribed route, someone else's creation, how can that be any more of an adventure than copying someone else's painting? Is a Winnebago the same as a covered wagon?

Why chop a bolt because *you* didn't need it? Perfectly good nut crack right beside it. A #7 wedge in at a twenty-seven-degree angle. Bomber. Falling! Ahhhh . . . pop! Ahhhh . . . I'd just as soon be safe. There is low-risk poker, after all. There are low-tar cigarettes. Should there be low-risk climbing? The book says 5.7, A1, but it goes free at 5.10M. What the hell's wrong with doing it 5.7 A1? Nothing. Protection, ratings, chalk . . . they're all part of the game. Who cares? Isn't climbing doing your own thing?

Came down off that damned thing. That guidebook is incredibly confusing . . . shitty route description . . . got lost twelve times . . . had to leave a sling . . . my best one. Was it Moses or Batso who said, "I don't give a rat's ass what anyone says about my route." Really! God bless the holy guidebook! Chapter XIV from the book of Roper; Arch Rock . . . funny how that little green book can have such effects on people. Maybe the next author can ask first ascenders from now on whether they want "their" route "ruined" by subsequent ascents or not. If they don't well, " . . . this unpopular, devious, dangerous, rotten, unprotected route is not recommended. . . . " Funny, I thought it was A1 when I did it. Rather fun, you know.

The Yosemite days make me think of the dawning of man. The Valley fills me with such happiness and elation in revealing all its splendors to us lowly creatures. I'm so surprised that Sentinel hasn't crumbled at the obscenities we—yes, you and I—have written upon this once-virgin valley floor. Is the view from Glacier Point real? Is the sight from the Wawona Tunnel to be believed? We are all in heaven already and don't even know it. We must all pause and let our minds capture the magnificence set before us. Surely this must last?

Sunday afternoon crazy fat momma ride out of the park-noisy-motorcycle-camper-slip-stream-volkswagen-ago-go. Whee! They're gone. No more day-glo sneakers and golden pitons strung on peeling necks. Back to the hardcores. Bums. Dirty. Think I'll do a climb. Anybody seen my hammer?

1975/76

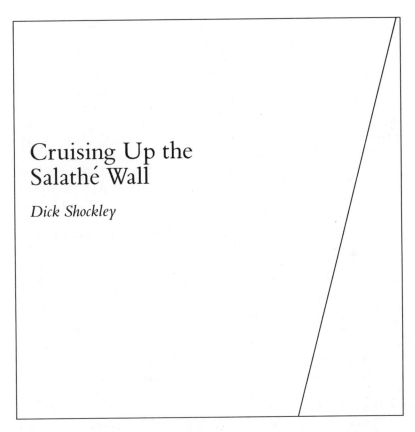

Cruising Up the Salathé Wall

Dick Shockley

Sayings come and go, and like the seasons, they never repeat themselves exactly. In the back of my mind I can hear someone singing, "Climbing is a drug, and I neeeeed a fix. . . . " But right now asphalt is all around me as I sit in the Oldsmobile dealer's waiting room with other stranded souls, waiting to have my U-joints replaced. It could take hours. My mind reverts to the route. The city fades away. I shrink to a mere speck, a dot carrying a big sack up to the base of the monolith, El Capitan.

We are well prepared, with a minimum of two quarts of water per man per day, rye-crisp crackers, a six-pack, anchovy paste, kippers, wheat-berry bread, cream cheese, canned fruit, salami, chicken-salad spread, a few illicit goods, and even toothbrushes and toothpaste. We are stoked. The late May days are so fine that I never want to go back to work, and the view of swollen waterfalls and a band of purest white around the valley rim, results of heavy snow from a recent storm, is in itself worth the trip from San Diego.

Rick is an old hand. At twenty-three he has already done several Grade V and VI routes in Yosemite, including first ascents; he has also spent two summers in the Alps. He wishes to climb the Salathé Wall on El Capitan. I am eager, because I love climbing and walls are new to me. In eight years of climbing in Southern California, I have been to Yosemite only twice.

But already there has been a tragedy. We were walking to the base early one morning, thinking about nothing and pleased by the five deer who serenely greeted us near the stream. We were planning to fix three pitches that day. We looked up and saw a climber in or near the Stoveleg Cracks on the Nose. We watched briefly and resumed walking. Then we heard a loud, tearing sound, like a falling rock, and it seemed to last forever. We backed away into a clearing in fear and looked up again. The climber we had seen was gone. It could not be. The sun shone and the birds chirped. El Cap, enormous and neutral, was silent.

"Shouldn't we go over there?"

"No. Let's wait here, Dick. We can't do anything for him."

"Karl is probably over there anyway." Karl has just taken a twelve-hour bus trip up from San Diego to climb the Nose of El Cap.

A minute later, Karl walks out of the woods and says he has seen a body.

"Just one? Was he soloing?"

He goes away and comes back. There are three bodies. He feels sick from the sight and smell and does not want to do the Nose anymore. He looks close to tears. They hit so hard they broke rocks.

Later we learn that the three climbers were from Minnesota. We had met them the preceding night in the campground. They were not entirely inexperienced on big walls, but for some reason they were not going up, but rappelling. That seems to be the bad part, the most dangerous. Pam, a girlfriend of one, is now alone in this vacation paradise, surrounded by huge rock walls, swifts, and violet-green swallows, by tourists with Winnebagos and cigars and poodles, alone with her misery. She has to drive home alone.

El Capitan just abides, perhaps waiting and listening for events of greater significance, such as an ice age, or a reversal of the earth's magnetic field, or the cooling of the sun. Rick and I plod on over to the start of the Salathé and leave Karl to his defunct dream. What can we say or do? We do not yet have a haul bag. Maybe we can borrow his. Idiots. Two specks, throwing it all to the wind.

Four days have passed since the accident. We have climbed to Mammoth Terrace and strung our ropes back to the ground from Heart Ledge. We are ready for the summit push. For one long day we jumar, climb, haul, and belay. We want to reach El Cap Spire (the twentieth pitch) by night; this will require ten pitches of climbing above the end of our fixed ropes. We hope to reach the summit with only two bivouacs. Eric Beck, the archetypal climbing bum (in the words of Chris Jones) now turned economics graduate student, says "speed is safety on a wall." To follow this dictum, we have diligently studied the supertopo he gave us.

The ground drops away and becomes indistinct. Huge cornfields spring up in our minds as we remember Eric's ascent of the wall with Keith Bruckner. Somewhere on the lower wall, Keith had remarked—out of the blue—to Eric, "One could easily grow corn here." A classic line, considering their elevation. Of course, I do not blame Keith for being infatuated with corn—but why corn? Why not alfalfa? Why not just say, "Man, it sure is wet and muddy here."

We move on up. The infamous Ear Pitch is not too wet, and above it I flail on aid up the amazing Double Cracks. We are now just a short distance below the Alcove, a blocky ledge one pitch short of El Cap Spire. It looks as if we can't make our intended bivouac site, but by now we don't even want to, since a party of two is already asleep there. Earlier, we had almost caught up with them; we wonder if we can slip past them in the morning. How fast are they compared to us?

Direct aid on overhanging rock is tiring beyond my comprehension, even using a sit-harness to rest. I am both startled and humiliated to feel my lips tingling from the exertion, my stomach muscles knotting, my fingers cramping and useless after the long pitch. I sob curses at everything while tugging at knots, trying to set up the belay and haul. They can probably hear me from the Spire, but I cannot help it. I am grateful that I do not faint or lose my lunch via the technicolor yawn. Finally I get the rope tied off. Rick begins to jumar, and from somewhere I find the strength to haul. Maybe I should have been running ten miles a day instead of eight.

It is dark by now. By the light of his headlamp, Rick leads a 5.9 jamcrack-squeeze chimney to the Alcove. I recall the fellow who told us about popping out of this crack in the dark and plummeting forty feet, but Rick reaches the Alcove without incident. Once I arrive, I turn fetal, too exhausted even for a beer. Around midnight I awaken and slowly and painfully manage to drag most of my body onto a flat bench of rock.

In the morning I have recovered. Since our route lies on the southwest face, the sunrise is hidden. Nevertheless, faint strains of Mozart, Bach, Ravel, and Robbins are heard as the warming light creeps through the valley. We argue heatedly over the choice of composers and appropriate passages. A beautiful smoky mist from the controlled-burn areas on the valley floor slides along the Merced River. (The signs along the road read "Management Fire—Do Not Report," and I longed to acquire one for my office, where it would fit right in and be appreciated every day.) Eventually the party above us moves on, and with no excuse for delaying longer, we cruise up the giant chimney behind the Spire.

Late in the day I stare at the "Wet and Slimy Pitch." My new Gore-Tex cagoule comes out, and I tape the wrists shut to keep the water out. It goes into my ears, eyes, and nose instead. We give this pitch a new, more explicit, name—several in fact—and are thankful it is the only mossy, ugly pitch on a thirty-six-pitch route.

We sleep on the Block. This sloping ledge is only five pitches above El Cap Spire, but we have fixed some ropes higher so that tomorrow we can jumar quickly in the cold early morning. The awesome landmark called the Roof is visible from the Block and looks quite interesting. Above the Roof we expect slow progress up the overhanging Headwall. It would be nice to be off tomorrow night, but ten pitches seem like a lot when they're mostly aid.

The party above us has become Gary and Rusty. They have stayed well ahead of us, and we will probably not pass them. Far below us, we can make out another party, or maybe two. We hope one pair are our friends Mike and Dewi, but we cannot communicate or see well enough to be certain. For luck, I tape a joint to a can of kippers and leave it on the Block with a "Mike" and an arrow scratched into the gravel of the ledge. (Later, sitting in the meadow below with a telescope, we saw two climbers ahead of Mike and Dewi. Oh, damn! We fear they scarfed the offering, as I would have done. But it turned out that the upper party perceived the spiritual depth of the gift. "It was really neat," Mike told me later. "They were two Frenchmen, and they yelled down, 'I theenk yore frehns 'ave leff you sometheen'.")

Chuck Pratt on the first ascent of the infamous Headwall Pitch. TOM FROST.

Gary and Rusty sleep on tiny Sous Le Toit Ledge, as if to expiate their routefinding error earlier, when an obvious-looking crack lured them right; the route to Sous Le Toit is hidden as a short pendulum around a corner to the left. We tried once to warn them, then subtly cruised up to the ledge. We knew that Sous Le Toit is a one-man lie at best, so we soon returned to the Block. It seems, however, that Gary and Rusty *prefer* pain. They hauled their bags up the low-angled slabs beneath Mammoth Terrace, for example, whereas we cheated and merely climbed those pitches with a few extra ropes, traversed over to Heart Ledge, and rappelled to the ground, leaving the extra ropes. Later we jumared back to the ledge with our loads, a tactic which got us onto steeper rock sooner and thus eased the hauling problems immeasurably. This was Eric's suggestion; at first I did not grasp its wisdom, but Rick pointed out to me that at least half the work on a big wall is hauling—so why not make it as easy as possible?

Gary and Rusty have been on El Cap for four days already. Gary says, "Once I'm on, I want to stay on." I guess that's okay. As I examine my dry, cracking cuticles and sore googies (small flesh wounds on the back of the hand which result from poor crack technique), I inform our new friends that we actually followed the procedure of Robbins, Frost, and Pratt on their first ascent in 1961. Gary and Rusty are not swayed by this fact. I recall the Belgian party that we overtook low on the route because their haulbag was being torn to ribbons, but I keep this to myself. After all, we are not here to compare methods, compete, argue, or criticize. We are here to get off as soon as possible.

Rick and I have a small private party on the Block.

"Don't you think we ought to save some of this for the summit?"

"Hmmmm. No."

The third day dawns. Last night was very chilly, like the previous one, but passable. I discover that I did not roll over the edge in my sleep. From now on, though, I really should stay tied in. There simply wasn't enough extra rope last night. Several bars of Stravinsky whistle by; I catch a strain of the Firebird Suite.

"Yarrrgnm. Sigh. Waaummmmnngg. Shrtpz. Ahhhhh. Well, friend, let's cruise."

To judge from the noises above, Rusty and Gary have begun climbing. It is time to move, but it is still cold.

"Okay, I'm almost ready. Just let me get this extra gear packed."

"Let's boogie."

"Cruise or bruise."

"Succeed or bleed."

"Top or chop."

"Summit or plummet."

"Make haste or tomato paste."

"Finger locks or cedar box."

"Consummate skills or heavy bills."

"Climb in style or fly a mile."

"Unravel the mystery or soon become history."

"Endurance or insurance."

"Keep your head or hospital bed."

"Lunge or plunge."

"Get the knack or face a smack."

"Underclings or angel wings."

"Nail the seam or giant scream."

Rick moves off the Block, jumaring toward Sous Le Toit Ledge. When he gets there I untie the rope from its anchor on the Block, hook my jumars onto the rope, and swing out over the spectacular exposure. My oh my, this isn't just three times higher than my local crags. This is another world. The cord stretches. . . .

Once on Sous Le Toit, we can see the Roof clearly. It almost begins to look reasonable and is even smaller than I thought. But the route goes around to its right. Why have I always assumed it went left? On second thought, it looks horrendous. Eric's topo indicates that the Roof is fixed but requires a long reach at one spot. We start up again, nailing two steep aid pitches while carefully watching Gary and Rusty as they climb and clean the Roof. When it is time for Gary to haul, Rusty cuts the bag loose. Rick says, "Now check this out, Dick," and I am immobilized as I watch it swing out from under the overhang. It takes a year. The Roof is indeed enormous. The scene calls for an ultimately personal phrase of self-expression: "Hooooooooo Maaaaaaaaaaaan!!"

During the morning, tourist buses stop in the meadow below to watch while I relieve myself. I hope they have a good scope, but for some reason—perhaps the complete irrelevance of anything of flat ground to our current state—I neglect to look over my shoulder and smile and wave at them. There must be a hundred spectators. Ants.

Last night I realized we had dropped nothing up to this point, and said as much to Rick. With typical foresight he pointed out the foolishness of the remark. Today I drop a carabiner and a pin. Bad. Then Rick drops a nut. They all make a pleasant, whirring sound, but it is so steep they fall beyond hearing before touching rock. We could scream "Rock! Rock!" all day long, but no one below could hear, for the wind is wrong. This is why one should not hang out at the base of El Cap when there are climbers above. Clip, clip, grab the haul line, swing out on the wall past Rick (good lead, Dad), and here at last is the Roof.

It starts out easily, and then I am standing in air in my aiders. This is almost fun. A little bit, anyway. Smile for a photo and try not to think how embarrassing it would be if one of these shitty old pieces of webbing were to . . . no, no, please don't think those thoughts, just the other kind, the pleasant ones . . . and concentrate on the moves. Move on. Eric's topo claims there is a place for a two-inch bong at the lip. Where, Eric, where? I search for long minutes, swinging in the breeze. Rick huddles shivering in the shade of the overhang. My spirits drag and so does the time. A fixed sling lurks just out of reach beyond the lip. All I need to do is grab it. Unngh. Shit, still too far.

Finally, in frustration, I lunge some fifty feet or so up overhanging friction holds, battle an avalanche of boxcar-sized blocks, hook a fingernail on the frayed wisp of rotten webbing, and clip into it only to find that the eighth-inch cord is attached to a may-pop stopper. A pop here would have a spectrum of consequences: psychological, physical, sexual, theological. For example, Rick might take over the lead. He tried once before, low on the route, but I drew a knife and threatened to sever his rope. My perspective returns as soon as I clip into the next fixed piece, a sturdy copperhead. Whew! Well, in all honesty, that was not too bad. A pretty simple pitch actually. Casual, even trivial. Look at that bag swing; easy hauling here.

Now we face the ninety-five-degree Headwall; six pitches remain. Rick nails and nuts onward, up the overhanging rock. There is supposedly a big ledge—Long Ledge—two pitches higher, but from here there is absolutely no sign of such a sanctuary. Across the valley, shadows on Middle Cathedral Rock mark the passage of time. It is growing late, almost 4:30. As I hang from my harness, I recall the overwhelming indifference of El Capitan. Toward the three boys from Minnesota. Toward us. I know this bears remembering, and I eye the anchors again and again. I am ready. The wind blows the haul line almost horizontally across the smooth, golden rock. We are climbing in the only crack for as far as the eye can see on either side. I want to stop time and absorb this forever. The insane swifts cavort in the wind.

I smear on glacier cream, face away from the hot sun, eat Starbursts, examine my anchors yet again, have a sip of water, and count the number of ways to sit in a harness. The pitch is long and strenuous, and I feel for Rick. The wall appears foreshortened since it overhangs so much. Soon the haul line is swaying fifteen feet out from the cliff. Finally Rick is done, and I come up, noting that several of his placements were tricky, if not tricky-difficult. Now I swing into the short aid lead toward the still-hidden Long Ledge. From the extreme right end of this narrow ledge, Rick nails and nuts up a crack, which will bring us to a ledge only two pitches from the top.

As Rick climbs, the texture of the rock changes: knobs appear. For the first time in eight pitches, it is possible to make a free move or two.

My last lead. As the sunlight begins to leave us, I start up a crack in a big hurry, taking all the wrong nuts. Eric's topo says laconically, "Pretty pitch." I realize I have screwed up when nothing fits. I curse the crack into remote regions for being the wrong size. With practice, I have developed a ritualistic, five-word obscenity to deal with recalcitrant cars and cracks or nonlinear partial differential equations. Finally Rick stills my rage and attaches the necessary nuts to my haul line. Then I am free, jamming a gentle crack into the last belay stance, an alcove below Pratt's Crack.

Darkness comes, but a full moon dispells it almost immediately as Rick squeezes up the 5.9 summit pitch. So much of the climbing is good that I wish there were time for me to climb the pitch instead of jumar it. Exultant yell: "What a finish!"

"All reet!" I reply.

I can barely hear him now, but he is probably ready for me to jumar. I know that the end of the difficult climbing comes very suddenly and obviously he is there. Only one way to tell for sure: jumar. It is tight in the crack, particularly with a pack. Then we are together again and I feel weary, but only one trivial pitch remains. The holds are huge, and then I see a tree. The summit tree. Then many trees. Can it really be? It is very bright. Rick and the haulbag arrive safely. Since the slabs are low-angled, the hauling is difficult. I get a few more blisters and open up the old ones, but so what?

We are alone. Rusty and Gary have disappeared. The terrain is nice and flat here. We hang our equipment all over the big tree and I settle down for a few pipeloads. Always room for a little more elevation. There is very little to say. No sounds arise from the valley, but we spy an endless chain of headlights coming up the Fresno Road. We are both satisfied to be around trees, to have the harnesses off, to be silent.

Sleep.

The Salathé Wall has seen at least one hundred—and maybe two hundred—ascents through the years. If any particular feature marked our climb, it was the absence of any remarkable features. We drove to the Valley, hung out a little, did the route, hung out a little, and departed. But to paraphrase a famous mountaineer, adventure is a sign of incompetence. Not all climbers would agree, of course, but I feel that this simply reflects different opinions on what constitutes adventure, or maybe what constitutes incompetence. I was certainly satisfied and wanted nothing more. Our lessons were short and simple: prepare well, wear tape or gloves to spare the hands (it was three days before we could comfortably close our hands), and climb fast.

One afternoon, shortly after we had arrived in Yosemite, we drove to the meadow below El Cap to check out the route. I was staring at it—feeling vaguely terrified—when a tourist in a Hawaiian shirt asked if I saw any climbers on the wall.

"Yeah, I think I do."

The cliff was covered with parties. They were on the Nose, the Shield, the Dihedral, the Muir. Dale Bard and Ron Kauk could be seen working on a new line near the North American Wall.

"They gotta be nuts, ya know?"

"Right."

"You'd never get me up there."

I could hardly argue with that, and since I am agreeable by nature anyway, I said:

"I agree. I think so too. They're all just maniacs, hanging up there on the sheer face and climbing up ropes that could come loose any time or break. It's just like asking for death. Pretty sick, man. Hey, I mean no way, Ray."

As a rule, this type has a gigantic Winnebago, cases of beer, and daughters that stop your heart in midthump and provoke thoughts of . . . well, as I was saying, Rick wandered over and we chatted a bit. The tourist loaned us his binoculars to look at the madmen on the cliff. But as Rick and I quietly speculated about the route, the man fell quiet, and a look of confusion, suspicion, or possible awareness dawned on his features. He yelled across to his wife:

"Hey, Ruth! These guys are gonna scale that mountain!"

1980

3

NINTH HIGHEST

Editors' Introduction

American mountaineers were slow to reach the Himalayan heights. Although several early expeditions made bold attempts on some of the world's highest peaks, by and large this theater was the province of European climbers. Only sixteen 8,000-meter peaks exist, according to the most recent listing. And only one, Hidden Peak, was first climbed by Americans. This event took place in 1958, not long before all the giants were at last climbed.

The next generation of mountaineers sought unclimbed faces and sweeping ridges. Americans kept pace in this new game, one major prize being the first ascent of the west ridge of Mount Everest in 1963.

With this sterling achievement, Americans caught up. And they also caught up in the realm of Himalayan literature. Tom Hornbein's *Everest: The West Ridge,* published by the Sierra Club in 1965, remains to this day one of the most evocative of all the expedition books.

By the late 1960s expeditions from around the world were seeking out the thousands of lesser unclimbed Himalayan peaks. Yet interest has never flagged regarding the peaks that rise above 8,000 meters. That mystical altitude—in feet the unmemorable number 26,247—is a magnet, a test. Those who ascend beyond this barrier enter a world of little oxygen and unforgiving storms, and the human body, not meant for this sort of torture, begins to suffer, to die. Yet people still persist in marching upward into the "death zone."

Ascent rarely focused on Himalayan climbs, for reasons now unknown to us. An exception, however, was our coverage of Dhaulagiri, the world's ninth-highest mountain. This peak is not only high; it is an isolated monster, subject to horrendous storms and winds. Rising to 26,795 feet, the massif in central Nepal was well known to early explorers. Indeed, the French expedition of 1950 that climbed the first 8,000-meter peak, Annapurna, had targeted Dhaulagiri as its main objective. But so convoluted were the approaches to this peak that the French turned to the easier, lower mountain twenty miles to the east.

Once the approaches to Dhaulagiri were charted, the mountain itself was not technically difficult: it was climbed in 1960 by a Swiss/Austrian expedition via the northeast ridge, now the normal route.

Such a huge mountain obviously had other routes, and one dramatic-looking line was the long and complex southeast ridge. In 1969 an American expedition led by a master of organization, Boyd Everett, approached this savage ridge. Low down, however, a climbers' nightmare happened: an avalanche killed two Sherpas and five expedition members, including Everett. The only survivor of the avalanche, Lou Reichardt, later wrote: "We had only an instant to seek shelter before it consumed our world. . . . It was a scene of indescribable violence, reminiscent of the first eons of creation."

One of the members of the trip, James Janney, who survived because he was lower on the mountain that fateful day, wrote a soulful reflection for *Ascent,* and it appears here as the first piece in our Dhaulagiri trio.

As a memorial to this expedition, a second trip took place in 1973. A large and competent group tried the southeast ridge, still unclimbed, but the difficulties proved too severe. As a consolation, three members reached the top by the regular route. It was the third ascent of the mountain, and the first time Americans had stood atop an 8,000-meter peak in ten years.

In 1974 *Ascent* came out with several pieces dealing with aspects of this expedition, one of which, "The Ridge," by Andy Harvard and Todd Thompson, is reprinted here. The climbers in this piece, who are attempting the southeast ridge, are not referred to by their full names. For the record, in order of appearance, they are Peter Lev, Del Young, John Roskelley, David Peterson, Jeff Duenwald, Jim Morrissey, Drummond Rennie, Ron Fear, Lou Reichardt, Terry Bech, Del Langbauer, and Tom Lyman.

Our final selection, previously unpublished, demonstrates that daring routes up 8,000-meter peaks still exert a magical pull on climbers. By the late 1980s several excellent routes had been done on Dhaulagiri, one of which was the eastern face, a wedge rising between the southeast ridge and the normal route. Four youths arrived a few years ago to attempt this enormous wall. A self-sufficient group, they planned to dash up the face without fixed ropes or Sherpa support. But the mountain had other plans, as it so often does. Kitty Calhoun Grissom, one of the most accomplished of the new wave of American mountaineers, tells of storms and sorrows, avalanches and conflicts.

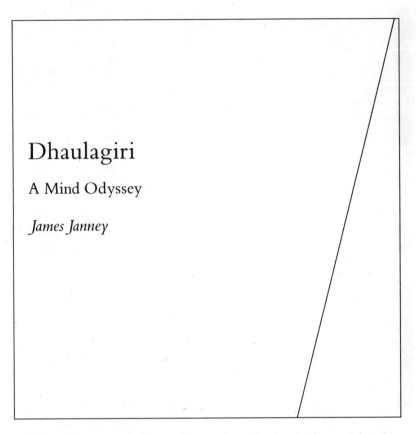

Dhaulagiri

A Mind Odyssey

James Janney

The white mass below rolls up the valley, mingling with other clouds above it, delivering its six-pointed message softly. Slowly each flake falls, lingering, before being flicked up by a slight breeze, not eager to reach the earth to be metamorphosed into water. The snow begins to fall fast, yet it is soft, feminine, gentle. The snow is cathartic; it is the calm after the violence, the silence after the avalanche's boom. Perhaps it was sent to us as a weak apology, as if Nature might be embarrassed at having taken so many at once, or perhaps, even more bizarre, for sparing Lou. The snow, at any rate, seems appropriate and beautiful.

As if in intentional countermotion to the snowfall, I ascend, though also lingering, thinking of those who have been free like the snow and now rest within the earth. This quiet emptying of the clouds seems to be both a white reminder of pale death and also a peaceful assurance of continuation—a confirmation of lives to come, lives which will attempt to carry on pieces of their spirits.

Looking up Dhaulagiri's southeast ridge; the northeast ridge is the right skyline.
ALLEN STECK.

Seven of my friends have died. Ice hunks formed from similar soft snow fell on them and crushed them unmercifully. Only Lou survived to tell those of us below. The clouds sense the tragedy and send snow. They pay their respects, as does the full moon, which now peeks sheepishly through the clouds, kindly assisting the forlorn search for any sign of life. We ascend. The procession, the wake, is good for us. Submerged in the pain of our upward paths, we forget some of the shock, some of the inexplicable ugliness of what has happened. For a time we forget the questions which may never be answered.

Yesterday, the day before their forever, my senses enveloped each's presence with sight. My senses incorporated each's sound in hearing. Now, totally unknown to my senses, they are dead. Dead. I cannot see, hear, or touch them. Understanding the reality of their death is like seeing a vacuum, like listening for an echo which is never returned. Somethingness disappearing into nothingness; the final period of a sentence which was never completed. The full moon will wane. It speaks of the paradox that life also wanes. Life, even at its height, cannot escape the fact of death. In fact, lived at a mountaineer's rhythm, life tends toward death. Pushing hard against life, the seven have been pulled away by death.

We live in a world of cycles. *Samsara* it is called in Buddhist Nepal. The cyclical make-up of existence. Water to vapor to snow, perhaps to ice, to water. The ever-changing moon, never constant yet always repeating itself. The wheel of life and death.

I ascend only to descend again. My footprints point upward and concur with others which have recently ascended. My footprints, after the ceremonial search, will return. Other's footprints will not. I make the ritual pilgrimage. For them the pilgrimage is over, cut off before completion, before maturation, some might say. Others will say they were cut off at the peak of involvement, of intensity, suggesting that the real joy of action is the process of achieving and not the achievement. Best, then, that they were cut off during the act and not the aftermath. Me—I do not know.

I do not know. My mind does not help, for it sends me on a wild shock trip. I cannot stand up even on an easy snow traverse. I become aware that now my sight has become round and the snow looks like an ever-changing concavity as I try to walk. Now my eyes are like tele-photo lenses and focus only on small depth-of-field sections—first on my blue padded knee against a washed-out backdrop of snow, then on a precise snowflake which is falling five feet beyond. I do not know.

The night comes, cuddles with us, and passes; I do not sleep. I do not really exist, but the living must return. They do, although only with hesitant steps weighted with a curious guilt about being alive when others are dead. Yet these steps are also filled with a strange joy, a thick, heavy joy about being alive and able to carry on what David, what they all stood for—a certain energy and vitality which caused them to die, yet which made all which went before bearable and more meaningful. Thoughts crystallize, perhaps too sharply.

It is not for us to ponder "Why him" or "Why not me." It is not for us to attach beautiful phrases apart from the fact as if to justify or attempt to give meaning. It is not for us to turn in desperation to some convenient concept of God which we neither accept nor understand. It is not for us to look above or beyond the incident, but to look directly, though seared by pain, into the undeniable fact of this accident.

There were five sahibs, and two Sherpas. Now seven no longer exist. Each was here for different reasons: some for pure adventure; some for companionship; some to prove something to themselves; some to gain a reputation; some to gain money; some only on a lark. All were trying to make up for a lack somewhere else in life; all were trying to complete themselves. All were human beings with many faults, yet all were there because they had the vitality to escape ordinary endeavor. They were attempting to find the answers to complex questions and to find out a little bit about themselves in this environment where they did not belong.

They could never have realized how much they took from us when they died, nor could they have realized how much they gave us. We take the energy and vitality of their souls and of their dreams. Taking a little bit of each individual which truly inspired us, we incorporate it into our lives, along with a knowledge of their faults, and descend. And continue living.

It is a time to look and a time to see. The pine forest with its fresh smells which permeate so deeply. The rhododendron. The clumps of grass. Nepal's spring breath. Down below it is spring, the youngest of the seasons. It bestows upon us its spirit. It is a time when the yaks are giving birth to their young. Though the evening comes, it is a time of newness, of recycling, of rebirth. As we descend we hear the sound of dogs barking. The candles within the homes cast a soft light, a quiet light on the families huddled around them. The children, young and inquisitive, greet us: "*Namaste.*" Nice. For all the hurt we are more aware.

Downward we go: down. Down past familiar places where we had stopped along the way. Each prominent rock or bend in the trail initiates a force which prompts me to recall a conversation during the inward trek. Floating through my mind, the incidents fall into harmony with the river below. We had been marked as fellow travelers on a path we had dreamed of for many years. We went along that path with mixed feelings about our objective, yet with definite pleasure in the fact that this unknown mountain had brought us together. We had looked forward to knowing Dhaulagiri intimately, but the basis for our pleasure was not really centered upon this mountain, but upon other mountains. Other climbs. Women. Photographs of New Hampshire ski slopes. Personalities of South American peaks. Martians in B.C. And even the horrors of the Alcan Highway. It was not so much what the immediate mountain brought us—that would have come later. We all brought, as Ross had said, these past experiences and ourselves, and made home wherever we were. It was a simple home, a nice home. Once more I hear the river.

Down we continue, past places where I had eaten with men now dead, had joked with those men, had sweated with those men. There are new footprints now but they do not matter any more than ours will; the footprints will disappear. The river will keep flowing, filled with a never-ending supply of glacial silt. The ecology of the valley will not change with their deaths. But one day the river flow will be altered only so slightly by a tattered piece of cloth or a fragment of bone which has re-emerged from the white cave of its tomb.

Similarly, those of us who are walking back will not ostensibly change that much. Yes, we are preoccupied now and will be for months. But that preoccupation will pass. Except at those times when something, some incident or situation, will recall what has happened in this past week. The flow of our private river will then be altered and the man in us which has been added, the certain maturity somehow bred by tragedy, will emerge, making that small flow more sensitive, more able to respond with feeling, more able to be alive.

1970

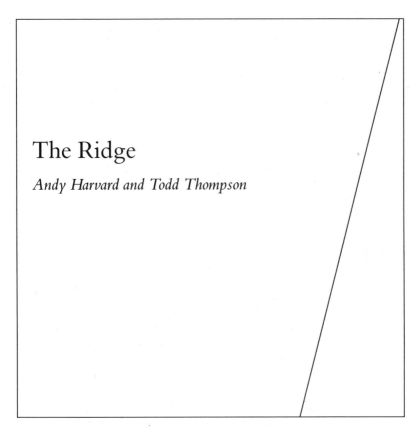

The Ridge

Andy Harvard and Todd Thompson

The storm was giving Lev and Young a hard time on the face. Heavy snow was falling by mid-afternoon. Ice breaking off from the hanging glacier to the left of the Hourglass made terrible noises, but it thundered harmlessly down the gullies alongside the route. Breaking cornices on the ridgecrest above were a threat, but an unlikely and unpredictable one. New snow accumulated and then sloughed regularly down the route, however, and it was in these powder slides that Lev and Young were climbing. Young led up over thin fifty-degree ice from Roskelley's high point to the bottom of the Hourglass. Lev made a very fine, short lead, the ninth, over a fifty-five-degree bulge into the center of the Hourglass. Climbing conditions were bad. They climbed between slides that swept over them, plagued by wind which blew spindrift in all directions. But this was the climbing for which they had come so far, so, oblivious to everything but the immediate, they kept on. It was dark when they finally descended, and the trail back to base camp was covered with fresh snow, so they started to dig a snow cave at the cache for a cold night's bivouac.

At base camp over a dinner of Calcutta Beef Peterson, joking speculation grew into serious concern for their safety. Two parties left the comfortable tent armed with headlamps and hot tea to retrieve the lost climbers. The rescuers stumbled around in the darkness and fog, anxiously calling to each other over the wind, tripping on equipment, tying into the wrong ropes and generally providing more excitement than the rescuees. Some who went out returned exhilarated by the night's beauty; others were exhausted by its fierceness. Those who remained in camp sat with candles at the door of the eating humpy, alternately cynical mountaineers and fathers with teenage daughters out late. They made hot tea to revive the sufferers, but drank it themselves.

Lev and Young arrived at camp under heavy escort, making laconic, understated comments about the day's climbing. They demonstrated the requisite nonchalance of climbers who have just been forcibly rescued. Morrissey articulated his relief in a shower of criticism for staying out late, mixed with lavish praise for a job well done. Both rolled off tired ears. Leisurely starts and the daily increase in the length of fixed ropes were leaving little time for climbing before the daily storm. Duenwald mischievously eyed the next day's team: "Tomorrow, you get up at three." Peterson gave him the finger, and Harvard choked on his tea, but nobody disagreed.

We considered the establishment of a camp at the cache below the ropes to reduce approach time, but, though half the face was finished, we were still on vague terms with the ridge, so we maintained a tentative, waiting posture until our knowledge and intimacy should increase.

The momentum of our expectations, built on nine days of mercurial activity, was suspended the next day by heavy snow. The day was devoted to reading, writing, talking, eating, or sleeping, all conducted at the same slow pace and low level of emotional involvement. Occasional harried trips were made to the drifted-in latrine on the edge of camp. Running to the latrine, Anderson fell into the garbage pit. Appearing at the door of the communal tent, his hair, beard, and clothes thick with powder snow, he said, "Hah! I didn't know there were any pigs up here." Morrissey, inside the tent, cracked an impish grin and returned, "Yeah, they dig holes all over the place, you have to watch out." It snowed three feet during the day.

The southeast ridge people, the technocrats, quietly discussed the objective danger of the route, that danger over which a climber has no control. The danger on the face was not excessive, but analyses varied according to the safety-mindedness of each man. A few were prepared to take great personal risk for the sake of the route; others found serious risk unacceptable. In any case, willingness to take understood personal risk was not the central issue. The varied backgrounds of the team meant that nearly half of the members did not have the experience to judge the danger for themselves, but would be exposed to it repeatedly in carrying loads to Camp I at the ridgecrest. What might be an acceptable amount of rockfall for an alpine ascent when one is exposed to it only once could be unthinkable for the repeated exposure of load carrying. The length of the ridge and the projected number of camps dictated that about two hundred loads be carried up through the Hourglass to Camp I. As the season progresses, the route deteriorates and rockfall increases, endangering the heavily traveled fixed ropes. Those who could judge had to decide what was justifiable risk for the expedition. . . .

Storms make men reflective and drive them into themselves; if a storm lasts long enough it will cause a man to discuss his most closely guarded concerns with his fellows. While the gale force wind rattled and swelled the tent, we turned to speculation. Rennie and Duenwald, who lead complex, specialized professional lives, saw the expedition as a simplified version of the world they knew at home, which afforded them the rare luxury of contemplation. Duenwald saw simplicity as an absolute good. "I feel very, very good," he sighed. "There have been few times that my life has been so pure and simple as the last few days. The absolute simplicity of life is becoming my goal." Harvard maintained that introspection and self-awareness should be possible during a busy, professional life. Duenwald told him to wait until he had a wife and kids. Smith thought that was all very nice, and said that the expedition gave him the only real opportunity he had other than weekends to follow his "avocation" of climbing. Lev thought that too much reflection was unhealthy and would only admit to being on a trip for fun. He pursued the theme of simplicity to say that a man has a greater chance to operate as a successful human being in the simplified context of the mountains than in the "outside" world. Fear, meanwhile, wrote in his diary, "The peace, the stillness, the beauty—the basic life. A time for learning and a time to think! To the north is the border of Tibet, to the south roll the plains of India, to the west is an old friend Dhaulagiri II, and to the east is Annapurna! The Himalayas, my love! Mountains are my only trouble besides women."

Reichardt poked around between the foodboxes looking for a chess piece that Ron had lost.

Thompson prodded the topic from simplicity to happiness, observing that happiness is the unachieved goal of everyone. He called it bovine stagnation, and said that as a goal sought by all the world, happiness is a pimpery. Duenwald accused him of devaluing everything that wasn't painful. Rennie said that happiness was important to him, but identified two kinds: the blithe happiness of the ignorant, and the disciplined happiness which rises above pain the way the fourth movement of Beethoven's Ninth Symphony grows from the previous movements. Searching for an example in literature, he decided that few writers understood happiness, or were capable of expressing it. Bech was reading Mann at the time, so Rennie began to hold forth on Germans as a bad example. Lev remembered that he had once been a Mann scholar, so he challenged Rennie more on principle than on conviction. Apart from literature, Lev identified happiness with selflessness, saying that happiness increases with responsibility.

On afternoons like this one, the Sherpas wisely stayed clear of the sahibs' tent. They probably sensed that once inside, they might never emerge again. Tea was served through the door. As the conversation lazily continued, the smell of popcorn drifted into the tent. We all ignored it for a while, then Morrissey stirred himself, walking stiffly toward the door of the cook tent. Startled Sherpas looked up to see the Bumba, face set and arms folded across his chest, bigger than life in mock anger. "I didn't know we had any popcorn left. *The sahibs like popcorn very much,*" he said slowly, distinctly emphasizing each word. Then he turned and stalked back to his corner. A bowl of popcorn appeared. Then another, and another, then pots and bucketsful—we cried mercy amid cheers from the cook tent.

That evening, with all sixteen climbers wedged into the dining tent for dinner, talk turned again to the conflict about the routes. The ridge was occupying only two men at a time, making most everyone else idle and impatient. Anderson and Bech were especially anxious to start carrying loads to the site of Camp I on the spur. Duenwald argued that working on the spur then would waste energy that would be badly needed in a few days on the ridge when loads started to move to Camp I on the crest. It was generally agreed that we could start the spur later in the month and still reach the summit before the monsoon. As a compromise, April 15 was set as the day to begin work on the spur. It meant that the problems on the southeast ridge must be resolved in the next six days. . . .

Lev's snoring was the only sound in camp that otherwise clear and quiet night. Langbauer and Roskelley were to start early on April 13 and attempt to reach the ridgecrest. Duenwald was to go up after them and make a final judgment on the objective danger that affected the route. Some climbers still expressed grave doubts concerning the feasibility of the route because of the danger. The fixed ropes, only ten days old, already showed signs of serious wear. Ropes came under harsh scrutiny during a rappel, when the climber must watch and feel the rope as he slides down; we were noticing cuts, occasional crampon holes, and an unexplained flattening of the rope sheath. The crucial variables on the ridge were the weather, the imminent arrival of the monsoon, and the objective danger. The ridge fanatics were anxious, uncertain, hopeful, and vulnerable. Doubt crept in.

Langbauer and Roskelley left early on the thirteenth. Driven by an urgent sense of mission, they reached the top of the sixteenth pitch by nine o'clock. Roskelley led off on the remainder of Young's six-hundred-foot spool, going two hundred feet on forty-five-to-fifty-degree ice, then led the eighteenth pitch, which steepened a few degrees toward its end, within eighty feet of the ridgecrest. While the members and Sherpas who remained in base camp watched them closely, Thompson noted in his journal, "I stand in base camp and watch the figures struggling competently high on the route and see that they are fragile. They are like our puny notions of honesty, beauty and the free act juxtaposed with the simple mass, the resistance and negation of this mountain. The resistance of the mountain to our efforts, even the wind alone, deny us as incisively as clods of earth landing on the top of a coffin deny life. I stand in base camp amidst the negligible material implications of an idea and know the hiatus between the concept of the southeast ridge route and physical possibility; between the line the eye follows on the mountain, and the gradual one-hundred-fifty-foot sections that mark a day's work."

Langbauer led the last bit, which tilted back to just over fifty degrees, to the ridgecrest at 21,500 feet. His hands in snow–clotted Dachstein mitts gripped the narrow ridge as easily as they could the back of a chair; he looked over—13,000 feet down the other side. The south face dropped away at sixty-five degrees; suddenly, he was very tired. He chopped a two-foot-square platform on the top of the ridge for his

On the Hourglass, the steep ice face leading to the southeast ridge. LOWELL SMITH.

belay anchors, eased a leg over, and straddled the ridge. The ridgecrest was sharp, steep ice, corniced here and there, as far along it as he could see in both directions. Tired and dejected, he thought he heard laughter. The smile and the irreverent laughter of David Seidman loomed in his consciousness. . . .

Roskelley and Langbauer stayed a few minutes on the crest, then started the long series of rappels. On the way back to base, they paused at the cache to pack the personal belongings stored there; they knew that they would not be back again, that we could not climb the southeast ridge of Dhaulagiri. It was a long, melancholy walk up to the col. . . .

We did not want to believe that the Dhaulagiri expedition could not climb the southeast ridge. Without the ridge, the expedition made no sense to many of us. We were cast adrift. Duenwald asked Harvard, Lyman, and Thompson to go to the crest to assess the route themselves. Roskelley and Langbauer would have liked to have been proven wrong.

The weather was not stable enough early on the fourteenth to go to the ridge, but loads were carried to Camp I on the spur as they had been the previous day. Quiet, vaguely desperate meetings took place in tents around camp. Some members were so committed to climbing the ridge that they began to consider establishing a camp under the cornice and climbing and living on the ridge as long as possible; if there was to be a failure, let it be a glorious one. . . .

Harvard wrote, "I think we should go for a little way, but I am alone in thinking that—the expedition has focused on the spur."

While part of the team reveled in the progress on the spur, the other part languished. It was not easy at first for the men who wanted so much to be on the ridge to work on the northeast spur with conviction. It seemed ridiculous to have thirty-two people and tons of air-dropped equipment at 19,300 feet in the Himalaya to make a third ascent. "It seems to me that the third ascent of a mountain by the old route is hardly worthy of comment. Well, at least Doubleday won't be able to use *Ascent of the Impossible Ridge* as a title for the book; that's one consolation," someone ventured. "Maybe they won't want a book at all," said Jeff. . . .

There is no clear line between success and failure. We seemed to fail, yet . . . there was more in the event than simple failure. We wanted to climb the ridge, but we did not need a heroic ending. If anything, antiheroism was the attitude we found most comfortable. We tried more than we could do; that was enough.

1974

A Wall of Gray Clouds

Kitty Calhoun Grissom

We awoke from the deepest sleep in two months to discover a blizzard raging outside the tents. Now? Just as we were ready to head for
home? Throwing down three feet of new powder, Dhaulagiri had not
finished with us yet. Two days earlier, three of us—Colin Grissom,
John Culberson, and I—had stood atop the mountain, elated but tired
of fighting avalanches, storms, and the cold. Now, safely back at base
camp, along with John's brother, Matt, we naively thought our difficulties were over. All we had to do was send our sirdar, Bir, to collect
porters from Marpha, a village only twenty miles away.

But the blizzard temporarily stopped this plan, forcing us to wait it
out. Meanwhile, our food was running low and our morale was falling
like the barometer. We wanted to go home. Be home. But finally the
weather cleared, as it always does.

"I'll go with Bir," Matt begins, "but we'll need some help breaking trail."

A long silence follows. "I'll go with you," I volunteer, trying to muster enthusiasm.

"Bir told me some Swiss trekkers passed through here on their way to Marpha," Colin says. "Before the storm. They'll be moving again by now, and once you reach their tracks you should be able to make time."

"I think we can make Marpha in a day and a half. I hope so, anyway," Matt replies.

Hours later, traversing an endless glacier, the three of us are bitterly cold. My feet feel as though I am shoving them into a freezer with each post-hole I create. Fighting the bottomless snow with every single step, we are moving at a slow pace, even by a snail's standard. Emaciated from the efforts of the past eight weeks, I crave a well-deserved feast and rest. But I obviously can't do this now, so I force myself to continue. Our immediate goal, French Pass, seems no closer than it did an hour ago.

Only after we climb out from the shadow of Dhaulagiri and move into the warm sunlight can my thoughts escape from our current predicament and drift back to the beginnings of our expedition. The four of us had been electrified back then, for none of us had ever attempted an 8,000-meter peak. Only I, in fact, had ever been to the Himalaya.

The monsoon had just ended and the foothills teemed with humidity and life as we began our approach march. Women toiled in the rice paddies that clung to the hillsides while squealing children romped in the dirt. The villages, clusters of one-room mud houses, were shielded by large trees. Old men squatted in the shade and chatted.

Higher up, we emerged from the world's deepest gorge, the Kali Gandaki, into a broad valley. The prevailing winds here had produced a rain shadow in which little grew except scattered sagebrush. Not far ahead lay Marpha, the last village on our approach, where we learned firsthand of that bane of so many expeditions: porter strikes. Half our porters refused to carry their loads any farther and demanded their pay. A shouting match developed between Bir and the deserters. While the rest of the porters egged on the troublemakers our liaison officer, Hary, feeling left out, decided to take charge.

"Kitty, I will talk with you and Bir. Now, please," he demanded. It took forever to negotiate terms, but in the end half our porters left and we replaced them with mules. Our remaining porters then demanded to be paid twice as much as a mule, even though the mule carried twice as much.

Finally, we left town with ten mules and twenty porters. As we wound higher into the mountains, forests merged into alpine meadows, which blended into barren scree slopes. Although we were tantalizingly close to the mountains by now, they remained obscured by the gray clouds that lingered after the monsoon.

Upon reaching our campsite at Kalo Pani, a rocky basin just below 17,000-foot Dhampus Pass, I felt sick. We had climbed into the realm of high altitude, where the unacclimatized are often seriously punished. Humility overcame me; I wondered if our plan to climb the world's ninth-highest peak alpine-style was just a fantasy.

Once over the pass, we dropped into Hidden Valley, a place of isolation and beauty. Only the wreckage of a plane revealed the presence of the outside world. A few hours later we clambered over French Pass and descended to the edge of a scree-covered glacier, where the porters unloaded the mules. The four of us eagerly jammed our packs with gear and followed some porters who knew the way to base camp, an hour away. I could hardly wait. Every night during those ten months since I had first seen Dhaulagiri I had fervently hoped I would have the opportunity to climb the incredible east face via the MacIntyre Route.

French Pass is getting a little closer, and I focus all my remaining strength on reaching it. It had taken us only two hours from the pass to reach base camp on the approach. But now, struggling through the unconsolidated snow, neither Matt nor I can break trail for more than a hundred yards before having to trade leads. Bir seems unable, or unwilling, to help. At dusk, ten hours after leaving base, we reach the elusive pass and descend the other side into Hidden Valley.

Matt takes the lead and I stumble along his tracks under the moonlight. My fingers and toes succumbed to the cold long ago, and I sense that frostbite is close. "Matt, I can't keep this up," I call out. I am embarrassed that I have become a burden.

"Okay, we can stop here," he reassures me. I watch helplessly while Matt and Bir erect our small tent. Not many words are spoken. We have no water or food and I sleep fitfully.

The next morning I awake nearly as weak and cold as I was when I arrived. The sun has not yet risen as we stagger through the chill toward Dhampus Pass. Below it we are surprised to find a large French camp.

"Yes, the Swiss were stranded here during the storm," a burly Frenchman explains. "One of the women got pulmonary edema. They are moving very slowly. They probably got to Kalo Pani last night."

Spotting the tracks of the Swiss, we follow them over the frigid pass and drop down to Kalo Pani. Here, for some reason, the Swiss left a tent rolled up in the middle of their recently abandoned camp. We are ravenously hungry, so Matt goes over to the bundle in search of food. I stretch out to soak up the warmth of the sun, finally peeping over the ridges.

"Matt," I joke, "one day you'll be snooping around and find a body." Suddenly, he is as still as a statue. Then he gingerly feels the bundle from one end to the other.

"Christ, it *is* a body. The woman—she died." We look at each other in disbelief. Death comes so swiftly, without warning. I think back on our close calls.

Base camp was barely visible through the thick blanket of fog. A large Japanese expedition with a permit for the standard route on the northeast ridge had already occupied the best campsites on the disheveled glacier. As we began our search for other sites we heard a crash from above. It sounded like several tons of ice were coming straight for us; we ran like scared rabbits. Then it became quiet again. We hadn't been at base camp for ten minutes yet. What an inhospitable place!

Hary didn't like the site either. Having read about altitude sickness he declared that he had all the symptoms: poor judgment, loss of coordination, nausea, and headaches. He wanted to descend to Marpha and carry out his duties from there, but that would not do. He would consume large quantities of beer and meat, and we would have to pay the bill. We sent Colin, a medical student, over with a stethoscope to convince him that his worries were unwarranted.

Later, we trooped over to visit our Japanese neighbors. Over cups of tea we explained that we had a permit for the east face and would be climbing up to the Northeast Col and traversing across the east face from there. The Japanese said we could share their route through the icefall to the col, but only if we contributed a couple thousand feet of rope to the cause.

"No problem," we replied as we said our goodbyes. Since we had thought the icefall would be no big deal and had planned to climb the east face alpine-style, we brought only 300 feet of rope. We thought about this dilemma and then went to speak with two nearby Spaniards, sole local members of a spread-apart expedition. Both were incapacitated: one had dysentery and the other had an infected blister. We graciously offered to fix the route through the icefall for them if they would donate a couple thousand feet of rope. The Spaniards readily agreed.

For two weeks we helped the Japanese forge a trail through the icefall and hauled supplies up toward the Northeast Col. At the end of this period we finally dumped our loads at the 18,700-foot col, relieved that our days of slogging back and forth along the glacier were finished.

"Let's go look at the MacIntyre Route," John shouted.

We made a short traverse over to a viewpoint. Colin got there first. "It doesn't look all that good," he said quietly when we arrived. Accounts of the first ascent in 1979 by the late Alex MacIntyre and friends described a coating of snow and ice that lay plastered over the rock for nearly the entire route. The tongue of ice that usually bisects the east face had not completely formed; water slithered over bare rock on the lower 2,000 feet.

Given the current conditions, we could not possibly do the climb. After the others had left, I sat and wept.

That evening's discussion was a somber one. "I don't think we can possibly do the MacIntyre," I began.

"Hey, don't we even want to try?" John asked.

"What about the Yugoslav Route off to the right?" Colin wondered. "It looks in good shape."

"We aren't prepared to do the MacIntyre in these conditions," I repeated. "And the Yugoslav Route is just a variation of the northeast ridge. If we can't climb the east face why not try the standard route? Or we can start up it, then make decisions later." Heads nodded in agreement.

All we lacked now was permission from the Japanese to climb with them on the northeast ridge. A few days later at the Northeast Col, while digging out our camp after a recent storm, we watched the Japanese ride out a large avalanche 1,300 feet above us. Fortunately, everyone survived and they began descending to the col. Though sobered by the incident, we saw a unique opportunity. As the Japanese arrived in camp, somber and shaken, we queried them about sharing the northeast ridge. "Yes, but you go first tomorrow," they said, grinning.

Two days later, Colin, John, and I clipped into the Japanese fixed lines with intentions of pushing the route past their high point. Colin and John were approaching the top of the fixed ropes when I heard a loud CRACK! echo across the slope. I glanced up to see the two of them flailing on a sliding wind slab, the fixed rope coming down with them. Diving into self-arrest, I desperately hoped I could hold their fall. Seconds later, forces beyond my control snapped me into the void.

Somehow I managed to self-arrest again, but another jolt jerked me from my position. A dull pain reverberated through my body as I tumbled down the slope with increasing speed. I covered my head in an attempt to keep it from being injured. Panicking will only make matters worse, I thought, trying to suppress my emotions as I prepared for death. Suddenly, I came to a stop.

Voices hollered from below, "Kitty! Kitty, are you okay?" I attempted to move but was pinned like Gulliver by the fixed line. "I think so," I shouted back, "but I can't move until you unweight the rope. Are you okay?"

A long pause. "Yeah. . . . Just a minute and we'll come up."

I turned and looked upward. The pickets anchoring the fixed lines had ripped out one by one; only the last had held, preventing a three-person fall to the glacier 3,000 feet below.

The fixed line loosened and I began to untangle myself. My axe had pierced my jacket, but fortunately had gone no further. Except for a rope burn through the elbow of my jacket, I saw no other signs of damage. Colin and John arrived, haggard but wide-eyed. Colin held up a deformed carabiner. "My harness carabiner unclipped from the line and caught on John's harness," he said with a grave expression. I stared at him, assimilating the words, the meaning, the consequences.

"I've twisted my knee," Colin continued, "and John has a bruised hip. We were all lucky."

As we stumbled down to our camp at the col, a lone figure moved steadily toward us. Matt had witnessed the entire accident in horror. He was as shaken as we were.

That night I took off my shirt to look at my elbow, which felt strangely damp. The rope had burned through my clothes and into my arm, leaving a raw area with a penetrating hole in the middle. A wave of nausea swept through me.

In the morning, before retreating to base camp to rest and recover from our injuries, we apologized to the Japanese for wrecking their fixed lines. They replied, "Japan in avalanches; America in avalanches. Spain go first next time."

Bir, who had lingered in the French camp for one more cigarette, catches us just as we are leaving Kalo Pani.

"Come on, Bir, we're going to help the Swiss break trail. The trekker is dead."

The tracks lead across a high ridge, the same way we came in, but then mysteriously turn down toward a steep valley. Are the Swiss taking a short cut we don't know about? If their route goes, we would drop below the snow line quickly and could be down in Marpha today. If not, we would have to retrace our steps, which would cost us precious energy and time. Our empty stomachs being the deciding factor, we decide to gamble on the unknown route.

Shortly, we meet a porter for the Swiss who confirms our hunch. Furthermore, he says, we are in good hands; their sirdar has been down the valley before. Now that we are on the last stretch, downhill, our sagging spirits and energy recover. We quickly descend past the listless trekkers to take over the post-holing.

Eventually, we break free from the snow and arrive at a high alpine meadow. Happy to be on dry ground, we scurry down the slopes, which funnel into a ravine. As this gully steepens and becomes choked with fallen trees and underbrush, we worry that perhaps the route has become overgrown and impassable. The heat grows oppressive. Crashing through bushes and vines, we at last come to a sheer cliff. I become frantic as my fears unfold. There has to be a way around the cliff; otherwise we'll have to climb back up several thousand feet to regain the longer route to Marpha. This does not seem fair. Haven't we suffered enough?

Grabbing exposed roots and vines, we pull ourselves back up the steep slope. The three of us split up, desperately hoping to find a way around the barrier. But our efforts are unsuccessful. In fading light we climb back up the gully in search of a flat place to sleep. We camp with the Swiss, whose sirdar guarantees that he will lead us out in the morning. I am restless and cannot control my desire to get out of this hellhole.

At dawn, while we wait for the Swiss to finish packing, one of them anxiously asks us if we saw the body. I look at the distraught man: he is struggling to control his emotions, but his grief overwhelms him. "That was my girlfriend," he sobs. "Her children paid for the trip to celebrate her fiftieth birthday. She loved the mountains," he continues, as if reliving the story might help him cope with the pain. "She wanted to reach your base camp, but she got sick as we crossed the first pass. We were stuck during the storm, and then she was too weak to walk. We had to carry her back over the pass. She died just as we made it to the other side. This is my worst nightmare. All I want to do now is to go home!"

I sympathize with the man and pray, if only for his sake, that we'll find a way around the cliff band. Although neither Matt nor I have much faith in the Swiss's sirdar, we are incredulous when he leads our group toward the same cliff that stopped us yesterday. We sit down in disgust to wait for their return. Bir and some porters soon come back with a report that they have been halted by the cliff band but will continue to look for a passage. The sirdar, he says, has not been down this valley in fifteen years.

Matt and I decide that if the sirdar cannot find the path in two hours we will desert the Swiss group and strike out for Marpha on the only route we know: the high traverse. Since I want to save my energy for that possibility, I look for a shady spot to rest. What a crazy place to be stuck!

Our morale weakened with each rest day in base camp. We had to go back up on Dhaulagiri soon or else quit. The winter jet stream was expected to arrive in less than two weeks. Though we had already abandoned hope of climbing the east face, we could still climb the northeast ridge if we hurried.

We climbed back up to Camp 1 with two Spaniards who planned to go all out for the top. At camp the Japanese informed us that their expedition was finished. The snow conditions had deteriorated, and a major snow bridge that led around the re-formed wind slab had collapsed. The Spaniards continued up, undaunted. With mixed feelings, we followed them up to explore alternative routes. The Spaniards crossed the wind slab without hesitation and kept ascending. Since the slab could release again, Colin, John, and I chose to sneak across the lower edge of the crevasse that marked the top of the wind slab. Here Matt turned around, thinking it too risky. We continued and established a moderately safe passage.

The four of us returned the following day to leave a cache at 23,000 feet. Beyond, the fixed lines continued across still more wind slabs. Concerned about the avalanche potential, Matt cached his load and descended to Camp 1 while the rest of us attempted the questionable slopes. Upon our return to camp, we were astonished to see Matt preparing to descend.

"It's too dangerous," he said. "I'll wait for you at the col."

John's voice filled with tension. "I wish you'd come with us. We've been through a lot together already; please don't quit now."

Matt shook his head. "Be careful," he warned, as he embraced each of us. Then he left.

Two days later the Spaniards appeared at our tent, at 23,000 feet. They had made it to 26,200 feet but one of them had taken a fifty-foot fall and both had sustained minor frostbite. They wanted some medication for the descent.

What would happen to us? I wondered as I staggered up to the site of our last camp at 25,000 feet. In our oxygen-deprived state it took hours to chop out a tent platform in the ice. Numb fingers fumbled with the tent poles while the wind tried to rip the tent from our grip. That night, teamwork reached an all-time low as each of us struggled with basic chores.

On the summit day, a wall of gray clouds moved slowly but steadily toward us. We plodded up the north face, winding through bands of rock littered with remnants of old fixed line. Leaving the security of camp and venturing onto slopes higher than I'd ever been on filled me with curiosity and fear. How long could my body function in the increasingly thin air? Would I have enough strength left for the descent?

As we punched through calf-deep snow I sank into a rhythm: six gasps for air, four steps forward, six wheezes, four lurches. Near the top of the face we dropped our packs and continued, our newfound energy coming from the belief that we were near the summit. Images of previous climbers on Dhaulagiri faded in and out of my mind. As we mounted the knoll we thought to be the top, we saw a rocky outcrop just ahead that appeared even higher. But the closer we came the farther the summit backed away.

We stumbled at last onto the rocky point. Below us, the south face dropped precipitously for thousands of feet to a glacier. We'd made it! But the climb had drained me of all strength and emotion; I was in a stupor. During our brief stay we took the obligatory summit photos. Since we didn't have a flag, John waved a dirty handkerchief.

Descending, drunk from the altitude and grossly uncoordinated, I felt an overwhelming urge to sleep. We collapsed like robots in the tent at dusk.

The descent to the col the next morning was treacherous. The wind had blown spindrift into our tracks and we made many annoying plunges through the breakable crust. We had little patience for this torture. As we neared the col Matt appeared, overjoyed to see us but satisfied that he had made the correct decision.

During the night it began snowing lightly and the clouds grew black. Bent under our loads, we left the Northeast Col for the last time. A large avalanche had swept the north face and buried our tracks across the upper part of the glacier. We made our way through the debris and reached the fixed lines at the top of the icefall, where Bir was waiting to help us. As he began taking some of our loads the realization of our accomplishment struck me. I had wanted to climb Dhaulagiri so badly, but I never let myself imagine making the summit because I didn't want to be disappointed. I knew the chances of success were slim. Now I was ecstatic; nothing could upset me.

I hardly recognized the icefall: large seracs had tumbled chaotically. Both the Japanese and the Spanish expeditions had left, and base camp was deserted, except for some trekkers. That evening, we celebrated over fried potatoes, Tibetan bread, and hot chocolate spiked with whiskey. Someone would leave tomorrow for Marpha and return with porters in two days. We slept well that night, oblivious to the storm, which had become a blizzard.

"Kitty, they found the path," Matt yells. I want to hug him but decide it might be premature. Instead, I rise to my feet and join the line of trekkers who are being led down a tunnel through the thicket. We emerge onto a hidden, grass-covered ledge traversing diagonally downward across the cliff. The valley floor is not far below. Finally, a chorus of cheers ring out as trekkers and climbers alike step out onto the gravelly plain.

1993

4

A SENSE OF WHIMSY

Editors' Introduction

From the very first, we at *Ascent* had a strong desire to inject doses of humor into our publication. The absurdities of mountaineering were legion; thus there were obvious opportunities for writing humorously about the sport, both in fiction and nonfiction. The problem was finding the material. Few American climbers wrote in this genre, perhaps because they were too serious, too deeply enmeshed in the factual aspects of their adventures. Or maybe they simply lacked the necessary skills.

Europe, however, with its abundance of climbing writers, had much to offer. Thus, our first issue featured Bernard Hollowood's parodic "Pens Over Everest," a funny vignette in which an expedition diarist finds the effort more than he can handle. Here also we presented the macabre drawing *L'enfer des Montagnards,* by the noted French writer-illustrator Samivel. Tucked in the back was a cartoon by Sheridan Anderson, the first of his many creations that would appear in *Ascent.* Sheridan's talent as a humorist was extraordinary, and his work soon began to appear in many publications in the U.S. and Great Britain. A collection of his climbing cartoons, with accompanying text by his "literary counterpart" Joe Kelsey, was published in 1989 under the title *The Climbing Cartoons of Sheridan Anderson,* five years after Sheridan's untimely death.

Writers and illustrators soon began to send their humor pieces to *Ascent,* and these submissions certainly entertained the editors. Tom Higgins, not normally known as a wit, sent us "In Due Time," a morality play in three acts that sets up well-known Yosemite climbers and traditions for humorous, almost satiric treatment. Mark Twain's "The Conquest of the Riffelberg" and H. G. Wells's "Little Mother up the Mörderberg" were recommended by friends. That these stories, and many others as well, were not included in this volume is no reflection of their quality, for all are worthy creations.

First in our collection here is the hilarious vignette "Druggs in Himalaya." As expedition doctor, Drummond Rennie finds himself in Kathmandu, scurrying around the local bazaars looking to replace his lost medical kit. After he sees a strange brown man in a grubby white turban dispensing assorted powders, he buys a little blue book in which the magical powers of the substances are explained. Rennie is a fine writer—no doubt about that—but he is nearly upstaged by the druggist-translator of this Nepalese version of *The Pharmaceutical Basis of Therapeutics*.

Our next contribution, "Dedo de Deus" (Portuguese for *Finger of God*), consists of two delightfully humorous stories, one written by Malcolm Slesser and the other by E. J. Henley. The stories, which originally appeared a year apart in the *Scottish Mountaineering Journal*, concern the ascent of a large granite spire near Rio de Janeiro by a hastily assembled group of climbers with, as it develops, quite different temperaments and abilities: Carlos Costa Ribeiro, a Brazilian climber of some renown; the inexperienced American physics professor Henley, (inexplicably called "Harvey" by Slesser); and the doughty Scottish mountaineer Slesser. This twin treatment of the miniexpedition proves to be rather amusing, as the events experienced by the two protagonists appear quite different in the retelling.

Next is Harvey Manning's "Leadership," a whimsical treatment of the many problems that leaders and their followers face on climbing courses in the mountains of the author's home turf, the Pacific Northwest. After seeing the bloody results of his students' attempts at self-arrest practice, Manning concludes, "neither a leader nor a follower be. Climb alone."

On no other mountain in the world do the absurdities of mountaineering accrue to such an alarming degree as on Denali, or "Big Mac," our very own mountain of Himalayan proportions in the Alaska Range. Eric Sanford's entertaining account of his ascent of the West Buttress Route is less a record of his own adventures than a collection of vignettes describing the tribulations of the bewildered and often naive mountaineers he meets along his way: the hapless Japanese who bring tomato stakes instead of aluminum pickets; the Polish mountaineers whose stove blows up; and the group whose food cache is consumed by ravens.

Denali—the high point of North America—draws mountaineers from all parts of the world, and though most expeditions are serious and highly experienced, others arrive at base camp without proper equipment or necessary skills. Some of these latter groups, of course, make the summit and have a good time: they are the lucky ones.

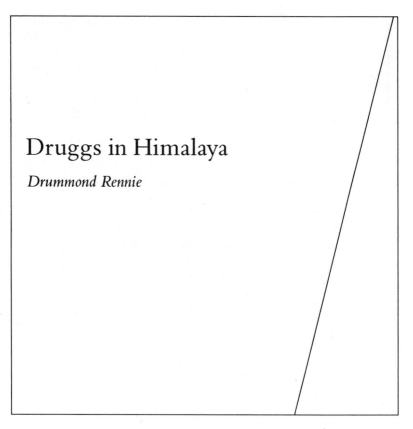

Druggs in Himalaya

Drummond Rennie

The expedition was poised to move. The years of planning, preparations, selecting the members, designing equipment; the months of
training, raising funds, hiring porters, engaging Sherpas, buying, begging, and borrowing gear, were over. Everyone was in Kathmandu.
Tomorrow we could be on the trail, headed for the high Himalayas,
and tomorrow we would be, except that our eighteen tons of equipment, shipped four months before, was completely lost. For a week we
searched frantically, establishing progressively that it wasn't in our hotel, wasn't at the embassy, wasn't in Kathmandu, indeed, wasn't even
in Nepal.

The average expedition IQ being around 170, mutually exclusive
contingency plans began rapidly to proliferate. Clearly, we had to assume that everything was lost for good and, unless we had come halfway round the world for nothing except to return with sheepish grins,
we would have to equip ourselves urgently. A walk through the bazaar

Retired Nepalese pharmacist working through his mid-life crisis. THOMAS LYMAN.

soon convinced us that if we wanted to, we could get the finest British oxygen, German boots, French rope, Swiss altimeters, American carabiners, and Nepali dysentery. My duty, however, since I was expedition doctor, was to provide medical supplies.

The hospitals, missionary or otherwise, operating on a shoestring, could not reasonably be expected to supply anything. I trucked off despondently into the noisy bazaar, jostling moodily through the crowds and trying to identify which wooden hovel was most likely to be a pharmacy. A knot of people blocked my way, so I elbowed in until I could see what they were staring at: a little brown man in a grubby white turban, squatting on the floor before a brightly painted backcloth. In front of him, separating him from the crowd, were thirty or so rusty sardine cans, neatly arranged in two rows, and each filled with a powder: yellow, brown, green, ochre, red, or black. The man, talking loudly and emphatically, was rapidly ladling out spoonfuls of powders onto squares of paper, mixing them, adding drops of clear fluids from old Nescafé jars and then with a deft twist furling each paper into a

cone. Frequently he would turn and point out important features on his
back-cloth—a charming scene of gray mountains and white pagodas
crowded with highly colored men in combat, or perhaps conversation,
with angular giraffes, foolish lions, aggressive snakes, hemiplegic an-
telopes, saucy apes, rearing elephants, and (as big as the elephants)
loathsome scorpions. Business in paper cones was brisk.

Here, very obviously, was the pharmacy. My problem was that neither Cambridge nor London nor Chicago had adequately prepared me
for this. What were these mixtures? I had left *The Pharmacological Basis
of Therapeutics* at home—anyhow it would be quite useless here. Suddenly I noticed a stained blue booklet on the ground beside the pharmacist. Interrupting his flow of Nepali words and universal gestures, I
bought it and opened it. It read: "PRICE—LIST OR Vanaspati Druggs
IN HIMALAYA, certified by Dr. M. B. Poolsingh F.C.P.S.D.P.H. &
Hy." I took it back to the hotel for study before returning to make my
purchases the next day.

At the hotel there was relative peace, the quiet broken only by the
sounds of scaffolders outside and of fornicators within.

The booklet was half in Sanskrit, half in English. On the inside of
the front cover, upside down, was stuck, incongruously, a colored
postcard-sized portrait labeled "Aaron Burr, circa 1794," and at the
back a photograph of a nameless Indian bodybuilder clad in an athletic
supporter and flexing his muscles at the camera, circa 1955.

The Little Blue Book was refreshing reading. Pick up any medical
journal in the States and look at the advertisement for any drug.
Those federal agencies have real power. Every claim is qualified by
"may . . . in some patients . . . temporary." It must not be used in the
young, the old, the obese, the neurotic, the pregnant, or those with
high or low blood pressure, allergies, or a tendency to liver, lung, or
kidney disease. "Warnings" are followed by "Contraindications," then
by "Precautions" and "Adverse Reactions," with subsections on Overdose and Habituation and Addiction, spinning out what the advertisers
call a "Brief Summary" into seventy-eight closely packed lines of small
print. Obviously, the drug is probably useless and you're darn lucky
not to kill the patient.

In contrast, the Little Blue Book radiated total optimism because the
drugs had an infinite range of action. "Weariness in body, paleness in
complexion, pain in waist or stomach weakness, palpitation of heart,
fattening, gastric troubles, enlargement of stomach, constipation, boils,
phlebitis. All such and other diseases will be cured for ever in life."

There were no contraindications, no side effects, no warnings—and never any possibility of failure.

I wanted a general pharmacopoeia and I was not disappointed. Opening it at random, I read "For Paralysis pains of joints psrains gas, muscle troubles, skin diseases, pour on the palm and you will tind in coozing out from its backside. Also good for failling hait, white hair etc. It is use for baidriess. The use of oil (Jindigutti) will grow hair long ans silhy. Price Rs. 2/—per tola.

"No 10. Hair-Enlarging Tonic Oil Ranghori," an oil of fourteen herbs will "turn silver hair darl-black. All other diseases of the hair or head will automatically be cured. Apply with Chopra oil."

No. 12 was specific for "Paralysis or Joint-Catching gastric trouble" and No. 8 for "Nightfalls and memory" (useful on the mountain), and "married bliss."

I was worried about pulmonary edema at high altitude, which came under the heading "Aesthema" or "Asthama." "Dose—Shilajeet 10 tolas, Madanmasta 1/2 tols. in honey. It can in beattle-pan and gives a pleasant small. Temedies all funt diseases."

Shilajeet was also good for "Diabetis. One doze daily in stale water" and "On bleeding and Unbleeding piles"—such a bane at high altitudes. Another problem high up would be "everlasting cold and headache round the clock when the body grows thinner and thinner." Use Formula 5, and Formula 6 for "Blood Purification and Leprosy. People have white, yellow, black or red spots. They suffer from Axjma and Itch which can be cured and the whole body begin to shine as polished.

"Tamarind, juggery, cocumber and half-boiled oil are discarded" when the medicines are taken. My Oxford Dictionary had no entry between *Juggernautish* and *Jugging*. But they must have meant jagri—a crude sugar made from the sap of East Indian palm trees. I did not see any difficulties with these prohibitions, nor with "celibacy should be observed during this period of medicine—forty days for Tila Oil No. 1." After all, we would be several weeks away from any women. This might lead to problems in itself, but there was Formula No. 15, "General Tonic for Mental Imbalance" for when "people begin to tear clothes, fling stones on others, talk at random, keep mum or murmur to themselves. Their tongues twist."

At first I had thought that Formula No. 3 would be better for this enforced celibacy. This was listed as "General Tonic for General Deficiency of Women." Unfortunately, it was not what it claimed, but merely something to "cure stomach weakness for ever, keep the mind intact during pregnancy and bring radiance to the complexion." There was no question, however, that there would be this deficiency, so back to Shilajeet Pure which is "found in the Himalayas. . . . it being a favourite of monkeys has to be obtained with much difficulty to test the best."

The book did not stop there, however. Like every other marketable book ever written, it dealt principally with sex. This might seem irrelevant to my purpose. But I was going to be the whole doctor, dispensing advice for the future as well as drugs for the present. We might be stuck in Kathmandu for a long time while we tried to track down the gear. And anyhow, I might garner a few hints. Shilajeet was good here, in Formula No. 9 "General Formula for having issues. Even if you been childless for 25 years," after the dose "your nursery will be filled with the laughters of the youngone." As a side product there are "fructifying harmones in the semon." Take for sixty days. It sounded like a Harvest Festival.

This did not seem likely to be much of a worry to the expedition. Nor was it likely that we would need Tila Oil, No. 11, for "any kind of looseness or want of flavour or erection or sensation in the productive organ of man which is removed by this ointment. Its curve, or thinness or other sort of weakness will also be removed due to this ointment." The cause is "excessive riding or cycling." But forty days of No. 11 rubbed on the "concerned organ" and "he will have sufficient power to satisfy his life partner." Also "stiffens loose breasts."

Under "Oil for Outward Rubbing" Tila curiously "rubbed to the uterus" cures shortness, bulging and tapering, and "discorder due to hand or toemuch female enjoyment flexible nerves etc. To be rubbed twice a day would give full pleasure married life. Even in old age Tila give a added pleasure." Rs. 2/—per tola. "Tila gives fram to the deformed breast and rubbed for viginal disordeis for 40 days would give pleasures of youth."

The expedition members were, it seemed, overachievers and I felt that more relevant would be "Ishk Ambar. Benefits A man can after its use, keep prolonged company with many a fair sex, without feeling any sense of fatigue. He will have muscular energy like an elephant, he will be inflammable like fire, will have sweetness of voice like a peacocks and will be nimble like a horse. His eyes will be as sharp as those of a vulture. His treasure of human potential fluid will be added in planty. His heart would be amorous and he would feel immense satisfaction after intercourse. It will also give healthy and handsome progeny" who can then be given "No. 4 General Tonic for Infants," which will "develop their memory power, produce blood in their nerves and radiate their faces with fresh zeal."

I had just drawn up a list of twenty-two drugs from Adarak to Sobhai, enough to guarantee all of us long life, perfect health and interminable ecstatic sex, when Jim came in. "The gear's all been found," he said. "Tomorrow morning, crack of dawn, you go to Pokhara to unload and sort the stuff out."

I put the Little Blue Book sadly away. It was late. I'd never find the pharmacist at this time of night. I went off to see Boris about a drink.

1974

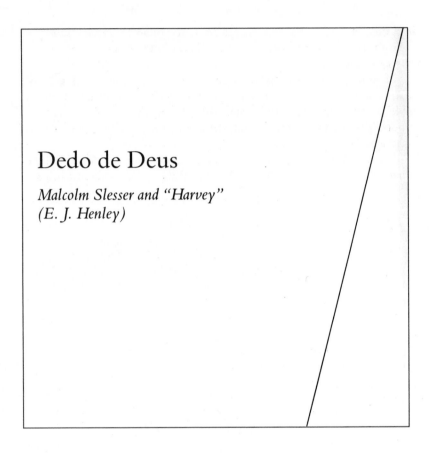

Dedo de Deus

Malcolm Slesser and "Harvey"
(E. J. Henley)

MALCOLM SLESSER:

A tendency to indulgence, whether in food, mountains, or liquor has, happily, always been a feature of the members of our Club. Never are we better than when flouting danger or offsetting some discomfort with the knowledge that in the valley lie groaning tables and exquisitely distilled malts. Age may alter the relative balance of such immoderation, but the Club spirit is unassailable. It will be perceived, therefore, that I, an aging member surrounded by the bald granite precipices of Rio de Janeiro with gin at five bob a bottle, experienced little difficulty in fitting into my new environment. It is true that when viewed on a cold winter's night in Scotland, pictures of these sun-drenched precipices draw forth fire and bold talk. But when seen in reality with the sun almost vertically overhead and temperatures oscillating a degree or

Carlos and "Harvey." MALCOLM SLESSER.

two about the hundred, the alternative of a Brazilian gin tonic in half-
liter mugs seemed the saner course. Nevertheless my SMC conscience
would twinge now and again when the sun set behind some glorious
vertical precipice, or when one day poised behind a beer on the summit
of the Sugar Loaf (it has a *téléphérique*) I suddenly saw the Finger of
God. I felt an instant admonishment. Moreover, it was an American
professor, a stranger to climbing, who brought me to its foot.

The Dedo de Deus (5,300 feet), to give it its Brazilian name, is a six-
hundred-foot finger of vertical granite set on top of a steep jungle-clad
spur, the second of a series of five peaks that grace the east flank of the
Organ mountains some fifty miles from Rio city. It was climbed first
in 1912 by Aceio de Oliveira and a large body of comrades in the days
before incoming Czechs and Austrians gave Brazilian climbing the tone
it has today. It was time I too climbed it, for Brazilians on learning of
my pretensions as a climber would smirk and say, "Ah, but have you
tried the Dedo de Deus? Of course, it is only for experts!"

Harvey's Chevrolet purred its expensive U.S. way through the deserted streets of 4:00 A.M. Rio with myself and Carlos Costa Ribeiro in
the back seats. Carlos, a student of physics, was a renowned climber,
having had a go at the recently discovered highest mountains in Brazil
on the Venezuelan border. As a youth in Austria he had been introduced

to *kletterschuhe* and dolomite. Harvey and he talked about the benefits of communism while I slept.

We parked at a roadside shrine at 2,500 feet in the depth of the slowly wakening forest, and looked up to see the momentary sun blush on the Finger, which poked censoriously out of a palisade of trees. One day, I thought in the putting-off frame of mind 6:00 A.M. always instills in me, we must have a go at the east face. Thank God, the normal route is round the other side. For several hours at least, one could press on assuming it was easier.

"That's our way," declared Carlos, pointing to the east face. "The original route would bore you."

Tamely and silently I followed him as he led into the jungle along a vague trail designed for pygmies. However, five minutes into the jungle and the plants on the floor gave up trying to live. One could stand up without being swiped in the eye by bushes, or throttled by hanging lianas. A prey to fears, I looked anxiously about for anacondas, rattlesnakes, or cor-de-rosas, and faced with what strength I could the thought of beating off Oncas.

The first pitch loomed out of the gloom, a sebaceous groove whose crucial move was executed by a monkeylike swing from the fragmentary root of a once-noble ipé tree. I was soon to learn that were it not for trees, Brazilian climbing would be impossible.

More gloom. Then slabs, and for a moment we broke into sunshine and saw the north wall dripping with cornices of moss, gravatas, and other nameless growths that lent an air of fester outdoing Coire Ardair at the height of summer.

Another half-hour of gloom and sweat, and then Carlos paused.

"We leave sacks here."

Personally, I never felt less like parting with my belongings. Reluctantly I changed boots for PAs, and draped on a few tape etriers and a hammer and pegs.

"You won't need these."

I smiled. Reports I had heard of Brazilian belay techniques would have scandalized Tennent, far less the author of a slide-rule work on running belays.

Carlos then led across an avalanche chute. These are common hereabouts, though mud and old trees take the place of snow. The debris is unstable and often can be jarred into further movements. The consequences are too awful to contemplate. Soon we were on mud of inconceivable steepness, barely held in place by a lush growth. With one hand on the north face, we slithered, groped, pulled, yanked, sweated, and clawed our way up mossy grooves, rotting trees, and holdless chimneys. Harvey did it all on his fingers. Carlos enjoyed antigravity. Then suddenly I was face to face with a mass of deep red orchid blooms, and it was worth it. Soon shouts from ahead spoke of light, and following a tunnel in some dense bushes I found my two companions sitting on a small rock tower looking up at the east face of the Finger of God.

It seemed to be composed of four totally detached pieces of rock that, like some child's puzzle, fitted together into a mountain. What route there was must lie along the interlocks.

The climbing, when it came, was delicious. Here, right on the Tropic of Capricorn, even at 4,700 feet, there is never any frost. The rock, though the finest granite, is almost totally lacking in incut holds. Nor does it ever have the roughness of a Chamonix slab. Rather, it seems to have solidified from a pitted syrup, and been upended. The few cracks lay along the interlocks or where massive chunks had broken loose. Resolute trees had managed to worm long tough roots far into the interior of the Finger and I found them useful as runners and belays. Much needed too, for my companions showed a complete lack of interest in such procedures. Harvey had no experience, and was in any event by this time utterly exhausted. He had climbed fully two thousand feet from the car largely on his hands. Carlos used ritual belaying. I looked for peg-cracks and found none. The drop beneath us was impressive; the landing a green umbrella of branches.

Harvey was breathing stertorously, and Carlos was lassoing spikes in Whymper fashion.

We reached a cave and thankfully crawled into the shade.

"Up?"

"Out."

Out right under an overhang I saw the first of several bolts. Like half-inch carriage bolts, these Brazilian things are made to last and to take the weight of about ten people. The whole philosophy and safety of Brazilian climbing hinges around them. The rock being holdless, it is their answer, and not a short-term one.

Harvey allowed his eye to dally a moment, and then undid the rope and started down. The Luso-Scottish elements, scandalized, called him back pointing out the commonplace that the party does not split up, adding the rider that the majority were in favor of going upwards. Harvey, no traditionalist, gave way only when he found we wouldn't give him a rope to rope down. Carlos led, and vanished. Whatever instructions he subsequently offered were lost in the wind, and Harvey was dangling on the first tape before he had time to reconsider. I fear we were brutal. When Harvey wisely announced that he had neither strength nor skill for this sort of thing, and that he would come down, Carlos instantly slackened the rope. Harvey slid wildly to the right, and, being a scientist, was at once aware that gravity was going to spring him out under an overhang, and not back to me.

"What do I do?" he shouted.

"Impossible to get back," I shouted encouragingly.

But Harvey was a U.S. citizen, and Carlos knew how to give a friend a helping hand. The grunts that ensued might have lured a female hippopotamus. And when my turn came I appreciated the difficulty. This pitch, called the *Maria Cebolla*, was led by a Czech immigrant called Drahomirubas. What he held on to while putting in the expansion bolts is a mystery. The last twenty feet are a slanting crack between an overhang and a vertical wall calling for uncritical faith in hand jams. I found Carlos contentedly gazing at the view, belayed to a cactus whose roots I was able to lift with one hand.

Thereafter we climbed within, not on, the mountain. Often as much as ten feet from the outer face we chimneyed for two long pitches, crept up a slab, and reached the top of a plinth. A huge rock crevasse, overhanging above us like a bad rimaye, was all that lay between us and the top. We climbed it the only way anyone has yet found—by a ladder. Half a century's weathering had exchanged iron for rust, but to make assurance doubly sure, the top was tied with decayed electric flex to an expansion bolt.

The summit is as flat as a navvy's thumb, with a forest large enough to keep visitors in firewood for decades. We all, for various reasons, were very happy. From here one can see some of the superb faces on the north side of the range. Some, like Garafao, are virgin and over fifteen hundred feet high. We dined off gammon (from the PX) and bruised pineapple and slid down the ladder for the start of the descent by the *voie normale*: a series of chimneys on the west face with ledges between. Harvey wouldn't climb, so we had to rappel. He lost his spectacles, and their glassy tinkle could be heard from the bowels of the mountain for minutes after. On the third rappel, the steepness of the pitch, and the absence of foreground nearer than one thousand feet, caused Harvey to ask for a safety line, and my rope was put in play. I had descended and was enjoying a quiet contemplation of cavorting mists and mysterious walls, when the rasping noise of Harvey's skin on the rope stopped, and he started gurgling badly. The safety line had jammed in a carabiner.

I shouted to him to haul himself up on his arms while Carlos freed it, but his arms were done.

"Cut the rope," he demanded in a high-pitched voice that was not like him at all.

"Wait a minute." One is not born in Aberdeen for nothing. Moreover, Tiso's was at least eight weeks' postage away. I climbed up and tried to lasso Harvey and haul him onto a higher ledge. However, having discovered a solution he was single minded in demanding it.

"Cut the rope"—a cry which, as he slowly went blue, he modified to "Cut the rope. I'll buy you a new one. I'll buy you as many ropes as you like, but cut the rope. . . . "

I nodded, and Carlos cut, and Harvey landed drunkenly beside me, while I coiled forty feet of useless nylon.

There were no hard feelings. The dusk was brief and beautiful, and we groped down the festering jungle on all fours, and made the road three hours after darkness. I had been neither attacked nor bitten. Next day, Harvey, a good colleague if ever there was one, offered to send to New York for a new rope. "Forget it. Just one of those things." We worked on, while his cigar smoke coiled lazily in the cold air of the air conditioner.

"Malcolm, you get whisky?"

"No." To all except diplomats it was eight pounds a bottle in Brazil.

"A case any good to you?"

If the Finger of God wagged at me, I never saw it.

E. J. HENLEY:

Professor Slesser's version of our ascent of Dedo de Deus and of how he transformed an old, frayed, nylon rope into a case of Chivas Regal is badly in need of elaboration. His overly modest account of what surely must be acclaimed as the "rope trick of the year" hardly makes him out to be the rogue and blackguard he really is. Indeed, the true saga of how a feeble, middle-aged, New York City cliff dweller whose previous highest ascent had been to the top of the Empire State Building (in an elevator) found himself nearly strangled near the end of a tortuous 5,300-foot, fourth-degree climb (the great Herzog called it "very challenging") may be of interest to readers. It may also serve as a deterrent to other novice climbers who may be foolish enough to trust Malcolm Slesser.

I freely admit that I went of my own volition; indeed, it was I who suggested the near-fatal climb, and introduced Slesser to Carlos Costa Ribeiro, our Brazilian guide and gracious host. It was, in fact, my second attempt at Dedo de Deus. Ribeiro and Mauro Andrade, who was then one of my graduate students at the University of Brazil, had attempted to yank and shove me up the "tourist trail" to the top of the rugged peak the previous month. The fact that Ribeiro and Andrade, two of the strongest, most resourceful rockclimbers in Brazil, had not succeeded in hoisting me more than five hundred feet over the well-trodden trail to the summit is an accurate testimonial to my physical condition and skill as a mountain climber. I still recall, with a warm glow, how Ribeiro and Andrade walked over to me as I lay panting and prostrate on a gentle forty five-degree slope and said with typical Brazilian tact and *gentileza,* "Professor, at times when climbers are faced with insurmountable obstacles, they show more courage by retreating than by going on."

It was in a naive, American spirit of Rotarianism that I introduced Ribeiro to Slesser and offered to drive them to the base of Dedo de Deus. It was my intention to walk with them to a comfortable vantage point and then enjoy a picnic lunch and a restful afternoon with a good book, leaving the climbing to the professionals. In preparation, I loaded my knapsack with two bottles of Beaujolais, a small roast chicken, biscuits, a package of Gruyère cheese, containers of cole slaw and potato salad, carrots and cauliflower, a tin of Toll House cookies, two pears and an orange, silverware, napkins, and a tablecloth, an autographed copy of Professor Slesser's *Red Peak,* my camera, a pair of high-power binoculars, sneakers, a first-aid kit, mosquito repellent, an inflatable cushion, a box of Suerdicki cigars, and a flask of Remy-Martin. The cognac, wine, and cigars were, as I recall, chosen with some care since I had to consider the *bon vivant* tastes of my erstwhile Scottish friend.

The ninety-minute drive behind us, we arrived at the base of the mountain at the uncivilized hour of 5 A.M. I did not partake of the conversation in the car, partly because I was too sleepy, but mostly because it was in a foreign language, mountain-climberese. There was a certain amount of semiabrasive verbal sparring since Slesser had never climbed in Brazil, and he was understandably curious to learn what the Brazilians considered to be a difficult climb, and what techniques were used.

We cast a few coins in the fountain next to the shrine in memory of the climbers who had died attempting to scale the formidable peak, and then began the four-hour trek to the base of the Finger. Had I not been struggling unsuccessfully with the tropical underbrush, a heavy knapsack, and a pair of ill-fitting mail-order boots, I would have noticed that we were taking an entirely different route to the one Ribeiro, Andrade, and I had taken three weeks earlier. Adding to my confusion was the fact that I was perspiring so much that my glasses were fogged, and I was suffering from what Jack Benny once called the clothing sickness— my tongue was coated and my breath was coming in short pants.

At approximately 9 A.M. I practically fell into Ribeiro and Slesser, who had been racing along ahead. They had removed their knapsacks and were pensively scrutinizing the thousand-foot high rock pinnacle which loomed up immediately ahead. It was a heroic sight; I felt like a roach at the foot of an obelisk.

I was very grateful to Ribeiro for having taken us to see this epic view. After consuming some food and a bit of cognac and snapping some photos, I suggested we move around to the other side of Dedo de Deus, where we could begin our ascent. The conversation, which had previously been carried out in English, Portuguese, or German, in all of which I am relatively proficient, suddenly lapsed into French, leaving me voiceless and voteless. It was apparent, however, that Ribeiro was having a difficult time convincing Slesser that an ascent was even remotely possible. It involved, as it turned out, pulling one's way up about seven hundred feet of a ninety-degree slope, followed by a thumbhold traverse across thirty feet of the exposed face and finally a series of two-hundred-foot French chimney wriggles up ten-inch-wide, damp openings inside the peak.

There were four reasons why I did not spread my tablecloth right then and there: 1) It was too early in the day; *Red Peak* could not possibly hold my interest for more than four hours; 2) the first few hundred feet of the ascent promised to be fun, since much of it could be accomplished by climbing up the branches of trees which grew in miraculous fashion in the granite rock (this also made it look deceptively safe); 3) I had already consumed half a bottle of wine in an attempt to maintain my water balance; 4) I had become somewhat emotionally involved in the contest.

There was much talk of the equipment which would be required. The two professionals donned hand-tooled leather boots and appropriate paraphernalia, and I was outfitted with a pair of canvas-topped bedroom slippers with rope soles called *alpagadas,* which cost fifty cents and are usually worn by impecunious fishermen. There was a long discussion of whether or not Slesser would need expansion bolts and pitons, but ultimately he was dissuaded and set out only with muscatons, wedges, and an old ninety-foot rope which looked suspiciously like the one I had seen his wife hang the laundry on. Ribeiro also carried a ninety-foot rope, but for some reason they did not want me to take my brand new thirty-meter nylon rope.

By some untold miracle, I managed the first seven hundred feet. The procedure was roughly as follows. Ribeiro would shimmy gracefully up a crevice or tree and then fix a rope so I could pull myself up. My legs never touched the side of the mountain. I was, however, making good use of my knees and elbows, which were a bloody mess. I do not know how Slesser negotiated the climb because whenever I reached Ribeiro, I collapsed in a soggy heap. No one was paying any attention to me at all. Slesser was alternately complimenting Ribeiro on his artistry as a climber and then berating him for his complete disregard for safety precautions. Ribeiro was romantically involved in the thrill of climbing and the glories of the vistas. It took us approximately three hours to negotiate the seven hundred feet and to reach our first crisis; we were at the point where it was necessary to traverse the open face.

The *jeito* for reaching the open face was to crawl along the branch of a small tree. If done properly, the tree bends and drops you against the side of the cliff whereupon is fastened an iron spike. As you clutch the spike and pull yourself out onto a barely perceptible ledge, the tree moves away from you; it is literally a point of no return unless one is wearing a parachute. It was an ideal place for me to settle down with my remaining bottle of wine and book. Why didn't I?

The traverse, incidentally, is named the *Maria Cebolla* ("Mary Onion" is a literal translation). "Maria Cebolla Day" in Brazil is the equivalent of the American "Sadie Hawkins Day," where the ladies are allowed to marry any man they can outrun. It is descriptive because the traverse slopes steeply up; hence, it must be negotiated quickly without loss of forward momentum.

When I proposed that I stay and wait for the two protagonists, Ribeiro, who had already negotiated the traverse, argued that it was not safe to descend via the Cebolla. I then offered to meet the duelists at the foot of the mountain if they would let me borrow one of the ropes for the descent. This was vetoed by Slesser because Ribeiro had fixed one of the ropes for the traverse and had left the other one as a belay (the fixed end of the belay, as it turned out, was tied to a cactus). I was given no choice; I became an unwilling participant in an unscheduled Olympic event.

It took us four hours to climb the remaining two hundred feet. Although most of the delays were due to "Harvey's" cramps, Slesser's desire to recover two twenty-five-cent wooden wedges which Ribeiro and I would willingly have abandoned proved to be a major hang-up. It was almost five o'clock and nearly dusk when we started our descent. The simplest way down would have been to rappel; however, this would have deprived our two adversaries of the challenge of racing down the chimneys, so back into the bowels we went. At this point I had the good fortune of losing my glasses. I say good fortune, because I am considerably myopic and without my glasses the descent was much less terrifying.

It was dusk-turning-to-darkness when the final and fateful crisis came. We were confronted with a forty-foot rappel, the first five and the last twenty of which were free fall, for the cliff had a negative slope. Slesser was the first one down. He eschewed a belay—largely, I suspect, because he did not trust either Ribeiro or me to secure it properly.

I followed with Slesser's rope as safety looped around my chest. My rapid, giddy descent was interrupted violently approximately eighteen feet from the bottom. The safety rope had tightened in a vice-like grip around my chest and I was spinning like a top in midair. The belayed and the fixed rope (both of which were in the same carabiner) were tangled and knotted!

Despite my total lack of climbing experience, I immediately made the correct diagnosis and with what little wind was left in my crushed chest, I called out bravely, "Cut the safety rope, Carlos."

"Don't you dare," bellowed Slesser, "that's my rope. It cost seven pounds."

What took place in the next twenty minutes is too bizarre and shameful to recount. It was patently obvious that Ribeiro could not pull me up; I could not detach the safety rope without endangering my life by releasing the rappel; there was no way that Slesser could get to me, since I was four feet from the cliff in midair.

I am convinced to this day that had I not offered Slesser a case of Scotch I would still be hanging battered and bruised above the foot of Dedo de Deus. If Malcolm Slesser saw, as he wrote, the Finger of God wagging at him as we left the scene, it was because Deus was saying "For shame! For shame!"

1974

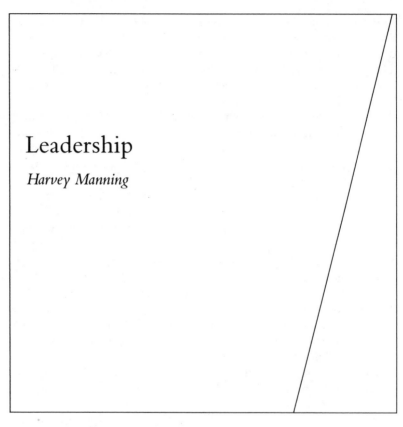

Leadership

Harvey Manning

Leaders have a different look from followers. They get it sometime while being potty-trained or tumbling around a kindergarten play-room. Once they get it, they have it always. People who don't get it early never do.

Leaders have different heads from followers. Ditto.

Followers don't have the look. If they masquerade as leaders, they yell and bully, thinking that will make up for the lack of look. Followers don't have the head. They make bold decisions, thinking that will make up for the lack of thinking. Followers-become-leaders, false leaders, are her-maphrodites despised universally, by none more than themselves.

Deliberately or otherwise, climbing schools insinuate that leading is more admirable than following and thus spawn false leaders. This is particularly so of a school staffed by unpaid volunteers, perpetuated through the principle of "each one teach one." Putting back into the school what one has taken out is a moral imperative. Climbers seeming

120

to have the capacity to lead are expected to do so, are scoundrels if they don't. Because true leaders are rare, false leaders are manufactured in wholesale lots, frequently to the regret of all.

Consider, for example, the first climb I led for the Climbing Course, Mt. Garfield. A half-hour from the cars we ran into a cliff. A true leader would have chosen the quick and simple end run. I bravely led my twenty-five followers directly into the cliff, up a gully which briefly in the wake of melting glaciers had been a clean gash in the granite, a series of fifty-foot walls broken by neat little chimneys, but these thousands of years later was a vintage low-elevation Cascades mix of brush, dirt, gravel, and rotten logs.

The unroped party was strung out over several hundred vertical feet when we heard a plaintive call, "Help! Help!" Investigation revealed that Bill, disliking my trashy gully, had attempted the naked cliff. He was spreadeagled, fingers quivering, knees doing the sewing machine.

I was about to send a team to rescue him when came a many-voiced shout, "rock! rock! rock!" In the gully above something was smashing and crashing; under my boots the earth was quaking. Each of us lunged for one side or other of the gully. BOOM! BOOM! BOOM!

All but one were pressed against granite. In the middle of the gully I saw Don turn to this side, find it solid climbers, turn to that side, likewise. I saw him turn to look up at approaching Nemesis, then turn to face the valley and, as if a swimming pool awaited, swandive from the brink. Below a forty-foot wall was a narrow ledge where he'd make his first bounce, then several more walls down which his body would thud-thud-thud.

"My God! My God! My God!"

I thought *I* was screaming. Certainly the scream was in my brain. But my mouth was shut. The scream was up the gully. I recognized it as Ray. I was glad he was screaming. *Someone* should express our grief.

Graceful as a bird Don soared, head first. Then in midair he performed a magnificent tuck and roll and was now falling foot first. He surely was going out in style. He hit the ledge with his feet and crumpled toward the edge. Not quite over. He stood up, smiling sheepishly.

But Ray continued to scream. Not for Don. For himself. In passing, the chunk of granite, big as a stuffed-full Trapper Nelson, had crushed him against granite of the gully side.

I asked Vic and Tom to lead the party to the summit of Garfield, which they did. I led Don (a sprained ankle only) and Ray (in shock from internal injuries but ambulatory) and several followers with undamaged flesh but shattered nerves back down to the road. Their peril was not ended. While pounding a piton for a body-lowering anchor, I

Party descending snowslope on Mount Rainier. JIM STUART.

broke the hammer handle. The steel head buzzed like a bee between the skulls of Don and Ray.

At the road somebody thought to ask, "Say, whatever became of Bill?" I didn't know then, nor want to know now. Presumably, for good or ill, he got un-spreadeagled. I couldn't vouch for it, never having seen him since the rock crashed down the gully. Years later I read an article in a climbing journal by a person with the same name—the same person, I hope.

The reason I didn't give up my masquerade, and the Climbing Course didn't give up on me, was that the fallible leader, though theoretically as self-contradictory as an imperfect God, was unadmitted but accepted. By necessity. Without congenitally fallible false leaders to supplement the few true leaders (who may have occasional bad luck but less often are blundering fools), the school would have to close. I was expected to continue leading and rather than be ostracized, I did.

Descending Mt. Constance, to save the time-consuming donning of crampons for a slope of steep, hard snow, I boldly commanded my followers to lie prone in self-arrest position and do controlled belly flop glissades. One team was unable to follow orders and lost control; the three of them hit a rock, one splattered, and we were the rest of the day hauling a bloody (but living) body off the peak.

Even when not personally present, I influenced events. Scheduled to lead Hibox, I scorned the usual trudge up Box Canyon Creek and the dull scramble to the summit in favor of an elegant high line from Lake Keechelus, traversing Margaret, Rampart, and Alta on the way. At the last minute I was called out of town on business. My substitute led the group of thirty-five along my imaginative route, wrongly thinking that I'd previously taken it and that the trip was reasonable for a weekend. At least the party reached the road in time Monday to call Seattle before the rescue team left town.

I earned a reputation as a leader of interesting climbs. Practice trips, though, were my masterpieces. My students returned from a rock practice up Ingalls Creek, at a new and unscouted site belatedly discovered to be a hell of head-splitting granite garbage, resembling the troops retreating from Bull Run. Weeks after a dynamic-belay practice I had arranged (but was prevented by circumstances from attending), half the student body was still hobbling around on sprained ankles; the serious casualties were limited to one broken leg and three cracked vertebrae. I led a Nisqually Glacier ice practice and we ran out of bandages, one in every four students mutilating his/her calves with crampons.

Snow practices were my specialty. Once, in Commonwealth Basin, a spell of unseasonable May sunshine had caused unusually fast snow which gave exceptionally good self-arrest practice. While exulting in the best sliding I'd ever seen on a practice (and going about yelling, "Faster! Faster! Don't roll into your arrest until you're going *really fast!*), I noted a girl lying at the bottom of the slope at the end of a line of red snow. Rushing to render first aid, I saw blood on her axe spike and a scarlet splash on her pants, plus a hole in the pants, both at a point on the inside of her leg far above the knee. Out of regard for my sensibilities, if not hers, I yielded first-aid duty to a female and got on with my leading. I ascribed the accident to pure awkwardness until blood was flowing all over the basin, five more axe spikes stabbed into five more insides of legs far above the knee, and dozens of bruises and pants holes in the same place. I realized I hadn't warned the students to keep the lower hand at the very end of the axe's shaft; in the high-speed arrests the spikes had pivoted around hands and gone into thighs. None of the wounds was disabling; one lad, though, came within an inch of being unmanned.

On another Commonwealth practice, conditions were more typical for May: a tempest was blowing and the snow was a bog. Only through new heights of bellowing and blaspheming did I expel all 150 students and instructors and group leaders from tents and snowcaves. When other members of the faculty suggested it was no fit day to wallow in the snow and perhaps the practice should be cut short, I declared this was what practices were for—to give beginners a vivid picture of what sort of sport it was they thought they wanted to take up. I toured the several practice areas, chasing blue-faced students and instructors from shelter of subalpine trees into slashing rain-sleet-snow. I had a paroxysm of rage on finding two instructors and a group leader building a fire! I grudgingly permitted them to keep it going when a physician explained he'd diagnosed three students as near death from hypothermia.

Shuksan was the end. In the evening I assembled the party of thirty-odd and told them we'd depart at 6 A.M. In the morning I awoke at 5:30 and yelled, "Rising time!" Just once I yelled. After years of yelling I *heard* myself. My loud, ugly voice too grossly violated the serenity of the meadow. I left camp precisely at the advertised time. Alone. After years of harassing people out of bags, on this morning, so calm and free, I said screw it and sauntered slowly up Shuksan by myself, savoring the peace and quiet. Gasping and sweating, they caught up with me at the entry to the Fisher Chimneys and harangued me for shirking my duty. I resumed my role as leader (false leader), a snarling, loud-mouthed bastard, and got them up the peak. But due to the late start, not until next day did I get them off the peak. Personally, I enjoyed the night on the rocks, the stars blazing so brightly, and then the light of the rising moon looking so ghostly on cliffs and glaciers. But I wasn't asked to lead any more climbs.

Stick at climbing long enough and one is likely to be dragged into the Great Leadership Debate. It happened to me when we were producing a new textbook for the Climbing Course.

The first draft of the leadership chapter was written by Frank, who saw man as deeply flawed. Individuals he liked and respected. The group, the climbing party, he viewed as a dumb beast that must be kicked and whipped and hollered to the summit.

Franz was offended by Frank's Hitlerism and volunteered to write a second draft. He was a key member of the editorial committee; I had no qualms about welcoming his offer and thought Tom a worrywart when he privately warned, "You know, Franz doesn't *believe* in leaders."

So his draft proved. Franz conceived a climbing party as a commune with one mind and spirit, each decision properly being made by whatever person was at the point at the time it was required. To encourage "leadership" was to profane the freedom of the hills.

No matter our private sympathies; we were preparing a textbook for a school. We asked a third opinion from Dave. Having once been on an expedition where the leader refused to lead, and as a result of climbing the peak essentially single-handed and having lost his toes and nearly his life, Dave was a convert to leadership. His draft, the final and published one, was a synthesis, saving much of the sweet idealism of Franz, but tempered by the sour realism of Frank.

As for me, I drifted into the third way. Neither a leader nor follower be. Climb alone. Things worked out so well I soon found I no longer had to climb at all.

1975/76

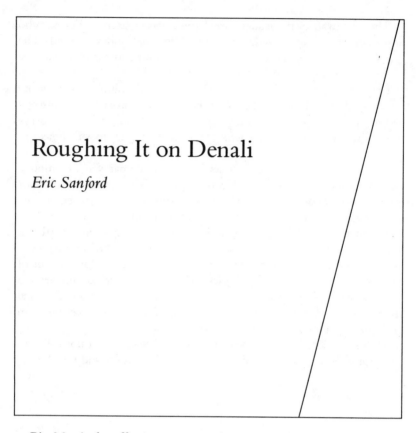

Roughing It on Denali

Eric Sanford

Big Mac is the affectionate name given to two hundred trillion tons of rock sandwiched between one hundred trillion tons of ice and covered with half a trillion tons of garbage. Some have called it Mount McKinley; the natives named it Danolly, the Smelly One. I called it crazy while wondering what the hell I was doing in the village of Talkeetna, waiting with three friends for the flight to the base of the great white mountain. I knew I would be in for some strange experiences; McKinley is not only noted for its weather but for its oddball human element.

The undeniable fact that Denali—to use the more proper native name—is the highest peak in North America, as well as the continued misconception that a "tourist" route leads to the summit, lures an endless horde of naive mountaineers to Talkeetna each spring and summer. A more comical mishmash of misfits could be found only in Chamonix, Kathmandu, or JFK International. Misfits are basically harmless at those places, but at Denali a forty-minute flight deposits unprepared and bewildered climbers smack in the middle of ten thousand square miles of rock and ice; the shock when arriving is substantial. (At least in the Himalaya one must spend a few weeks walking to get to the mountains—there's no other way.) Technically, Denali offers a choice: the purists and the foolish walk, but the lazy ones—say ninety-nine percent of the total—choose to fly.

April 16 brought good fortune. After only one day of waiting in Talkeetna, Cliff Hudson, fresh from a nonstop, thirty-eight-hour poker game, shoved the four of us and our gear into his two-seater plane. My headrest was a can of "Chateau de Chevron."

The bobbing and weaving airplane made a final dive and slammed down onto the glacier. I plopped out of the plane like the cork from a bottle of champagne and rolled off into the snow, stiff and green. Cliff lit a cigarette, gazed wistfully into the sky, and wondered if he could get in at least ten more trips before dark.

Suddenly the horizon was alive with commotion and color. Running and stumbling toward us, screaming insanely and waving their arms wildly, were ten Japanese. We stood staring in amazement; it was a sight reminiscent of northern Iwo Jima. As they got closer, I tried to decipher their spirited yelling: it sounded like "sticket" or "cricket" or, perhaps, "picket." Picket? Aha, that was it. Picket! But what did it mean? Were they all on strike? Were they building a fence? Was it the name of some Caucasian general who had offended their ancestors? I got ready to dive back into the plane.

Our visitors were climbing all over themselves, each trying to be the first to grab our attention. A leader emerged and, in his fastest and most polite Japanese, recited the history of the world, or something similar. When I appeared puzzled, he started all over. One word kept popping up in his story: *picket*. And the crazy fellow kept pointing up at the Cassin Ridge.

Finally it dawned on me what was going on. Pickets! The guy wanted our pickets. When I pointed questioningly toward our pile of gear, the entire group began jumping up and down, jabbering all the while. Planning their trip in Japan, they had misinterpreted the Park Service equipment list and brought two dozen tomato stakes instead of climbing pickets. Finding them somewhat unsuitable for ice belays on the Cassin Ridge, the Japanese were willing to barter anything in their possession. I declined their offers until I was hoarse. I didn't plan to create an international incident, but what the hell were we supposed to use if we gave them our pickets—tomato stakes?

Hudson, standing by his plane and ready to leap in if a rumble developed, had a don't-you-little-devils-even-consider-it look on his face as he watched one of the Japanese troops fondling a wing strut. The leader launched into another tirade that I was sure was his technical explanation about how easily the plane could fly minus those cumbersome struts. Wouldn't Hudson enjoy seeing his struts put to the honorable cause of helping conquer the mountain?

Finally we escaped. Hudson escaped. The contingent from the Land of the Rising Sun retired to their huge, camouflaged World War II tent to plan their next move.

The next day began late. Actually, the day began on time, but we were a bit slow realizing it. The temperature at eight o'clock hovered at thirty below; since it was early spring, the sun didn't hit our edge of the glacier until midmorning. We spent the late-morning hours warming up and organizing our loads; we knew we should take advantage of the clear weather to move some gear up toward the mountain.

It was easy traveling along the glacier, and we sang and laughed and snapped pictures. The singing and laughing ceased, however, as the route began attacking the mountain in earnest. Above the first rise—the first of several thousand to come—was a rather strange sight: either the Park Service had set up a raven-feeding station or else someone's food cache was being vigorously and thoroughly trashed by the huge scavengers. Half a dozen immense birds, obviously well fed, were screeching and fighting over every scrap of food. What had once been the supplies for ten climbers was now a chaotic mess strewn over several acres. I made a mental note to bury our supplies ten feet deep, not wishing to face the embarrassment of later having to explain that our failure was due to ravens.

As we wearily approached base camp late in the day, I looked up and spied a large, self-suspension dome tent slithering merrily down the glacier toward us; a moderate breeze and slight incline made its journey easy. Then, stumbling over the horizon, came a wild-eyed, half-naked man, one hand holding up his knickers to his knees and the other gesturing wildly for the tent to stop. As he frantically yelled at us, his trousers dropped to his ankles and he crashed onto the snow.

We quickly surrounded the mischievous dwelling and towed it back to its owner. It seemed he had stepped out for a quick trip to the latrine, and the tent, held down solely by the weight of his sleeping bag, had decided to go for a stroll. You can't really blame the tent; lying in the same place all day long can get pretty boring. Later, I heard the man mumbling something in Russian about "capitalist pig air currents."

Early the following morning, as we grimly ate our breakfast of sweet, sticky gruel, the crisp morning air was shattered by an explosion. I quickly analyzed the possibilities: the Japanese had decided to take our pickets by force; the mountain was actually a dormant volcano and had picked this day to erupt; or perhaps a monstrous crevasse, filled to the brim with garbage, was experiencing heartburn. But I hadn't considered reality.

We watched in awe as two Polish climbers flew out of their tent just moments before it burst into flames and was vaporized. Smoldering in the charred remains was a large double-burner propane stove that looked like it had been pilfered from a Winnebago. The five-gallon propane canister fell to Earth a few minutes later, having completed a speedy orbit of the moon.

The crafty Japanese, never ones to miss a trick, immediately converged on the hapless Poles and began chattering, "Pickets? Pickets?" Within minutes the dejected Poles had lost most of their climbing gear.

That day, while trudging up the glacier over endless and deceitful hillocks of snow, I was reminded of factory work. If trudging were a job, you couldn't pay me enough to do it. Clever me, I do it for free.

As we approached Camp 2, I noticed that we had some new arrivals: a young couple who must have been on their first outing, since their clothing and equipment appeared brand new. Any conscientious climber will let some favored piece of ancient equipment slip into his wardrobe to demonstrate he's been around forever.

I slumped down on the snow and said hello to the young folks. Noticing that the woman's face was beet red, I offered her some sunscreen. "No, thanks, we've got plenty," she replied, pointing to a large bottle of Johnson's Baby Oil. We talked some more and I discovered that the couple had been traveling along the glacier for eight days from base camp, having gotten slightly off course: their first two camps were actually located *below* base camp. I figured it would take them eight months to climb the mountain at that rate. I didn't mention it, just wished them luck.

The sun was appearing about five minutes earlier each day, much to my pleasure. One morning, as we luxuriated in the warmth, two skiers appeared on the horizon. We watched enviously as they carved smooth, graceful turns down the fresh powder covering the glacier. As they got closer, it seemed that only one was making smooth, graceful turns; the other was apparently practicing survival skiing.

They soon reached our camp, and the wobbly skier collapsed in the snow. The other delivered a more formal greeting: "Hello. Nice day, isn't it?"

"Yes, it certainly is," I replied. "Say, is your friend there okay?"

"Well, actually we had a bit of a problem up above, and he seems to have a slight cut on his face. We don't really have much of a first-aid kit. Do you think you could look at him?"

We gathered around the moaning man and rolled him over. A little problem? His face was split open from eye to chin, and his swollen tongue stuck out where he had once had some front teeth. We spent an hour stitching him up. Since he was close to going into shock from the loss of blood, we lashed him to one of our sleds and headed down toward base camp to arrange to have him flown out.

His companion mentioned something about trying to ski up the mountain in a day and his buddy falling at Windy Corner and grabbing a fixed rope that turned out not to be fixed and tumbling a thousand feet down the glacier tethered to a pair of windmilling skis and stopping five feet above a huge crevasse by digging his elbows into the ice. Skiing around Windy Corner? For an encore maybe he'll try riding a bike down Hoover Dam!

Soon we arrived back at base camp, which by that time resembled Grand Central Station. Twenty new arrivals from a Seattle-based climbing school had just been dropped off, presumably by a 747. As we approached, they all stopped whatever they were doing and stared at us with a hey-what-are-you-guys-doing-here? expression on their pasty white faces.

After the novelty of our arrival wore off, they went back to the matter at hand—issuing ice axes and crampons to everyone. Most of them stared at this gear as if they had never seen it before. One lad insisted his pack was already too heavy and that a friend had told him he didn't really need those spikes anyway. Still another chap emerged from an army-surplus pup tent wearing full camouflage fatigues, an olive-drab helmet complete with netting, and a belt canteen. I hoped I would get to see him drink out of a metal canteen at twenty below. The Park Service questionnaire had asked, "Do you have your own equipment?" He had undoubtedly answered, "Affirmative, sir."

As we sat and waited for the rescue plane to arrive and take the skier away, a plump, assertive woman approached me, apparently assuming I had something to do with the Seattle expedition. "Say," she said angrily, "what's this about sharing a tent with someone else? I didn't pay $1,900 to share this stupid little tent. There's hardly enough room in there for me! What do you mean by supplying only ten tents? I told you people I wanted a private tent, and I mean to have one. I don't care if you have to go out and buy one! You hear me?"

I assured her I totally agreed and that I would rectify the problem right away. She stomped off across the glacier.

Nearby, four climbers were clumsily setting up their tent while roped together. Obviously, they had heeded the advice in *Freedom of the Hills:* one *never* walks on a glacier unroped. Like the action in a three-ring circus, so much was going on that I found it impossible to absorb it all.

As we continued to wait for the plane, our casualty kept staring into a mirror, tilting his head this way and that, and asking if we thought he'd still be good-looking. And did we think he'd have much of a scar? And did we know the name of a good plastic surgeon in Anchorage?

The plane landed in the fading daylight, and we loaded the poor wretch into it and headed back to Camp 2, arriving at midnight. An entertaining day.

Another morning, another tedious haul. As we flopped down after the exhausting carry, we realized we were not alone: a hundred yards away, a large party was putting the finishing touches on a gigantic igloo that must have taken a full week to build. We set up our modest camp and went to visit.

Their igloo resembled the Astrodome. I poked my head inside and saw room for twenty climbers, though only two were dozing at the moment. "Howdy," I greeted the occupants. "Did the game get rained out or am I here on the wrong afternoon?"

One of the men propped himself up on an elbow, squinted in my direction, grunted, pulled his sleeping-bag hood over his head, and flopped back down. Perhaps he didn't speak English.

Outside, another member of the party appeared, and we all sat down and had a cup of tea. "Say," I began, "those fellows in the igloo seem rather beat."

"Ya, they're not going any further. I told them for six months to get into shape, but no way. All they wanted to do was eat and drink and play cards and watch the 49ers. To hell with them. They can sit here and freeze for all I care. I hope they end up in a crevasse. The rest of us are going to the top!"

As we sipped tea in the soft evening light, another climber appeared on the glacier above us and began threading his way down through a maze of crevasses. For several minutes I watched him weave in and out of the creaking mass of ice.

"By the way," I asked my host, "is that fellow with your party?"

"Ya, that's George. He just went up to have a look around."

"Alone?" I queried.

"No one else wanted to go."

"Isn't that a bit dangerous?" I continued.

"Dangerous? Why?"

"Well, what if he should fall into a crevasse?"

"Oh, that's no problem. He's wearing his beeper."

"His beeper?"

"Ya, you know, one of these." He reached into his pocket and pulled out a Skadie Avalanche Traceiver. "Haven't you ever used one of these before?"

"Well, yes, I've used it before, but not in crevasses."

With a bored look he continued to explain. "It's simple. If anyone falls into a crevasse, we know just where to look for him. See, you simply turn this dial and put this earplug in and listen for the beeps from his unit. They'll lead you right to the crevasse. Using the Skadie means you don't need ropes anymore."

"Oh. Now I understand. . . . Yes. . . . A good idea. . . . I wonder why no one else thought of that before?" I turned my attention back to the wandering climber, thinking that at least he wouldn't be dead *and* missing in some bottomless crevasse; his friends would know exactly where the body was. I also wondered if they had access to a hundred mile extension cord—the battery life of a Skadie is only five days.

We bade the group good night, not wishing to wait around for the inevitable rescue.

At Camp 3 we decided to make only one carry per camp until we were in place for a summit bid. The thought of trudging up and down Big Mac simply to shuttle our food a little farther up was not at all appealing. I was beginning to feel—and probably smell—like a burro.

We packed huge loads and began to trudge up the 3,000-foot wall to Camp 4. Since we didn't have our Skadie beepers, we opted for a more conventional style of climbing: we used ropes.

At 13,000 feet we reached a long, icy traverse above a steep drop. A series of reddish brown blotches just beneath the ice fell into the abyss. I immediately flashed on the climber with the broken face and shuddered as I peered downward.

Farther along, I came upon the fixed rope that the "beeper bunch" had installed earlier and told us about. I gave it a tug; it seemed solid, but force of habit made me ask for a belay anyway. I clipped into the fixed rope, which was secured at the near end by a shiny new ice screw, and gingerly started across. As I reached the opposite end, my heart missed a beat: the rope wasn't attached to anything. It had simply been stuffed into a hole, where it had frozen into place. Fixed? Those idiots had "fixed" only one end of the rope! It reminded me of the last time I had my car "fixed." I gave the rope a sharp tug, and it popped out of the hole and dangled uselessly in space.

We had been on the mountain more than a week, and it was time for a rest day. I slept until the first rays of the sun hit the frozen tent, then turned over and slept another hour until the tent was a dripping mess. Finally, I oozed out of my bag and stepped outside into the brilliant sunlight. Clad only in my red long johns and huge white bunny boots, I decided to wander around. Climbing to the top of a nearby rise, I was surprised to see other signs of life: garbage lay strewn around a crudely built igloo.

Feeling sociable, I strolled over to greet the occupants. As I reached the entrance, a scruffy head appeared, followed closely by a raggedly clothed body. He spoke first. "Like, hey, man, how's it goin'?"

"Er, fine," I responded. "How about you?"

"Hey, man, it's a real bummer, you know? You got a cigarette?"

"Ah, no. I don't. Sorry."

"Hey, man, that's okay. Like, I've been trying to get off this hill for like two weeks, you know what I mean?"

"Er, no, not really. . . . What happened?"

"Well, like, I had to kill all my dogs, you know, man, and. . . . "

"Dogs?"

"Yeah, man, my sled dogs." He motioned over to the far side of his igloo.

I glanced down and swallowed hard. Scattered about the igloo were pieces of dog. Bones and tails and feet and eyes and ears were frozen in the snow like the fossilized remains of a slaughterhouse. My gaze continued to the top of the igloo. There, impaled like a pagan war token, was a dog's head. My jaw dropped a foot.

Dog Head Bob, as we later named him, caught me staring. "That's Charlie, man. He's the best dog I ever had, so, like, I gave him the best place, you know?"

Nauseated, I shook my head in agreement. "How come you killed your dogs?"

"Well, man, I ran out of food, you know, and then I got my feet froze and the sled's stuck up on the hill, you know, and my old lady can't get it down and . . . "

I turned toward the steep slope rising behind us and could barely make out a solitary figure struggling with something next to a mammoth crevasse. I turned back to Bob, took a step back, and tried to comprehend the situation.

"Yeah, that's my old lady up there. She's still trying to get that old sled down so we can get outta here."

I found myself staring at his feet. His huge boots looked like some-one had taken a shotgun to them.

"Yeah, man, I borrowed these boots from this guy, you know, and he said not to worry about the holes and stuff. But I guess they musta leaked or something because I froze my feet."

He pulled one of his feet from the worthless boots, and, indeed, it was swollen and discolored. "Man, like I can't even fit any socks on, you know?"

We conversed for a few more minutes and he told me how he had heard about this guy who wanted to drive his dog team up Denali, but that he, Bob, a trueblood Alaskan, had decided to ace this other guy out, but he had run out of food halfway up on account of his dogs, who weren't exactly keen for this trip, and so here he was with no more dogs to eat, and did we have any extra food he could have?

I told him we were fresh out of dog meat but that perhaps the ex-pedition right behind us might have some.

I returned to camp and related my amazing tale. Everyone thought I had finally gone off the deep end this time; but one by one they ventured out to talk to Dog Head Bob, and each returned shaking his head in awe. We spent the rest of the day drying out our gear and trying not to think of sled dogs.

Both the sun and Dog Head Bob were still asleep the next morning as we pushed on up the icy slopes. Several million miso-secs later (on a long climb, each day is divided into many millions of "misery-sec-onds" instead of hours; each miso-sec is slightly longer than the pre-ceding one), we crested a ridge at 16,000 feet and slumped into the snow for a rest. Above us, a weary-looking threesome were making their way down a steep, wind-sculpted ridge. Their progress resembled a slapstick version of tug of war: the leader would stumble forward, pulling the rope taut and yanking the following two climbers off their feet. The last man would retaliate with a violent yank. The poor fellow in the middle was being cut in two by the oscillating antics.

Assuming they were returning from the summit, I inquired about the conditions. It seemed that they hadn't made it past their camp at 17,000 feet: their summit food had been packed next to the white gas, and the escaping fumes had permeated all the food, resulting in a pile of inflammable mush, some rather strained relationships, and a terminated expedition. I urged them to raid our small supply of emer-gency food at 14,000 feet and give it another try, but the thought of

Pilgrimage toward the summit of Denali. BRIAN OKONEK.

retracing their steps up Big Mac didn't appeal to them. We said good-bye and watched as they started down, tugging and swearing with each step.

We continued to inch our way up the mountain: one step, one breath, one step, one breath. Rest five minutes, gather some energy, then one step, one breath. At 17,000 feet we came upon an abandoned snow cave piled high with candy wrappers, torn plastic water bottles, and pieces of frozen Ensolite. It wasn't an appealing place, but we were glad to set up camp out of the frigid wind. The wind howled all night, and no matter how often we plugged the cave's tiny chinks, spindrift spread over everything.

The summit day at last. At six o'clock, as we left our cave, the thermometer registered a toasty minus twenty, and the winds were of the gale-force variety. The snow swirling around my feet made the ground itself appear to be moving—a boiling caldron. Time became meaningless, movement imperceptible. Each step forward was an instinctive movement as my toes felt for the incline ahead.

At some point my ankles didn't flex quite as much; the angle had eased. The top? I eagerly peeled back my furry hood and looked upward for the first time in hours. A few yards away was a pile of junk: the summit!

Clouds and snow swirled around us. Razor-sharp crystals attacked every spot of unprotected skin, but I couldn't complain: this was the experience I had come for. The sweat and toil and uselessness of struggling to the top of this inelegant mound was the ultimate act of nonproductivity, and I had loved every minute of it.

The view? Well, I'm sure it would have been quite magnificent if there had been one, but, alas, the mist was thickening by the moment; the only view I had was of my own feet as they turned and pointed downhill.

It was time to undo it all and head back down the mountain. Down past the cluttered snow cave and the wind-scoured ridge. Down past the gaping crevasse with the woman tugging at an ice-encrusted sled. Down past the dog-head igloo and the unfixed rope. Down past the climbers who would not move. Down past the beepers and the creepers, the eager and the tired, the friendly and the fierce. Down past a dozen expeditions, large and small, fast and slow. Down past rotting supplies and quarreling ravens. Down past tugging guides and submissive clients with sunburned eyes and ears. Down, down, down. . . .

1984

5

FORAYS INTO FICTION

Editors' Introduction

English-language fictional pieces on mountaineering have appeared sporadically for a century. But until recently these novels and short stories did not sit well with mountaineers, who often ridiculed the silly plots and technical mistakes. Never once in the early days did believable climbing action gain center stage in a work of fiction.

Many of these early works were published abroad. A comprehensive study done recently by Audrey Salkeld and Rosie Smith shows that of some two-hundred-thirty English-language short stories involving mountaineering—some written a full century ago—only a dozen were published in the United States before 1967, the year *Ascent* first appeared.

Obviously, American climbing publications cared little about fiction. With momentous real-life mountaineering events occurring worldwide, writers and publishers alike must have regarded mountaineering fiction as senseless. Why invent heroes when climbers were actually braving icy couloirs and stoically enduring the deaths of their comrades?

Having grown up feasting on Jack London and Ernest Hemingway, we at *Ascent* savored exciting adventure yarns. Early on we wondered: Could we get at the heart of climbing through fiction? Could climbing fiction be written well enough to capture the interest of our readers? We decided we had to try, since a writer of fiction can manipulate real events to engage readers and reveal truths about the human condition in ways a mere chronicler cannot.

Our first experiment, a reprint from *Punch* magazine, appeared in our opening issue. "Pens Over Everest," by Bernard Hollowood, was a satire of a typical Everest expedition, pre-dating the similar and now-famous *Ascent of Rum Doodle* by four years.

More fiction followed, and by the early 1970s our readers could find tales of imagination in nearly every issue. Fiction writers, those dispossessed souls without an audience, began to seek us out.

Caught in a pleasant trap, we realized that since we had started to publish fiction, we were expected to continue. After all, who else would publish these tales? Over the years, readers and reviewers began to take notice of our gambit—and, to our relief and satisfaction, they generally approved.

Our first story here is by the most creative person ever to labor at *Ascent,* Lito Tejada-Flores. This voluble jack-of-all-trades greatly influenced the direction of our articles and design in the early 1970s. Ever willing to take chances, Lito naturally submitted the first piece of staff fiction, a short oddity of word-plays we made him place on the inside front cover, where it would cause as little harm as possible. But the very next year, undaunted, he gave us "Rojo's *Peón*," a far more orthodox story, and the one included here.

"Icarus," our second feature, was crafted by Ian Rowe. We had long been enamored of Scottish writers, and of Rowe we said in our contributors' section, "Ah, those literate Scots, may they breed copiously." Rowe spins a tale of two vulnerable climbers, each of whom thinks the other is the best climber in the world. Toying with his protagonists' emotions, Rowe gives us a glimpse into a macho world.

Next comes "The Rock Gods," Joe Kelsey's well-honed allegory about future Yosemite inhabitants. The idea for this tale slipped into his brain one day as he searched without result for a piton he had dropped earlier from the heights. Who would eventually find it? he wondered. And what would this person make of the strangely shaped object? "My story," Kelsey later wrote us, "focuses on the roles in which we 'mortals' cast Royal Robbins *et al.,* and how we let their achievements set upper limits on our own ambitions." Some translations may be in order: the Bird King, the Ice King, the Santa Claus, and the Devil are, respectively, Yosemite legends Royal Robbins, Yvon Chouinard, Chuck Pratt, and Warren Harding.

Our final selection in this chapter proved to be a milestone for *Ascent.* The fiction we had used before 1974 was short, often just one or two pages. So when Jeff Long, a tall stranger from Colorado, handed us a seventy-page untitled manuscript, we hefted it—and blanched. "Better be good," we growled. With the help of our friend Michael Charles Tobias, we toiled with Long to pare the beast down to manageable size. The result was the still-long but wonderfully surrealistic fable we named "The Soloist's Diary." We now regard Long as perhaps the finest wordsmith we have ever published.

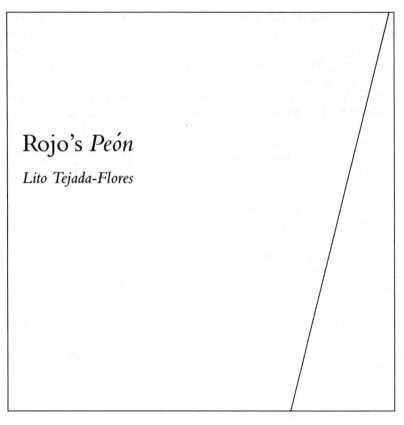

Rojo's *Peón*

Lito Tejada-Flores

Rojo's *peón* sits gray and silent on his big gray horse beneath a gray and angry sky. There is rain in the air, and wind, always wind, and the mended inspected fence stretches downhill from silent horse to silent cabin below. Rojo's *peón* looks at the mountains of cloud with tired wrinkled eyes; other mountains are hidden beneath these mountains of gray cloud. No one in these parts knows his real name, except perhaps Rojo or Rojo's father who hired him; not even Rojo's bookkeeper who pays him ten-thousand pesos every two months when he comes down to the *estancia* house to get provisions for his *puesto*. There was a time when Rojo's hands called him "*el Chilote,*" as if to say "that no-good Chilean," but that was before he cut one of them across the face with braided whip and rode away without a word, and that too has been forgotten. He is too old, Rojo's *peón*, for fighting or gossip or memories; he can still mend fences, ride his giant horse, keep the sheep from wandering too far up into the mountains. The years and the wind have abraded the rest. *Cosas patagónicas,* Patagonian things: time and bad weather, summer and winter, the little cabin unchanging, the wind that sweeps out of the mountains like the broom of God, *el viento blanco, el viento azul,* the white wind, the blue wind, this hard country south of the pampas at the edge of these hard terrible mountains. Up there now, those *gringos* from Buenos Aires . . .

Motionless on his statue horse, Rojo's *peón* lets his wrinkled gray eyes move across invisible mountains beneath swollen clouds: *el Fitz, la Torre,* the tower, and the big white one and then the pass. It is insanity to go up there, so much ice, so much rock. When I was a boy we climbed, but the hills were brown and burning by the coast; we scrambled with the sun on our backs and the sea down below, blue like my horse's eyes, sparkling glass, the white walls and tin roofs of the port spread out, and our house, the third shack down in the little *callejón,* fronted with plywood packing crates from Japan, our plaster virgin by the door with her flowers, little white flowers in a blue can of Esso marine-weight oil. Where did I find those flowers on such scorched brown hills? *Devociones de mi juventud,* boyhood devotions, and now I only live on horseback, and it's starting to rain. Too many, too much, these angry clouds. . . . And where is Chile today? On the other side of the mountains, across the ice and the sea too, I think. Lost like an old man, an old man on his horse watching the storm get worse, a daily occurrence here where there are so many storms, *cosas patagónicas.* . . .

But why did the old man refuse to lead our horses up here to base camp? Surely he must have known where to find the path, the *sendero,* and it took us a day of searching in the rain. They say he's worked for Rojo for thirty or forty years, or his father, Rojo's that is. Rojo's *peón,* that stupid old man just sitting on his horse like he was deaf and dumb, and Nestor talking to him so slowly, not at all like he does back home in BA, or anywhere. . . . And now he's been up there for a week, Nestor and that German, and it's storming so hard, I'm trying so hard not to worry. . . . The wind snaps another dead branch off another tree; it falls on the wet ground beside the two orange tents.

The little camp at the upper edge of the forest, five or six miles from the grassy hill where Rojo's *peón* sits on his horse in the rain. The little camp right up under the *cordillera,* just below the moraine of the glacier that snakes up towards the high rocky peaks, the *cerro* such-and-such, *el monte* something-or-other, and behind above them all, the tower, *la Torre.* Why did we ever come? We were so comfortable in Buenos Aires, so happy. She is crying in the little shelter of fallen logs covered with plastic tarps. The fire has gone out again and Julia doesn't care. She's been trying to keep the fire going for two days now, as the storm gets slowly worse and worse. But Julia is only a city girl, a Spanish lit major from Vassar, here to study the gauchesque novelists, Zavala Muñiz, Benito Lynch. . . . But spending a year in South America is one thing, coming up here to this horrible place is another. And the wedding next month? My parents are flying down on the fifteenth and Nestor said . . . and afterwards he promised we'd spend a month on his family's ranch in Missiones. There aren't any mountains there, are there? . . . But Nestor is so rich, why does he have to do these. . . . More tears, more wind shaking the trees overhead, more rain.

The pile of wood that she dragged up so painfully is completely soaked now. The whole forest is a monochrome blue. In the clearing, where only a week ago they could see *la Torre* and all its satellite spires, there is only the belly of a great gray cloud hugging the earth. Yes, almost a week now. And Nestor spent that whole first afternoon chasing a lamb that had wandered this far up the canyon. I wouldn't look when he killed it, but I did help him barbecue it, a regular *asado*, just like some band of old-time *gauchos*, but what would they be doing up here? They'd have more sense. I bet that old man hasn't come up this far in thirty years. . . . I'd rather have my nature in smaller doses. Sunday afternoon in Palermo, with all the flowers and Nestor being really adorable, like he can be sometimes, telling me how much prettier I was than all those Argentinian girls all around, all those couples so happy in the sunshine, so safe, and afterwards driving back into the city for supper in one of those open-air steak houses, all in a row down by the river. . . . What a spring, and in such a city, how could I have resisted? And Nestor's so perfect really; it's almost a cliché being so tall and dark, so charming. And I was so flabbergasted when he actually proposed and now, but oh, oh Jesus but I hope he's okay. This awful storm, this . . .

Awful storm indeed, like all Patagonian storms, becoming indeed more awful the farther one gets from the plains, from Rojo's *peón* on his sad still horse in a thickening drizzle; up through the forest and past the two trembling tents and the weeping blonde girl, where the rain comes tearing in windy sheets through the sad blue trees; up onto the glacier where a million snowflakes are trying so hard to fall, only to be scooped up by the wind and tossed another thousand feet in the air to try again. A full-blown Patagonian storm riding out of the wet emptiness of the *hielo continental*, the continental icecap, on the back of an antarctic wind, one of the thousands of Patagonian things, *cosas patagón-icas,* which either turn men into philosophers or kill them.

The wind more than anything else is Patagonia. The wind that be-comes visible as it hurls torn shreds of cloud in all directions at once, twisting, turning, doubling back, then roaring straight on in from the west with its freight of snow and frost. West wind, northwest wind, southwest wind, the devil's own wests. The wind owns everything here, this range of peaks, *la Torre.* We were crazy to think it could have been ours, even for a day, and we needed at least a week of good weather. A crazy gust of laughter shakes his cold body and passes on the wind. He hangs onto his rope that in turn hangs down out of the clouds and the swirling snow, leans forward and rests his forehead against the hoarfrosted rock. Half the time he climbs with his eyes shut, his goggles have been torn off somewhere, this morning? yesterday? Now he opens his eyes and sees nothing but moving whiteness. He leans on the rope, rubs his hands in the wet gloves, calls up: All right, Hansl, I'm down, *du kanst hinunter kom*—What's the matter with me? Why do I keep calling to him? Of course Hansl can't hear me, Hansli's dead. Why do I keep forgetting he's dead? I must be in worse shape than I thought. Those two pitons just ripped away, like they were noth-ing, and he just stood there, half-covered by the avalanche, slowly slid-ing down the wall, scraping away the snow as he went; the bastard didn't say a thing, just looked up. . . . And he had half our pegs and all the extra rope, the bastard! and I'm supposed to get down all this by myself, another thousand meters, ha . . . but Nestor is too cold to laugh, and laughter becomes a hysterical trembling that shakes his body on its small holds. He has to grip the rope even tighter in a moving white vertigo. Little avalanches cover him. His red cagoule, like a priest's robe, is torn, wet, and frozen.

Nestor is so cold, so exhausted now, that there are many things he no longer understands. He is a middle term in a series of events that seem to him to stretch out far beyond this storm, beyond *la Torre,* beyond . . . but the directions, the beginnings and ends, escape him, are only confused by so much snow. The letter from Munich three months ago filled with Hansl's naive enthusiasms: the two of us, you who know those mountains so well, rush tactics, overwhelm it, one big push, how can we lose? How can we lose? That's what she always said to any objections. Her stuffy New England family? Well they came around, didn't they? Children? How can we lose, you so dark and me so blonde? This goddamn snow! I can't see if I'm anywhere near the col. Snowing too in Bariloche when I met her: the little tea-room on the Avenida Mitre, right around the corner from the Vizcacha, all the instructors down from *la Catedral* laughing in the corner in their blue parkas. Jorge, Diki, the Petrovic brothers, so warm in here the windows are all steamed up, can't even see the snow outside and there's Julia, all lonesome-blonde in the corner. The old German waiter will be back in a minute with his silver tray all full of pitons and slings so I can go on down, go home now it's so late. . . .

So long, so late, and they said they'd be back Thursday, two days ago, but Nestor's so strong he must be okay. Everyone knows he's the best climber in BA; they're jealous of him with all his friends at the television. I remember those stories in Bariloche even before I met him: so arrogant, you'll see. . . . And then in that tea-room after skiing, he just walked right up to my table, of course I was almost the only girl in the place, but so charming, really, and those drunk ski instructors making their slangy cracks I couldn't understand, thank goodness. . . . I can't understand it, why does he want to climb these awful mountains, *la Torre* especially?

Those days of good weather, when we could see it looming up there at the head of the valley like a great big—no, I can't say it, my up-tight petit-bourgeois upbringing I guess. . . . Oh my God, what am I talking about? to whom? And look at everything all soaked down here and it's starting to snow. Oh dear, that means it's getting worse, and the fire's still out. What if they should come back right now, I'd better, oh, why, why would anyone want to do such a crazy damn-fool thing? No one can climb these mountains. No one will ever climb *la Torre*.

No, no, he shakes his head and turns his horse in the rain. Rojo's *peón* knows that no one will ever climb *la Torre*. People were not meant to climb these terrible mountains, nor these mountains meant to be climbed by *los hombres*. *Poco a poco se gana el cielo,* little by little one gets to heaven, but not by climbing mountains, not this sky, this heaven, there are too many clouds, there is the white wind. Up there it's always winter, and hard and terrible.

Even this storm has grown worse as he watched: the wall of clouds blacker, more twisted by the wind. It has all happened before: year in year out, deep snow in June and July, by November the thorny *calafate* turns green for horses and sheep to graze on, but even when the sky is blue the wind howls down out of the canyons, there is no peace in this land, these are not mountains for men to climb. And last year, those little men who came from Japan they said; they stayed three months at the foot of the mountains and went away with sad faces. We are going home. Enough of this foolishness, watching invisible mountains. *Tú entiendes, cavallo mio?* You hear me, oh my horse? Rojo's *peón* is stubbornly proud of having resisted the *voseo,* the funny grammar of the pampas; he still says *tú.* But it has been easy enough, he has hardly talked to a soul these last twenty years. Long ago he wanted to remain a Chilean, not to accept their ways. But it no longer matters. He even drinks *mate* now; they give it to him in two-kilo paper sacks at the *estancia.* In his cabin the black kettle is waiting on a black stove. A man must drink something hot. *Vamos,* let's go down.

But that *mate* is so awful; it's the worst thing here in Argentina. Thank heavens Nestor drinks it with sugar, and Hans, of course, he can't stand it, like me. I'll just make some old-fashioned Liptons if I can only get the fire started. Why is everything so hard? And my hands are ruined, look: all scratched and black-and-blue. . . .

Soaked worn abraded fingers, so many hours, days in wet gloves: sore, then numb and frozen, painfully thawed to be soaked again. So cold, so hurt, my poor hands. It's getting so I can hardly hang onto this rope. That's it, just keep banging them against the rock, one at a time, till the feeling comes back. Then I can pull this damn thing down and make another rappel, another! Christ, how many more to the col? and our fixed ropes, if they're still there. . . . And then a few more hours down to the glacier, easy going back to camp: the tents like giant orange butterflies in the dark blue-green forest, no more wind, Julia running out crying, a fire, tea, Julia taking off my boots and thawing out my feet. . . . It's so warm here with my head between Julia's breasts. Why doesn't Hansl hurry? It's direct: the rope comes right down to the tent, right out of the clouds. He should have an easy time; once you're dead, you see, you don't weigh anything, just floating down. . . . Julia, don't cry so much! Julia, I thought about you up there, at night in our bivouac caves, coming down, even on that broken ledge where the rope got stuck. . . . Julia, we'll make love later on, I'm so tired, too tired, and I can't feel anything in my feet, my hands, Julia. . . .

But Julia is in the tent, lying on her sleeping bag, crying quietly to herself. The fire is burning again, but already starting to sputter; an unwatched pot of tea is boiling slowly away, turning black in the smoke. Rain and snow are falling together; everything is wet. . . . Late-afternoon clouds are already congealing into darkness; nothing has changed. How many hours of light? even here, so far south. . . . And if Nestor isn't back, doesn't come back this afternoon, then what? and why do I only think of Nestor, not poor Hans? and why *poor* Hans? And oh God, what's going to happen to me up here? Of course I know the trail down. . . . But tomorrow, if he doesn't come tomorrow, or the next day . . . and I haven't even told him about the baby, of course, I wanted to wait till after. . . . But I promised myself not to think about Nestor getting hurt, dying, oh. . . . Her blonde hair half-wet half-tangled on the damp blue nylon of her bag, buried broken beautiful face, weeping muffled but steady; the rain muffled but steady, dripping down a thousand tree trunks; the wind muffled but steady. Another branch snaps, falls.

Up in the clouds, the memory of sharp needle-like peaks hangs like a bad dream. Or a good dream, but anyway only a dream, twisted by the wind. Another small avalanche covers Nestor where he stands on the broken ledge. The cold snow on his face wakes him up. Once more he starts to kick his boots against the rock, bang his hands, one at a time, against the snow-covered rock. Nestor looks up. The rope is still hanging down, still stuck; somewhere up there in the clouds the little knot has jammed at the edge of an overhang, in a crack. Jesus how can I tell? ¡Hijo de la gran . . . son of the great whore who bore it! Nestor rocks back and forth, dizzy, cursing without conviction. Things are beginning to repeat themselves. How many times already has he tried to pull down the rope? As soon as the feeling returns to his hands he can try again. Hurry! It looks late already and Hansli had the bivouac sack in his pack when he fell. No shelter tonight. And no room to sit down on this stupid ledge. But if I can't pull this goddamn rope down it doesn't matter, it doesn't matter if I can live through another night, it doesn't matter if I fall asleep again. . . .

Sleep: I must've dreamt of Julia. Well I can always dream, but it isn't just a dream. I know there must be a fire down there, tea boiling in a little black pot. Julia must be awfully worried, poor girl. I should have left her in BA. Even life in camp is too tough for her; the tents look like giant orange butterflies coming closer through the trees. . . . No, no, I won't let it happen again. My hands are starting to hurt, a good sign. In a minute I'll try again. ¡Hijo de la gran puta que lo parió! Two days ago the two of them had been so close to the top, the great ice mushrooms, of the summit and then. . . . But no, Nestor himself is no longer sure if they made it or not. When did this storm start? when will it end? In a minute I'll be there. Julia's waiting in her sleeping bag, warm and naked. I'm almost home. . . .

Rojo's peón is almost home. His horse ambles down a little wash and up the other side. It's raining lightly and there's his cabin, his puesto. Rojo's peón has been thinking of the gringos from Buenos Aires, up there on la Torre. No, they are only men, as I too am a man. They are not able to do such things. No one can climb la Torre. And that pretty blond, *la rubia,* what can she be doing up there? what crazy dreams drove them to come here? to go up into the clouds? . . . I too, but my dreams are only of the sea. My dreams are full of sunshine, the dreams of an old man, dreams of youth, just dreams. . . . There is so much one cannot explain. Patagonian things. *Cosas patagónicas.*

1971

Icarus

Ian Rowe

Where did
He go
Id
Ego

An apocalyptic sunset exploded down the city street, crazy-angling the paving stones and blowing black to the ground the hunched, doomed shadow of William Goat, the best climber in the world, in the autumn of his life. The best, that is, to all but himself. A waddle behind came Fatima, his woman, brought back from the Karakoram for a lifesmanship gambit and a pair of old boots given to her father, a fakir who had said with what had seemed admirable fatalism, "A man would drown should he raise his head to the mountains while wading in the river." Now she lived in a converted slaughterhouse and was known as Fat Ima. One boot for a pair, thought Billy, and he laughed bitterly against himself.

The trouble was that Billy thought that Murray Snurd was the best climber in the world. In fact, he was the second-best climber in the world and regarded Billy as a demigod.

Billy was going to the pub for his weekly humiliation by Murray Snurd, who called him William and had never dared to call him Billy. Snurd was approaching from another direction, equally dreading his weekly humiliation at the hands of Goat. He knew that Goat would sit arrogantly by himself at the bar while the sensuous and desirable Fatima would flaunt her body and the regular customers would drool into their beer. Goat was unapproachable.

Billy's mind followed a familiar spiral of depression. Snurd never had a place for him in his car on weekends. He had waited for the invitation for years, but Snurd would not even speak to him in the pub. It was all too predictable. He knew that the group would polarize; the wives and girlfriends at one end and the men at the other. The wives and girlfriends were all delicious and he longed to pat them on their silken knees. And all the while Snurd would hold his group around him and plans would be laid without Billy's participation. He had not wanted to solo the south face of Everest without oxygen. Why doesn't he call me Billy?

Why does he call me Mr. Snurd?

But perhaps tonight was the night. He was fresh from the north face of the Eiger and Princess Anne had really enjoyed it. He quickened his pace and turned into another street. In the window of a bookshop he saw Snurd's latest book, *On Alp and Slagheap*. Another optimistic balloon burst. Why hadn't he thought of slagheap climbing?

Fat Ima's veils obscured her vision and she bumped into the crestfallen climber at the window. Billy delivered a short punch and dropped her to the pavement. Wasn't he more working class than Snurd? Brought up on slagheaps? He flung the prostrate Ima across his shoulder with the ease of supreme fitness and strolled into the bar.

"Here she is, Bob, keep her happy." A murmur of drooling appreciation rippled through the bar and menisci shivered in old men's glasses. Billy straightened his snakeskin caftan and entered the lounge.

He had calculated his arrival so that he would not be first. When he saw the empty lounge he was as alarmed as he would have been seeing an only, distant runner fall from the rock face at some thin crux. They could not have changed pubs without telling him. He tapped his watch anxiously. Then he twigged; it was a day early. The worst had happened. It was Wednesday and Snurd came here regularly with his bird, Nikki Van Bokker, beautiful black-booted Bokker, Queen of the Veldt and Miss Outspan, 1968. To be caught here would be blatant bootlicking; he had to get out fast. He spun round, tripped on the carpet, and fell heavily against the door, which opened with a crash and precipitated him into the arms and bosom of Miss Van Bokker. He was beyond help, torn asunder by the conflicting emotions of mortification and lust. Snurd spoke slowly from behind.

"Hello, Billy. Fancy bumping into you like this."

Billy knew he could never match wit like that. A sick, stupid smile forced itself to his lips as he got up. He blurted, "I have just fallen for your bird."

Snurd knew he could never match wit like that. He could have hit his bird at that moment. How could he make amends? To Billy's surprise, Snurd laughed and asked what he wanted to drink. Billy took a half-pint so that he could escape as soon as possible. Then they were sitting up at the bar as he had always wanted to do, with Nikki Van Bokker, the Queen of the Veldt, exquisitely cross-legged between them. His beer went down in painful gulps and then he heard those long-awaited words . . . lift . . . this weekend . . . the Ben. He gagged. His eyes watered and between the coughs he was agreeing to meet Snurd that very Friday and they would be off northward, revving through the starry night, speeding hedgerows seeming to keep time with the rock music beating from the radio. The smell of car, fish and chips, and cigars. Nirvana.

Snurd could hardly believe his luck and felt as if he wanted to shout. True, Billy had snorted sarcastically, but nevertheless the arrangement was made.

Billy could do little for the rest of the week. Next day he was out trapping hedgehogs, which he gave to Tinkers in exchange for underarm skin grafts for his research in the Department of Sexual Deviation at the University of St. Giles, but his nose was not in it. Already he was on the Ben, sniffing the cordite as hammer pounded rock and pendulous cliffs toppled with the impact against erosive eternity. He was, as usual, isolated at the pub the following night, despite the fact that Snurd had spread the word. The beast is warming to us, they thought, and a few glances of friendship were cast in his direction. Billy, as ever, made a false interpretation; but, whereas in other weeks his misery would have increased, tonight he was immune to his self-persecution. His mind's eye saw himself tied to his idol by an almost divine cord, the silhouette of fragile men carving their destinies from the unwilling, ungenerous precipice.

And that Friday night he stood with Ima at the rendezvous. The realization grew that this could be his last opportunity to seize his solution. But he was prepared for everything.

Fat Ima crooned tunelessly under the wistful cloud of her breath, words of her homeland and village, execrable hovels in the flood plain of the large river, which reeked of sheep and smoke from juniper fires fed to the blue sky through the intricate lattice work of the open chimneys; she thought of the meager, waving crop of maize brought to the water mill in colossal loads on the shoulders of small, dhotied men, or of dusty travelers pattering through the village on infinitely sad, timeless donkeys. And of the handsome strangers who had arrived with strange talk and devices which whirred and snapped as she veiled her face from their infidel view. They had taken her away and now only her chants could serve to evoke what she had known, random snatches of dialect exhaled and dissolved into the snell frigidity of an Edinburgh night, where no echo returned from the gray walls which towered above the tacky pavements.

Billy Goat, the best climber in the world, shivered inside his down jacket, as he had done a thousand Friday nights at this spot; he sensed the nostalgia of many weekends which had yielded superb climbs, physical triumphs yet pyrrhic victories of the spirit. The irony never failed to precipitate his Monday depressions, which over the years had extended so that now he had forgotten the simple joys when everything was new.

And all because of Snurd. At every contorted twist and turn in Billy's quest for unity, at every new experience hewn from an ever-deviating creativity, some action of Snurd's would be seen as better and at a higher plane of existence. There was so little now that Billy had not done that the fear of creative exhaustion intensified his fears. Yet tonight . . . this weekend, perhaps. . . .

Snurd's cheap little car bubbled around the corner and came to a flatulent halt, the near side bumper knocking the rucksack from under Ima's fat backside and sprawling her across the pavement. She picked herself up with the patience of centuries. Snurd jumped out and groveled apologies to her. He knew he would never make her now. Ima, in turn, was astonished that the infidel even acknowledged her presence. Nikki Van Bokker turned a sympathetic, inviting glance toward Billy, whom she now realized she desired above all else. Billy, in turn, knew that they were trying to be funny, and burned with humiliation; that sarcastic look of desire in Nikki's eyes . . . they were friends, these two; how mercilessly callous, how contemptuous of him!

To Snurd's surprise, Billy started to load the car as if nothing had happened.

Billy did not expect that Snurd would let him load the car, after stupid Ima got herself in the way.

They were off. Billy sat nervously in the back seat, picking his nose. "Nikki," Snurd said nervously, "give Billy a tissue."

No one spoke until they reached the hut, though Billy wept silently. Nothing more could happen to him, save that Snurd would not climb with him.

Yet Snurd had made a decision. In view of his inferior ability, he would climb with Nikki, and Billy could indulge his well-known predilection for soloing.

Billy had also made a decision should Snurd refuse to climb with him. He had prepared.

The night was silent in the black hut under the black cliff, a dance of cocoa mugs on a greasy table. A melange of kerosene and fear. And each person slept on their decision.

The morning came. Outside the hut, Snurd said, "I won't climb with you, Billy. I would be better with Nikki, who is more my standard." He desperately hoped for a contradiction.

None came. Goat watched them go and bitterly savored the skill of Murray Snurd. This was the final rejection. So be it. He turned and walked into the hut, stepping over Ima in the doorway. He picked up his rucksack and walked purposefully up the corrie to the big cliff, a cloak billowing out behind him, a dark stain of sweat curiously emphasizing the large S on his chest. He had to fly. Elated and invincible, he stood at the foot of the cliff with no motive but the ultimate. *Shazam Boom,* he yelled, and ran up the first section of vertical rock. Some yoga, breathing slowly through one nostril and exhaling through the other, thinking of the void and the non-him. The trance came and he moved up the rock in an orgiastic harmony of spirit and body, taking the impossible ways and eliminating the un-eliminatable. Then he was poised on the top and the sun shone golden in his hair and his shadow danced on the grass far below. Out of his cloak he drew a can of petrol and laughingly poured it over his head. A match was burning in his outstretched hand. He gave a short snort of triumph and contempt and ignited himself in a soft explosion. He pushed forward into a dive and fell in a magnificent crescent of flame.

On the grass below lay Snurd and Ima. He had left Nikki Van Bokker up on the mountain and was fulfilling his wildest ambition.

Through his burning eyes Billy saw their writhing bodies. And then he realized it all. He knew at that moment that he had always been in the lead. Still was. The King. Thirty-two feet per second per second burning King. He flailed his legs around, trying to get feet first, flapping his arms to put out the flames. Poor burning dead superman.

1972

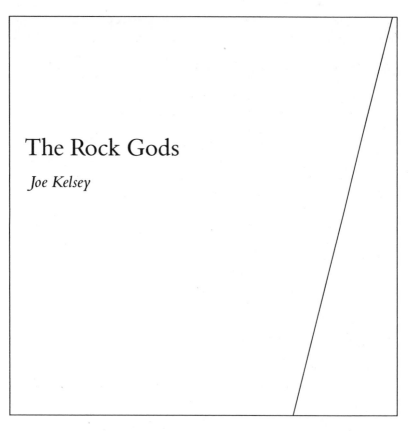

The Rock Gods

Joe Kelsey

The legends told how long ago, before the Great Mist drifted up from the west, killing most of those in its path, there had dwelled in the Valley a race of gods. The name of the Valley, Yoza-mity, was said by the wise to mean, in an ancient language, "Where the Rock Gods Climb."

The Gods were powerful, but their power, and indeed, interest, was restricted to Yoza-mity, and they had no control over the winds, so during the passage of the Great Mist they ascended the high walls surrounding the Valley and disappeared, leaving behind a small band of followers and their mortal ruler, the Coo-ree. Their Priest dressed in green and wore a wide-brimmed hat.

The best remembered of the Gods was the Bird King, and the Priest possessed an item of blue-colored footwear believed to have belonged to this deity. The Bird King was known as a lawgiver, and laws that seemed arbitrary or absurd could be explained as having been spoken by the Bird King. Two other Gods, small in stature but great in power, were the Ice King and the Santa Claus. The Ice King was the blacksmith of the Gods, and the Santa Claus was a jolly bearded fellow known both as a climber of chimneys and as God of the Vine. Most cultures have their evil spirits, and the evil spirit of Yoza-mity was the Devil of the Early Morning Light. He was a comic character, and in several myths defied the laws of the Bird King, only to be humiliated.

Many of the names of the rock formations derived from legends of the Gods. The largest rock, El Salathay, was named for the progenitor of the Gods. He in turn was descended from a wood-elf named Myur. The formation at the head of the Valley, shaped like half a dome, was known as Tissy-Ack, an old word meaning "Where the Bird King and a Lesser God Waged Battle." The name of Sundial Rock, the prominent cliff on the south side of the Valley, apparently referred to a method used by the Gods to tell time.

Since the regrouping of the Tribe after the Great Mist, people had occasionally found near the bottom of cliffs strange artifacts: pieces of rope, bits of strong fabric in the shape of tape, and strangest of all, spikes of steel with a curious hole in one end. These relics were given to the Priest, who locked them in a chest with the blue shoe. He called the spikes God Pins and said they had been forged by the Ice King. No one knew what their use was, but it was said that only Gods were permitted to use God Pins. It was said by some that the Priest had a picture that showed a God sliding up a rope.

It was not known whether the Rock Gods had really made any laws regarding conduct on the floor of the Valley. The Priest and the Coo-ree invoked the name of the Bird King to keep respect for their laws. Legends told only of laws forbidding the use of God Pins and permitting no one to leave ropes hanging from cliffs, or in any other way desecrating the walls. These arcane rules were transformed in time into one restriction that everyone could understand: Mortals were forbidden to climb on the walls of Yoza-mity.

The subjects of the Coo-ree were content with their simple pastoral existence and had no desire to climb the cliffs. They felt secure under the protection of the Gods and had no urge to leave their Valley. The people spent busy lives catching fish and tending the orchards and the bears. (The bears had been domesticated and were fed garbage. They provided the people with milk, meat, and fur.) Many generations had passed since the Great Mist and legends of the Gods were accepted without question. But as life became easier certain young people, who were spared the difficult labor of their elders, became cynical and doubted the existence of the Gods. They told each other that the Priest had made the blue shoe and the other relics himself.

Another result of the improved standard of life was that young people had more time for play. Among their favorite pastimes was the climbing of trees and boulders. Two young men, Memph and Gnienst, became particularly adept at climbing and mastered almost every stone in the Valley.

Inevitably perhaps, the attention of Memph and Gnienst turned to the great walls. They approached the bases of several cliffs to study possibilities for climbing. At the base of El Salathay they found a pale pink rope attached to a God Pin. Its stiffness suggested great strength.

The rope was important because a problem existed on long climbs that did not exist on boulders. A fall from a boulder rarely caused injury, but a fall from a cliff could be more serious.

Gnienst thought of a way to use the rope to prevent long falls. One climber tied to each end of the rope, and only one climbed at a time. The other was fastened to a tree or large block and ran the rope from his partner around his waist.

At the bases of some cliffs they found God Pins. Gnienst thought about them and guessed that Gods had hammered them into cracks in the cliffs. No one had realized this before, because no one had looked at the cliffs closely enough to see cracks; the Priest saw only the perfect shapes of Tissy-Ack and the other rocks and would consider the idea of flaws to be heresy.

Gnienst would have used the God Pins, but Memph did not want to hammer things into the rock. Memph was not one of the cynical youths who doubted the existence of the Rock Gods. He had always felt reverence for the Gods, and though climbing seemed an extension of this reverence, hammering iron into rock seemed an insult to the Gods.

Gnienst also devised a refinement that would allow the climber going first to go farther without risking a long fall. Pieces of the God's tape could be tied into loops around trees, rock spikes, and even stones wedged in cracks. The rope would pass within the loop; the climber could only fall twice his distance above the last loop.

And so it came to pass that one morning before dawn, not wanting to be seen, Gnienst and Memph quietly approached the base of a cliff. They had selected what appeared to be the easiest route on the north side of the Valley, to the left of the Arches of the Bird King.

As he approached the Arches of the Bird King, emotions tumbled through the mind of Memph. He felt the exhilarating combination of anticipation and doubt, curiosity and ambition. But beneath all was dread. Living within limits imposed by religion was a source of serenity. Memph's relation to the world had been defined by the laws of the Gods and the walls of Yoza-mity. Much has been said about fear of failure, but little about fear of success. If he and Gnienst succeeded in climbing out of the Valley, they would no longer be subject to the laws of the Gods. They would be free to go in any direction. The possibility of such freedom turned exhilaration into an awareness of the cold dawn.

Memph would have turned back, but his thoughts were interrupted by their arrival at the cliff. They had to decide where to climb and chose a chimney that appeared to be easy. Gnienst tied himself to a rope, took several loops of tape, and began to climb. He climbed one hundred feet to a large ledge, and it was time for Memph to begin. Memph saw that the climbing should be easy, but he was tense and clutched the rock. He gasped for breath after struggling over a large stone wedged in the chimney. The climbing was difficult because he feared the Gods.

Above the chimney, Memph and Gnienst untied from the rope and followed a stream bed for a few hundred feet. They reached a steep wall and tied on the rope again. It was Memph's turn to go first.

Going first was good, because Memph had to concentrate on which way to go and where to place his hands and feet. Soon he forgot the Gods. The simple joy of climbing returned as he moved upward.

So the climb continued. The route proved to be easy, until the boys reached a small ledge halfway between the Valley and the rim. Above them was a slab so smooth that at first it appeared only Gods could climb it. But beyond a slab to the left was a series of ledges that led to a large tree. Crossing the slab proved to be difficult, but no more so than many of the boulders.

Beyond the tree was a corner with a very rotten log across it. The log was used with apprehension: Gnienst remarked that it could not last another winter. Above the log the climbing was again easy.

On one ledge Gnienst could find no tree or block to which to tie himself, and he feared that he would be pulled from the ledge if Memph fell. But he found a stone that would fit into a crack in such a way that it could be pulled out only by lifting. He tied the rope around the stone, and while Memph climbed he thought about his invention. Now they could protect themselves in many places if they carried a sack of stones. Gnienst thought about other cliffs, even the great face of El Salathay.

The climb continued, and soon Memph crossed dirty ledges into a dense forest. Here they unroped and scrambled to the rim.

Memph and Gnienst looked out from the rim over the Valley and felt a joy never known to the simple folk below. They had risked much, physically and spiritually, and they had succeeded. They stood where only Gods had stood, and they could go wherever Gods went.

But neither Gnienst the technician nor Memph the philosopher had thought beyond the rim of the Valley. They had not planned their descent, and the treacherous route down the gully to the east diminished their feeling of equality with the Gods. Still, when they reached the trees and ran through the forest of the Valley floor, they savored the exquisite pleasure of defying a higher power and getting away with it.

They had gotten away with nothing, for they had been seen on the sacred cliffs and were summoned before the Coo-ree and the Priest. Both the Coo-ree and the Priest were livid with rage because someone had gone where it was forbidden to go. For their part, Memph and Gnienst exhibited the arrogance of those who have felt the Gods' special grace. As a result, Memph and Gnienst were banished from the Tribe.

The exiled climbers made camp in the dust beneath Climbing Boulder, across the Valley from Sundial Rock, and here they planned another climb. Would they have climbed again had they not been banished? Though they truly loved to climb, it was alienation from the Tribe that committed them to the other world, the vertical world.

Memph remembered his impotence before the Tribe and contrasted it with his joy as he had coiled the rope above the Bird King's Arches; he knew that he could be happy only when he was on a wall. He now knew a different religion, based on the impersonal hardness of granite, the religion of the Rock Gods. The religion of the Gods was not the religion of the Priest; the Gods had their own beliefs. Why else would they have devoted their lives to climbing?

This insight into the religion of the Gods was the closest that Memph ever came. Memph could not be a God because the Gods had come first. A person seldom has the time to become a God. The feeling passed and the time had come to prepare for El Salathay.

The best route appeared to be the south buttress. Gnienst convinced Memph of the need for God Pins, for though they had a sack of stones of various sizes, the stones did not always fit. Indeed, the Gods had cleverly widened cracks at intervals in such a way that God Pins just fit into the holes.

Climbing on El Salathay was different from on the Arches. It was seldom possible to climb on the rock itself, so Gnienst either jammed a stone or hammered a Pin every few feet, attached a loop of tape, and stood in the loop. Memph had to remove the stones and Pins so they could be used again.

This process was made easier by another of Gnienst's discoveries, a piece of equipment unknown to the Priest. It was a metal oval with a spring gate. The boys had two, which they called Ovals and used as links between God Pins and loops of tape.

Memph let Gnienst go first, because he was better at mechanical problems but also because Memph did not have his heart in the climb. He was impatient while Gnienst worked slowly up the cliff, and when his turn came, stepping from loop to loop and loosening Pins, he was not happy. Hammering God Pins into the rock was irreverent; stepping into loops of tape was not climbing, and Memph felt that what he was doing was wrong.

He felt no better when he reached the stance, and he asked his friend to go first again. Gnienst himself was discouraged because the climbing was going so slowly. They had dried bear meat and several bearskins of water, but it seemed unlikely they would reach the first ledge, called the Nostril, where they planned to spend the first night. With this in mind Gnienst quickly arranged the stones, Pins, and Ovals, and began to climb.

Gnienst never completed the second rope length. The young men were intent on the problems of the rock, and so had not seen the clouds gathered above them. Of a sudden, while Gnienst was clipping a loop to a God Pin, a bolt of lightning struck the rock. Flames flashed from the God Pins; Gnienst was briefly senseless and the current passing down the rope jolted Memph.

The vengeance that Memph expected from the Gods had come to pass. Continuing the climb was not considered; both youths could think only of returning to the ground. The rope was tied to several hammered God Pins, and while rain fell, they lowered themselves down the rope as the Gods were said to have ascended ropes.

Wet and repentent, Memph and Gnienst returned to the Village to ask forgiveness. The Tribe felt the Gods had punished as they saw fit, and that further punishment would insult the Gods, so the youths were accepted back into the community. (Also, the simple Yoza-mity tribesmen liked a good story and regretted missing the tale of the Bird King's Arches.)

Gnienst was to become a renowned bearherd and invented a yoke by which bears could pull wagons. Memph became Priest and restored to the religion of the tribe the relevance it had lacked for many generations. He did not forbid climbing, but rather taught youth to treat rocks with reverence.

Memph expressed the sentiments of all the people of the Valley when he said that the Rock Gods were indeed merciful. A bolt of lightning had been mild retribution for defying the laws of the Gods.

1974

The Soloist's Diary

Jeff Long

. . . *not to imply that I wish to specify the degree of pain and passion with which I die, nor the actual manner of death, nor even its approximate instant. But to control my death's quality . . . to have mattered, one mute perception spanning the ages which this remote tirade against the rock has paradoxically rendered eternal, wrought in its own inconceivably lonely vast body.*

Today: performed a most elegant movement. It was yesterday, I think, that I threw away all but twenty feet of rope.

Sound is the most tenuous of things: untouchable, deceiving, hiding in shadows, covering its damp tracks with echo, cacophony, history hanging on its subtle dark pallor or harmonies, a night which ridicules vision. So too I have trouble these days in hearing beauty. It is years now. All the rock is as it appears: a barrenness ending in human things with warped and mangled flesh, pale veins and tendons utterly void of strength. My nostalgia is infinite. My heritage of vacuum in the rich somber architecture of nature. My desire an impossible return.

Long ago I spoke with other wretched ones. One swore he remembered start-ing from waves, another from the desert. Still others mentioned primeval for-ests, rice terraces, lagoons; and another, a remarkable figure, yelled to me ages ago from across a crack that he had been born on the wall and was trying to find his mother somewhere high above him. I arrived by crude error and, forever, here. . . .

I can vaguely remember starting to climb. Reduced to myths, I suffer on the rock. Various amnesias blot the tissue of my memory and de-prive me of a heritage, making me into a creature of the rock. By climbing an infinite height we have created an infinite depth and our pasts have become doubtful.

But still . . . still it seems as if there was once a period of beginning, a time when the dead climbers seemed grotesque as they hung from the crack or became bones upon small ledges. Years of dedicated horror have eaten that innocence away. The ground is no longer visible, nor its image, and even the horizon is obscured by dense low mists. There are no sides to the wall. There is no summit, which is our first dilemma.

We climb because it's what we did. For a long time now we've per-suaded ourselves of our humanness by fluctuating and challenging the rock with our stifled personalities and raging diversions. There have been seasons of religious intent and seasons of ennui and of hatred. Our eyes flashed those days of flux, but the days are different now. Every-thing seems ancient. The days are indistinguishable from the rock and our eyes have nearly mineralized. We no longer take pride nor find pleasure in pretending. We no longer change. We simply climb.

So there was a world I knew. It consisted of the rock and the sky upon my back, of my strength, of Aaron and Gareth, of the cold nights, and water bottles and pitons, ropes, hammocks, and fading things. They recede more and more. Within me I feel a far-belowness. There are caverns in me that are marvelously daubed with thick, phos-phorescent pigments and rich echoes, places that hide me from the wall and this gagging subjection. It is a sheer journey, a mercy of myself to myself. My mind, receptacle of images, is at once a holy strife. Half-formed characters grope their way into shimmering position. Many present moments but only one past, a darkened sanctuary.

In the mist there was nothing to see, only ashen forms a few yards distant. Unjointed shadows that faintly resembled things of the normal world existed down there. What seemed like a tree swimming before us was sometimes a tree; at others it was a thin strand of erect rock; sometimes it was nothing. Even the trees were without roots, free to wander. The outer world had disappeared. We were submerged, the brief scents, cool trees, and wet rock . . . without form. Only our touch was above suspicion in that place.

We edged cautiously through the forest, our huge packs looming up in perpetually slow light, with gray tails of mist gliding behind, attached to our thick, veined shoulders. Those wafting tails of mist were true ghosts, I suppose, dismal and pathetic remnants from earlier ages in nature. We felt this. They were no terrifying apparitions at all, just impotent little driftings without more purpose than to absorb all echoes, all definite perception, and all our thoughts. Everywhere we were relentlessly hung, pursuing and pursued.

We came across a tree with a patch of its bark shaved away. In the polished oval of wood there was carved a deliberate figure, a calligraphic revelation, a single character that seemed simple but was incomprehensible. I found it; it was one of the first nights. There it was suddenly, an impression, a solemn insolvent word deep in the mute forest, but as to whether there was meaning in it? Yes, I think so; but from that fossil I knew then and ever will, nothing. It was not to be the last of such scriptures.

It was a forest of petrified wood. Even the cold trees, their green needles hanging in a semblance of life, seemed forever frozen and empty of life. Petrified. Every tree stood faintly, fog-moistened and brown in the grayness. Each tree was a grotesque climax of the gloom of that place, and in a similar way the spectral birds with their dimly flashing colors increased rather than diminished the loneliness of that land. When the slight sound of their beating wings came plummeting between the trees, we weren't raised out of the silence but only reminded of it and sunk deeper into its glaze.

Two ancient climbers were there, all rotted from aging and from the eternalness of apathy that was the fog. We were passing through the forest when suddenly we came upon them, two bent little figures squatting dwarfishly over a tiny birth of orange flame that was licking meekly at their world. There was no noise, not even spitting or crackling from the little fire. We watched them in silence, in astonishment, not knowing at all what they were. (Later we would know that they had descended while there was still a way back, an equally fatal course to take.) Both of them were clothed in rags; each had draped long scraps of old cloth over the shoulders of their parkas, shredded and emptied of feathers, vacant and flat. Both were wearing pants heavy with mud and holes, and both were barefoot in the cold, their feet flattened, cracked like baked mud.

Standing there apart from them and their flame, I had to struggle to keep from choking, and my mouth was slack and whistling hollowly with my ruptured panting. I could hardly force air into my lungs, and I was hard at forcing it back out again. It was them and their fire; something in the separate baseness of it strangled me. There they crouched with their tangled hair wet, matted in heavy clenching nests upon their shoulders. They weren't talking. They were just crouching intensely over the flame, absorbing its meaning, squatting under, within; possessed by the mist.

We withdrew silently and went far around their little circle with its handful of contemplated flame, away from the primality of their neanderthal scene, away from the awfulness of their underworldness and their abysmal degeneration, and especially away from the fact of our similarity.

Gareth came to camp with a human bone nestled gingerly in his open hands. We followed him to a broken hut built of granite and rotted pine. In its shadows lay a thin skeleton half-buried, a layer of dirt covering its legs. Something in the hasty nature of its covering imparted an air of breathlessness to the scene, as though near death the man had hurriedly dipped himself into the shallow grave. We stood about looking at it for a few minutes, then Aaron and Gareth drifted away. I stayed waiting while the earthen skull stared sightlessly into the depths of the wasted ceiling. I was filled, for the few moments I contemplated the hollow sockets, with something beyond myself, but soon, discerning no message, I left the sepulchral shadows and reentered the mist. Night came. We had no idea where the rock wall began. We'd searched for days in the mist, groundbound. Now we ate our rice, carrots, onions, drank our tea. And sat by the fire.

Mosquitos, the lips and arms of succubi, their opaque wings humming, sang at me in the darkness, luring me from my veil of smoke. But I wouldn't leave the fire. Feeling the black air on my cold back, I knew somehow that if I so much as closed my eyes to the light of the fire, the night would devour me. I could do nothing but cling to the fire. Out there was some character of the void and seemingly I was the only one of the group to sense it. I said nothing to warn Aaron and Gareth; instead I hugged the flames with my worried brow, afraid, protecting the others with my fear. I heard popping, clattering noises and whirled about to face the night. I grabbed a thick stick and mumbled hoarsely, but there was nothing. Later in the night, when the others slept, something touched my shoulder. I was instantly alert. But again it was nothing. My horror: It was far worse being touched by nothing than by any something. The nothing offered no substance, no resistant solidity to belie oblivion. I can remember that. I was new to voidness then.

We found the wall and soon after the preliminary crack. A queer beach spread out before the wall. We thought at first we'd come upon the site of some massacre or a gruesome sacrificial field. There were men lying everywhere, not in any dense abundance, but randomly scattered all about. Some were more recently dead and were only partially eaten and decomposed; others were only bone or shadow. The remains lay positioned so that we were unnerved at times when one or the other of us suddenly tripped over the hidden bones of an unexpected body. There was no predicting where to set our feet. Grass and brush were everywhere; the bodies were anywhere. We were, as children, stunned. It was my first exposure to dead bodies, and it was a grisly first. The limbs twisted in terrible directions, skulls were bashed and empty, parts missing. Tropical birds and ravens had long before settled on them and had picked away their eyes. Animals had since died and had been buried, so to speak, on the dead compost of the skeletal piles. This too I remember, how the animals fed upon and died upon a single substance.

Lying everywhere were weathered pieces of manila, nylon, refuse, words.

We should have known. They were fallen climbers. We looked up and acknowledged the rock. It was above us irregularly, and hardly visible for the mist. Gareth drew a circle in the air and pointed upward; Aaron secretively scratched a figure into the dirt. This terrible deadliness was a new dimension to climbing for all of us. In climbing we'd always known an elusive risk, but such rampant danger? We'd assumed a dignified nonchalance before in the presence of rock. Here, though, was a graveness. There are victims of accident and there are victims of something more (something of themselves). These were like so many mites shaken off an animal. Other occasions would arise in my future, occasions for my will, but by the time those sediments and springs of seeming freedom initiated balance, or ties to the earth (in apparition),

I would long since have been swallowed by my choice, and circumstances would never again permit a contradiction of this. Naively I opted for the wall as I treaded its beach of grass and lost ones.

We groped about at the base of the rock wall, seeking out the proper crack to begin climbing. We knew of it but had no method of finding it. It was in fact merely a climber's tale that had fertilized our venture. The vague rumor of an unclimbable wall . . . but we could see nothing for the mist. Nevertheless, from the root of the abruptly rising rock we could sense that it was a huge wall, and too that it was occupied. From the base it was an empty slab, no sight or sound coming down, yet we could easily feel its population. We put our hands to the rock and knew that somewhere above us were other climbers touching its glabrous angles.

For two days we wandered along the base of the wall, searching for the primary crack, craning our heads back to stare upward into the mist and to imagine the great wall. Amidst the scree, the congestion of dead shattered things slowly grew. That afternoon we were touching the crack. It was horrible. There was a cozy simplicity then, sanctioned by such a mass above us, an unseen thing. There was no drama in the beginning. We were unsure of everything and had set no regimen for the ascent. We inserted our pins into the crack and ascended. And there upon the rock was the vision of the outside. Everywhere were dead climbers and climbers' things. Ropes hung from hanging bodies. The sky was rock.

Scarcely above the thickest of the mists appeared immense, inverted platforms of granite that blocked our sight upward and looked impassable. We had never encountered anything like it before. The entire wall just changed directions and flattened out as an endless ceiling, a panoply. That they are territorial gates which allow progression but no descent is possibly the greatest factor that traps us here on the wall, but something more prevents us from even attempting to retrace our path to reach the ground again. We took several months to sew our way across the ceilings and can never retreat. The roofs composed an agglomeration of hundreds of down-vaulting rotten bulges and overhanging crumbling dihedrals requiring innumerable fixed anchors. Had we been able to see through the mist before starting, we would have witnessed this catastrophe of nature: a flat, horizontal wall thousands of yards above the ground, extending along a parallel over the forest for miles, with nothing to suggest that the entire colossus shouldn't topple as a mountain in itself to Earth. Its confusion is indescribable; my accounts have oftentimes been discounted by Aaron, and his by Gareth, for we each formed perspectives and fears of the overhangs, none the same, none even consistent within themselves. There were, hanging from the rock, thousands of geometries which we had to skirt, but there were so many and they were so varied. Forms seemed to recur as we wove about beneath baffling plates of rock, doubting our paramnesias. The filaments of color, the membranes that laced the ceiling like wafers, were static, but their effect was disturbingly animate. As we negotiated the stone roofs, we were closed upon by the rock. As soon as the last man had finished cleaning the pitch, we would look back in the direction from which we'd come and would know we were lost backwards, that we could only move by ascending, by going outward. We had come out of a myth, an elder Earth, and felt wrongly, fatefully, about it from the instant we were suspended.

Then one early gray dawn we could see the ending of the roofs, and we perceived a summit awaiting us over the rim. Before the ground below disappeared, I was struck by a last real vertigo while surmounting what we thought to be the last of a seventy-day wall-roof. I was on the pitch leading. I mantled onto a long and wide cup of amber flakes, but as I did so I was confronted by two tiny, insane things. They were crack animals such as we ate, but something in their extrafamiliarity was abnormal. One opened its beak and shrilled at me, its black tongue lapping vilely. I backed away, one hand on the wall for balance. Wildly they sprung about, in a frenzy at my trespass. They were just crack animals, no larger than my hand, smaller than many I've killed, yet they had me backed against the rock. I went to my knees and began swatting at them, swinging my free hand at them with a fierceness to balance my fright. But they came on anyway. Their insistence was all the more intimidating; I'd never before had a crack animal chasing me, always they only hid. They pattered about in little circles, striving to drive me off their world. By chance I tapped one with my fingers and the creature was lifted up and across the lip of the basin. It shrilled feebly, then sank away. The other paid no heed and that one too, as light as a pebble, was caught with a swipe of my hand. It fell and I watched. And for the first time, still spastic from their miniature aggressions, I realized something of what was meant by my height. The yawning panorama had absorbed them valuelessly.

Suddenly I understood what danger I was in. Hitherto believing I had escaped by climbing apart from the world, I was reprimanded with sickness for having diluted a truth; there can be no escape from the ground, it would say, that womb, that voracious pit all spread out below in mocking. I froze and dizzied, became faint and desperate for solidity. I wanted the reassuring pressure of something firm against my body. I wanted total security of compassion in matter. I fell onto my belly, but as I lay prostrate it seemed my back might somehow betray me, perhaps fall and pull me with it. I clutched deeper and unhappier into the slight turf of the basin, then carefully, very slowly, I rolled onto my back. Crossing my arms over my chest, I cautiously looked into the sky, but it was all empty, depthless too, full of content (its blueness) but barren even of cloud, a formless form. I lay pinned hysterically on a platform in the thin mist, a last dream before the rock became the sky and the earth disappeared behind me and under my body, in both directions and backwards. I closed my eyes and lay miserably on my back, throbbing with wild intuitions of the hungry earth and the hungry sky absorbing me into its granitic eternity. We began coming upon decaying parchment fragments like chronicled flotsam on the rock. Folded or tucked into old haul bags, or tied within pieces of plastic that hung from the wall, we usually found these mementos in some isolated spot, rarely in the company of other journals. The dead men presumably preferred it that way.

Later we found several pairs of men wrapped in homosexual postures . . . tender deaths. And there were some signs of brutality, as in the case of one climber who'd been thrashed with a hammer. And brawls, verbal destruction, even two lynchings, all strung as twilights of inconsummate longing upon the rearing, unspeaking rock. Several of the journals mentioned tales that a certain climber, upon reaching "a summit plateau," kept on climbing, hanging slings and carabiners on tree limbs, playing out his few remaining meters of rope through ascenders as he crawled immortally over rocks and tree roots that carpeted his horizontal stone. At times he grew desperate as he maneuvered upon the ground; at times he was confident of his safety. He slowly perished that way, carrying the wall with him.

Toward the bottom many complained of banshee whispers. But gradually the individual ascents, each one toward the lassitude of varying degree, forced upon them all the realization that much of what was thought to be external (ghosts and screams) was in fact internal. However, it was hardly a soothing realization. Each climber had become an isolate, a centered organism with its own pantheon of unsharable, internal phenomena, accumulating a private transparency, echoes reshaping a convulsing and writhing world, effecting interior disasters (or salvations) whereby the climber would untie and return quickly to the blurred ocean and the soft humus below.

We continued on up the headwall. The months of progress over it were like research through vague tombs, daily efforts to recapture a past figure's deeds and character in some prehistoric network. Gareth began assembling biographies, Aaron began compiling a grammar of linguistic cores. We read of men, of the signs they had used to appease their restlessness, and then we destroyed their diaries and the scraps of the wall's history have long since blown away.

Except for the idea and reminders of our solo climber. Nearly every journal we read included two separate passages regarding this gentle creature. Everyone on the wall seems to have acknowledged him at some point. His story is like a branch.

Crudely put, he began as a beginner. Some of the journals swear this climber had never climbed before. Apparently he just approached the wall, then simply banged his way up the rock, a process variously interrupted for food, rest, and night. His style was comically inadequate, as testified to by journal italics. He was slow and an early doom was predicted for him by the many climbers who continually passed him. He was described as friendly and impeccable. Several climbers urged him to retreat from the wall. He didn't. One party had to revive him from a coma brought on by exposure after a short fall. They stayed with him on a ledge for two days, urging him to get off the wall, and then climbed on. He followed slowly. In time he crossed the first great overhang and was thereby committed for the rest of his life to climbing the rock wall. His history becomes a blank for some time until a record of terrifying notice about his transformation. Perhaps he had found some hidden couloir with its own crack system and meditated there. It's not unlikely that he came into contact with the legendary Taoist climbers, or the yamabushies. I don't know. No one knows. The next mention is of his ease and his beautiful style, and awed descriptions of his smooth speed. He was said to have climbed naked, even on cold days when everyone else was suffering in their down jackets; one or two journals spoke of him climbing without the use of hands. One climber swears to have seen him ascending without touching the rock at all.

There are tales of cryptic chanting and foodlessness. Some say he required no water but fed instead upon sunlight and his own saliva. One passage speculates with rather extreme detail and rhetorical treatment on the possibility that the soloist reached a top. The fragment is abstract but painstakingly defines the soloist lodged in a landscape of ascension "serenely reflected." After hopeless deliberation I considered it highly probable that the summit had indeed been reached by the soloist. I stared up the wall to its governing horizon of rock and sky and was pleadingly thrilled. If the summit truly existed, and if the soloist had reached it, then obviously there was a chance that we too would find it. It had a tremendous impact on our morale and pace. We covered large stretches of rock each day for many weeks, believing we could almost see it, but soon enough our excitement was played through and the tedium we had grown used to again resumed. We slowed our pace, climbed more methodically, hauled the foodsacks and water, the hammock, winter gear, our pens and paper. Little by little our new-found energy was sapped and expended. In its place we were left with a transient faith. That was enough, to believe there was a summit. . . . Years seemed to have seeped into my core . . . the delirium of pastness, an impetus beyond memory.

Many climbers were left abandoned when their partners died, and for a while they'd carry on. Not as well, but at least for a while. We found traces of one climber who had taken off horizontally, knowing his suicide, seeking desperately perhaps an edge or corner to the wall. His packet of notes described the pathetic ambition; we know nothing about the actual attempt. He questioned the value of upward ascent and bravely, we thought, separated from the vertical flux. He left the traffic of the wall and became alone twice over; first he was cast into hermitage by his partner's death (a sliced rope, we read), and then he tossed away all hope of reaching anywhere on the regular route, climbing sideways, wandering across the face. The cracks were few, though, and doubtful. His notes could have been anything: diversions, a dirge, dreams, a hoax. We wondered if he ever reached an edge to the wall. And as we wondered, we too began to sense the ritually fatal power of our dreams.

We climbed and found no summit. In winter it was too cold to climb so we settled on a huge forklike outcrop. Each winter morning we would wake coldly and everything around would be frozen. The lichen would be frosted, and the thin bed of water made into streaked glass. I later learned how to concentrate on the particles of sunlight and fire myself with their semblance of heat. We had nothing to burn. So we emerged from our bags and gathered close together to talk. To make warmth, or at least collectively to forget the cold.

But silence came. One bitter morning something happened. We gathered, shivering, standing in a tight circle, our hands tucked in the bellies of our sweaters, and we tried to talk. But terrible day, terrible sun . . . my first word became a white vapor, a netherness. Our winter breaths were marked by clouds of frost, a common fact of winter, one about which we'd never before cared. Until this day. "Gareth," I said. And there Gareth hung, there he vanished in a puff of frost. We started, then gaped as it hung and drifted a little higher, finally evaporating. Before our very eyes the word withered. We all heard me say the word, each of us understood what I meant by it, but suddenly, breached by our space, it was emptied of inertia, of its semantic value. It was no longer the same, it was humiliated by the vaster elements, condemned to limbo. (Aaron later added the phenomenon to his grammar.)

We were astonished. We blinked.

"Gareth," I said. This time we tracked the punctured cloud anxiously. The breath of frost rose again, but again it came apart. Our eyes deepened. The word *was* for a moment, but then it wasn't. It went nowhere. It was inaudible music, a particular cadenza which was for us an artifact, an instant of locality beneath the compromise of matter. The whole affair is almost not worth mentioning, but . . . you see?

Strange. As we got higher and left below us the mist, and eventually the clouds too, and as the sun was less and less filtered, colors disintegrated. I can't make distinctions between particular colors anymore. There is the sky color, no matter what color. And the rock is constantly the color of rock. Even we climbers and our multihued gear have lost color.

One day we would be in a gigantic chimney-crack, or again we'd find ourselves coaxing holds from an incipient groove, or squatting upon a ledge or hanging lazily beneath small, shading overhangs. But it was all the same rock, and only our experiences and perceptions fluctuated. After a while it seems the world froze and that the flux we sensed was merely internal and practically unreal. For a moment time has fallen asleep. At some other point we were born. Now, solidified like rock, time is ethereal and volatile as the sky. We climbed upon time as though it were mineral, and as we did we breathed it and our bodies exhibited time's marks. Our grayed hair dozed in lengths.

We had long since escaped the pit, when suddenly it stirred and rose up after us. Some of the very old journals we'd collected had records of the mist ascending the wall. Those earlier men had described demons and angels that flew about within it, hunting, haunting climbers. The mist, it was recorded, was filled with musics and scents, and now and then the sound of heavy objects fluttering down through thick air, or banshee screams of other climbers. They described peculiar agonies and frequent suicides. Gareth and Aaron and I meticulously read the accounts, but none of us could understand why the mist should be of such consequence. It seemed to us that the tracts concerning the mist were more like fairytales that wearied climbers had invented for their survival.

But the day came when the wet smoke rose. Serenely it rose up, fathomless, extending for miles up into us, swirling about our ankles and knees, then drifting on high above, swallowing us on our wall. In it were the brilliant wet colors we'd known below, and there the agony began, for the vivid colors wrought memories we'd forgotten. Images flooded and exhausted us. After the first desperate days we became more and more vacant, and climbing was at last impossible. We found a large, flat tower of rock and made our camp there and for a long time hovered in our opiate, the mist, engulfed in the past, moist nostalgias; its rich texture even softened the callouses on my hands, ruining them. When I touched the rock they shredded like springtime fingertips. Aching, limbs would collapse not just from weariness, but from emptiness.

In the morning we would wake and excitedly begin chattering to one another, trying urgently to relate each valuable detail of our night's dreams. The excited lesions of speech would quickly fall away as we collected ourselves in sad dissipation and sat closer together, one by one describing our nocturnal utopias. It was private territory and we each knew it would be a violation of the dreamer's sacred cosmos if we dared offer a word of interpretation. Instead we'd nod ambiguously and wait several minutes before the next would set in with a dream, eager to spin it out.

Frequently, by the time our dreams had been told, half the day was gone. Though the sun was layered with heavy mist, we could still discern its relative position by its lighter aura in the murky sky; thus we could mark our days. After the dream-telling was done, we would retire to separate parts of the ledge, maybe to exercise on the rock or to sleep, but usually just to sit and remember. And later, when the sun was going down for the night, and the mnemonic afternoon was expended, we were visited by spirits. Those which other climbers had called demons and angels came to hover by and talk to us individually. We each had a personal conclave that hung by us; as mine was invisible to Aaron and Gareth, so theirs were to me. They were pit phantoms come to convince us to return to where we'd risen from. Mother phantoms came, and various succubi, and old friends showed their tender concern for me. Even philosophers and poets would come up to talk with me. They appealed to my passions and my reason, arguing and cajoling, debating, kissing my head. I sat hunched up, my eyes squeezed tight, listening and sometimes crying a little, envisioning past loves and duties, recalling ideals I'd once championed. They were sweet echoes, but I felt a need to deny them all. What of the future, I would ask the phantoms, and they would flicker hesitantly before ignoring my words. My firmness would dissolve and I'd remember all the good things, all the fine pasts, just by sitting there against the wall, sighing. At last I flailed my arms against the phantoms when they demanded I dance in the air with them. My knuckles began bleeding where I'd knocked them violently against the wall.

I stared at my blood and many things rushed into place. Rough hair, nails broken, hominidal fears at night, and hungers, yes, the bloodness being the great hunger. I licked my knuckles clean and watched as more of my own blood welled up. I began lapping the scrapes, drinking of myself. Hunger seeped through me, and when the phantoms circled again I croaked at them to leave me. Look at me now, I warned them. They re-formed out beyond the ledge. You rest, they whispered, we'll leave. But I knew they'd return. Dreams and seasons have no evolution.

I glanced about. There were Gareth and Aaron, one lying in his bag, the other sitting in a corner smiling. I wanted to scream to them of the danger. Instead I went to Aaron, shook him gently, and pointed to the wall. His eyes were glazed in distance and his smile seemed permanent, but he nodded his head and murmured assent . . . tomorrow, tomorrow we'll climb. When I shook Gareth he struck at me, weeping.

So with pieces of sling and old rope I lashed him fast to the wall. He didn't mind much. He struggled, but not with meaning. He was too possessed by the mist.

And next day, early in the morning I shoved and pushed Aaron awake. I was frightened that he might continue his depthless smiling, so I beat him. That morning we began our escape.

The first day we ascended only a short distance, but most importantly we began bleeding again and feeling ourselves as bodies and not as dreams. Each afternoon we'd return to the mist-enclosed ledge. Gareth recovered day by day, but still tended to collapse into reverie, so we kept him tied to prevent his suicide. We climbed each day, surrounded by the mist, shoving our way through its melancholia, fixing ropes for the coming day when Gareth could sanely join us.

I sat on a ledge for a long time, the rope draped around my waist and piled at my feet in loose coils as Aaron led above. Somewhere far below me Gareth was waiting for us to come sliding down to him with food. But I came awake instantly. Something about the rope insisted an end to my stupor. No words had been spoken, no warning, but I was suddenly alert to a tension burning down from above. Maybe the rope conducted the tension, maybe it was the air that was adhesive and saturated with urgency. And suddenly it came in an eruption of space. The rope's tension collapsed on itself as I clenched it anxiously. One moment there was tautness and demand streaking down into my hands; in the next I was left holding a limp substance, useless and without strength. Aaron was falling. The stillness woven deeply in the fibers leapt and the rope jumped fiercely; my palms screeched, taming the motion, searing, stopping the serpentine speed into sluggishness and final stasis of smelt flesh and inertia. I heard a distant slap high above me. Aaron had finished falling. The rope began pulling insistently at my waist, weighted on its far end. I set against it and wrapped it about my thigh, wondering why and how long the fall had been. In a minute there was the grappling sensation of lessening pressure, followed by a vibrating tug, and then a relaxation of the invisible pressure pulsing through the cord. Finally the hard pull eased, its tautness properly restored, fluid rather than enmeshed in the drastic sleekness of weight. I began working in the slackness as Aaron revived himself and started up the crack again.

From somewhere I remembered how immediately before the fall the air had been warm, the sun directly above me. But I was beginning to shiver with the coldness, and the sun was low by the time the rope released itself once again. Another crashing. This time the slap came two times quickly as I held the fall, then sounded twice more just before I felt his total weight pulling violently against my waist. This, I could feel, had not been a good fall.

I waited for Aaron to call something down, but he didn't. He said nothing, just his weight. Invisible, existent only by the proof of the rope, he revived himself again. I could feel the rope jerking and releasing as he tried to pull himself into a prehensile position. Again I forced pain away from my burned hands, oblivious to the chill about my throat, demanding the same patience that dominated our life on the wall. I waited. Finally Aaron found a hold and the rope became unweighted again. I waited more. And while I lurked in my shadow (the pre-night), I heard what I had never dared to hear, an end to hope. It came like a small, dry bat through the fog; a groan, a tiny, bleached noise, muffled, half-sheltered by its shock, smothering. It was a memory, stars blowing hilted, stars in their cobalt flood of fear and aloneness infecting me in the night. An acute hum. I hit out, thrusting in every direction at the frightening blindness, and by chance my hand struck the rock. The spell snapped; there was rock, and my consciousness was restored, transfigured. My eyes came open. I could feel the rope again, and bit by bit I let the rope slide through my hands, running it as smoothly as my braking palms would allow. I worked him down through the mist gradually. Our sun was pallored, buried in the universe, already hinting at its usual bile black. One knew simply that one was; if he heard voices, or groans, he was conscious, and nothing more, of another, less verifiable existence. Aaron didn't answer. I continued letting out the rope.

At last I could hear his feet scraping weakly at the rock as he tried vainly to keep his balance against the arcing wall. And his hands kept slinging against the opaque, moonless stone. I continued lowering him. Finally his slumped body materialized, all wet and dark. On his head was blackness, a frigid blue shimmering, and his sleeves were also wet and bloody. I pulled him onto the ledge and laid him out. The mist became verglas and illuminated his epileptic form. The gray cold was at its margin. Drained by the night, I knelt and manipulated him down an overhang toward insomnial Gareth.

For the fallen one, days were spent in the heap of his drugged, lacerated half-corpse. But soon enough he could drag himself about, and would lie gazing out into the mist, numb with his private thoughts. He slept, pampering his scabbed face even in his sleep, careful not to touch a large bald patch where his scalp had ripped. On a few fingers the nails were pulled off, while on the rest, the cuticles had burst and bled, and his knuckles were flayed. A few times we had to kick him hard before he's come awake from his delirium. But Aaron never really recovered from his fall, for though his wounds healed they were poisoned by the mist, and he was skittish and impacted with nightmares. One day the mist began to recede. Just like that, and we again became indistinguishable from the rock, and knew then we had risen slightly further.

We found a female mummy. She left no diary or notes. She was dried and dessicated after many years from hanging upon the wall. Tucked in her nylon hammock, she was well-covered with a thin silvery poncho that had at one time been painstakingly sewn as a lid to the hammock, but had long since been partly opened to reveal this precious corpse. Her hair was still long and beautiful, golden and soft. Short phrases of poetry were inscribed in the stone, and a multitude of names covered the rock above her head and chest, wreaths and bouquets of remembered loves that were immortalized here and dedicated to this one. How many had passed this way, brutal and hardened by the elements, and lifted the torn flap to witness her? Had there been even an intimation of company? But no, instead, each moving fragment of a body on this glossy wall, dissuaded by worn faith and weariness, persists deathlike to its own final isolation, there to be devoured by loneliness and gravity. For a moment, peering reverently at the body of this dusty and lofty female, I was gorged with her delicate process, her every grace. The fine woman. And the rock pushed at me with its slickness and with its fine-flaked, deep, deep sterility . . . but the woman, she never pushed toward death; instead to her own vanities, her clutching thighs, her fertility and population. I am her child, but what labors must I undergo to forget her? Some would challenge the contradiction on sheer principle and insist that consistency either is or is not valid. I never suffered as I poised between the rock and the female, but I can never eliminate that possession which was their harmony.

Another season of nailing and bouldering above our ledges transpired and we entered a weird, vertical plateau, still believing in the soloist and the escape he represented. Artistic exercises suddenly flooded the rock. There were carvings, bas-reliefs, etchings, poetic and philosophic engravings, statuettes, and figurines. Curiously, they all seemed confined to a particular zone, its area covering roughly three hundred square feet. It began and ended with no reason, its perimeter was not dictated by an encroachment of bad rock nor was it lined with cracks. It just ended, top, bottom, and side, by common aesthetic agreement. Climbers had religiously fixed pitons and bolts throughout the zone so that those hapless ones who followed would not accidentally chip or scar the art pieces while climbing through. All we had to do was snap our etriers onto the provided pins and we could easily ascend the vertical museum. We spent some two months in the region, rappelling and wandering about the abutments and fineries, returning to our hammocks each night to await the day when we could again resume our discoveries.

Everything was carved out of the wall rock. Pitons and drills had been skillfully wielded by the sculptors and masons, and the work had been beautifully polished by the wind. Some of the pieces were fragile, subject to destruction but at least temporarily surviving the elements.

All of the pieces, whether poetry or sculpture, reflected the medium of rock and the unavoidable reason for climbing forever. Everything was immediately apparent to us. But where had all the energy for this work arisen? Some of the pieces were overtly human creations and consisted of major rock workings, with heavy chiseling methods, while others were less forceful. These last works were milder compromises between natural design and human interpretation. Of these, some works were simple mineral patterns that were emphasized and highlighted by chip-out around the borders. The most gentle of the man-rock compromises were what we called the shadow creations. These offered grave difficulties to the understanding. Upon first glance they seemed just misshapen knobs, chicken heads, crystals jutting abnormally from the surface of the wall, but after some time we discerned that at certain moments the sun cast from these knobs particular and significant shadows which would stray sinuously across the granite entabletures surrounding them. The shadows were ephemeral, of course, and the work was only complete for a few minutes each day, but they were the most precious and abundant of works in all the zone. The more I became familiar with the shadow creations, the more I discovered in them. To my amazement I found that some of the knobs had been so carved as to give off a shadow pattern of one sort in the morning and an antithetical pattern in the afternoon. But then one day our hearts nearly burst when we recognized our own shadows. The rock, the immovable sun were devouring us in our introspection. Naively we had conceived of our immersion as a source of invention; it was our last intelligible clue.

In the mornings, with the first rays of sun, we would begin climbing. While Gareth and Aaron started up the crack, I would pack the sleeping bags and hammocks, rig the sacks for easy hauling, then jumar to where the others were waiting or climbing. I'd haul up the gear, fix it to the pins, and wait. Or climb, then wait. Or wait, then climb. The three of us could cover ten or twelve pitches in a period. We made leisure into a doctrine, trying not to sweat because water was so precious, breathing as regularly as we could, following the rhythm of our bodies religiously, and surviving by being conscious of that process of survival. When we came to what looked to be a sure death pitch, we would clamor for the lead, anxious to contradict our lethargy. But even death pitches lost their possibility and we'd sometimes hang for days, becalmed at one point and lacking all desire to do anything. We'd hum to ourselves all day as we lay, tightly pressed against the rock, in our hammocks, noting our passive miseries, sucking on pebbles, staring blankly at our hands or the similar sky. But these spells would grow heavy with their own unique tedium and soon enough we'd begin climbing again just because it was something else to do. Seasons passed.

A winter was approaching. Still, we were nowhere. Still following the primary crack, many pitches beneath us and no top, only the dull sky overhead and beneath us; no deviation from the grievous music that would rattle our afternoons.

And then, the first instance in over a year, curled and dead, self-buried beneath a shelf of rock and loose stones, lay a naked, still shimmering climber. I mantled frantically up onto the miniature pedestal and caught sight of his body, and after fixing the rope for the others to follow, I unburied him. His flesh was cold, yet it was still pliable, and when I caught his hand it was limp and flexible. The fingers would bend or straighten when I worked them, as would all his joints, and with a start I noticed that there wasn't the slightest sign of discoloration or rotting. A saint, canonized? Some monk of the mount who had overextended himself? The corpse was not only intact, it was also undead. It smelled sweetly, like pine, and though it was dry it seemed fresh, even unctuous. And yet it was a dead thing. It didn't breathe nor could it move. It was affixed in a limbo midway between deadness and life. It was *ready* to move; it was flexible and unrigid, but it was unable to actually initiate the movement it seemed to contain. It was a wonderment, but at second thought it was a terrible thing, a boneless, cold mass. It had bones, and was in every way a human body, but because of its preservation it seemed empty. It showed no sign of escape. Most terrible of all, when Aaron and I dragged it from its recess and pulled one of its eyelids open we discovered it was lacking an iris and pupil. It looked as though the eyeball was pure, white marble, unveined and with a dull sheen to it. I could, I swear, even see the tiny crystals in its surface. But neither Aaron nor I would touch the eye.

And Gareth was behind us, gasping and snarling, tossing and wrenching his ruined wild head. I looked to Aaron for help, but he had pendulumed to an adjoining belay area, frightened immediately by what we both must have accented in our ancient suspicion, the finality of Gareth's despair. All that night I was left on the ledge with Gareth and his madness. Aaron stood desperate, waiting somberly and shivering only some yards across and below. Gareth kept his head-shaking on and refused to answer his name, keeping his clasped fists in primal hidden postures of innocence and disbelief. Man, I said, What man? But he only shook his head and wept on, snarling; so I tucked the unthinkable damp corpse back beneath its covering of rock and snapped myself into a piece of anchored sling lest my peril in Gareth's presence be realized this night.

Then I walked to the limit of the sling and reached my hand out to Gareth and pulled him to me and hugged his tense head against my shoulder for our first contact in years. With this motion he groaned once and, weeping, gave over his fists to me quietly and at last. It was the journal, a mere few paragraphs of language, but it was the solo climber's own journal and at that we all three were cast irrecoverably into infinity.

1974

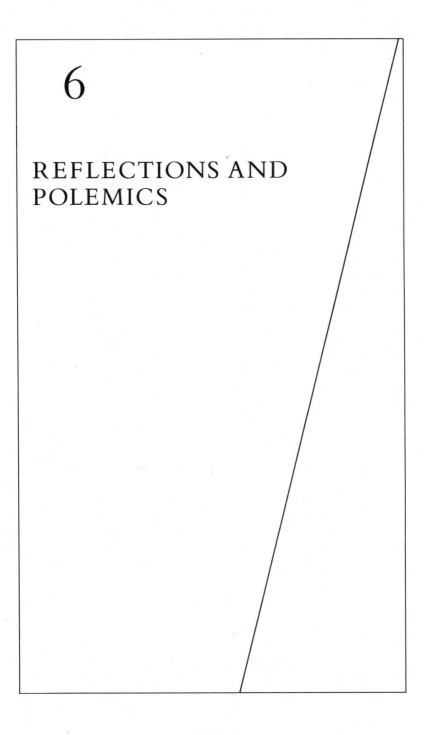

6

REFLECTIONS AND POLEMICS

Editors' Introduction

One of the delights of being an *Ascent* editor has been the opportunity to present essays concerning the ideas of climbers who, plagued by some obsession, decided to put their thoughts on paper. Some of these essays were devoted to ethical issues, a few were critiques of climbing literature genres, and many were meditative in character. Two went so far as to criticize institutions important to climbing in America: Chris Jones's essay on the American Alpine Club appears in this chapter, but space did not permit us to include Pete Sinclair's thoughtful essay "Behold Now Behemoth," a critique of the climbing management policies of the National Park Service.

Our first piece here, Doug Robinson's soulful "The Climber as Visionary," is a pensive examination of the role the sense perceptions play in mountaineering. Much of the joy of climbing can be traced to the tactile and visual experiences that accrue to climbers during their ascent. The slow accumulation of these positive experiences lead to an overwhelming contentment that is often of greater importance to the climber than reaching the summit.

"Reflections of a Broken-Down Climber" is the counterpoint, for here are the musings, ravings even, of the action-oriented, nonvisionary climber Warren Harding, whose charismatic, iconoclastic style has won him favor with a large part of the climbing community. This story, a precursor to Harding's farcical book *Downward Bound,* is largely concerned with his controversial 1970 ascent of El Cap's Wall of the Early Morning Light and subsequent recriminations concerning the style in which it was accomplished.

Twenty-two years after its publication, Chris Jones's "Who Needs the AAC?" still retains its relevance as a critique of the conservative faction within the American Alpine Club, which to this day resists liberalization. Jones's basic premise was that the AAC, which had remained static at around 2,000 members, should have sought to keep abreast of the burgeoning mountaineering activity in America by increasing its membership. But this was not happening—and it still isn't. Conservative members of the Club's board of directors still argue that the AAC is meeting the needs of American climbers by publishing the highly regarded *American Alpine Journal*, funding a viable publications program, representing American climbers overseas, operating the Teton climbers' ranch, and promoting a recently adopted rescue insurance program for its members.

But some extremely important needs are not being met. For instance, the board voted against further funding for the Access Fund—formerly an AAC committee, but now an independent group—which has as its principal goal the preservation of climbing areas throughout the country, a goal accomplished in part by maintaining a dialogue between land managers and climbers. By this act, the AAC leadership appears to be abandoning the concerns of mainstream climbers, whose numbers are now estimated at 150,000. It is possible, however, that the current president, Jed Williamson, may change that.

Our next piece takes us out of the political arena. Woe to those who enter their climbing history into a word processor without a diligent perusal of David Roberts's quintessential critique of climbing autobiographies, "Patey Agonistes." He demonstrates that dangers abound even when writers of moderate skill try to piece together the events of their climbing lives. Roberts discusses the good and the bad elements of several autobiographies in his typically acerbic, professional style.

Portraying climbing as an art form is a daunting task, but Harold Drasdo makes an admirable case for such an assertion in "Climbing as Art." Imagine you are watching a solo ascent of the horrendously difficult Astroman in Yosemite Valley: the event could easily be considered a vertical ballet, every movement executed quickly and perfectly, like the movements of a celebrated ballerina. And, as Drasdo posits, the soloist performing this is a kind of artist.

When Tom Higgins wrote "Tricksters and Traditionalists," he probably didn't realize that the conflict over disparate climbing styles would still be raging nine years later. The traditionalists condemn the tricksters with almost evangelical fervor, while the latter struggle along trying to find a way to climb hard new routes without getting seriously injured in the process. The dispute is, ultimately, unresolvable; we can only relax in Warren Harding's "Rock of Ages Home for Old Climbers" and marvel at how rockclimbing in America continues to evolve.

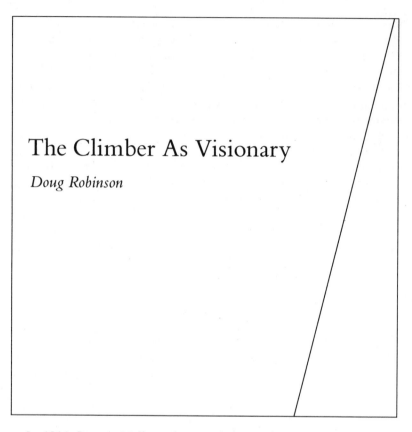

The Climber As Visionary

Doug Robinson

In 1914 George Mallory, later to become famous for an offhand definition of why people climb, wrote an article entitled "The Mountaineer as Artist," which appeared in the British Climbers' Club Journal. In an attempt to justify his climber's feeling of superiority over other sportsmen, he asserts that the climber is an artist. He says that "a day well spent in the Alps is like some great symphony," and justifies the lack of any tangible production—for artists are generally expected to produce works of art which others may see—by saying that "artists, in this sense, are not distinguished by the power of expressing emotion, but the power of feeling that emotional experience out of which Art is made. . . . Mountaineers are all artistic . . . because they cultivate emotional experience for its own sake." While fully justifying the elevated regard we have for climbing as an activity, Mallory's assertion leaves no room for distinguishing the creator of a route from an admirer of it. Mountaineering can produce tangible artistic results which are then on public view. A route is an artistic statement on the side of a mountain, accessible to the view and thus the admiration or criticism of other climbers. Just as the line of a route determines its aesthetics, the manner in which it was climbed constitutes its style. A climb has the qualities of a work of art and its creator is responsible for its direction and style just as an artist is. We recognize those climbers who are especially gifted at creating forceful and aesthetic lines, and respect them for their gift.

But just as Mallory did not go far enough in ascribing artistic functions to the act of creating outstanding new climbs, so I think he uses the word *artist* too broadly when he means it to include an aesthetic response as well as an aesthetic creation. For this response, which is essentially passive and receptive rather than aggressive and creative, I would use the word *visionary*. Not visionary in the usual sense of idle and unrealizable dreaming, of building castles in the air, but rather in seeing the objects and actions of ordinary experience with greater intensity, penetrating them further, seeing their marvels and mysteries, their forms, moods, and motions. Being a visionary in this sense involves nothing supernatural or otherworldly; it amounts to bringing fresh vision to the familiar things of the world. I use the word *visionary* very simply, taking its origin from *vision,* to mean seeing, always to great degrees of intensity, but never beyond the boundaries of the real and physically present. To take a familiar example, it would be hard to look at Van Gogh's *Starry Night* without seeing the visionary quality in the way the artist sees the world. He has not painted anything that is not in the original scene, yet others would have trouble recognizing what he has depicted; the difference lies in the intensity of his perception, heart of the visionary experience. He is painting from a higher state of consciousness. Climbers too have their "starry nights." Consider the following, from an account by Allen Steck, of the Hummingbird Ridge climb on Mt. Logan: "I turned for a moment and was completely lost in silent appraisal of the beautifully sensuous simplicity of windblown snow." The beauty of that moment, the form and motion of the blowing snow, was such a powerful impression, was so wonderfully sufficient, that the climber was lost in it. It is said to be only a moment, yet by virtue of total absorption he is lost in it and the winds of eternity blow through it. A second example comes from the account of the seventh day's climbing on the eight-day first ascent, under trying conditions, of El Capitan's Muir Wall. Yvon Chouinard relates in the 1966 *American Alpine Journal:*

> With the more receptive senses we now appreciated everything around us. Each individual crystal in the granite stood out in bold relief. The varied shapes of the clouds never ceased to attract our attention. For the first time

we noticed tiny bugs that were all over the walls, so tiny they were barely noticeable. While belaying, I stared at one for fifteen minutes, watching him move and admiring his brilliant red color.

How could one ever be bored with so many good things to see and feel! This unity with our joyous surroundings, this ultra-penetrating perception, gave us a feeling of contentment that we had not had for years.

In these passages the qualities that make up the climber's visionary experience are apparent: the overwhelming beauty of the most ordinary objects—clouds, granite, snow—of the climber's experience, a sense of the slowing down of time even to the point of disappearing, and a feeling of contentment, an oceanic feeling of the supreme sufficiency of the present. And while delicate in substance, these feelings are strong enough to intrude forcefully into the middle of dangerous circumstances and remain there, temporarily superseding even apprehension and the drive for achievement.

Chouinard's words begin to give us an idea of the origin of these experiences as well as their character. He begins by referring to "the more receptive senses." What made their senses more receptive? It seems integrally connected with what they were doing, and that it was their seventh day of uninterrupted concentration. Climbing tends to induce visionary experiences. We should explore which characteristics of the climbing process prepare its practitioners for these experiences.

Climbing requires intense concentration. I know of no other activity in which I can so easily lose all the hours of an afternoon without a trace. Or a regret. I have had storms creep up on me as if I had been asleep, yet I knew the whole time I was in the grip of an intense concentration, focused first on a few square feet of rock, and then on a few feet more. I have gone off across camp to boulder and returned to find the stew burned. Sometimes in the lowlands when it is hard to work I am jealous of how easily concentration comes in climbing. This concentration may be intense, but it is not the same as the intensity of the visionary periods; it is a prerequisite intensity.

But the concentration is not continuous. It is often intermittent and sporadic, sometimes cyclic and rhythmic. After facing the successive few square feet of rock for a while, the end of the rope is reached and it is time to belay. The belay time is a break in the concentration, a gap, a small chance to relax. To climber changes from an aggressive and productive stance to a passive and receptive one, from doer to observer, and in fact from artist to visionary. The climbing day goes on through the climb-belay-climb-belay cycle by a regular series of concentrations and relaxations. It is of one of these relaxations that Chouinard speaks. When limbs go to the rock and muscles contract, then the will contracts also. And at the belay stance, tied in to a scrub oak, the muscles relax and the will, which has been concentrating on moves, also expands and takes in the world again, and the world is new and bright. It is freshly created, for it really had ceased to exist. By contrast, the disadvantage of the usual low-level activity is that it cannot shut out the world, which then never ceases being familiar and is thus ignored. To climb with intense concentration is to shut out the world, which, when it reappears, will be as a fresh experience, strange and wonderful in its newness.

These belay relaxations are not total; the climb is not over, pitches lie ahead, even the crux; days more may be needed to be through. We notice that as the cycle of intense contractions takes over, and as this cycle becomes the daily routine, even consumes the daily routine, the relaxations on belay yield more frequent or intense visionary experiences. It is no accident that Chouinard's experiences occur near the end of the climb; he had been building up to them for six days. The summit, capping off the cycling and giving a final release from the tension of contractions, should offer the climber some of his most intense moments, and a look into the literature reveals this to be so. The summit is also a release from the sensory desert of the climb; from the starkness of concentrating on configurations of rock we go to the visual richness of the summit. But there is still the descent to worry about, another contraction of will to be followed by relaxation at the climb's foot. Sitting on a log changing from klettershoes into boots, and looking over the Valley, we are suffused with oceanic feelings of clarity, distance, union, oneness. There is carryover from one climb to the next, from one day on the hot white walls to the next, however punctuated by wine-dark evenings in Camp Four. Once a pathway has been tried it becomes more familiar and is easier to follow the second time, more so on subsequent trips. The threshold has been lowered. Practice is as useful to the climber's visionary faculty as to his crack technique. It also applies outside of climbing. In John Harlin's words, although he was speaking about will and not vision, the experience can be "borrowed and projected." It will apply in the climber's life in general, in his flat, ground, and lowland hours. But it is the climbing that has taught him to be a visionary. Lest we get too self-important about consciously preparing ourselves for visionary activity, however, we remember that the incredible beauty of the mountains is always at hand, always ready to nudge us into awareness.

The period of these cycles varies widely. If you sometimes cycle through lucid periods from pitch to pitch or even take days to run a complete course, it may also be virtually instantaneous, as, pulling up on a hold after a moment's hesitation and doubt, you feel at once the warmth of sun through your shirt and without pausing reach on.

Nor does the alteration of consciousness have to be large. A small change can be profound. The gulf between looking without seeing and looking with real vision is at times of such a low order that we may be continually shifting back and forth in daily life. Further heightening of the visionary faculty consists of more deeply perceiving what is already there. Vision is intense seeing. Vision is seeing what is more deeply interfused, and following this process leads to a sense of ecology. It is an intuitive rather than a scientific ecology; it is John Muir's kind, starting not from generalizations for trees, rocks, air, but rather from *that* tree with the goiter part way up the trunk, from the rocks as Chouinard saw them, supremely sufficient and aloof, blazing away their perfect light, and from that air which blew clean and hot up off the eastern desert and carries lingering memories of snowfields on the Dana Plateau and miles of Tuolumne treetops as it pours over the rim of the Valley on its way to the Pacific.

These visionary changes in the climber's mind have a physiological basis. The alternation of hope and fear spoken of in climbing describes an emotional state with a biochemical basis. These physiological mechanisms have been used for thousands of years by prophets and mystics, and for a few centuries by climbers. There are two complementary mechanisms operating independently: carbon dioxide level and adrenalin breakdown products, the first keyed by exertion, the second by apprehension. During the active part of the climb the body is working hard, building up its CO_2 level (oxygen debt) and releasing adrenalin in anticipation of difficult or dangerous moves, so that by the time the climber moves into belay at the end of the pitch he has established an oxygen debt and a supply of now unneeded adrenalin. Oxygen debt manifests itself on the cellular level as lactic acid, a cellular poison, which may possibly be the agent that has a visionary effect on the mind. Visionary activity can be induced experimentally by administering CO_2, and this phenomenon begins to explain the place of singing and long-winded chanting in the medieval Church as well as the breath-control exercises of Eastern religions. Adrenalin, carried to all parts of the body through the blood stream, is an unstable compound and if unused, soon begins to break down. Some of the breakdown products of adrenalin are capable of inducing the visionary experience; in fact, they are naturally occurring body chemicals which closely resemble the

In the Needles of South Dakota. STEVE ROPER.

psychedelic drugs, and may help someday to shed light on the action of these mind-expanding agents. So we see that the activity of the climbing, coupled with its anxiety, produces a chemical climate in the body that is conducive to visionary experience. There is one other long-range factor that may begin to figure in Chouinard's example: diet. Either simple starvation or vitamin deficiency tends to prepare the body, apparently by weakening it, for visionary experiences. Such a vitamin deficiency will result in a decreased level of nicotinic acid, a member of the B-vitamin complex and a known anti-psychedelic agent, thus nourishing the visionary experience. Chouinard comments on the low rations at several points in his account. For a further discussion of physical pathways to the visionary state, see Aldous Huxley's two essays, "The Doors of Perception" and "Heaven and Hell."

There is an interesting relationship between the climber-visionary and his counterpart in the neighboring subculture of psychedelic drug users. These drugs are becoming increasingly common and many young people will come to climbing from a visionary vantage point unique in its history. These drugs have been through a series of erroneous names, based on false models of their action: *psychotomimetic* for a supposed ability to produce a model psychosis, and *hallucinogen,* when the hallucination was thought to be the central reality of the experience. Their present name means simply "mind manifesting," which is at least neutral. These drugs are providing people with a window into the visionary experience. They come away knowing that there is a place where the objects of ordinary experience are wonderfully clear and alive. It may also be that these sensations remind them of many spontaneous or "peak" experiences and thus confirm or place a previous set of observations. But this is the end. There is no going back to the heightened reality, to the supreme sufficiency of the present moment. The window has been shut and cannot even be found without recourse to the drug.

I am not in the least prepared to say that drug users take up climbing in order to search for the window. It couldn't occur to them. Anyone unused to disciplined physical activity would have trouble imagining that it produced anything but sweat. But when the two cultures overlap, and a young climber begins to find parallels between the visionary result of his climbing discipline and his formerly drug-induced visionary life, he is on the threshold of control. There is now a clear path of discipline leading to the window. It consists of the sensory desert, intensity of concentrated effort, and rhythmical cycling of contraction and relaxation. This path is not unique to climbing, of course, but here we are thinking of the peculiar form that the elements of the path assume in climbing. I call it the Holy Slow Road because, although time-consuming and painful, it is an unaided way to the visionary state; by following it the climber will find himself better prepared to appreciate the visionary in himself, and by returning gradually and with eyes open to ordinary waking consciousness he now knows where the window lies, how it is unlocked, and he carries some of the experience back with him. The Holy Slow Road assures that the climber's soul, tempered by the very experiences that have made him a visionary, has been refined so that he can handle his visionary activity while still remaining balanced and active (the result of too much visionary activity without accompanying personality growth being the dropout, an essentially unproductive stance). The climbing which has prepared him to be a visionary has also prepared the climber to handle his visions. This is not, however, a momentous change. It is still as close as seeing instead of mere looking. Experiencing a permanent change in perception may take years of discipline.

A potential pitfall is seeing the "discipline" of the Holy Slow Road in the iron-willed tradition of the Protestant ethic, and that will not work. The climbs will provide all the necessary rigor of discipline without having to add to it. And as the visionary faculty comes closer to the surface, what is needed is not an effort of discipline but an effort of relaxation, a submission of self to the wonderful, supportive, and sufficient world.

I first began to consider these ideas in the summer of 1965 in Yosemite with Chris Fredericks. Sensing a similarity of experience, or else a similar approach to experience, we sat many nights talking together at the edge of the climbers' camp and spent some of our days testing our words in kinesthetic sunshine. Chris had become interested in Zen Buddhism, and as he told me of this Oriental religion I was amazed that I had never before heard of such a system that fit the facts of outward reality as I saw them, without any pushing or straining. We never, that I remember, mentioned the visionary experience as such, yet its substance was rarely far from our reflections. We entered into one of those fine parallel states of mind such that it is impossible now for me to say which thoughts came from which of us. We began to consider some aspects of climbing as Western equivalents of Eastern practices: the even movements of the belayer taking in slack, the regular footfall

of walking through the woods, even the rhythmic movements of climbing on easy or familiar ground; all approach the function of meditation
and breath-control. Both the laborious and visionary parts of climbing
seemed well suited to liberating the individual from his concept of self,
the one by intimidating his aspirations, the other by showing the self
to be only a small part of a subtly integrated universe. We watched the
visionary surface in each other with its mixture of joy and serenity, and
walking down from climbs we often felt like little children in the Garden of Eden, pointing, nodding, and laughing. We explored timeless
moments and wondered at the suspension of ordinary consciousness
while the visionary faculty was operating. It occurred to us that there
was no remembering such times of being truly happy and at peace; all
that could be said of them later was that they had been and that they
had been truly fine; the usual details of memory were gone. This applies also to most of our conversations. I remember only that we talked
and that we came to understand things. I believe it was in these conversations that the first seeds of the climber as visionary were planted.

William Blake spoke of the visionary experience by saying, "If the
doors of perception were cleansed every thing would appear to man as
it is, infinite." Stumbling upon the cleansed doors, the climber wonders
how he came into that privileged visionary position vis-à-vis the universe. He finds the answer in the activity of his climbing and the chem-
istry of his mind, and he begins to see that he is practicing a special
application of some very ancient mind-opening techniques. Chouinard's vision was no accident. It was the result of days of climbing. He
was tempered by technical difficulties, pain, apprehension, dehydration, striving, the sensory desert, weariness, the gradual loss of self. It
is a system. You need only copy the ingredients and commit yourself
to them. They lead to the door. It is not necessary to attain to Chouinard's technical level—few can or do—only to his degree of commitment. It is not essential that one climb El Capitan to be a visionary; I
never have, yet I try in my climbing to push my personal limit, to do
climbs that are questionable for me. Thus we all walk the feather
edge—each man his own unique edge—and go on to the visionary.

For all the precision with which the visionary state can be placed and
described, it is still elusive. You do not one day become a visionary and
ever after remain one. It is a state that one flows in and out of, gaining
it through directed effort or spontaneously in a gratuitous moment.

Oddly, it is not consciously worked for, but comes as the almost accidental product of effort in another direction and on a different plane. It is at its own whim momentary or lingering suspended in the air, suspending time in its turn, forever momentarily eternal, as, stepping out of the last rappel you turn and behold the rich green wonder of the forest.

1969

Reflections of a
Broken-Down Climber

Warren Harding

Climbing would be a great, truly wonderful thing if
it weren't for all that damn climbing.
  John Ohrenschall

As I sit on the veranda of my quarters at TM Herbert's Rock of Ages
Home for Old Climbers, enjoying my Graham crackers and warm
milk, I think about the past eighteen years. . . . My rise and fall as a
rock climber . . . what a fine person I used to be . . . where did I go
wrong?

Finally I realize what's wrong with me . . . why I'm rather oblivious to many of the things around me. It's simply that I've spent too
many nights and days dangling from Yosemite's granite walls. My
once keen analytical mind has become so dulled by endless hours of
baking in the hot sun, thrashing about in tight chimneys, pulling at
impossibly heavy loads, freezing my ass off on long cold nights in
various examples of the "ideal bivouac gear," so that now my mental
state is comparable to that of a Peruvian Indian well stoked on coca
leaves. . . .

Warren Harding. GALEN ROWELL.

I've been at it too long . . . thought that when I'd cleverly run in front of a rapidly moving truck (September 1969) I'd be spared any further indignities (such as climbing). But my badly smashed right leg recovered sufficiently to allow me to pursue this ridiculous activity.

A couple of years ago I had met a rather unsavory character name of Dean "Wizard" (Wizard?) Caldwell. As our acquaintance dragged on, I discovered that we had much in common. For one thing we were both rather lazy . . . an important quality of the serious climber. We talked much of past glories and future plans but for the most part didn't actually do anything. Grandiosity of our plans seemed to be directly proportional to the amount of booze we would consume at a sitting. One night in the Mountain Room, completely taken by Demon Rum, we decided we would climb El Capitan's Wall of the Early Morning Light . . . The Big Motha' Climb!

We knew it was quite safe to indulge in such talk since neither of us was capable of climbing anything. . . . Dean had some badly torn ligaments, result of stumbling over a tree stump while walking to the potty room in Camp 12. My right leg was still pretty bad . . . weak knee would barely bend. Tried a new climb, east edge of Royal Arches, only got out about forty feet. We adopted the name of "March of Dimes Climbing Team."

Fall—beginning to get worried now . . . physical condition has sufficiently improved; we can stall no longer. Began carrying loads up to the "base camp"; cloak of secrecy surrounding our activities . . . "great hairy giants" were all around waiting to annihilate any trespassers on "their route." Fearfully, Wizard and Batso skulked around the valley. Difficult to be discreet carrying things like twelve gallons of water, big sacks of food, bivvy gear, six hauling bags, and the like. Eventually got things sorted out and bagged up. Led and fixed the first two pitches.

Then, of course, the weather turned bad . . . sitting it out at Dave Hanna's place we were shocked to learn that the dreaded Royal Robbins had suddenly appeared in the Valley . . . what now? Would he come charging up the wall . . . just plow us under? Desperately, we moved out.

Almost predictably, rain started falling as we reached the top of the first pitch where our five hauling bags were hanging. . . . So in mid-afternoon we set up our first bivouac . . . bat tents with plastic tube tents over them. It soon became obvious that we had vastly underestimated the time that this venture would take us. Fortunately, we had also greatly *over*estimated the amount of food and water required for a day's sustenance. We had figured twelve days stretchable to fifteen days. (Turned out to be "stretchable" to twenty-six days.)

End of second week . . . things looked different—very bad! We'd been on a rock wall longer than anybody else ever had (at least in Yosemite) . . . last two days in a wretched state of soggification. As the fifteenth day dragged on, still raining, we realized we were in a very critical position. We were only about halfway up . . . at the bottom of the Dihedrals, where our hopes of finding a good crack had come to nothing.

Our mental and physical condition had somewhat deteriorated from the effects of the soaking rainstorm, the general wear and tear of bashing our way up fifteen hundred feet of the hardest climbing we'd ever experienced.

Dave Hanna and Pete Thompson came up to the base of the wall. . . . Bullhorn voices from below informed us that the weather forecast was not very encouraging: clearing tomorrow, but another storm on its way. . . .

We pondered the situation as the rain continued through the day and into the night. Realized it could take another ten days to go the rest of the way. Carefully inventoried the rest of our remaining food. We'd have to radically reduce our rations if we were to stretch them out to even come close to finishing the climb.

But the thought of giving up the climb seemed simply unacceptable. It wasn't at all hard for us to make up our minds to press on . . . somehow try to make it. Another factor . . . the thought of trying to descend the fifteen hundred feet of mostly overhanging wall with our gear made us retch!

Next morning we informed Dave and Pete of our decision to continue. They seemed to feel we were insane but . . .

Weather cleared . . . a day to get dried out and reorganized, then come to grips with the Dihedrals. Only took us five days to get up this delightful area . . . lots of A4 nailing, bolting, riveting up overhanging bulges. On about the twentieth day we heard unfamiliar shouts from below. The shouter identified himself as TM Herbert.

"Hi TM—Good to see ya! What're you up to?"

"We've come to rescue you!"

"Whaaaaat?"

About this time Dean (leading) noticed ropes being lowered over the rim about eight hundred feet above. A great deal of shouting ensued. Most of our—uh—"rhetoric" would be unprintable in all but the most "advanced" periodicals. We did make it quite clear that we were fine, had the situation well in hand, were not about to be rescued. Fortunately those in charge of the rescue operation elected to suspend the effort, thereby sparing everyone some rather bizarre scenes: rescuers landing on Timothy Tower to find "exhausted" climbing team enjoying a fine minifeast of salami, cheese, bread, and an entire bottle of Cabernet Sauvignon (Christian Brothers, of course) all in a beautiful moonlit setting. Dialogue. "Good evening! What can we do for you?"

"We've come to rescue you!"

"Really? Come now, get hold of yourselves—have some wine. . . ." The action could have gone anywhere from there . . . a quiet intelligent conversation with the would-be rescue team returning in the morning via their fixed ropes. Or had the rescue team been overzealous, a wild insane piton hammer fight might have followed. For we were very determined not to be hauled off our climb. We'd put too damn much into it to give up now! The hard part was behind us.

We were still feeling quite strong in spite of being on very slim rations for the past week. Perhaps our minds were becoming a bit fuzzy, though . . . had dark, cloudy visions of the National Park Service being influenced by envious, money-hungry climbers who would like nothing better than to fill their pockets with $$$ while removing two clowns from a climb they didn't deserve to be on. The wall would remain (with all the hard work done) in a virginal state, awaiting a team of super climbers who could do it in real style. . . .

So onward and upward!

Finally there was Dean battling his way up what we hoped would be the last pitch. But as he came to the end of the climbing rope, still about sixty feet below the rim, the day too came to an end! Frustrating— disappointing to be so near and yet have to wait until the next day, but no use taking a chance of blowing it now. . . .

Next morning I was totally unprepared for what I saw as I floundered up the last overhang onto the ledge at the rim . . . a veritable army of newsmen, friends, would-be rescuers (and a beautiful girl, Beryl Knauth). As I anchored myself to the ledge, I suddenly felt an overwhelming feeling of emotional release—sort of came "unglued" for a moment. Pulling myself together, I joined the happy carnival atmosphere that prevailed at the summit: batteries of camera snouts trained on us, gorging ourselves on all the food and champagne! All sorts of friends and well-wishers, ecstatic kisses and embraces— what a marvelous little orgy! Only thing lacking was a Mexican mariachi band!

But if I could have foreseen what would happen in the next few months I might have been tempted to say, "Oh, screw it all!" and bail off the top—well not really! With all the bullshit there were a lot of good things.

But there were ominous cluckings from certain pious experts about the degenerative effect on climbing of all the publicity attendant on such a climb. It would tend to attract hordes of unworthy persons to the rock walls and mountains—got to reserve all this for us "good guys." Keep the masses out! Maintain the esoteric image of climbing, raise the standards, etc., etc. . . .

It comes to mind that climbing is rather commercialized, certainly highly publicized, in Britain. Has this resulted in total deterioration of British climbers and climbing areas? It's my impression that it has not! Apparently Britain's relatively small climbing area is quite heavily used. Is the countryside becoming one huge garbage dump? I've been told by those who have been there that it definitely is not. Why? Could it be that the people, even though they are large in numbers, have come to know and love their mountains and desire to take care of them?

Elitists will argue that it is necessary to discourage the masses from mountain areas. No doubt this would work quite well in a feudal system where a small nobility had complete control of the peasantry. But such is not the case—theoretically, at least, this country operates as a democracy. . . . All, worthy or not, have equal right to the public lands. Again, theoretically, the use and preservation of our mountain areas would seem to depend on the vote of the masses. How, then, can we expect the support of the average citizen in conservation if he is told the mountains are too good for him, that they should be reserved for a minority of self-styled "good guys"?

Perhaps the hope of the "Valley Christians" lies in some form of regimentation patterned after the meticulous system of climber control so magnificently conceived and employed by the Soviets. Apparently well-structured training programs are carried out—screw-offs quickly weeded out!—examinations and ratings given, climbs assigned only to the properly qualified—everyone kept in his place!!

But this is digressing . . . back to what's important: climbing.

Why did we climb the Wall of the Early Morning Light as, how, and where we did? . . . I had always felt that the route should follow the right-leaning cracks in the lower section—traverse into the Dihedrals, then roughly straight up. This was not prompted by Comician ideals but rather by some undefinable esthetic attraction this particular area held for me. As with some other routes—Leaning Tower, Half Dome, South Face—I was not concerned about how many bolts it might take. It was simply that it appealed to me and I wanted very much to climb it!

With the storms—three in all—food shortage, and, most significant of all, the rescue fiasco, the whole thing, reflected by the press, captured the imagination of the public. Oddly enough, the "high adventure" magazines, such as *True and Argosy* showed only the mildest interest . . . maybe it was just a glorified flagpole-sitting exhibition after all.

But whatever it was (the real climbers knew!) there definitely was general interest. An exciting, fun-filled whirlwind tour of public appearances followed our return to the Valley. Fame and fortune were ours!—though I did seem to be getting quite a bit more of one than the other; like my share of the proceeds—$1500 for four months' work. It didn't exactly seem like a get-rich-quick scheme. Anyway, at least there was great professional satisfaction: I had advanced from my lowly status of unemployed construction worker to the enviable position of unemployed TV star!

The emotional and monetary aspects of something like the aftermath of the Wall of the Early Morning Light are little short of amazing! Whether they like it or not, the principals involved suddenly become a business organization (or perhaps, a disorganization!). Some personalities can change significantly, others don't. Warm friendship and camaraderie can be replaced by cold contempt and suspicion. Happy laughter can turn to nervous, polite chuckles.

But we all know each other better now . . . for whatever that's worth. I still believe that it's entirely possible to work with the various commercial aspects of climbing without destroying the flavor.

Do I really want to, though? What is this climbing trip all about, anyway? Does it really matter if a particular climb is done in any particular "style"? Is there one "true code of ethics" that is admirably suited to all climbers? There are those who profess to have the real answer. In other fields, so did Jesus Christ, Karl Marx, and Adolf Hitler!

I have often been asked why I seldom, if ever, write my views on all this ethics business. In thinking about it, I realize I really don't give a damn. If all or most other climbers feel a need for the comfort and shelter of structured thinking—if there are those who feel a need to establish and promulgate these principles and lead the masses to a better 1984-ish life, fine with me! I still feel inclined to do my own thinking. As long as the VC don't get their own secret police and employ Spanish Inquisition methods, I won't worry about being imprisoned, stretched on a rack, forced to confess my sins, and then burned at the stake as a heretic. Rather, to the self-appointed gurus, I say: Bugger off, baby, bugger off!!

As I observed earlier, I'm entirely fed up with all this crap about bolts, bat-hooks, press releases, commercialism, etc., etc. . . . At a trade show in Chicago, Dean and I received the electrifying news (rumor?) that RR and Don Lauria had just completed the second ascent of the Wall of the Early Morning Light, and had chopped out all the bolts and rivets; all this in only six days!!

Naturally, many people at the show asked our reaction to this. At the time, the best we could come up with were weak little attempts at humor: "Oh, well—they're just faster than us. Chopping bolts? Whatever's fair," etc., etc.

But the questions still came, especially upon returning to Yosemite Valley.

"Well, Harding, how does this grab you? What do you think about the bolt-chopping thing?" Frankly, I hardly knew what to say or think. For one thing, it didn't seem worthwhile to go to all the trouble of finding out what had really happened. . . .

Still, some people thought that I should be concerned about all this— shocked, offended perhaps. Fact is, I don't give a rat's ass what Royal did with the route, or what he thought he accomplished by whatever it was he did. I guess my only interest in the matter would be the possibility of some clinical insight into the rather murky channels of RR's mind.

Perhaps he is confusing climbing ethics with some fine (obscure?) point of prostitution morality . . . like, perhaps, a one hundred-bolt climb, e.g. Tis-sa-ack (or a hundred-dollar-a-night call girl) is very proper; but a three-hundred-bolt climb (or a three-hundred-dollar-a-night call girl) is gross, immoral, or whatever. Or maybe Royal has gone the way of Carrie Nation—substituting hammer and chisel for hatchet! And then again, maybe it's got something to do with rivets—I don't know. In a way, I feel sorry for Royal (a veritable Alpine Elmer Gantry) with all these problems, bearing the responsibility of keeping rockclimbing the "heavy," complex thing it must be. . . .

Many years ago, when I first started climbing, it really seemed like fun. I truly enjoyed busting my ass trying to somehow get up something like Lost Arrow Chimney . . . or picking out a new route . . . but always feeling good about it. But suddenly it just seems like a drag. Maybe I should have stuck with sports car driving. . . .

Perhaps this turned-off feeling will pass; the relaxed atmosphere in the foothill location of Rock of Ages is conducive to mending the soul. It's good to be in such fine company . . . Al Steck and Steve Roper sitting at a table playing checkers, mind and vision too dim to cope with the rigors of chess . . . Chuck Pratt wiling away the hours conducting some imaginary symphony orchestra. Truly beautiful to see Earth Mothers, Jan and Beryl, bustling about in their long pioneer gowns, looking after the old fellows. . . .

The sun is slowly sinking, another day is drawing to a close. All the old climbers are putting away their toys and games, soon will be drifting off to their quarters to await the cheery call to dinner. Perhaps some of the more daring will have a small glass of Red Mountain.

I remain in my chair a bit longer—I try to probe further back through the years . . . before the Wall of the Early Morning Light . . . but it all seems like "I've seen this movie before" . . . always the good guys versus bad guys. Maybe I should have played cowboys and Indians; only trouble is, I'd surely have been an Indian!

1971

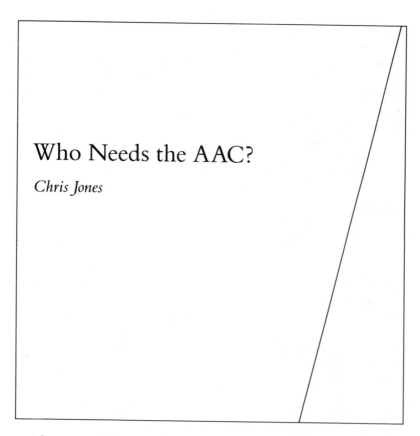

Who Needs the AAC?

Chris Jones

Almost every country that has mountaineers or mountains also has a national alpine club. The first of these was founded in England in 1857, and is still known quite simply as the Alpine Club. Today national alpine clubs may be broadly divided into two types—those modeled after the original Alpine Club, with restricted or elitist membership policies, and those with completely open membership. Ostensibly both these types of organizations are national clubs, with bylaws saying just that in eloquent language; but whatever the lofty aims of their founders, the key question is whether or not they are fulfilling their role in the fast-changing world of the seventies.

Just what should a national alpine club be doing today? The bylaws of the American Alpine Club (AAC) state admirable goals: "The objects of the Club shall be: the cultivation of mountain craft; the encouragement of climbing and exploration; the promotion of good fellowship among climbers; the dissemination of knowledge concerning mountains and mountaineering through its meetings, publications, and library." It is only on further reading of the bylaws that one discovers that these objects and facilities are to be restricted to "those who have made mountain ascents which the Board of Directors shall consider acceptable." This closed society was obviously acceptable to our founding fathers, but today I would say that it is at the root of most of the shortcomings of the AAC.

Some say that because there are qualifications it is an honor to belong to the AAC. This is absurd, for though the requirements are daunting and tedious enough to exclude many, they simply are no measure of mountaineering competence by today's standards. However, the true test is not whether a policy of open membership might offend some conservative diehards, but whether or not it would be beneficial to American mountaineering.

Since the AAC is recognized by climbers, our government and foreign governments, as the official body representing U.S. mountaineers, then what it does is rightly the concern of not only those few who happen to be both qualified and members, but climbers at large. Those who specialize in rockclimbing, those mountaineers who do not aspire to technical climbing, and those who are simply mountain enthusiasts—they all have a stake in what the AAC does, yet they have no say. They are disenfranchised. The concept of a closed society that works on behalf of all climbers seems indefensible. It is an anachronism. Five or ten years ago, climbing in the U.S. was a sufficiently minor activity that its adherents were able to do pretty well as they pleased—a few eccentrics were of no concern to the authorities. Today this is no longer true, and tomorrow it may well be far worse. Regulations and controls are proliferating, access problems hitherto unknown have cropped up, and rescues are costing the government considerable sums of money. In my view only a strong, well-financed organization can effectively promote the interests of climbers, for when the crunch comes who really gives a damn for the views of nine-hundred odd "fresh-air sniffers"?

The work that the AAC does do is largely hidden from climbers, so that a brief summary is probably of interest. The club has two committees, among others, which act as a liaison with both the National Park Service and the Forest Service, and much good behind-the-scenes work is done, notably the negotiations leading to the recent opening of the Grand Teton Climbers' Ranch, perhaps the best single thing the club has achieved. There is a publications program which produces an excellent journal and some good-to-indifferent guide books, while one of the club's best projects is the award of modest cash grants to enterprising young climbers—a fine idea. Expeditions receive some support, but in general only the official stamp of approval required by certain foreign countries. The club possesses an excellent library, and is beginning branch libraries in Seattle and Denver, a plan that needs vigorous support and encouragement. In addition, the club responds to immediate problems, such as the Dhaulagiri tragedy and the Peruvian Andes earthquake, appropriately and in good time. Finally, day-to-day inquiries from the public and media are answered.

One will notice that these programs are not solely for the benefit of members of the club, but are of real concern to all climbers. For the sake of argument, let us imagine that the AAC has become an open club, with a membership in the tens of thousands and consequently an income in the hundred-thousand-dollar range from subscriptions alone. This large membership would enable us to negotiate with the government, and others having jurisdiction over climbing areas, from a far stronger position than today. Relations with the Park Service and Forest Service are absolutely crucial to the future of climbing in the U.S., for by executive edict these agencies could make climbing virtually impossible. The ludicrous regulations at Devil's Tower, Wyoming, are an example of bureaucracy gone berserk. Currently the AAC reacts to situations, rather than being in on the inception of new plans. The Teton Ranch, for example, was initiated after a number of years when climbers were harassed and even jailed for remaining beyond the camping limit, while the touch-and-go situation in Yosemite is always dealt with after the conditions have become intolerable, rather than before. At present, rescues in the national parks are generally carried out by rangers in combination with climbers, for which the climbers are often reimbursed. How much longer the NPS will be willing to foot the bill on these operations is a moot point—those in Yosemite are costing tens of thousands of dollars annually—and indeed it was recently suggested that a party would be billed for an attempted rescue in Yosemite. Motorists are required to carry insurance or post a bond, as are others engaged in potentially hazardous pursuits. Should the Park Service decide this would be desirable for climbers, there is no economically attractive way that the present AAC could offer insurance, whereas a greatly expanded club would certainly be able to do so. One of the chief arguments for the proliferation of restrictive regulations is that the NPS does all rescuing and has to pay the costs. An insurance scheme, then, could go a long way to preserve our freedom to climb as

Sheridan Anderson's sardonic view of climbing organizations.

we choose. The fact that rescues are currently free and that most insurance policies do not yet have an exclusion on mountaineering should not be taken as a permanent state of affairs, as some companies already exclude mountaineering from their coverage.

A prime task of the enlarged club would be a far more vigorous conservation effort, with the whole thrust directed to the protection of mountain areas. Equally important, and far more vulnerable, are the small outcrops, often near large cities, which need our constant attention to ensure public access and enjoyment.

The construction of mountain huts, although it may seem a contradiction to the above, on close analysis may be found to be beneficial. Certain studies have suggested that widespread and indiscriminate camping is more destructive of fragile alpine areas than properly planned and constructed mountain shelters. It may well be that Americans, looking to Europe and elsewhere, will decide against mountain huts, but the debate should at least be started.

In considering guide books, the club is currently able to say that lack of money prevents them from revising or reprinting guides. Yet with sufficient turnover, a publishing program would be self-supporting—the more popular guides underwriting the more obscure ones—and authors could be paid to get the job done properly. The present AAC guides to Canada are an obscure mass of footnotes which require a reference library to decipher, and are quite unsuited to the need for concise, up-to-date information. Other club publications on technique would be welcome, as a mass of misinformation from authors of dubious distinction is flooding the market.

The idea of branch libraries is excellent, but at present there is no chance that the program will flourish, for as an AAC newsletter says, "We do not have any money to purchase books and are completely dependent on contributions." An incredible situation. Apart from well-stocked libraries, the expanded club would be able to furnish information, maps, and vital personal contacts to small groups attempting to penetrate the red tape surrounding the Himalaya, or simply needing data on some obscure corner of the Rockies or Bolivia. None of this information is available now.

The greatest single expense for parties climbing in distant ranges is often the air fare. With the increase in charter and group travel, the club could offer reduced-cost flights not only to the Alps and the Andes, but also the Himalaya. In this way small groups, who have no desire to go in for publicity and fund-raising campaigns, might well be enabled to climb in the ultimate mountains—the Himalaya.

Finally, a progressive club would be able to begin a mountaineering fund similar to the Mount Everest Foundation in Britain. The MEF arose from the financially successful 1953 Everest climb, and now uses that money in turn to support numerous parties, both large and small, on worthwhile enterprises. Certain groups, such as the recent Annapurna South Face Expedition, have considerable support from the MEF, and will thus return a portion of their profits to the MEF to be used once again.

Even if a considerable number of current members of the AAC thought an open club along these lines were desirable, we should not be optimistic as to its likelihood. Organizations are incredibly resistant to change—they fight to remain as they are—they are dynamically conservative. Established organizations have a great advantage in meeting demands for change: they endure, they continue, while the demands tend to be ephemeral.

One minimum change that would probably be proposed (it seems to offend the fewest numbers) is to establish a federation of mountain clubs. This would allow the AAC to carry on exactly as before, while being less of a threat to the autonomy of existing clubs. This was precisely what happened in Britain when the Alpine Club, similarly faced with the need for innovation, formed the British Mountaineering Council (BMC). The members of the BMC are not, on the whole, individual climbers, but clubs and other organizations. With such an arrangement there is very little financial support and the council remains totally remote from the bulk of climbers. All the tedious and unglamorous jobs have been placed under its jurisdiction, while the very nature of its makeup has attracted climbing bureaucrats and safety-mongers to its hierarchy. The result has been wholly unsatisfactory, as the people who run the BMC imagine that climbing is all about safety, and that a zero-accident year is climbing's main goal.

Here in this country the AAC leadership is aware of the changing situation of climbers and their organizations. In 1970, outgoing AAC president Nick Clinch said,

> With today's tremendous growth in climbing we are faced with an inevitable increase in problems. We cannot shift these problems from our shoulders because there is no place else for them to go. In American mountaineering the buck stops at the American Alpine Club. This is a large load for a relatively small number of members, but we are doing the best we can within the limit of our resources. . . . We are being overwhelmed. Consequently we must do the following: increase the dues . . . increase membership while maintaining the membership standards.

The obvious solution, surely, must have occurred to many members, for what is so sacred about the "membership standards"? These holy standards are being allowed to cripple the club in terms of both numbers and dollars; but far more important, not only the club but American mountaineering is being shortchanged.

Many climbers feel that the existence of organizations is contrary to the spirit of climbing. Yet single climbers, individuals in a complex

society that increasingly controls our actions, can best defend their free-
doms through collective action. And this, in the final analysis, is the
real justification for organizations such as the AAC.

To the question of who needs the American Alpine Club, a revital-
ized American Alpine Club, I would say we all do; and to fulfill its
expanding role the club will need as many of us as possible. The leading
spirits of the AAC are men of good will, dedicated to American mountaineering. It is our contention, however, that they need to develop a
new and wider vision of the future. If they fail to do so, the club and
its idealistic younger members will suffer, and American mountaineering will lose one of its greatest opportunities.

1971

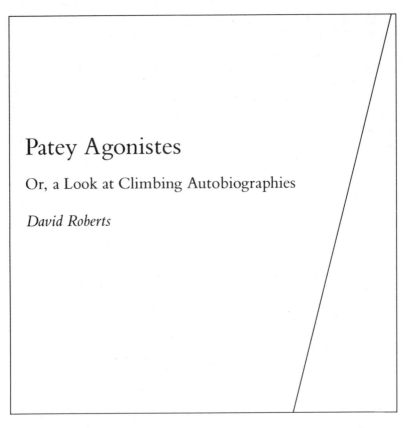

Patey Agonistes

Or, a Look at Climbing Autobiographies

David Roberts

A couple of centuries before mountain climbing got invented, Benvenuto Cellini began his autobiography thus:

> No matter what sort he is, everyone who has to his credit what are or really seem great achievements, if he cares for truth and goodness, ought to write the story of his own life in his own hand; but no one should venture on such a splendid undertaking before he is over forty.

Words to give ordinary mortals pause, but not climbers. Like Benvenuto himself, the best mountaineers are egomaniacs. Hence it is not surprising that, among the genres of our belles lettres, from Mummery through Dougal Haston, an honorable place has long been occupied by the autobiography. Some of the boys, especially of late, have fudged a bit on the quaint old Florentine goldsmith's prescription of four decades under the belt before taking up the pen, but what of it? Climbers live fast, die young, burn themselves out at thirty—but continue to care for truth and goodness. And great achievements? Why, the first solo moonlight descent of the Abendliedspitze in winter? The *direttissima* sans Sherpas on the north face of Chogolagiri?

Alas, the fact of the matter remains, no mountain climber has yet written a good autobiography. This essay, via a somewhat reckless tour past a dozen of the most interesting landmarks of recent years, will try to uncover some of the reasons.

One of the foremost is that Benvenuto was right about the forty years. Climbing autobiographies are written, usually, by men (and an occasional woman) who are still in the thick of it, climbing hard, keeping up their standards, fighting off mellowing. In short, too close to their subject to see it well. Another basic flaw stems from the form which every autobiographer seems to choose, whether out of habit, imitation, or simple laziness; namely, a chronological recipe of major climbs and expeditions. VS Pritchett, the English writer who waited till his late sixties to begin his own autobiography, warned in a lecture once that "chronology is the death of a vast amount of autobiography." The writer, he argued, ought to view what he is doing as "conducting a search," not "traipsing down chronology." His words are apt for mountain climbers, who think of their own careers in calendar terms ("let's see, '68, that's the year I did . . . ") and so the life itself, the vital shape of it, gets lost in the ticking off of successive accomplishments.

So impersonal, in fact, are most climbing autobiographies, that one could well paste together from them a kind of Standard Life, and thus do away with the need of writing any further ones. Start with the Anemic Childhood, say from Hermann Buhl's *Lonely Challenge*. The boy who, inept at sports, weaker than all his playground chums, accused of being a sissy, finds in adolescence in the solitude of the mountains an overcompensator's paradise. Proceed with Early Poverty and Crazy Stunts. Any of the British Rock and Ice gang will do: Dennis Gray's *Rope Boy*, perhaps with an anecdote about Don Whillans pounding the crap out of a belligerent motorcyclist twice his size. The names dropped are always names like Brown and Whillans; and the implication that driving to the crags is at least as dangerous as climbing befits the mystique of meteoric youth.

Interrupted by—First Encounter with Death. Kurt Diemberger's *Summits and Secrets* can be plugged in here. Erich has fallen from the Dent du Geant. Musings like "What was the point of it all—?" substitute nicely for the real sense of tragedy young climbers seem incapable of feeling. (Them as which do feel it, get out of climbing early: hence no autobiography.) This unpleasantness stomached, we come to the

Tiger Days (early twenties): impossibly fast times on old classics, insatiable hunger for climbing, the perfect partnership discovered. Lionel Terray's *Conquistadors of the Useless* suffices, with its vignettes of Lachenal and himself burning up the Alps.

Fame (at last). And with it, the first strange tones of public modesty ("we were fortunate in having so little rock fall") fused with the discovery of an inner invincibility. Chris Bonington's *I Chose to Climb* explains how, on the Southwest Pillar of the Dru, it came to him that, "however bad conditions become, whatever goes wrong, I could extricate myself." Fame leads logically to First Himalayan Venture, which must be narrated only in a tone of sour disillusionment. Buhl, turning his back on the weaklings on Nanga Parbat, is the classic prototype. But a Walter Bonatti (*On the Heights*) can steal the show from the summit party by bivouacking alone on K2; and a Joe Brown (*The Hard Years*) can deflate Kangchenjunga by implying that it was a piece of cake.

Somewhere about here, life intrudes in the form of Marriage—to a hitherto-unmentioned, henceforth-hazy female. The proper handling of this touchy subject is to tack it in at the end of the chapter, like a P.S., as in Dougal Haston's *In High Places:* "One other significant event that year—I finally married my girl-friend Annie." An Annie warrants at least two or three sentences in the remainder of the book, as, for example, when she carries gear up to the base of the climb. Children, if they ensue, merit perhaps a sentence apiece, or a snapshot, dandled on the hero's knee.

On to other things. There are, alas, too few new worlds to conquer, and fame and marriage have taken their toll. The climber does well to undergo, at this point, a Deeper Experience in the mountains. Diemberger discovers "the fourth dimension," and, chin in palm, concludes that "Time encompasses even space." Even the down-to-earth Brown uncovers prehistoric skeletons in Persian caves. The Deeper Experience is closely allied to the Richer Fulfillment, a must for all autobiographers who do not chase the retreating will-o'-the-wisp of ever-rising climbing standards. Eric Shipton puts it well in *That Untravelled World:* "After Mount Kenya I became less and less concerned with the mastery of technical difficulty, or even the ascent of individual peaks, but more and more absorbed in the problems and delights of movement over wide areas of mountain country."

And at last, a Summing Up? But no, climbers autobiographize too young to look back from the rocking chair. Terray, writing a few days before his fortieth birthday, came close to striking a valedictory note:

Don Whillans. JOHN CLEARE.

My own scope must now go back down the scale. . . . It will not be long
before the Alps once again become the terrible mountains of my youth, and
if truly no stone, no tower of ice, no crevasse lies somewhere in wait for
me, the day will come when, old and tired, I find peace among the animals
and flowers.

But he had to spoil it with a postscript explaining how the next year,
contrary to all his presentiments, he dashed off on three major expeditions—to Jannu, the east peak of Chacraraju, and Nilgiri. (And indeed,
a cliff lay in wait for him, just three years ahead.)

Only Bonington, it seems to me, has insured himself adequately
against the future. Having rashly published his autobiography at the
age of thirty-two, and with such *emeritus* echoes in the title, he may
have suddenly realized that he had sold the rest of his career short. A
problem neatly solved by Gollancz and himself in the title of Volume
Two: *The Next Horizon,* which appeared last year. The publisher's
advance notice points out that "for Chris Bonington there will always

be a next horizon"—promising limitless sequels with similar titles (*The Further Challenge? I Chose to Keep Climbing?*) in the Boningtonian future.

Are climbing autobiographies really so bad, so predictable? Worse, I submit; for a good thirty percent of your average *Lonely Conquistadors of the High Hard Places* belongs to a category duller than all the above: Route Description. To quote only a random sentence from Terray: "Another hard pitch led to an old ring-peg on the right bank of the ice gully." Or Bonatti: "A solid piton finally goes into the rock; I take a stance against the wall and belay my companion who is in the process of joining me." Such writing represents self-observation at its feeblest, equivalent, really, to the diarist who records: "Got up at 8:00. Brushed my teeth in the bathroom, then had breakfast downstairs. . . . "

What's missing, then? Virtually everything that signifies that climbers are real people as well as climbers. All the internal things. How does one's motivation change over the years, for instance? At twenty, the mountains seem inexhaustibly exciting; the only problem is how to get enough of them. At thirty-five, one calculates what trips are worth going on, what achievements would still be worth the risk, whom one can get along with,

What about fear, and the whole gray area of reluctance, ambivalence, the temptation to quit? Why does a Bonatti throw in the towel at thirty-five, after his finest climb, while a Terray goes on into his mid-forties, plugging away at the challenges that animate far younger men? Mountaineers have at last admitted that theirs is a highly competitive business (Haston is exceptionally candid about this, as when he relates hiding in a crevasse so that two Frenchmen won't realize he's coveting the same route they're looking over). The logical corollary, that climbing is a career in which ambition, status, and fame play essential parts, remains unexplored in the autobiographical literature.

The real meaning of a life spent climbing goes unexamined, too. It may be Mallory's fault that, when called upon to answer the old "why do you climb?" query, mountaineers, usually a tight-lipped bunch, wax instantly metaphysical. We get all kinds of fluff about being at one with the natural world, seeking inner limits, encountering the ultimate. Solemn musings about self-conquest, the brotherhood of the rope, self-knowledge through adversity. (Bonatti is so shameless as to talk of nature as a "school of character.") How refreshing it would be to hear instead an answer like, "It was that or life insurance."

No climber has yet seen fit to write his autobiography as a true *apologia*. Since the days of Leslie Stephen, the intelligent justifications for a life of climbing have been few, far between, and (*vide* Mallory)

cryptic, at best. "Why do you climb mountains?" is, to be sure, a silly question. But a reply like Haston's "From early days, I found that climbing was the only thing in life that gave more than momentary satisfaction," is a silly answer. Love of nature, by the way, seems to have little to do with it. Superclimbers are, on the whole, uncheerful about hiking, impatient with the weather, insensitive to the subtleties of landscape.

Most absent of all from climbers' autobiographies is a sense of the interpersonal. The usual impression conveyed is of a succession of tough, loyal, immensely skillful ropemates, for each of whom the author would gladly lay down his life—yet they blur together like Trojan warriors. Even the famous lasting partnerships go unarticulated. What a bland picture of Whillans emerges from *The Hard Years*. And though Terray is considerably better at capturing Lachenal, still, in an otherwise moving obituary, he can plumb the source of their magical affinity for each other only in the trite formula, "We were attracted to one another by our common passion for the great climbs, and before long we formed a team of unusual unanimity."

Perhaps this gawkiness about the interpersonal helps explain the shadowy role of the wife. Climbers *are* human: they fall in love and get married; and marriage changes them profoundly, as it does anyone else. On the whole, it undercuts the willingness to take risks. But to admit this, for the top climber, is to admit to turning soft. Hence the whole problematic area of the interpersonal stays veiled in climbing autobiographies. The poor fugitive wife is seen as we see Gulliver's: always there, presumably devoted, raising the kids, keeping quiet and at home the rest of the time. The mountains are the mistress.

So much remains to write about. Are climbers inherently intolerant of the gentle, domestic side of life? Or is there a perhaps peculiarly British reticence about discussing these things—since probably more than half of all climbing autobiographies ever published have been British? It is a curious fact that there is hardly an American example of the form. Miriam Underhill's *Give Me the Hills* and Dorothy Pilley's *Climbing Days* come to mind—both very British in slant. Has any male American climber in the last thirty years been so audacious as to think of penning his memoirs? (Perhaps at this very moment Royal Robbins is laboring secretively over a tape recorder, Fred Beckey has reached 1952 in his chronicles, Warren Harding is signing a contract with Grove Press.)

What kinds of people does climbing attract? No easy answer will suffice, for ours is an endeavor that hooks characters as diverse as Aleister Crowley and IA Richards, as disparate as Tom Frost and Cesare Maestri.

Climbers who write, while not genuine apologists, are lifelong "fans," devotees. Therefore, I think, they have never been hard enough (honest or critical enough) about climbing itself. Take the idea of the career. If climbing follows certain patterns that hold in other ways of life—the effort to rise from obscurity to recognition, for example—then can we not gain insight into climbing by looking at it with the half-jaundiced eye normally reserved for careers we despise, like those in business? Granted, no one is likely to get rich climbing. But how much of the reward of climbing comes, for a Terray, from "making it" as a sport hero in his own country? What does it do to a Bonington to become a TV celebrity?

Even at more modest levels, competition for status plays a strong role. Any local climbing area bears this out. A lot of mountaineers quit, or at least tail drastically off, after their "big climb." Surely a certain itch gets partly satisfied in the back-slapping of one's peers. Fame breeds contentment, makes it all the harder to go back to the square one of risk and hardship.

Why is climbing so easy for the young, so hard to keep up for the not-so-young? Even professional sports, one suspects, are not so ruthless. A hunch: between the ages, roughly, of fourteen and twenty-two, it is emotionally easier (for the average male in a Western culture) to risk one's life than it will ever be again. I married at twenty-four, and I know that my commitment to my wife (and, to a lesser extent, to my job) interfered with the old, easy commitment I could make to my climbing partners. It follows that I did my own most dangerous climbing before the age of twenty-four.

How much of the appeal of mountaineering lies in its simplification of interpersonal relationships, its reduction of friendship to smooth interaction (like war), its substitution of an Other (the mountain, the challenge) for the relationship itself? Behind a mystique of adventure, toughness, footloose vagabondage—all much-needed antidotes to our culture's built-in comfort and convenience—may lie a kind of adolescent refusal to take seriously aging, the frailty of others, interpersonal responsibility, weakness of all kinds, the slow and unspectacular course of life itself. What role do women play? For they can seldom become our ideal climbing partners, not even in this age of liberation.

A psychological study of top racing drivers concluded that, although well above average in intelligence, they ranked below average in tolerance of others' emotional demands. I suspect the same is true of top climbers. They can be deeply moved, in fact maudlin; but only for worthy martyred ex-comrades. A certain coldness, strikingly similar in tone, emerges from the writings of Buhl, John Harlin, Bonatti, Bonington, and Haston. The coldness of competence. Perhaps this is what extreme climbing is about: to get to a point where, in Haston's words, "If anything goes wrong it will be a fight to the end. If your training is good enough survival is there; if not nature claims its forfeit."

Of the books mentioned above, the best-written is easily Shipton's. His alone, in its early chapters, escapes the prison of chronology and begins to define a life in climbing as a life with shape, meaning, potential alternatives. Shipton headed Cellini, moreover: waited till long after forty to write his autobiography and so could see, especially well, the ironies of a lonely boyhood. A marvelous beginning—but only a beginning, for *That Untravelled World* sadly lapses into the usual chronological plod, loses focus, even though the writing remains urbane and sensitive.

The best of the books, all things considered, I think is Terray's. Despite pages of bluff, unskilled writing, despite a blurring together of climbs and an ill-disguised impatience to get the book done with, *Conquistadors of the Useless* (awful title) ends up conveying more of the truth than any of the other books. Terray writes well as if by accident: as when, with eloquent brevity, he follows up on the lives of his teammates in the decade after Annapurna, or when his sense of irony rises almost to outrage about the absurd climbing games he played for real against the Germans in World War II.

But I have saved for last any mention of the two books which, I believe—though neither is in the true sense an autobiography—come the closest to telling what it is like to be a climber. They are Tom Patey's *One Man's Mountains* and Menlove Edwards's *Samson*. Both are posthumous books, edited by others. Both are collections of occasional journal articles and miscellaneous poetry. There the resemblance ends; but it is worth pointing out that the lack of deliberate form has something to do with the success of each book. Neither Patey nor Edwards was consciously autobiographizing. Patey wrote to amuse a close brotherhood, those who understand mountaineering from the inside. Edwards, one guesses, wrote mainly for himself.

One Man's Mountains may well be the most entertaining climbing book ever written. By fusing the British tradition of intelligent, whimsically self-deprecating mountain writing (the vein of Shipton, Tilman, Longstaff, and Murray, at their best) with the fierce and rowdy iconoclasm of the Creagh Dhu and the Rock and Ice, Patey discovered a jocular voice all his own. It was an achievement that took years to polish, as the volume attests: the earliest articles, from the mid-fifties, are surprisingly straight and ordinary, with only here and there a flash of the wit that was to mellow into perfection in the articles and ballads of the late sixties.

His wife, Betty, who selected the writings, divides them into four categories: "Scotland," "Abroad," "Satire," and "Verse." Yet they are really all of a piece, all satire. Patey had strong talents as a writer: a fine ear for dialogue, the knack for characterizing in a single stroke, a sense of timing, and above all, the tragicomic gift of the balladeer. But his accomplishment emerges as all the more remarkable when one reflects that he milked all his best effects out of what really amounts to a single conceit: the climber as Quixote, tilting at *nordwands*. Take a single passage from "A Short Walk with Whillans." At the foot of the Second Icefield of the Eiger, besieged by falling rock, a storm gathering:

> Simultaneously with Whillans' arrival at the stance the first flash of lightning struck the White Spider.
>
> "That settles it," said he, clipping the spare rope through my belay karabiner.
>
> "What's going on?" I demanded, finding it hard to credit that such a crucial decision could be reached on the spur of the moment.
>
> "I'm going down," he said, "That's what's going on."
>
> "Wait a minute! Let's discuss the whole situation calmly." I stretched out one hand to flick the ash off my cigarette. Then a most unusual thing happened. There was a higher pitched "WROUFF" than usual and the end of my cigarette disappeared! It was the sort of subtle touch that Hollywood film directors dream about.
>
> "I see what you mean," I said. "I'm going down too."

What is so perfect about this scene? There is no point carping that this is not the way it really happened, that climbers are not quite so blasé in the midst of danger, that probably the rock didn't really knock the ash off the cigarette. This is the way it ought to have been, the distillation of tales brewed in pubs over decades, the stuff of legends. Patey was a mythographer. And so his Whillans has legendary proportions: what Gray, Brown, and Bonington all miss, trying so hard in their own books to tell the good vintage Whillans tales, Patey picks up in a page: it is he that discerns, unlike the others, the streak of morbid fatalism in the otherwise so thick-skinned hard man. Patey died in May 1970, in a rappelling accident on a sea stack off the north coast of Scotland. He was thirty-eight: too young of course, especially in view of the writing he might have done. But he left us one incomparable book.

The life of John Menlove Edwards, on the other hand, is the dark side of climbing autobiography. By the age of twenty-one he was doing hard new routes in Wales; during the decade from 1931 to 1941 he was (with Colin Kirkus) one of the two best rockclimbers in Britain. But the great failures of his life were professional and personal. His career was theoretical psychology. Though his brilliance led to considerable success as a clinical psychiatrist, his research (the real labor of his life) was rejected by the authorities of the day.

He discovered early that he was a homosexual. Two unhappy love affairs during his twenties are hinted at in his poetry. In 1935 he met Wilfrid Noyce (who was then seventeen) and taught him how to climb. He fell deeply in love with Noyce, and though the passion was necessarily one-sided, they climbed together intensely for several years and collaborated on two guide books. In 1937, on Scafell, Edwards held Noyce on a two-hundred-foot leader fall; two of the three strands of the rope were severed. Noyce was unconscious for three days and nearly died. It is impossible to calculate the effect of this accident on Edwards, for he never wrote about it, but it must have been profound.

The rest of Edwards' life is tragic. He spent much of it alone— engaging in Herculean swimming and solo rowing feats, or holed up for a year in an isolated cottage near Snowdon. He was a conscientious objector during World War II; because his grounds were agnostic, his application was at first insultingly rejected. He became paranoid, attempted suicide in 1945, and spent time in a mental hospital. In 1957 he collided on his motorcycle with a boy riding a bicycle; Edwards' arm was broken badly, and the boy died beside him in the hospital. Shortly after, with his arm in a cast, trying to sharpen a sickle, he sliced off the knuckles of his hand, severing tendons. He was stoical about the pain, but in early 1958 he committed suicide by swallowing potassium cyanide.

Samson was put together by Noyce and Geoffrey Sutton and privately printed around 1960. Their effort was to establish Edwards as a poet and prose writer of minor importance; and so the book has an annoying literary-critical tone to it (notes "explicate" the poems and articles). Edwards was not that good a writer: too cryptic and derivative and fragmentary to interest most nonclimbers. Yet the combination of his life (which half of the book goes to delineating), his climbs, and his writing make *Samson* a unique and fascinating work. His poems are, on the whole, less interesting than his articles, although occasionally a few lines capture his special way of seeing the world:

> You rock, you heaviness a man can clasp,
> You steady buttress-block for hold,
> You, frozen roughly to the touch:
> Yet what can you?

The articles are strange, to say the least: deeply inward, fact blurring into fantasy, breathless and obscure, with the sense of great strength violently repressed. The most interesting of them ("Scenery for a Murder") is a difficult parable-fantasy of a long Alpine climb with a shadowy *doppelgänger* named Toni, the young, beautiful, unspeaking partner, the better climber. At the end, Toni dies in a bivouac in the narrator's arms:

> Then his eyes went wild a little, they were a little wild always, and then he cried, sobbed out aloud on my shoulder. Not long after that he died.
>
> But murder, you say. There was no one else present, you say, no murderer. So? Nobody else? Have you forgotten the singing, have you forgotten the scenery, the wild scenery? . . .

His mountain writing is the most intense I can remember reading. Early, especially, he had a gift for humor, as in a lovely caricature of the Winthrop Young generation of gentlemen-climbers. But his real subject is inner conflict, self-doubt, fear: just the feelings climbers have the most difficulty facing head-on. There is no pride or vanity in his writing: the very strangeness of it lies in its obliviousness to the rest of the world. As early as 1941 he seems to have identified himself as a schizophrenic. One of his most haunting passages is about nothing more grandiose than backing off a solo climb only fifteen feet off the ground.

> Look at yourself I said, and do you know what this is, that it is schizophrenia, the split mind: I know but I do not care what I said: it is stupid: what could you do if you did get ten feet higher up, the rocks have not started yet to become difficult, take yourself off from this cliff: oh, this climbing, that involves an effort, on every move the holes to be spotted and often there are none, then every limb placed, the body set into the one suitable position found but with trouble, then with the whole organism great force must be exerted, before anything happens, and this is to be done while the brain is occupied sick and stiff with its fears: and now you have been doing this for well over an hour and a half and the strain must be telling: get down therefore.

1974

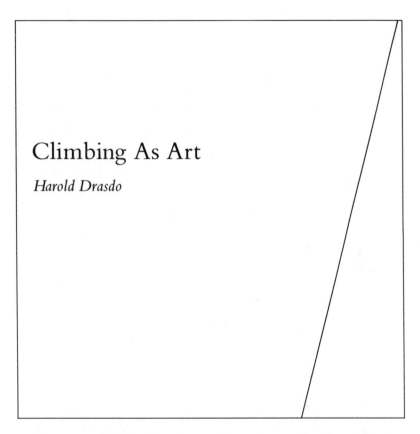

Climbing As Art

Harold Drasdo

Now to say that climbing is a creative act is one thing; but to say that a climb is like a work of art is quite another. To some it will seem that the comparison is good only within a very limited area of overlap. But I want to claim that the likeness is extensive and important and so I represent the suggestion one step at a time.

First, it surely has to be agreed that mountains and cliffs often impress us in the same ways as the great achievements of such arts as sculpture and architecture. In fact we often have no choice in describing them but to resort to comparison with these arts or achievements. This tendency is very evident in the early records of mountaineering in the form of conscious analogies. Modern writers are more likely to use these metaphors unconsciously but even today we find, for instance, ADM Cox having to liken the two great buttresses of Clogwyn du'r Arddu to a medieval fortress and cathedral in order to try to capture their fascinating antitheses of form. For every unnamed mountain which becomes Someone's Peak, another becomes Somebody's Tower or Spire or Dome or Pyramid. Its features are described and named as buttresses or pillars or ridges or walls or columns. These tectonic metaphors are the natural expression of our process of thought.

Or, instead of seeing the present shape of the mountain as resembling a type or feature of building, we are struck by the way it has been carved from a greater form. We do not have to anthropomorphise a titanic sculptor to see the sculptural qualities of mountains. We think of the forces of wind, water, ice, and lightning as tools because there is evidence everywhere of how the rock is being ground down, split, hammered, washed, and crushed—nature's processes which man appropriates and forgets where they came from.

But there is a limit to the reach of these metaphors. In fact, it might be claimed that cliffs and mountains are façades without shape or dimension until they are floodlit by human effort. Just as the Prince wakes the Sleeping Beauty, so the climber's touch brings the cliff to life. The more it is worked over, the more aspects are revealed and the more secrets suggested. And this mystery is never diminished. Every storm, every change in the weather resurrects and reasserts it.

To see the extent to which climbing invests mountains with significance, consider a hypothetical problem: how to write a symphony using as inspiration the North Face of the Eiger. Before the 1930s this proposition would have seemed an intangible and hollow exercise. But one can imagine that today a piece of music might easily utilize as its theme the 1938 route and would not strike many composers, especially those working in cinema, as too daunting an undertaking—the chief artistic problem might well be the avoidance of clichés, Wagnerian passages, a spacious exit, and so forth.

Climbs interpret mountain faces. A climb is the most human relationship possible with a mountain face. Climbs amplify the persona of a mountain. The more effort has been expended, the more increment to the mountain's character. The Hörnli Ridge is not desecrated by those half-million climbers who have ascended it. It is hallowed. The mountain might indeed be considered a holy place, as in many cultures it has been. The climber reveres each detail; he knows it as a monk knows his abbey or as the curator of a historic monument knows the parts of his building. Even on the meanest gritstone escarpment on the darkest, foggiest winter afternoon he tells off the buttresses, corners, and gullies one after the other, name by name or presence by presence as he passes underneath them. And every feature is charged with meaning.

Climbing on Indian Rock, Berkeley, California. JIM STUART.

In descending the easy slopes below a great cliff or mountain many of us cannot help but turn again and again to review its structures even when we know these structures like the backs of our hands. Or we trace the line we have just climbed upwards and upwards, over and over again, trying to grasp that line in its integrity and to establish its relationship to the cliff. Some of us find it impossible to make an uninterrupted descent however much the circumstances might advise this. We could look forever and make a fine art of walking backwards.

If we turn our attention to the climb now, rather than to the cliff, we see that it cannot be considered apart from its setting and that it can sometimes hardly be separated from its story. The world's most classic and celebrated routes—say, the Grandes Jorasses by the Walker Spur or the Nose of El Capitan—are preeminent because in addition to the technical merit of their climbing problems they are enlarged by their dramatic histories and, above all, they are superbly placed.

Look at the excellences of climbs such as these for a moment. We can conveniently use the first-named as our subject taking advantage of some remarks made recently by the man who first climbed it, Riccardo Cassin. The Walker is regarded as an incomparable route, Cassin rightly says, "for its continuous difficulties and for the grandeur of its development, as well as for its setting."

"The grandeur of its development." The expression stops us dead. Then we speculate on whatever nuances may have been gained or lost in translation. But next we wonder to what province of human activity an allusion is being made. Surely an aesthetic or intellectual metaphor is hidden here? The remark suggests an elevation of design and experience to disallow its use to describe a mere game. Does the idea come from music or drama? Is it as though there are identical processes involved when, say, a great symphony or tragedy involves and possesses the listener; and when climbers follow their route or, relativistically, the wall's huge structures unfold around them? (Each part distinct in character and fixed in sequence; the serial nature of the whole, once established, as irreversible as that of any familiar piece of music; themes hinted at, then taken up and developed: the diedre of thirty meters, the traverse of the ice bands, the diedre of seventy-five meters, the pendule, the Black Slabs, the Gray Tower, the Red Tower.)

Or does it come from the epic novel? "The grandeur of its development." A surprising thought, might we share it with an epochal game of chess or even with a superb mathematical proof? As though, going step by step beyond what had previously been imagined, there has been an extension of possibility to expand the consciousness once and for all time.

The Eperon Walker is one of the greatest climbs. But the very shortest routes on outcrops are tested to exactly similar specifications. At one time an absurd dialogue between British hillwalkers and rock-climbers persisted and echoes of the argument are heard to the present day. It was alleged that the really fanatical climbers—"rock gymnasts"—were utterly indifferent to the beauty of mountains. Whilst in fact no climb, however short, is agreed to have value and importance unless it satisfies certain uncodified but stringent aesthetic criteria—it must be difficult, it must be separate, it must be unique, it must not change, it must not incorporate the irrelevant. Difficulty, because the experience should not be cheaply available. Separation, because the experience should be inescapable. Individuality, because the experience should be distinguishable. Permanence, because the experience should remain on offer to others. Unity, because the experience should not be subject to interruption by other experiences.

In summing up these remarks on the attributes of good climbs, it seems to me to be incontrovertible that climbs offer rewards very like those of works of art. The great routes expand the consciousness, each one enlarges us. They live on in our minds for the rest of our lives. The very memory of these adventures can evoke powerful feelings. Our imaginations can recreate and perhaps surpass these experiences but first our senses must acquaint themselves with them. Only those who believe that true art is always moral or didactic will be able to reject this view on principle.

But if the climb is like a work of art, is the climber, then, a sort of artist? Yes, I say: though more often in an interpretive than in a constructive sense. In climbing, as claimed already, the two roles almost merge. But in either of these senses, why not? In movement, as though in dance? Certainly. I can imagine the brief orgy of tomfoolery and amusement the suggestion will inspire amongst some of my friends. It pleases me to entertain them for a moment. But no one who has seen something of the range of style and attack displayed by those who lead the hardest rock climbs could doubt for a minute that these experts exist on just the same plane as the greatest performers in the world of dance. Pavlova or Nureyev would stand anonymous amongst this company. In dramatic confrontation as though in the writing or staging of theater? But of course. What else is climbing about? Is a reach of the imagination like that of the novelist? No doubt. Every new route makes real an unexplored possibility and the epochal routes are made by those who have seen that a generally accepted or even unnoticed boundary can be crossed.

Perhaps this excursus on the nature of climbing has now become tedious and circular but certainly all sorts of speculations continue to suggest themselves. I have compared the art of climbing with that of dance. Yeats asks himself, in a famous poem, how can we know the dancer from the dance? When the room is cleared, however, all that remains is the idea of dance. To separate the climb, the climbing, and the climber may be more rewarding. For the climb has a physical existence independent of climbing and the climber; and it is capable of almost infinitely extendable description, both objectively and in terms of value, utterly different in degree to any description of a golf course or dart board, also existing independently of the player. I am sure that an analysis of both recreational and artistic activities along these lines would raise some interesting questions. But whatever their place in human activity, climbs and climbing exist uniquely and whether they are best thought of as a kind of art form or as a pastime almost dominated by its aesthetic components, they remain irreducibly fascinating and rich.

1974

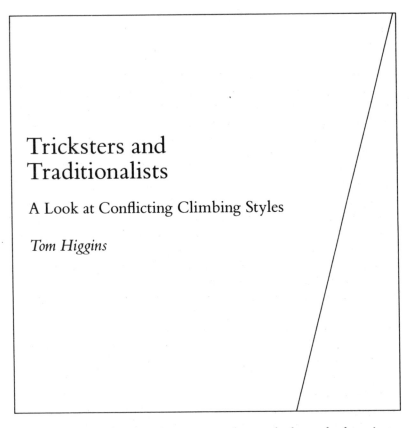

Tricksters and Traditionalists

A Look at Conflicting Climbing Styles

Tom Higgins

Colorado climber Pat Ament recently watched people dragging a thirty-foot ladder up scree slopes in Boulder Canyon. Were they on their way to a high-wire act, he inquired? No, no act; they just needed to preprotect a new route with a bolt twenty feet off the ground.

In Yosemite Valley, holds are chopped ("sculpted," say the defenders of the action) into the rock to allow tries at free climbing El Capitan. At the other end of the Valley, on Glacier Point Apron, a string of aid bolts is placed to protect free climbing on Hall of Mirrors. Reportedly, protection without aid was possible, but on a less direct line. The route is then touted as one of the greatest new free climbs in Yosemite.

In Tuolumne Meadows—in the high country of Yosemite National Park—routes on every major dome are done by placing bolts and pitons while on rappel, by standing on bolts to place others, and by creating bolt ladders to protect free climbing. In the latest Tuolumne innovation, leaders place protection bolts while hanging from hooks attached

227

to flakes and knobs. In the same area even the long-standing agreement to respect the protection style of the first-ascent party is weakening: a bolt was recently added to an established route on Daff Dome.

In every major climbing area in the country, it is possible to see climbers rappelling cliffs in order to preview crux sections of proposed new routes, to rehearse moves, and to place protection. When these climbers finally decide to do their routes, they often fall repeatedly and rest on their protection. The new protection devices, friends, encourage this behavior; since the protection is more easily assured, climbers can push closer to the point of falling.

Clearly, rockclimbing styles are changing. "Tricksters" are bending and altering the traditional rules of the climbing game. In the traditional style, climbers do not alter the rock in order to free climb it. Nor do they preview routes on rappel, or fix protection on aid or on rappel with the intention of immediately trying to free climb. Aid climbing is done to get to the top, not to set up a route for free-climb attempts. Likewise, in traditional style the climber might fall a few times trying a free climb, but he or she doesn't rest on the protection between attempts. The traditionalist knows there is a time and place to give up.

The conflict between tricksters and traditionalists is no small issue. Before 1970 there were few, if any, tricksters; nearly all the routes were done in traditional style. Now, tricksters are continually creating new routes with their controversial methods. Also, capable and respected climbers subscribe to the methods. Vern Clevenger tells of times and places he stood on protection bolts to place others and previewed or rehearsed while on rappel. Jim Bridwell has doctored rock selectively and has placed bolt ladders to protect free climbing. John Bachar rests on hooks while placing protection bolts. Reportedly, Ray Jardine "sculpts" holds on El Capitan. These expert climbers, of course, do not use the controversial styles everywhere or every time. They all have climbed ferocious routes in traditional style.

Nevertheless, respected climbers not only use the new styles, they defend them. In an article on face-climbing styles and standards in the 1982 *American Alpine Journal,* Bruce Morris reports that many climbers in Tuolumne now subscribe to "the construction of a line of technical difficulty at almost any price." He quotes "notorious local Claude Fiddler," who asks, "How can a route be worthwhile unless 'questionable methods' were employed on its first ascent?" Of Vern Clevenger, Morris writes: "He demonstrated a willingness to cheat selectively . . . as long as it extended the upper range of the free-climbing spectrum." The attitude seems to be, so what if protection bolts are placed on aid or rappel, as long as the resulting climb is a good one? So what if a flake or crack is slightly altered to make a great free climb? Why should climbers be bound by old rules—or any rules—when creating new routes or trying to free climb old routes?

The conflict between traditionalists and tricksters extends to methods of reporting new routes. Whereas climbers once agreed to report their first-ascent style openly, now information about style is not readily forthcoming. Some tricksters simply refuse to say how they did a climb, perhaps believing the style of ascent is no one's business. They may not lie about how they climbed, but often they remain silent about their style of ascent until asked directly. Their silence creates an awkward and misleading situation. For example, Morris remarks of a Tuolumne first ascent: "No one will ever know for sure whether [the leader] drilled all the bolts strictly on the lead." And referring to Pièce de Résistance, another Tuolumne climb, Morris states, "Only one bolt— but [the climbers] would never say which one—was supposedly drilled on aid." Other climbers acknowledge their aid ladders or rests on protection, but only to close companions. The information rarely gets into print. Journal articles relate heroics, not style, and modern guide books, short on history but long on route maps, contain few references to the style of ascent.

Climbers arguing for full disclosure of style perceive a glaring contradiction in the paucity of reporting. Why are tricksters so loud in defending what they are doing but so reluctant to reveal their style of ascent? It appears tricksters want a free ride on the backs of people climbing in traditional style. Because tricks are a relatively new phenomenon, climbers unaware of the inside story presume traditional styles were employed and give their respect accordingly.

It is time to reexamine the issue of climbing styles. The first question is obvious: why should there be *any* agreement about styles? The answer is equally clear: because these agreements safeguard the climbing enjoyment of others. Some agreements between climbers aim at facilitating the competitive side of the sport. Contrary to cherished belief, climbing *is* a competitive sport. Climbing a route all free, with limited protection, and on the first try means much more than climbing it after rehearsing moves or placing protection on rappel. Consequently, climbers should agree to reveal how new routes, particularly hard ones, were done. Only in this way can climbers test themselves by trying routes in the same or better style.

Climbers are not alone in making agreements about competition in their sport. Bagging game with a bow and arrow is much more impressive than with a rifle, and kayaking a rough river is a greater achievement than doing it in a tube raft. People participating in these sports agree to reveal what technique or style is used because the achievement and stature of those responsible are thereby defined. The achievements in any sport are remembered, written down, and discussed for many years. For that discussion to have any meaning, people agree not to imply they used a bow and arrow when they used a rifle, or used a kayak when they used a raft.

Other agreements guard against actions climbers find offensive. For example, when climbers agree not to paint their names on walls, blast out ledges, fix cables, or otherwise drastically alter the rockscape, they do so because most climbers are offended by the result. Similarly, many climbers are offended by an extra piton or bolt added to an established route. Upon finding such additional protection, they feel the same as they would coming across names spray-painted on the rock. A bolt and a pin added to a route at Lover's Leap, in California, once caused much debate. Several climbers still feel the protection should have been left as it was originally placed. The thirty-odd bolts placed on the regular route of New Mexico's Shiprock over the years so outraged climbers that one fanatic spent half a day removing them. On Yosemite's Lost Arrow Tip, six extra bolts were added in the 1950s to John Salathé's original ones. Some thought the bolts demeaned Salathe's efforts and should be removed. They were. In short, agreements between climbers about style are useful and important because they enhance or protect the climbing experience. Contrary to what tricksters say, climbing style is not a personal matter.

Of course, there is an exception to the agreement against altering protection on established routes: the first-ascent party may indicate better protection is needed. The Snake Dike on Half Dome provides a good example. Seasoned climbers, making the first ascent using marginal protection, realized only at the top that the moderate route was destined to become a popular climb. Therefore, they gave the next party permission to add numerous bolts, thus ensuring that beginners would have a safe and enjoyable time.

It is not only on established routes that climbing or protection styles are more than personal matters. The same is true for first ascents. There were once plenty of new routes for climbers to "hunt," so it didn't matter that some people used "bows" and others used "guns" to do the coveted climbs. Plenty of "game" existed for each. But now that

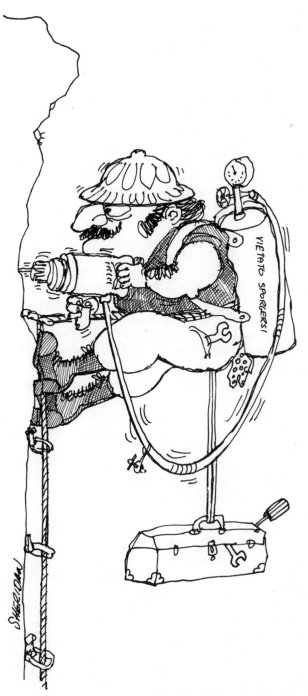

Sheridan Anderson captures Maestri's famous trick ascent of Cerro Torre.

game is scarce, climbers employing different styles are in competition for new routes much more so than in the past. A first ascent accomplished by preplacing bolts or pitons on aid or rappel removes the opportunity for another party to make the first ascent without using these techniques. The same is true for first ascents done by rehearsing or resting on protection.

Tricksters defend their actions by means of two popular but fallacious arguments. The first is that no matter how a first ascent is done, traditionalists can always climb the route in their preferred style. They can bypass protection placed on rappel, and they can try a route without rehearsing or resting on protection. In so doing, they can experience their own "first ascent." The problem with this contention is that it discounts the importance of first ascents for others. Removed forever is the unique opportunity for a first ascent in traditional style. Obviously, a special satisfaction comes from doing a first ascent, naming it, telling others the story, being recognized, and adding one's name and accomplishments to the history of climbs in an area.

Tricksters raise a second argument: "Tough luck." They say the first-ascent party always has denied others the opportunity for a first ascent, no matter what the style. To be sure, people using traditional styles do deny first ascents to others, including climbers employing the new tricks. The rebuttal, however, is simple: bullets kill more easily than arrows. Where game is plentiful, it doesn't matter who uses what weapon. But when game is scarce, it certainly does matter. Guns remove more game for bows than vice versa. It is for this very reason that bow users are allowed to hunt before the regular season opens. It is also the reason that certain weapons are restricted in hunting and fishing. Consider the rightful ire of a flyfisherman observing someone building a trap or dynamiting the water!

Not only do tricks remove opportunities, they create certain dangers. Where a first ascent is rehearsed by top rope and preprotected, for example, traditionalists may be endangered in subsequent ascents. Traditionalists may not be able to place protection on the lead and, not having rehearsed the moves, may fall at a dangerous point.

Again, climbing style is not purely a personal matter. It affects other climbers in various ways. On established routes, adding protection offends climbers who wish to do the route in its original style, or as the first-ascent party intended the route to stand. Consequently, many climbers still agree to honor the protection style of the first ascent. On new routes, both climbing and protection style can affect others as first-ascent opportunities grow scarce. In this case, climbers employing preprotection, rehearsing, and resting on protection are more easily able to do first ascents than climbers choosing not to use these styles. For all these reasons a majority of climbers prior to 1970 agreed not to employ certain styles on first ascents. If a route could not be done in the traditional manner, the prevailing agreement was to leave it for better climbers—or future generations—to try.

Tricksters should reconsider what their climbing styles are doing to others and change their actions. First, where preprotecting, rehearsing, and aid ladders are employed, they should be widely reported. Guide books and climbing magazines should report the style of ascent. Without this information, other climbers cannot know what challenge has been set before them. Trusting climbers who presume traditional styles of ascent may even be endangered as they try to repeat certain routes. Second, tricksters should stop using their techniques on new routes in areas where first-ascent possibilities are scarce and where other climbers want to employ traditional styles. Third, and as a last resort, tricksters might confine themselves to places where the opportunities for new routes are plentiful. In such places they are less likely to happen upon established routes they feel need alteration in protection or in the rock itself. If they want to preprotect, rehearse, or create bolt ladders for free climbing, their actions will not greatly inconvenience traditionalists.

The last two points are the most difficult for tricksters to accept. After all, they believe their style is applied only when traditional styles cannot be used. Perfectly capable of climbing in traditional style, tricksters feel they know its limits. They feel that few, if any, climbers will be deprived of first-ascent opportunities.

A recent case in point is the Bachar-Yerian Route on Medlicott Dome in Tuolumne Meadows. This spectacular route ascends a black water streak on a dead-vertical golden wall. The leader placed protection bolts while hanging from hooks affixed to knobs. The climb is superb, the line is direct, the protection is scanty; it is hard to imagine the route could be protected without resorting to a trick such as hanging from hooks. Surely, say the tricksters, no opportunity for traditionalists was removed in *this* case.

Perhaps the Bachar-Yerian Route could not be done any other way, except by rappelling to place the bolts. If all the routes done by tricksters were this impressive and difficult, there would be less to discuss. Within a few miles of the Bachar-Yerian Route, however, numerous examples abound of climbs where tricksters have removed very real possibilities for traditionalists. Handjive, on Lembert Dome, originally protected by placing bolts on rappel, lay well within the capabilities of climbers of the time to protect on the lead. Hoodwink, on Harlequin Dome, was first done with an aid ladder to protect free climbing. Traditionalists of the day could have done the first ascent without the ladder. Death Crack, once rehearsed by top roping, is now led occasionally on sight. Blues Riff, once protected on aid, is now done without this style. In the last two cases climbers of today were deprived of the opportunity for first ascents in traditional style. Other examples exist where climbers of the era, or those of the next generation, could have done—or would have wanted to try— trickster routes in traditional style.

The irony of the Bachar-Yerian Route is that John Bachar's usual climbing style suggests how the route might have been done to no one's objection. Since Bachar free solos routes of the highest standard, one gets the impression he put in his bolts for subsequent climbers. Suppose he had put in only those bolts that could have been placed without hooks and let climbers scratch their heads for years to come. Neither the traditionalists nor the tricksters could then object to losing the first-ascent opportunity to such a fine climber and so pure a style.

Whatever real or supposed opportunities were removed by the Bachar-Yerian Route, the style of ascent still creates a disadvantage for climbers preferring the traditional style. In the hands of lesser climbers, "hooking" is certain to remove ever more first-ascent possibilities for traditionalists of today and the near future. It is possible also that advances in protection technology will allow routes like the Bachar-Yerian to go without hooks, rappel placements, or aid ladders. Or perhaps more climbers will soon accept less protection, in line with Bachar's usual climbing style. The point is that tricksters should not presume to know the limits of traditional styles or styles less dependent on protection. Also, they should not presume to know how many climbers prefer traditional styles now or will in the future. Traditionalists may be a silent majority or weekenders who rarely have the time or contacts to make known their preferences. Considerable unthinking arrogance lies in the presumption that one knows the capabilities and preferences of everyone in the growing population of rockclimbers. Tricksters should also realize a first-ascent opportunity comes only once. Restocking can revive game populations for those fishing and hunting. But once the first ascent is bagged, it is gone forever. This fact alone should give pause to those who use weapons that others in the sport refuse to employ.

Unfortunately, much of the discussion about climbing styles is so off-base as to discourage serious debate. For example, tricksters say their style brings them closer to physical and psychic frontiers. Bruce Morris claims that to climb beyond "temporal ethics" is to take "mystical steps toward achieving a deathless super-consciousness." Does this Nietzschean rhetoric really clarify matters? Traditionalists say their style makes routes more challenging because there is less reliance on equipment and more emphasis on the act of climbing. Arguments go on endlessly about psychic rewards and purity of heart; it all sounds like a Sunday sermon. No wonder so many dismiss the whole matter.

The way to wake up the debate is to shift the focus from style to impact. Whether the bow and arrow or the gun provides the better experience is not at issue. The much-needed focus of debate is not what trickster style does for its adherents, but how it affects climbers who prefer other styles. In the economist's jargon, tricks create an "externality," a negative public consequence from private action. Traditionalists are getting less information than they want or need to measure achievements. They are finding scarred rock or protection altered from the first ascent; they are getting fewer chances to try their style on first ascents. These important, concrete issues can and should spur intelligent debate.

From such debate, climbers can get down to the business of mending old agreements or striking new ones. Everyone will be awake for the ensuing discussion. The tricksters will have their points:

- Who are traditionalists and why have they been so quiet if they perceive so much harm? How many are they?

- If traditionalists repeatedly fail to make a first ascent, shouldn't they agree to give us a chance?

- Will traditionalists agree that some climbs will *never* be done in their preferred style? If so, why should those walls be left alone forever?

And the traditionalists will have their points:

- How can we strike agreements with tricksters to ignore certain walls, areas, or established routes?

- If tricksters continue their ways, why don't they at least agree to report their style of ascent in articles and guidebooks?

- Should there be experiments with new bolting technology? Would climbers use the technology more to climb in traditional fashion or more to place aid ladders for protection? Or both?

Agreements among climbers about styles have changed and will continue to change. Although tricksters now dominate the scene in many climbing areas, they have not buried previous agreements favoring traditional styles. Agreements against tricks, for full reporting, and for preservation of established routes have a sound basis. They have protected the fundamental interests and experiences of climbers for many decades. Consequently, the agreements may have more proponents than tricksters know. At the very least, such agreements govern an older generation of climbers who still climb in the traditional style. Other proponents may be occasional visitors to climbing areas, who are numerous but not generally vocal about style. Also, a younger generation now beginning to climb will soon discover the reasons for agreements about traditional style. Many will be in a quandary about how new climbs are done. They will consequently find it hard to measure themselves against the challenge. And they will watch as beautiful, improbable walls succumb only to those who practice special tricks. It is likely that many in this generation will demand to know how first ascents were done, to try the "impossible" without resorting to tricks, and to experience the rock and protection of classic routes as they were originally. Perhaps it will not be long before demands for old and familiar agreements rise up like so many poltergeists. If so, what will the tricksters do? Agree or not? Abide or not?

1984

7

COLD RIDGES, WARM SANDSTONE

Editors' Introduction

North American climbing came of age during the 1960s. In rock-climbing meccas like Yosemite, the Tetons, and the Shawangunks, free-climbing standards shot upward like rockets, never again to go down. In the bigger mountains, especially those in Canada and Alaska, a new breed of mountaineer put up routes that surpassed the standards set earlier in Europe.

With this new interest, guidebooks and articles appeared. Although Americans still flocked to the Alps and the Himalaya, more and more of them turned northward. The number of significant alpine routes done in the Canadian Rockies, the Yukon, and Alaska from 1965 to 1975 is startling.

Ascent has featured many pieces about the Far North, several of which are included here. Our first selection, Allen Steck's "Ascent of Hummingbird Ridge," is crafted in the form of a letter. The beautiful ridge on Mount Logan's southern escarpment had never been attempted: it was horrendously long and the elevation gain was a staggering 12,600 feet. Six men spent thirty-seven days struggling slowly up the ridge, wondering daily if they were brave or foolish. They placed eleven camps en route while doing the ridge alpine style, a bold feat admired to this day. The route has never been repeated in its entirety.

The name of the ridge stems from a brief encounter with a migrating rufous hummingbird on Osod Buttress, low on the route. (*Osod,* a word we carefully avoided explaining in 1967, is an acronym for "Oh shit, oh dear"—a commentary on the level of commitment.)

As the lead article in the first issue, "Hummingbird Ridge" occupies a unique niche in *Ascent*'s history. And a sentence in the editors' introduction to the piece (not included in this reprint) subtly set the tone for our future credo: "The following letter recapitulates in tranquility the personal experiences of one member of the expedition, while a pitch-by-pitch account can be found in the 1966 *American Alpine Journal*."

Some climbers loathe snow and ice. Chuck Pratt is one such person, and we can imagine him shivering with disgust as he reads about adventures in the Far North. His preferred ideal, never attained, of course, is to take a few strides from the car, preferably across a flower-strewn meadow, and lay his hands upon a spire that shoots upward a thousand feet. The rock must be perfect, the ledges must be spacious, and the temperature must be in the low eighties. No clouds allowed, of course.

Pratt's "View from Deadhorse Point" concerns several climbing trips he made to the American Southwest, where he found that many of his conditions were met. (True, the rock wasn't too great, but one can't have everything.) With humor and remarkable insights about the mental aspects of climbing, Pratt leads us on a tour of his special world.

Our next story takes us back to the cold north country. In 1974 our long-time contributor Galen Rowell visited the Great Gorge of the Ruth Glacier, that Yosemite-like furrow that snakes through the "foot-hills" below Denali. Here he and his partners, David Roberts and Ed Ward, found a challenge diametrically different from the Hummingbird Ridge. Rising out of the glacier was an Alaskan version of El Capitan. About 5,000 feet high, the southeast face of Mount Dickey featured three things that El Cap didn't: bad rock, violent storms, and an ice cap for a summit. Rowell's account of the climb is subdued; obviously this climb, like the Hummingbird Ridge, was such a gutsy exercise that it humbled the participants and made them all too aware of their fragility. One theme expressed by Rowell seems especially relevant today: "Climbing can be a dangerous narcotic. Unsatisfied after the first flush of intoxication, many people become real climbing junkies."

We further investigate the phenomenon of such junkies in our final story, "Aurora." In this account Jonathan Waterman and his companions venture to what is perhaps the coldest place on Earth: Denali in winter. (Chuck Pratt would not feel comfortable here.) The Cassin Ridge had never been climbed in winter when Waterman and company trekked to the base a decade ago. The idea of doing something for the first time on a famous route—first solo, first winter ascent—becomes an obsession, a fix, for many climbers. And obsessions often have a way of changing people. Waterman's adventures on the mountain that almost killed him changed his life. Is his obsession over now? We would guess not.

Ascent of Hummingbird Ridge

Allen Steck

It is not the role of *grand alpinisme* to face peril, but it
is one of the tests one must undergo to deserve the
joy of rising for an instant above the the state of
crawling grubs.
  —*Lionel Terray, 1965*

Berkeley, January 1967

MY DEAR C:

A year and a half has passed since the events occurred that I am about
to relate, and even as I write this, I am acutely aware of the feelings of
disbelief and despair that we shared for a good part of the ascent, along
with other related certainties, such as incomparable effort, hunger, dis-
ordered beauty, and, at times, quiet companionship.

It was Long's consuming desire to climb this absurd ridge, ever since
his first visit to the Seward Glacier in 1953, and it was not long before
Wilson and I were drawn into the enterprise, little realizing how intense
an experience it would be. I recall that we wrote Evans while he was
still in the Antarctic advising him that he was drafted for the expedition
because we needed a Neanderthaloid super-being, heavily muscled yet
sound of mind, to drag us relentlessly to the summit. Coale and Bacon
joined us later, both of them excellent men of proper spirit and humor—good sufferers all.

The only photos of the ridge were aerials taken by Boyd Everett in 1964, and they were so dramatic that we simply could not cope with them. The terrain did prove to be a bit more gentle than these pictorial nightmares indicated; still, a mood of defeat developed early in the planning stages and persisted right through to Camp 4.

Long and I came in on the first flight and we took a few passes across the ridge to obtain some idea of the difficulties we would encounter. As we flew toward the mountain, a huge ice avalanche dropped from the crest below the east summit and we followed its course down the southeast flank as it grew to a massive cloud in the glacial basin two miles below. So overwhelming was the magnitude of this mountain that we could scarcely concentrate on the complexities of the ridge itself.

We landed at the base of the ridge late in the afternoon of July 7 and suddenly found ourselves quite alone as we watched the tiny airplane disappear into the vast glacial sea, the Seward Plateau. This was my first visit to the Yukon and the land of the evening sun. I was entranced at once with the spaciousness and compelling beauty of the place. For the longest time we just sat and watched Mt. Augusta and St. Elias in the fading light, but it was Mt. Logan, of course, that dominated the scene because of its proximity. The southern escarpment is over fourteen thousand feet high, the south ridge spanning this elevation difference over a distance of some six miles.

The others arrived on the following day and we were very soon occupied with the task of hauling our equipment up the glacier closer to the mountain. The weather had turned warm and in the days to come the cliffs lining the five-mile perimeter of our glacial cirque were alive with avalanches, some of which cascaded down over the rock with all the grace and vigor of our own Yosemite Falls. For several days we were undecided as to the best way to gain the crest of the ridge, which now was some three thousand feet above us. Avalanches gave a sense of urgency to this problem, but we minimized the danger somewhat by doing our exploratory work from midnight to 11 A.M.

There were anguished discussions at base about our chances of getting to the crest. We had to do something, however, and we eventually decided on Osod Buttress as being the most realistic approach and began to haul food and equipment up this monstrous thing. It was a ten-day effort and brought forth sufficient excitement for all, had we simply stopped here. The Shooting Gallery in the couloir was bad enough, but the two-hundred-foot Prow probably was the focus of agony as far as Osod goes. I shall not dwell on my own problems there, which were extreme, but refer to Evans's diary for the sheer drama of his solitary rappel off the eminence, as it happened some two thousand feet above base camp:

> . . . it again struck me as pretty darned ultimate to start off without belay on a single strand of ¼-inch line on a 200-foot rappel, the top 100 feet of which were free. I used a brake bar with two carabiners and fastened a Jumar to my seat sling for safety. About one-third of the way down my thumb slipped off the Jumar and it caught me and held tight. I could just barely graze the wall with one foot and could not raise my weight off the Jumar. Fortunately, I had my trusty Swiss army knife in my parka pocket so I wrapped the lower rappel rope around my body to jam it and cut the tie-off loop connecting the Jumar to my Swami. This, of course, bounced me down on my rappel brake, but I was able to grab the Jumar and release it and finish the rappel.

One can well share Evans's moment of intense careful thought as he chooses which of the two quarter-inch lines to cut—his rappel rope or the connecting sling. John is a remarkable person. A man of great energy and endurance with qualities of kindness and compassion that make for a good companion. Both he and Long had the "big wall" capability; that is to say, they could operate with equanimity under intense exposure and really impossible situations, where peace of mind hangs by such a fine thread. To be sure, we all acquired a level of composure to handle these things as time went on.

Osod Buttress was a taste of things to come; I doubt that we realized we would be living for thirty days on a ridge where, ninety percent of the time, anything dropped outside of the tents would immediately be lost. It is still a mystery to me why we lost only a few minor things like gloves, an ice axe, some first-aid equipment, instead of something more substantial like a tent or even Dr. Long, whose medical talents surely would have been missed. . . . Speaking of Long in this manner is indicative of the good relationship that we have formed over the many years we have climbed together. He is very ambitious; perhaps his greatest creation, as far as mountaineering is concerned, is having designed and promoted this particular adventure.

Camp 1 was eventually carved out of the ice, at which point we became aware of the ghostly configuration of the ridge beyond. Bad weather hit us here, but for some reason we moved out anyway. There was a compelling sense of urgency with us now that we were committed to the ridge. No time for wasted motion; no time for rest. Long and I fixed the lines to the top of the gendarme above Camp 1. Even before we reached the top, his creative mind had already envisioned the aerial tramway that was to haul all our loads across the gulf between this pinnacle and the cornice above Camp 1. On the following day Bacon, Coale, Wilson, and Long exhausted themselves getting the loads over the tramway and beyond the gendarme, while Evans and I laid the lines up toward Camp 2 . . . mostly in bad weather. The decision to dismantle Camp 1 in favor of an unknown site above was unquestionably aggressive. Evans and Long, in a moment of incisive thought, considered it too rash and shouted up to us to come back, but we were already too far up to hear.

Camp 2 was a desperate and fearful place. We spent seven days there because of severe weather. We could not leave the tents without going onto the fixed lines; the weakened cornice in back of the tents was not pleasant to contemplate. We were not too much closer to the summit than we had been at base, and our thoughts vacillated between advance and retreat. Who of us can forget Coale's wild scheme to tie all our fixed ropes, belts, and shoelaces into one huge rappel, should the need for escape arise? His rappel probably was just the sort of fantasy one might expect of the vigorous engineering mind. Frank really displayed a beautiful positive, fearless spirit at 2, which we felt was surely fraudulent but nevertheless endured. Bacon was performing well considering his rather recent recovery from a fall he took while leading in El Dorado Canyon near Boulder, Colorado. He was new to the expedition game. I was with Paul at the base of the Prow when sixteen loads were hauled up. We tied them on and Evans hauled them up by himself . . . a ten-hour job. The mind struggles now to comprehend the meaning of all this.

Jim Wilson, expedition philosopher and cook, who pronounced Camp 2 safe by postulating that the cornice, should it collapse, would not take the tents and its occupants with it, is a proponent of the "suffering" value to be found in mountaineering, the enjoyment of the sport being in direct proportion to this ingredient. Mountaineering for Jim has a sort of built-in, predictable pleasure value! Another certainty that comes to mind without too much thought is that of the unwashed body. At a lecture on the trip shortly after our return I recall that my aunt, a psychologist, suddenly sensed the lack of cleansing opportunity and asked me in astonishment, "You mean to say that you went thirty-seven days without washing?" The great mental forces that lead inexorably to mountaineering are well known to her, but going unwashed was a concept that she could not quite grasp.

I heartily recommend a week at Camp 2 for anyone desirous of experiencing the deep excitement of living. The view from the front porch was most peaceful as long as the eyes were closed . . . one could

evoke such pacifying images as lush, expansive, green meadows, tropical ferns, soft leaves pressed into moss. Open the eyes, and there you
have it, "contrast and the cult of danger," as Wilfrid Noyce once wrote.
"Observe that pronounced declivity there, James; lovely plastered
snow, icicles, splintered rock and dark evil ice . . . leading into the
depths . . . gives one rather an urge to gravitate, doesn't it? See that
vast glacial expanse; no living thing . . . the only forces at work being
the wind, the caress of the sun and the terrible crushing power of moving ice. A really classic example of what the geographers would call a
food deficit area?" "I would rather be back in Livermore fighting for
fluoridation," says Wilson, his eyes happily closed.

Through the ritual of democratic discourse we arrived at a temporary solution to the problems of Camp 2 by abandoning them for those
found at Camp 3. We permitted the Snow Dome to become our primary objective, but did leave a rather unlikely loophole: should we by
some strange combination of fortuitous events find ourselves across the
Traverse by August 2nd, we would go on toward the summit. It was
all a matter of food; we had to have it as far as surviving was concerned.
By the time we arrived at Camp 3 we had been out twenty-one days,
and while our loads were getting lighter thoughts of food were becoming more intense. Our cache on King Glacier, which had always bothered me, was intruding more and more into my thoughts. I can assure
you that there is no more disturbing thought than that of a food cache
on the great expanse of King Glacier.

Camp 2 was precarious, but Camp 3 was more exposed, though
without the excitement of the cornice, which, incidentally, had collapsed on the day of our departure. The weather turned really bad on
the carry to Camp 4 on the Snow Dome. I recall very clearly that Long
and I had discussed going down to collect the fixed lines below 4 that
evening, but decided not to, as we were certain that retreat would begin
on the following day. You may imagine our surprise when the storm
miraculously dissipated and we looked out onto the incredible Traverse
in brilliant sunshine on the following morning. It was the 31st of July.
Suddenly the summit seemed possible.

A shovel and an ice hammer were the only tools used to carve the
trail across the elegantly corniced ridge, some five thousand feet in
length (the ice axes being used simply to hold up the tents). During the
next two days it seemed as though we were suspended in mists between
the sky and the glacier seven thousand feet below, so thin was the ridge
crest at times. Coale and Long fixed the lines on the first day. The
technique used was novel in the extreme: the first man led on the fixed

rope, which meant that the leads amounted to six hundred feet at a time. It was exhausting work using the shovel and we found that what had taken some ten hours to carve could be traversed after completion in thirty minutes. Small cornices were simply removed from the crest by shovelling them away; a rather fearsome task, for they made such disturbing noises as they collapsed. The rest of us carried loads out onto the Traverse and Camp 5 was set that evening on the first level platform we had yet found on the ridge, a camp that carried the affectionate name of "Yukon Flats," for it was indeed expansive in contrast to the others.

On August 2nd, Evans and I set out to finish the last of the Traverse. It was a lovely day. Most of the time we were separated, because a six-hundred-foot lead is time-consuming. We spent lunch together and it was very nearly a disaster for Evans. We sat with our feet dangling over the edge and Evans had taken off a boot to clear the ice from the inner-sole. While thus occupied he dropped the boot and lunged forward to catch it as it was on its way down to the glacier. I was actually unaware of the drama that was unfolding until I saw Evans lunge . . . and fearing that he was falling, I too lunged and managed to grab his parka at the same instant his fingers caught the lace. Thus he was spared the joy of completing the ascent in his inner boot; a task, I must add, for which Evans certainly was not underqualified.

I drew the last lead, took the shovel and bade farewell to John. The air was still. The cornices and ice towers were balanced on a slender spine of rock, the culmination of this giant ridge that formed a seven-thousand-foot barrier between two huge glacial cirques. A soft mist rose to the east of the crest, though it did not quite reach over the top. I turned for a moment and was completely lost in silent appraisal of the beautifully sensuous simplicity of windblown snow. Equating beauty with audacity has many connotations in our lives; the concept seems particularly meaningful to me as I think back on this particular moment. Such capricious interaction of wind, sun, and snow!—the result made even more exquisitely delicate by gravitational forces. Snow is one of the most lovely manifestations of nature.

Each of us had our moments of rather personal involvement with this ridge and this seemed to be mine. This last six hundred feet would in some way unlock the trail to the summit. Moving deliberately and without hesitation, I began to excavate a path across the remaining cornices and ice towers. The thin quarter-inch dacron line tied to my waist led back to Evans who was now some three hundred feet behind. I was entirely alone. I was deeply absorbed in this work when a small cornice on which I was standing broke with a strange squeaking sound. The sensation of falling is not new to me, though here it was more unpleasant than usual. I certainly cannot explain why my left arm happened to be extended, unless it was some sort of futile reflex action directed toward flight, for which I had the wrong equipment. In any case, it was indeed extended and I found that I had stopped with my arm fortuitously draped over the ridge crest formerly hidden by the cornice. The shovel hung below me on the cord we had tied for just this purpose. I lay still for a moment, watching the broken cornice disappear into the depths, and began to assemble the pieces of my shattered composure. Rather unnerved by this event, I finished the remaining three hundred feet of the Traverse engaged in a unilateral conversation with the mountain, the first that I can ever recall. I explained forcefully, without restraint, that one of us was going to win and because of my shovel and uncontrollable desire, it would be me. Thus mentally fortified, I reached the end, called for John to come over, and together we surveyed the route up toward the summit before going back to Camp 5. The Traverse was completed!

Hunger was our companion now as we worked our way up through Camps 6, 7, and finally 8, just below the summit. We were on reduced rations to protect our margin of safety as much as possible, for we wished above all to be able to take a week of bad weather should it come higher up on the mountain as it did below. Emotional release was abundant on the day the lines were fixed to the summit plateau. The ridge was finished, the exposure gone. A four-foot picket, sunk to the hilt in the ice, still holds 2,400 feet of fixed rope leading down to Camp 8.

As we neared the summit the sun shone on us, beautifully diffused through thinning clouds in the upper sky. Words are such useless things at times, the mind preferring simply to be absorbent, drawing up impressions from all its senses. My eyes told me that Evans's tattered pants were in urgent need of repair; that Wilson's parka could use several trips to the dry cleaners. I saw too that my friends shared my great inner joy of the simplicity of this moment:

> this is another earth, another sky no likeness to that human world below.

to quote a Chinese poet whose lines will never lose their beauty throughout all human involvement on this earth.

Many persons have reached the summit of Logan with visibility down to less than fifty feet, while others, like ourselves, were blessed with unlimited views in all directions, the most lovely being a glimpse

Looking back along the infamous Shovel Traverse. ALLEN STECK.

of the Malaspina Glacier and Pacific Ocean beyond the summit of Mt. Augusta to the west. We faced this magnificent panorama with emotions reminiscent of similar occasions on other mountains; the more dominant feeling bringing to mind the familiar phrase: "Descendamus de monte ineffabile, in nomine Osodi," which, loosely translated, reads, "in the name of Osod, let's get off this unspeakable mountain."

The trip was far from over, however. We spent another two days getting down to our cache in King Trench whence our flight out to the civilized, culinary smells of the 202 Club in Whitehorse was undertaken. Surely the most exciting moment of our travels occurred as the tiny aircraft groaned down the glacier at full throttle, while Jack Wilson desperately tried to get the thing into the air before reaching the icefall which lay directly before us in paralyzing proximity.

You will have discerned that the venture was not without substantial emotional and physical impact. We do not deceive ourselves that we are engaged in an activity that is anything but debilitating, dangerous, euphoric, kinesthetic, expensive, frivolously essential, economically useless, and totally without redeeming social significance. One should not probe for deeper meanings.

I am reminded of an event that happened some years ago. I was with Pratt, Evans, and Long on the ascent of the East Portal of Ribbon Fall in Yosemite Valley. It was after the second bivouac, while Evans and Long were leading the Guillotine Flake. Hungry and thirsty, I sought solace in hammering the date on the rock wall at my back, when Pratt, sensing perhaps my momentary loss of composure, suddenly proclaimed with excessive emphasis to no one in particular:

"I could climb for a million years and still not know why I do it . . . why? . . . why?" he cried, beating his fists against the wall, "am I here?"

I was overjoyed at this vocalization, generated as it was by neither alcohol nor other mind-loosening agents, of a nagging question that had been bothering me for some years. I know now how I should have replied:

"It's the grubs, Pratt, those crawling grubs we must rise above!"

Affectionately,
ALLEN

1967

The View From Deadhorse Point

Chuck Pratt

Embedded in the red earth of an austere and isolated section of America's Southwest is a metal plaque commemorating the single point in this country common to four states. The Four Corners Monument, where it is possible to stand in Utah, Arizona, New Mexico, and Colorado simultaneously, is the geometric center of an area that has been frequented for more than twenty years by a subculture of desert-loving rockclimbers whose attraction to the alien beauty and legend-filled history of the area borders on the obsessive. Why the desert should exert such a fascination on a handful of climbers is a mystery to those who are not attracted to it, for the climbs in Four Corners, with a few remarkable exceptions, have little to recommend them. They are generally short—often requiring less time than the approaches, the rock at its best is brittle and rotten and at its worst is the consistency of wet sugar. Perhaps it is significant that desert climbing presents objective dangers not usually encountered by climbers used to more solid rock.

249

Although the dangers inherent in sandstone climbing are infinitesimal compared to those faced by the mountaineer, it is just these small-scale threats that are more suited to a rockclimber's temperament. Among the traits shared by virtually every climber who is active in the desert is the conscientiousness with which they avoid the Expedition Game.

The quality of the climbing, however, be it safe or dangerous, cannot by itself fully explain the desert's appeal. There have been too many California Desert Expeditions that have returned home without achieving a single climb yet judged the trip a complete success. A desert environment is maintained by an irresistible force whose nature cannot be penetrated by superficial efforts. To gain any lasting worth from what the desert has to offer, we had to learn to put our pitons and ropes away and to go exploring in silence, keeping our eyes very open. It wasn't easy. We wasted a lot of time climbing until we got the knack.

EASTER 1960

We are walking down a blood-red canyon called de Chelly toward the place where it intersects its twin. Everything around us is a shade of red—the walls, looming above us for a thousand feet; the sand beneath our shoes; the river, sluggish with its cargo of silt; even the dog that explodes from a nearby hogan to warn the canyon of our presence. His bark, echoing between the canyon walls and amplified by a dozen tributary canyons, becomes deafening and we hurry through his territory to escape the sensation of having climbed over a neighbor's fence into his backyard.

We pass an occasional oasis of color wherever a natural amphitheater in the canyon wall protects a grove of luxuriant cottonwoods, the bright green of their leaves made almost luminous by the red walls surrounding them like a fortress. Turning a final corner into Monument Canyon, we see Spider Rock for the first time. We already know that it is eight-hundred feet high but it is the proportion that excites us; slender and majestic, it rises from its talus cone like a crimson arrow aimed at the sky. On its summit dwells the Spider Lady, nourishing herself on the flesh of disobedient Navajo children, leaving their bones to bleach in the noonday sun. The Indian legend is a convenient explanation for the pile of white rubble seen on the summit of Spider Rock, and the Spider Lady, the Navajo equivalent of the bogeyman, is an equally convenient device for maintaining discipline among rebellious children.

Slowly we circle the spire to see it from every possible angle. We go mad looking at Spider Rock and so we climb it. I have memories of flared chimneys, bolt ladders whose bolts fall out under the rope's weight, Kamps stuck in a mantel position on a piton trying to pull his pantleg from under his foot, and the summit pitch, a lieback over a flake that looks amorous enough to come off in somebody's arms. For a while we stand on the summit, experiencing sensations that are nobody's business but our own and then start down, the first two rappels producing more adrenalin than the ascent. Retracing our steps out of the canyon we feel the temporary depression which accompanies an exhilarating experience that belongs to the past.

Returning to the cosmopolitan atmosphere of Chinle, we disguise ourselves as tourists and edge discreetly toward the ranger headquarters to find out how much of a stir we have caused, for we know intuitively that since we feel so happy, we must have done something illegal. "Are you the boys who climbed Spider Rock?" We can't tell if the ranger is merely curious or if he is trying to catch two criminals. After a long pause, Bob finally admits to the crime and the ranger invites us into his office for a friendly chat. He informs us that the Indians are infuriated. It seems a conclave of the most powerful medicine men in Navajodom have just completed a three-year ritual of removing the curse from Canyon de Chelly that was placed there by the first ascent of Spider Rock; that now they will have to start all over again and the best thing for us to do would be to leave on the next stagecoach or something.

On our way out of town we stop at the local trading post and I go in to look for an ice-cream bar. The place is filled with Navajos and within half a second the conversational hum drops to the point where I could have heard a feather falling. A shadow stirs in a corner and an Indian built like a buffalo looms above me as I lean for the door. "Did you climb Spider Rock?" he wants to know. "Why yes," I answer, reaching for the doorknob, "now that you mention it, I did. But there's another guy outside who climbed it too." Spread the guilt and the punishment might be less severe—the logic of Nuremberg. "What did you find on top?" Every eye in the trading post is upon us, every ear straining for my reply. It's bad enough to place a curse on the land by climbing Spider but to contradict their cherished myths of the Spider Lady would be going too far. "We found a pile of bleached bones on the top."

Climber leading on North Six-shooter Peak. RICK HORN.

Now it's so quiet I can hear molecules colliding in midair. Slowly I start turning the doorknob but the buffalo takes one step toward me and, demonstrating a remarkable intimacy with the nuances and connotations of a language not even his native tongue, asks, "What do you take me for—a fool?" and the room erupts into hysterical laughter. I gather the pieces of my patronizing ego up off the floor and carry them out the door in my hands.

Not bad for a first desert trip. I get up one climb—the finest in the Southwest—and I learn a couple of things about Indians. Best of all, I want to come back.

AUTUMN 1961

Dave Pullin and I are wandering through a graduate course in quicksand trying to find Cleopatra's Needle. We offer our kingdoms for a canoe at the stream crossings but we're stuck with an automobile and have to nurse it cross-country. About noon we find the bloody spire and start up with lucky me getting the second lead. It is very 6.0, the pins going in easily by hand and coming out just as easily under a load about five pounds less than I weigh. How to lighten myself by five pounds? Strip? There is a cruel east wind rising and the sky is growing dark with clouds. I send the hardware down and haul up one pin at a time. I stand on one and count until it pops out. Fifteen seconds. The higher I get the less time I have to place the piton and get off the thing before it grinds out. Halfway up I reach a bolt and retreat, leaving fifteen pitons shivering in a crack. We'll finish it tomorrow.

Christmas City. The snow is everywhere—just crept in during the night and decided to stay. Beneath the howling wind I can hear an occasional dull thud with metallic overtones, as though someone were gently beating Cleo with a hardware loop. I look out of the car window toward the spire, barely able to see it through the snow flurries. I see my rope slowly swaying from the bolt, and at the bottom of the rope is a ten-pound mobile of assorted angle pitons and carabiners. I mention it to Dave. "Shit, Pullin, every goddamned piton I put in got blown out by the wind during the night. This is no place for an Englishman." We retrieve the gear and, tranquilizing it in a corner of the trunk, drive to the nearest bar.

We are learning that the rocks of the desert are organic. The climbs in Four Corners have a quality of aliveness not usually associated with the inanimate world and for me that quality is becoming a source of increasing attraction. It is fascinating to view erosion as a process rather than an end result, for the wind can visibly alter a spire even as we climb it, and a good rainstorm will dissolve the softer sand into mud so that no two parties ever see the same summit.

Dave and I are disappointed about Cleo and we would like to stay in the bar and get blotted, but we leave when an Indian tells Dave, whose beard is rather gnarled and intermittent, that he looks like a paleface werewolf.

AUTUMN 1963

Shiprock, fabled monument, rises before us in splendor and silence, a tableau from the genesis of the Southwest, historical remnant of a unique volcanic violence which has created a collage of mountainous fluted columns, jagged arêtes and sheer orange walls that intimidate us into silence. Once on the summit, Roper and I can see for a hundred miles in every direction, but there is nothing to see but a vast plain of sand and sagebrush and a dozen miniature Shiprocks dotting the horizon. Then we hear the tom-toms. Or rather we feel them, a dull sympathetic response in the pit of the stomach which we eventually interpret as a drumbeat. Is this the prelude to a thousand shrieking savages circling Shiprock, launching flaming arrows at us? Are they waiting for us on the ground with their fires and sharpened stakes? We can see nothing stirring on the plain below, yet the drumbeat continues, insistent and sinister. We descend cautiously to be greeted only by silence and an empty desert. The drums are silent now and we joke about it, attributing the whole thing to imagination. Even so, we nearly break an axle driving back to the main road.

Moab is a small community in southeastern Utah, founded by Mormon pioneers and nurtured in modern times by uranium and potash. North of the town is the Colorado River on whose shore Roper and I decide to camp while climbing Castleton Tower and The Priest. I am just out of the army and Roper is just going in, so this trip will be our only meeting in four years. Each of us has two years of information and gossip to exchange, so we babble until the moon goes down. We are lulled to sleep by the night sounds: wind murmuring through the willows, the fluttering of a thousand leaves in the cottonwood above our heads, a ring of crickets competing with the frogs down by the river, where the deep currents of the Colorado flow westward to become cataracts.

We are going to try Cleopatra's Needle. Roper has already climbed it so there is little question as to who gets to lead the aid pitch—lucky me again. I am reminded of the last time I was here, with the Englishman, as my pitons fall out from under me, dislodged by the simple action of pulling up five feet of slack. The sandstone, disintegrating with each hammer-blow, rains down into my face so that I have to climb most of the pitch with my eyes closed. When the rain stops, I open my eyes standing on the summit, red from head to toe.

Roper prusiks up, cleaning with his hands, and not bothering to step onto the summit, he jumps into rappel and vanishes. I hardly give him time to get off the rope before I take off too and within seconds we are both on the ground shouting and jumping up and down as though we have just gotten away with the crime of the century.

A new day arrives and we drive around a corner to try Venus' Needle. We fail and instead of recognizing our failure as a sign that our trip is over, we become stubborn and drive vehemently to Canyon de Chelly. The snow catches us on the second pitch of Spider and we can no longer ignore the message. There is a time on every desert expedition when the end of the trip is signified by subtle changes either in our own temperament or in the environment. One morning the sky is somehow different or the sunset will be of such surpassing splendor that no climb can match it. Now that our two failures have brought us to a halt, we pay attention to the wind and migrate west with the clouds.

SPRING 1964

TM doesn't want any part of Cleopatra's Needle. He's heard stories about pitons being blown out by the wind so we try Venus' Needle instead. It's the same height as Cleo and the rock is just as soft, but TM hasn't heard any stories about it so that makes it okay. The last time we were here the weather was so cold we couldn't even touch the rock; the closest we could come to a desert experience was sitting in a theatre in Gallup, New Mexico, watching *Lawrence of Arabia*. TM attacks the first pitch vengefully and I can hear his ribs cracking as he tries to force himself through a narrow slot fifty feet up. There is a tumultuous mechanical clatter behind me and a pickup arrives with two Indians aboard. I am paranoid about Indians ever since the incident in the trading post and now here I am, lashed to an immovable desert spire while some gadget-festooned freak grunts and thrashes above me. One of the

Indians gets out of the pickup and strolls nonchalantly over. I untie from my anchor and brace myself for running. "We're looking for arrowheads," I volunteer. His laughter is profuse. "Well, you won't find any up there. I thought you were just climbing it." Then he gets back in his truck, says something to his companion in Athabascan and drives off, both of them laughing hysterically as they bounce away across the dunes. When I climb up to TM he wants to know what the Indians thought was so funny. "Oh, they thought we were looking for arrowheads." And then TM laughs too.

Spider Rock again. It's been three years since the last ascent so the Indians will have to bring the medicine men back for another ceremony. Rockclimbers have their religion too, but I doubt that we could explain it to them. We manage it in one day this time but have to rappel in the dark. Two rappels from the ground my mind cracks when an aid sling jams behind a block and I'm left suspended under an overhang trying to cope with a pack, two extra ropes, and a camera strap that is strangling me. TM shouts up fatherly advice during the lulls in my gorillaish ravings and I finally struggle back onto a ledge and start over.

This time no one seems aware of the ascent. No council of war from the Indians, no friendly chats in the ranger's office. We remain in the campground for two days and the only visitors we receive are a blind, arthritic donkey and the Chief Ranger's daughter, who is selling Girl Scout cookies. We stock up with enough to last us for the journey home and drive off. If it's this easy to get away with it, I think I'll climb it again.

SPRING 1966

We have come directly from Berkeley to Zion, a mistake, for the monstrous walls of Zion Canyon, more intimidating than those of Yosemite, have subjugated us into tourists. We abandon all thoughts of climbing and turn instead to the trails until we once again dare study the walls for routes. But it is useless; we are too small and the lines we have drawn to define the limits of the possible have not been drawn far enough out to include Zion. The place oppresses us and we leave, thinking that someday when we are younger and suction cups are in vogue we will come back and climb the Sentinel.

Remaining tourists, we enter the role with a passion. Southern Utah contains landscapes so alien to anything in our experience that we feel that we are traveling on the moon. Cedar Breaks, Bryce Canyon, Ko-dachrome Flat—areas where ancient varieties of sandstone have congealed like damp soot into formations so grotesque and fragile that climbing is out of the question; much of this country is for the eye only—great reefs of crimson rock, scalloped and capped with foam, stretch across vast areas of the desert plain like waves frozen in time at the instant before breaking. And there is the San Rafael Swell, an oceanic expanse of crumbling sandstone columns, sinuous and baroque, standing in clusters around Gothic arches, the whole merging into a larger pattern of plateaus and mesas which merge again into the timeless design of the desert's evolution. The horizons beyond Four Corners strain the limits of vision and of imagination. The desert can be comprehended only in its detail, for we are dealing with the sea.

SPRING 1967

This trip is going to be a strange one. For the first time we are taking a woman along on a desert expedition and I feel that ancient superstition of sea captains. "But this is a bird of a different hue," Roper assures me and I take his word for it as we arrive in Zion from Death Valley. The walls seem less intimidating this time, perhaps because we have no climbing plans until we get to Arizona. Still, we don't feel big enough for Zion—maybe next year, since we seem to be growing.

One last try at Spider. It will be Roper's first time and my third. We are wary of the Indians and the rangers both so we use a bit of stealth, finding the Bat Trail into the canyon. At the start of the trail we find a sign that states, quite unequivocally, "No Climbing." "Balderdash," I say and "Bullshit," says Roper and we turn the sign around so its blank side shows and proceed into the canyon. We will sleep in the canyon tonight, try to get up the climb tomorrow and back up to the rim and the highway without getting caught.

The early morning chill is destroying our resolve and we just about rationalize our way out of the climb when Janet contributes her opinion. "You guys are not only cowardly, you're soft. It really isn't all that cold and now that you're here you should do the climb." "Roper, will you please discipline your woman." He makes a fist but cannot look her in the eye. We glance at each other, then at the rock and silently begin to climb. We reach the summit when the sun is close to the horizon, casting Spider's shadow down the canyon into infinity.

SPRING AND FALL 1969

On the rim of an immense plateau high above the town of Moab is a newly constructed visitor center at Deadhorse Point State Park. Like most visitor centers, it was built on the assumption that a modern building, with picture windows and flush toilets, will somehow attract people to an area of scenic beauty which did not attract them before. Certainly the center was not built in response to the pressure of an ever-growing population, for very few visitors to the area ever see Deadhorse Point. Not the hunters who each season swarm into Moab to display their trophies and trade deer hearts for elk livers; nor the tourists whose schedules allow only for a trip through the uranium plant; nor do climbers reach Deadhorse Point, for there is nothing there to climb.

The visitor center houses drawings, graphs, charts, and working models all neatly and logically arrayed to explain the view from Deadhorse Point. Some of the tourists who do find their way to the Point wander through the building and then leave, without bothering to look at the reality itself; just as the tourists in Yosemite, content to remain in the security of the lodge, will watch movies of Yosemite Falls rather than walk the one-quarter mile to experience directly the spray from the second highest waterfall on Earth. Such is the level of their curiosity.

Approaching the edge of the world, we separate to experience the view in solitude. On the far horizon are the ramparts of a snow-shrouded range of peaks rising above the dark red expanse of Canyonlands National Park. Across the entire plateau all sounds are hushed and the desert colors, so bright and varied during the day, are subdued by twilight. Directly before us nothing is visible for the earth drops abruptly into an emptiness as vast as the sky. Slowly the view expands as we reach the edge, where a sand-stone cliff plunges below us to a sloping plain. We are standing on the summit of an incomprehensible series of steps, separated by sheer cliffs of sandstone. Far below, so distant that we cannot see its motion, is the silver curve of the Colorado River, performing its endless task without regard to night or day, the river and the land living in a unity that will last as long as time will flow.

There was a time when the view from Deadhorse Point was free. Now there is a small fee for the privilege, collected by a ranger dressed not quite in Lincoln green. Someone has to pay for the visitor center.

1970

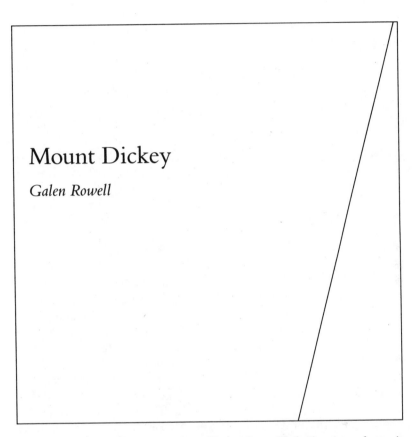

Mount Dickey

Galen Rowell

"There's no doubt that it was the hardest climb I've ever done; it strikes me in retrospect as just short of phenomenal how well we worked together. . . . Psychically, the thing has really gotten to me; I have dreamed for fifteen nights about Dickey. . . . Never has my subconscious been so caught up in a climb afterwards."

I have yet to dream about Mount Dickey. But then Dave Roberts is an expedition cat who has used up many of his nine lives in Alaska. He is also a survivor of the Huntington Jinx, a curse that darkens the history of America's most beautiful mountain. Huntington has been climbed only three times, all by different routes. At least two members of each successful Huntington team have subsequently died accidentally. Seven out of seventeen in all. One of Dave's party died during the descent. Another, Don Jensen, was killed in a freak bicycle accident in Scotland. Dave learned of Don's death minutes before flying to Los Angeles for an American Alpine Club meeting. At the same meeting we spontaneously planned the five thousand-foot rock wall on Mount Dickey for the next summer.

Dave had seen Dickey from a distance during his Huntington expedition. I had actually skied up to the base and touched firm granite—sparkling crystals in pallid quartz monzonite, a granite deficient in the pink feldspar that normally gives warm flesh tones. This technical point would later prove important. Seen from the air, the pink and the pale granite are easily distinguished. McKinley and Huntington are pink; they have perfect rock. The Moose's Tooth is pale; it has some of the worst granite in the world. But I knew Mount Dickey was good; I'd been there and touched it.

I was sure the mile-high southeast face would go if nature gave us the proper breaks. We needed four or five days of clear weather when the wall would be relatively free of snow. This meant June or July and a roulette game with the weather. I had talked about the climb with a group of friends from the West Coast, but as summer neared, each of them declined. By default, our party consisted of Dave, myself, and Ed Ward, a close friend of Dave's with considerable expedition experience.

Dave is right that our ascent went phenomenally well, but only if we compared outlines of plans to outlines of success. On the thirty-second pitch I thought I was further into the jaws of a trap than ever before. I learned an important lesson. I'd always seen truth in the adage, "The only thing to fear is fear itself," but now I realize that confidence can be a more dangerous adversary.

Earlier, I had seen this demonstrated after descending, with three companions, from the south col of the Moose's Tooth. I often wonder if we could have made it by bulldozing ahead with confidence. Many factors had contributed to our decision to quit six hundred feet from the summit. We had spent three days with four men in a two-man tent. A 2,500-foot headwall avalanched immediately after we had climbed it early in the morning. We had sat out one storm and saw signs of another moving in. Food and fuel were low. The rock on the upper buttress was the worst granite imaginable—bulging overhangs with the consistency of Crackerjacks. We had watched in horror as the most inexperienced member of the party nearly lost his boot off the col toward the Buckskin Glacier, four thousand feet below. No single thing had stopped us. Courage comes from faith, not logic, and our faith had been seriously undermined.

On the fourth day we had descended toward base camp on a glacier where several friends had remained behind and were met by a veteran climber, who asked if we made the summit. When we said no, he stared at us and said in all seriousness, "You chickenshits!"

We had been shocked. We later joked about being "chickenshit but alive," but the event had a deep-seated effect on our psyches. Next time, when trying to resolve a conflict between fear and confidence, we would hear that voice saying, "You chickenshits!"

I had always been proud of my intuition for trouble. Secretly I regarded it as more than intuition. Some kind of ultimate rationality had been bestowed on me. I saw life in counterpoint. I solved problems by hunting for hidden likenesses to things I already understood. I took photographs with the same eye for hidden likenesses, the dim outline of a meaning or the strong symbolism of a form. In climbing, I tried not to make decisions by rules of right or wrong, which are at best hollow symbols of judgment. I made decisions by immersing my thoughts until either fear or confidence shortcircuited logic.

Early in my climbing days, logic was most often shortcircuited by fear. I thought if I could only conquer fear, then I would accomplish wonderful things. I was never seriously hurt. Gradually, over a decade, confidence became dominant. Only occasionally was fear still strong enough to make me retreat.

With hindsight, I can think of numerous friends who must have gone through this same process. Climbing can be a dangerous narcotic. Unsatisfied after the first flush of intoxication, many people become real climbing junkies. In a study of risk-taking athletes, psychology professor Bruce Ogilvie concluded, "They are simply 'stimulus addictive,' that is they have a periodic need for extending themselves to the absolute physical, emotional and intellectual limits . . . of psychic ecstasy found by living on the brink of danger." Studying the effects of drugs, Andrew Weil concluded, "Tolerance is not a phenomenon associated only with drugs. In fact it looks as though human beings become tolerant to any pleasant experience that they indulge in too frequently."

Climbing junkies overdose on confidence. The Greeks called it hubris. Climbers gain confidence in the first place because their basically honest approach works. They discover a feeling of karma—not necessarily as an outside force, but a recirculation of their own actions. It becomes a self-fulfilling prophecy. Faith in one's honesty, confidence, and even immortality is gradually reinforced as climb after climb proves successful. Out of faith comes courage, not logic. And courage divorced from logic becomes hubris, in which arrogance etches away the old honesty. The good vibes of karma silently change into the false understandings of hubris.

The rate of attrition of climbing junkies is fantastic. Many die in the mountains, giving no clues about their terminal mental state. A surprising number stop climbing suddenly and become religious converts to various extreme faiths. Their friends are often surprised when this happens, unaware that their junkie companion has already been a captive of false understanding for years. Some survive relatively intact, destined to move slowly through life like some sort of lobotomized genius, searching through dim recollections of something the brain was once able to do that it will never do again.

I was relieved to find that after twelve straight years of Alaskan expeditions, Dave Roberts is not a climbing junkie. He is strongly motivated by fear, but still possessed with enough confidence to get into serious trouble. Like myself, he has chickened out of serious first ascents in the mountains and had questioning afterthoughts. Once, on a major alpine wall in Canada, Dave forced a companion to give up a direct new route and to traverse off because of avalanche danger. Most textbooks would stand foursquare behind his decision. When one person feels the dangers are too great, the party quits. But Dave wondered about his judgment: "Was he the fanatic, or was I the coward?"

Ed Ward is neither a fanatic nor a coward. He is one of those strong, silent types we love in movies and all but ignore in real life. Quiet strength is powerful only in front of a captive audience. Focused on a movie screen, or on a novel page, our attention is forcibly directed to the strange quietness of such a personality. In an actual group, we are most often drawn to people with flair. The comedians and the extroverts get more than their share of the world.

On Mount Dickey, Ed's quiet strength had a captive audience. To this day I don't know how many doubts ran through his mind. I only know that he seemed to make no snap judgments and never mentioned going down. He led quietly and efficiently both on free climbing and direct aid. I felt I was watching a movie in which Gary Cooper was on my side.

When we went to sleep on our first bivouac, not a cloud was in the sky. A few hours later dawn broke on cloud-locked valleys. White streamers crept up the Ruth Glacier and lapped the base of the mountain. Dave talked about going down; Ed and I were immediately defensive; none of us felt sure about either alternative. We had done more technical climbing on the previous day than on any day in our lives. We were twenty-seven pitches up the wall, nearly three thousand feet. With five fixed ropes at the bottom, we had climbed for eighteen hours, carrying the lightest loads we had ever taken on a big wall. A tent could not be pitched on the route, so our strategy was to climb fast and light during a break in the weather, rather than haul big loads slowly up the wall into almost certain storms. With twenty-hour Alaskan days, we expected to do the climb in three to five days.

At the bivouac site I outlined the scenario of going down. Rappelling safely meant leaving double anchors each time. If we left fifty nuts and pitons in place, our Alaskan climbing would be finished for the year. Also, we would be descending three thousand feet through the icing level. If the storm hit, ropes would almost certainly become frozen. We were enveloped in cloud, but occasionally a distant light-show of peaks flashed through the depthless gray murk.

We decided to continue. After several ordinary pitches we suddenly entered an open amphitheater surrounded by high walls of rotten rock. Much of the rock on Dickey had been of excellent quality. We had encountered only one section of really poor rock, and it had been low enough angle not to cause us great problems. Now we were surrounded by rock with the consistency of marbles held together by cheap glue. It resembled overhanging Crackerjacks, like the worst rock on the Moose's Tooth.

The only escape was a doubtful traverse around a headwall on the right skyline. It was Dave's turn to lead. He later wrote this description:

> We moved slowly in a blind chillness. I grew paranoid: you could almost get lost up here in the white-out, with thirty previous pitches below. At the top of thirty-one I was in despair. There was virtually nowhere to go; the rock steepened sharply on all sides, there were no aid cracks, my ledge looked like a dead end. I talked to myself and wasted time searching for an anchor. The impatient call came through the fog: 'Are the ropes fixed?' 'Wait a minute, goddamnit!' I yelled back, knocking in a fifth bad piton.

Soon it was my turn. The only hope was a long traverse. Not to make this pitch would be to admit defeat. Descending in the coming storm seemed impossible. Powered by commitment, I climbed up and out of sight around a corner. A two-inch crack split the face, aiming into an abrupt merger with perfect rock. I placed several nuts for safety, then moved up a short overhang until my hands were jammed in firm rock. At this point, while my feet were still breaking off chunks of rotten crud, I yelled for slack. The rope went up from the belay, then traversed rough rock and went up again. The rope wouldn't budge. I yelled again and felt the rope actually tighten. In the dull acoustics of the white-out, Dave thought I was yelling "rock" and that perhaps I had fallen. Pinned for long seconds on the overhang, I almost did fall before I finally made myself understood. The crack ended and another traverse brought me to the end of the good rock. As quickly as it had begun, it changed back into glued marbles. Anchor pitons were impossible to place. Bolts would have been equally useless. But thirty feet above me was a tantalizing ledge.

Bad conditions near the summit. GALEN ROWELL.

In another situation I might have given up. I was already above good protection, and the rotten rock seemed desperate. But the alternative seemed worse. I convinced myself that I couldn't downclimb the pitch and that thirty feet of sixty-five degree rock *had* to be possible. Up was the only way.

What lay beyond that thirty feet I couldn't guess. It *had* to be better. If not, we were finished. I told myself that the rotten amphitheater was an exception to the rule and around the corner we would find climbable rock.

A few snowflakes sifted through the murk as I took out my alpine hammer. I marveled at its versatility. I had never used it to cut steps in rock. I considered trying crampons, but the rock didn't seem cohesive enough. Pressure on the pick of the hammer dug out a wake of gravel.

I chopped big, crumbly steps—ugly round craters more than a foot in diameter with sloping sides. Each one threatened to roll out my foot as if I were stepping on a bed of ball bearings. Once again I could pull up no slack, so I descended to a rotten stance and began pulling up rope with all my strength. As ten feet came up, I tied it in an open loop in front of me. Soon five cumbersome loops hung from my waist so that I could untie them and provide slack as I moved higher. After ten feet I placed a worthless knifeblade in a crumbling seam. I knew it wouldn't hold but I clipped in anyway. The snowflakes diminished. I was glad, since I imagined that an inch of snow would make traversing the foot-steps impossible. As I moved higher the belay seemed worthless and the climb itself futile. I was a child building a sand castle while the tide crept up a beach already isolated from safety.

After an hour of fear and step-cutting I crawled onto the ledge. It was a severely sloping ramp with grooves at either end. I rigged a complex anchor system of poor placements and figured that I could counterbalance the system in an emergency by sliding off the opposite side of the ledge. My triumph in reaching the ledge was short-lived. Above, the wall was vertical and blank. The rock was so crumbly that I hacked out a sitting platform in minutes.

I answered Ed's and Dave's questions like a bureaucrat.

"How is it above?"

"Come on up."

"How are your anchors?"

"The ropes are fixed."

While Ed and Dave jumared up the ropes, I took several runners and leaned around the corner. I saw thick swirls of fog and occasional glimpses of a snow-covered ledge above and to my right. I had no inkling about the quality of the rock, except that it was much steeper than what I had just climbed.

Ed appeared on the ledge with an incongruous smile. I thought he was not really aware of the gravity of our situation. He seemed happy, quiet, and as controlled as ever. I told him that the route lay around the corner, and just after I lowered him out of sight, Dave appeared on the ledge.

Dave spoke freely about our position. The coming storm. The horrible descent. The unclimbable rock. The new rockfall damage to both our lead ropes. I realized later that I put on a façade and answered Dave's questions with smiles and assurance. I suddenly understood why politicians smile.

In his notes of the climb, Dave appraised my calm smiles in the same way I saw Ed's. To him, "the ledge seemed even more hopeless. A blank, crumbly wall loomed into the white-out above. Galen sat at the far end, as gravel trickled between us into the void. 'Where's Ed?' I wanted to say, and 'What now?' Would Galen admit it, that we had run out of choices? Or would he keep that blithe, cheerful countenance to the end?"

People who project false confidence constantly smile when they are being watched. From TV ads, pulpits, governments, and crumbling ledges in Alaska, the results are the same: things that shouldn't happen are accomplished with smiles. Toys are sold to children by showing the smiling faces of other children using them. Religion is dispersed, not from the searching moral centers of individuals, but from smiles of false complacency in a bitter world. The reality of government bears little resemblance to the smiles of a candidate. And on our ledge in Alaska, in a situation in which none of us belonged, two of us smiled while one showed his real fear.

I remember feeling very detached on the ledge. Everything seemed unreal. I felt a scary power that I could hold life at arm's length. It was like watching my own funeral. But I'm not very good at funerals, either. I try to be controlled. To fight normal emotions. But always something unexpected moves me. A tiny thought, a piece of music, the glimpse of a friend, alive.

Maybe the line between sanity and insanity is whether you start screaming the thoughts that everybody has but doesn't admit. Look at Dave. He's probably not half as scared as I am. People think if you don't talk about it, you're not anxious. Dave's done all those big Alaskan routes; so he's probably got more cools than either of us. But the Huntington Jinx. He might be really out of his mind. If we level with each other we'll both start whimpering. I'd better not agree with him or we're doomed.

We overdosed on confidence. Why did we ignore the warnings? The missing pink feldspar. Dave and Ed said the high clouds were often normal during clear spells. And the amphitheater, with its rotten chamber of horrors. Were we too far in to back out now? What if Ed's pitch doesn't go? What then? Rappel? Wait out an Alaskan blizzard? It could last ten days. Shit, I didn't even bring a down jacket. Just a couple of wool sweaters and a ventile parka to save on weight. Maybe McCarthy was right after the Moose's Tooth failure. Maybe the conditions *never* exist in Alaska to get up the giant rock walls. Sheldon says there's eighty feet of snowfall a year and more precipitation in summer than in winter.

This isn't courageous. It's not even fun. It's stupid. I don't want to be here. Hey, all you phony forces out there: I don't believe in you, but I will if you just get me out of here. I'll admit it. Yes, I am a chickenshit. Just get me out of here. Shit, we're higher than El Cap right now, and we've still got two thousand feet to go. Let me wake up. It's a bad dream. It's got to be. It's one of those miserable anxiety jobs where I've got lead in my bones and I can't get away from anything. Jesus, there are a lot of things I want to do. So much unfinished. It's all happening so slowly. It can't be real. It's not so bad if I close my eyes. Maybe Dave will think I'm resting. . . .

Ed's voice flinched me to attention: "Perfect rock! It goes!"

Less than a minute had passed since I'd lowered him around the overhanging corner. He was back on the same perfect rock I'd touched at the base of the climb a year before. The storm was holding back. It would certainly hit us, but we just might make it to that big ledge only a thousand feet from the top. We could wait it out there if we had to.

This time Dave's voice interrupted: "Congratulations. That was really good routefinding. It might be the crux of the climb. I don't see how you ever figured it would go. It looked hopeless to me."

I turned to Dave and smiled.

1975/76

Aurora

Jonathan Waterman

The finest mountain route in North America has long been a psychological watershed for alpinists. During the 1961 first ascent, Riccardo Cassin and his companions paid dearly. All of the team were frostbitten on the 9,000-foot-high Roman nose of granite that unyokes Denali's south face. On the summit they prayed for their deliverance and left a statuette of the Virgin Mary. Riccardo, veteran of numerous epics in the Andes and the Himalaya, returned to Italy with numbed fingertips and close calls burned into his long-term memory.

Six years later, several members of an expedition paid an even steeper toll for the first winter ascent of Denali: one died and the three who made the top were frostbitten. Art Davidson wrote a book, *Minus 148 Degrees,* titled after the extremes of temperature during their 1967 ordeal. I often defended the team's decision to continue climbing after their companion's death. But after meeting the summit climbers I thought it strange they never climbed together again. It appeared that climbing the mountain in winter—aside from the obvious risks to fingers and toes—could also jeopardize the integrity of a partnership.

From 1971 to 1982, another dozen teams vied for the second winter ascent of Denali. These expedition-style teams stocked camps, dug in during storms, weathered high winds, and grappled with their sanity. Some lost toes; others saw God. Four Swedes bickered and split up. A soloist later committed himself to an asylum. But no one reached the summit.

When Mike Young, Roger Mear, and I planned our own winter travail on Denali, we had advantages over the 1967 climb. Advances in technology had improved climbing equipment, while changing philosophies allowed us to climb the technically difficult Cassin Ridge alpine style, with no fixed camps or tedious load relays.

Mike was a Rhodes scholar just finishing medical school. He and I had spent two New England winters traveling around in our heatless Volkswagen, which inured us to the many cold belays we inflicted on one another. From the beginning, our friendship hung on the ultimate cold climb. We plotted obsessively and viewed all of our climbing as training for something bigger and better.

Mike applied two tactics to climbing from his track and basketball years at Yale: competition and confidence. Whether at the bottom of a climb or the top of the key, Mike shifted into high aerobic gear until the summit was in the bag or the ball was in the net.

Roger called such undue physical exertion "mindless graft." Nonetheless, following the tradition of the early British explorers, he flung himself upon the least-traveled passages of the world. When asked about his winter climb up the north face of the Eiger, he replied with typical understatement: "Right, 'twas a good climb, a wonderful place, you know?"

When asking Roger to join us on Denali, I mentioned that the game was not only to climb it, but to get up without blackening fingers or friendships. Roger said yes immediately.

Roger was irreverent and mischievous. He would ridicule us as we strained at pull-ups or endured ten-mile runs. Mike the Ivy Leaguer was initially piqued by Roger the Queen's jester, who was always rolling another joint, pretending to lose car keys, or sleeping late. But after their uncertain initiation, they soon became a vaudeville act, wholly complementing one another, inadvertently excluding me.

Shortly before our climb, I tore ligaments in my ankle but deluded myself by casting it with a stiff double boot. I frequently had nightmares of falling through clouds and cartwheeling over ice cliffs with a flopping ankle. Or the wind would wrench me away from the mountain as the air exploded from my lungs and I wafted into the stratosphere flatter than paper. I wondered, but never asked, about Roger's and Mike's dreams. For consolation I visualized us stepkicking and axepunching in rhythm up the summit ridge, higher than all of the continent, higher than birds fly, higher than rain or grass or any being of Earth.

In summer of 1980, Mike fell one hundred feet into a hidden crevasse below the Cassin and pulled his ropemate to the brink before he stopped. Mike climbed out unhurt. They retreated, although Mike wanted to finish the route alone. The next year I too jumped crevasses and listened to avalanches pulverize the glacier during my first stab at the Cassin.

Philosophically, mountains had become my college and family at age sixteen, after I read *Minus 148 Degrees*. Although it defied articulation, climbing fulfilled some deeply felt creative yearning. Climbing Denali in winter, I hoped, would fill that chasm of undefined and inexplicable need.

We argued the merits of our plans with anyone who would listen. We said that the southern ridge maximized our exposure to the sun. We told mothers, friends, and lovers—skeptics all—that we would be sheltered from the north winds that buffet the mountain in winter. With all the prescience of air-conditioner salesmen badgering Eskimos, we bragged that February and March have the longest days of the dark winter, and we flaunted equipment designs that should keep us warm at sixty below. Most people thought us cracked.

Among ourselves, we reveled in Mike's bull-like optimism, Roger's practiced hard-core alpinism, and my deafness to the meaning of misery. We were quite willing to push one another to the ends of the earth and agreed to brook no weaknesses. Consequently, when I contracted bronchitis just before leaving, there was no turning back.

On February 17, 1982, we flew onto the Kahiltna Glacier as Mike muttered about white beaches in the Caribbean. As we vaulted out of our ski-plane another team barreled into a second plane, so grim-faced after their failed winter ascent that they stared straight ahead, refusing to acknowledge our ebullient waves.

The wind blew a thirty-below-zero chill through my zippers and into my crotch like liquid ice. Since Mike and Roger pretended not to notice my coughing, I pretended that the spasms were mere sneezes. True to form, Mike strutted around without a hat, remarking on how warm it was. And Roger discovered a *Penthouse* stashed in his haulbag by some joking torturer.

We set up a tent and promptly snapped a pole. The cold would continue to break stoves and lanterns and zippers and boots and cameras. Even removing a mitten to tie a knot could cost you your fingers. Because our cockiness was the only way to disguise the layers of terror in our hearts, we never openly discussed the cold, which shadowed us like an omniscient being.

Denali's winter mood was completely unlike the more benign and sunkissed summer pastels. Even the sunset was violent: the orange light was plucked right off the mountain as it pulsed into abrupt nightfall. Unlike the perpetually lit summer climbing season, the sixteen-hour winter nights meant that camp chores began and ended in the dark. That night the Cassin Ridge stretched taut and arrow-straight beneath the rounded summit bow, tinted violet by stars.

In the morning we put our heads down and trudged into the relentless north wind, pulling loaded sleds ten miles toward the Cassin. We made pitiful progress. I coughed and limped behind Mike and Roger on the end of the rope, tilting back a bottle of cough syrup and chewing its frozen shards. Images of hot showers, warm beaches, and an ex-girlfriend plagued me like a toothache, while my ankle rode fat and unforgettable in its double-boot cast.

On the third morning our ten-foot-long snowcave tunnel filled in with wind-blown snow. Feeling a burgeoning morning urgency, I slipped out of my warm sleeping bag and struggled into my climbing suit, bracing myself for the inevitable hell outside. I wormed my way into the tunnel, shoveling and kicking back chunks of snow into our living quarters.

After twenty minutes of burrowing I poked my head up into a ground blizzard. When I stood up the wind blew me to my knees. Leaning into the gale, I staggered away from the cave and futilely searched for a windbreak. In this nether winter world where fantasy merges with reality, I imagined a toilet flushing; so I yanked off my mittens, unzipped my suit, and squatted until that loathsome wind blew me over and I was back in kindergarten, shame-faced, helpless, reduced to whimpering as I crawled back stinking into the cave. Unwilling to bear witness, Mike and Roger promptly exited and performed jumping jacks in the wind while I boiled my clothing.

Eventually, Mike tried to define the wind. As it whipped and whistled out in the tunnel, he waxed Shakespearean. With a sweeping gesture of his arms he announced that the wind was the breath of God. I never heard anything so untrue in my life.

On our fifth night we dug a palatial snowcave, with a customized "Quick Jonnie" chamber carved into the tunnel. Inside, Mike disgustedly swatted at Roger's clouds of burning dope—Roger assured us he would stop once we began climbing.

My bronchitis dried up and optimism warmed us as we approached the Cassin. Ten thousand feet above, the wind was like storm-driven surf. Its waves crashed and broke over the summit, swirling giant banners of foaming snow over the southwestern face. Our route, however, laid still and taunting.

Early on February 27 we emerged from a snowhole beneath the Japanese Couloir. Roger couldn't get over the bergschrund, so he stood on his pack, reached over the gap, and mantled up. We hoisted the packs up, chinned ourselves over, and pumped our legs, calf muscles screaming under huge packs, spurred on by the fear of changing weather.

It was impossible to avoid knocking plates of ice onto each other. When someone in the lead screamed "Ice!" the unhelmeted followers tried to duck beneath their packs. Four hundred feet up, Roger took a hit in the face and swore violently; his dark blood speckled the opaque ice like graffiti.

We swung our axes and kicked our feet repeatedly into the cold belly of the mountain. We were jumpy, nervous, yelling at each another to hurry. My left ankle felt good while frontpointing, but at each flat-footed twist electrical jolts shot up my leg.

We finished the 1,200-foot gully fumbling with our headlamps. The night hung above as if it were the mid-Atlantic becalmed: vast and black and mirror-still. We tied ourselves into pitons and made our beds on a narrow rock shelf, swinging and clomping our feet over the void with great delight. Getting off the avalanche-fired glacier and coming to grips with the climbing felt so nice that we temporarily forgot the business above.

The stove's flames licked at a pot full of ice. Two hours later we slurped down freeze-dried swill, and when Mike and Roger hurled my home-baked fruitcake into the void, I feigned indifference. We slept fitfully, wiggling toes and adjusting hoods, ogling the full moon as if it could offer the warmth of a lover.

Several hours before dawn we started melting ice for tea. Getting out of warm sleeping bags and pulling on frozen boots made us shut our eyes, clench our stomachs, and flutter our breath. Packing up was awkward with mittens, so we would take them off, make an adjustment, then rewarm our fingers in our armpits; our feet felt blocky and sore and distant.

Mike and Roger raced to the east, axes squeaking in the Styrofoam snow. As Roger led a hundred-foot cliffband with down-sloping 5.8, Mike and I looked away, cringing as we thought of Roger's seventy-pound pack. His crampons raked the rock like fingernails screeching on a blackboard. Then, after a dutiful curse, he was up.

We followed him onto a long ridge that sliced the sky and, to my delight, made the wind hum in subjugation. *Au cheval* along this corniced arête, we kicked steps into the snow and ice for hours, weaving around cornices, oblivious to the space beneath. We laughed and taunted one another; I sang at belays. The mountain gave us what we had come for, and as we straddled it and held it and gently kicked it, I loved it more than I have ever loved a mountain before or since.

On such days you can see every snow crystal sparkle. You can even hear music, although the most elegant orchestra could play here and be horribly underdressed. Some might say that we had too many endorphins rushing around in our heads or that we were surfing a tsunami and staring down at our own reef of mortality, but those people will never hug sun-warmed granite in sub-zero cold, gnaw icicles from their moustaches, or hazard that a mountain and its wind have become a living, breathing entity.

We knew that we would suffer soon enough, but we did not know that the winter climb would prove to be a link to our later lives. Climbing the Cassin in winter put Mike's medical schooling in perspective, developed the pacing for Roger's march to the South Pole, and inspired my writing career. Even a decade later, I am still a captive of this climb.

Our competitiveness was one unfortunate by-product of both the climb and our personalities. The tension surged like a hot current along our climbing rope. If we didn't flash the Cassin, we would have to answer to weather conditions beyond any of our experiences. So, fervently kicking around a cornice, then running across a knife-edge, I pulled Roger off his feet behind me; snatches of blasphemy attached to my name blew past me in a fiery breeze.

That night's campsite was the only flatness of the route. Instead of pitching our tiny tent we jumped into a crevasse and chopped out a snowcave. Later, bathed in eerie ultraviolet glow, Mike and Roger gagged on freeze-dried chili and dumped it into the crevasse's bowels. I forced mine down, hoarding every calorie.

As we slept the wind gusted and swirled and shook at the cave entrance like a wolf worrying a caribou's flank. By morning our sleeping bags were frosted with snow.

There, at 13,500 feet, the climb became our only focus. We were married, chained, and bonded to Denali because a lesser dedication would have been dangerous luxury. Once we climbed higher, retreating during a winter storm, or even surviving a storm, seemed unthinkable. We had to get up.

That day the climbing was superb, albeit strenuous. After fun moves I'd shout, "Boy, that'd be great with light packs!" Roger and Mike replied with glowering anxiety on their faces. We clambered over tawny granite and gray ice, pinching rock with one hand, swinging an axe with the other. We rested on ledges, calves burning, chests heaving.

Because we couldn't afford to rest and acclimatize properly, we all had minor altitude illness. It was a question of getting pummeled by a storm, weakening to the cold, and being kited off by the wind versus dealing with headaches, weakness, and loss of appetite. We took the latter course, and if the cold had only tickled before, now we could feel its talons prickling our skin. Fear actually constipated me.

At the end of our third day of climbing we chopped a tent ledge into steep ice. Since it was too crowded for three, I built a separate platform with snow blocks and clipped into an ice screw. Then I lit the stove, put on a pot of ice, and hid inside my bag. Either gusts of wind blew out the stove, or the pot needed more ice, so I would emerge from my embryonic cocoon, shivering and hating the cold. My fingers turned wooden and the blood crept back all too slowly as I winced and thrust icy digits into my crotch.

When the northern lights first appeared, I dropped the lighter in astonishment. A single ghostly strobe swept the horizon. Then the entire sky filled with tracers. I yelled, nearly knocking off the stove, while Roger opened the tent. Outer space was raining translucent bands of jade and saffron, stealing time and the cold away from us, reeling us beyond the bounds of our banal earthbound existence. Dinner somehow got cooked but had no taste; I no longer felt the cold.

Sleep was an elusive pursuit, so I gave a running commentary of the colors to Mike and Roger, burrowed inside their sleeping-bag wombs. I studied the heavens, raving like a lunatic.

I refuted Mike by saying that the wind is not God's breath, but Lucifer's; the northern lights are the aura of God. Every manmade monument—from Buddhist temples to cathedral frescoes to Louvre paintings—will remain forever artifices, forever cast into the shadow of this night and its aurora.

Although Roger and Mike kept rolling onto one another inside the tilted tent, their grumbling—like the neon glow of Anchorage—was eclipsed by the sublime specter that blazed above and around us. I felt lifted and freed from earthly cares, while my anxiety about the next day was replaced by exhilaration and spiritual awe. Finally, the world was born anew as the northern lights dimmed into dawn.

The days blurred into one another. We grunted up rock pitches, leaning heads and knees wearily on the ice, always guessing how much further. I kept looking over my shoulder, wondering when the Great Fly Swatter in the sky would squash us like the insignificant insects that we were.

When Roger dislodged a boulder from a long chimney, he screamed "Rock!" and I shrunk under my pack. The forty-pound missile crashed a foot away and bounced fifty feet down, then crashed and gathered more rocks, pounding down until I could no longer see them. Ozone filled my nostrils. I imagined falling with the rocks as if I had become the clipped bird of my nightmares, down past the blinking blue eyes of tottering seracs, feeling the air burst from my lungs as I cartwheeled through wreaths of cloud and bounced off slabs of pebbled granite and slammed into the maws of the crevassed glacier below, finally free.

The falling rock had come and gone in a flash, but when fear is constantly thrown in your face and adrenalin surges through your vessels all day, you no longer recognize when you are supposed to be afraid. Roger shouted "Sorry!" and we blithely continued up the chimney together.

As the climbing became less difficult we grew weaker from the altitude. The thermometer read forty below at 16,500 feet, so Roger hid our "negativity indicator" in the bottom of his pack. Though we wore every piece of clothing we had, the wind came right through our customized suits. I didn't envy Roger, who was harassed by a headache and nausea that evening, taking his turn outside the tent like a Third World cur.

Morning fell loud and clear. We packed the rope away and I began stepkicking up a long couloir. Mike and Roger followed on my heels, grousing about the distance between my hard-won steps. So I cursed back at them—our tacit mode of climbing communication. Near the couloir's top, I felt dizzy and let them pass.

Stomach acid clung to the back of my throat. After a brief rest, panting over my ice axe, I raced upward with a pulse drumming in my head. Lost in an other-worldly spell, I stepped on a patch of windslab snow, which broke away beneath my sore ankle and started me sliding. The world flashed around me: distant icefalls and endless peaks and cobalt sky whirled with flying saucer clouds. I jammed in my axe pick

Climbing on the Cassin Ridge above 15,500 feet. DON FREDRICKSON.

and clawed to a stop. Through the fog of my pom-pom head and my now-throbbing ankle, I forced myself to concentrate, then climb.

I caught up to them at 18,000 feet only because they had stopped. We chopped out a platform, then set up the tent, continually looking over our shoulders at the sky.

Inside my sleeping bag I assumed a praying position and whispered, "Please, please, please give us one more good day." In the grip of forces beyond your control, righteousness and prayer come to agnostic lips as if you had been born thumping the Bible. Such alchemy is frequently denied afterward, but during the heat of action it shrinks your skin with all the swiftness of a frigid baptism. No one could deny that Denali rose higher and whiter than any church on Earth.

We slept deeply and it dawned miraculously clear.

Up, up we went. The tempo of the drumbeat increased in my head. My feet turned leaden. I could not find a rhythm, let alone go more than one step at a time. Mike and Roger yelled for me to hurry up but I could barely move, so after cursing like brigands they pulled gear out of my pack to lighten my load. Still, I stumbled back and forth, woozy with Denali's thin air, a derelict destined for the gutter.

Finally, after a paltry thousand feet, they stopped and chopped a platform. When I arrived, their anger hung indelibly, like the calm before a great storm. They could have gone on to the top. Bivouacs this high on the mountain were foolhardy, maybe even deadly. But short of being dragged I could not go on.

We piled into the tent. I was too weak to talk. My world spun and dipped and hovered as I held my head and tried to find my breath. Mike plied me with tea while Roger looked out the door and analyzed the sky; they took turns looking out the tent as if something were coming to get us. I'll never forget their wide eyes, the creases on their foreheads, the tension that shook the tent like the wind. Even sick, I knew how worried and scared and tiny we were.

I had destroyed our speedy climbing formula, so I closed my eyes and let sickness spin me away from the bitter realities into unconsciousness. That night the tent became a frozen coffin. We tossed and turned and rolled onto each other throughout the long, long night.

Just before the dawn I dreamed of drowning. I came alive thrashing and lunging for my sleeping-bag zipper, desperate for air. I sat up and realized that fluid had infiltrated my lungs; I could only steal panting breaths.

While the stove roared, Mike changed socks. His two big toes were black with frostbite, but when Roger peered closer, Mike yanked the socks back on. "Oh," he said, "it's nothing."

Stuffing my sleeping bag seemed to take hours. After breakfast, they left the tent, so I zipped the door shut, steepled my hands together, and begged for good weather and the strength to survive the coming ordeal.

Mike overheard me. He knew. "You say something, Jon?"

"No," I said, my breath bubbling. "Nothing."

I followed their steps, oblivious to the sea of clouds that had arrived, oblivious to the passage of time, and acutely aware of the terrible heaviness of the gravity that repeatedly sent me sprawling to the snow.

After several hours Mike and Roger topped out, dropped their packs, and walked the anticlimactic fifty yards to the summit. When they returned, they were not amused to see me crawling down below.

Mike jogged down and relieved me of my pack. Twenty minutes later, I finished my crawl to the summit ridge. I looked briefly upward, but on this day my success would be measured in survival, not a summit. I could manage only two steps before collapsing over my axe and fighting for the privilege of breathing. The wind was mild but the cold was vivid, and despite wearing three sets of layered mittens we couldn't touch our metal-topped axes. Somehow it registered that my toes had frozen.

We plungestepped down and after a dozen strides I was completely winded. Even the descent of Denali's standard route was going to be a battle. Roger and Mike were too cold to wait, so I urged them onward. After several minutes I caught my breath, although sitting down in the hundred-below temperature didn't seem to improve my mood. I shivered violently.

I had to pace myself. Breathe twice for each step, then rest for ten breaths. Again, again, and again. I forced myself into the rhythm, eyes locked on my feet. It became a game: how do you move forward when you can barely breathe?

Mike and Roger watched and waited as long as they could in the cold. They shouted at me in shrill voices, alternately mad and caring, then left me behind to keep me walking and ward off their own chill.

At Denali Pass I rested a long time, terrified I would fall asleep and never wake up. Just before dark, I caught up to them at 17,000 feet. Roger was curled outside the tent, so I crawled in with Mike. The tent shuddered with the cold, so I didn't bare my skin for more than a few seconds. Even while exhausted I could still enact my preprogrammed warming functions: brush off snow; remove Gore-Tex suit, mittens, boots; get in bag; dry feet; warm toes with hands. I turned on my headlamp. "Wait a minute," I thought. "White toes! Frostbite?" I massaged my swollen bluish ankle and toes until I fell into a sleep racked by coughing.

Strong winds blew in daylight and clouds as we fixed cocoa in the tent. Mike looked me in the eyes and told me I would die if I didn't get down. Then he dressed me like a child. I stumbled off into the wind as they pulled down the tent.

The sky darkened. Taking only three or four steps at a time was disheartening, but I thought I might get down. Mike caught up, then passed me, while Roger stayed with me, cajoling and coaxing me downward. At 16,200 feet I batmanned madly down the fixed ropes, stopping constantly to catch my breath, not sure how much longer I could continue. I tried to downclimb the bergschrund neatly, but in my sickened torpor I fell and landed next to Mike. He laughed—I'll never forget his laughter and the emptiness of our fallen friendship.

In the past, our partnership had rarely suffered because we had always been strong together. For seven years I had envisioned us laughing and hurting and starving and lusting after ice-blasted mountains that no one else gave a rat's ass for. Although we would later be hounded by the media and receive letters and phonecalls of congratulations, as I recoiled below the bergschrund I thought our expedition was a rout.

I lay gasping on my pack. In my delirium I suggested calling for a helicopter; Mike suggested leaving me. No sooner than the words left our mouths, the swirling clouds parted and we saw climbers below. The seriousness, the commitment, and the isolation all disappeared. We smiled for the first time in a week.

As we stumbled down, some Brits walked uphill with congratulations and hot tea. I stared at them, speechless, exhausted, elated. They pumped our hands. We looked up at the mountain wondering if we were dreaming. Someone helped me untie from the rope. "We're alive," I said to no one in particular. Later, in a snowcave, we warmed up and the mountain disappeared. While their nurse massaged my toes, the Brits confessed that when they had first seen us they thought we were crazed because our expressions had been those of asylum escapees.

In the morning Mike was angry, no longer willing to wait for me. His blackened toes mandated immediate descent. Fortunately, I had recovered in the thicker air, so we roped up and raced one another down the low-angled slopes.

We reached our 7,800-foot cache that afternoon and dug out some food. Mike apologized and said the frostbite was his own fault. But I wondered how we could ever set things straight. The words froze in my mouth and we both acknowledged without speaking that this climb had wrecked our friendship. Concealing our disappointment, we glutted ourselves with canned ham and pineapples. Then Mike reminded us of his toes, so with distended stomachs we packed up and trudged toward basecamp in the gathering dusk.

Darkness hit quickly, and we became puppets jerking along to the pull of the rope. Unlike Mike, Roger and I had no snowshoes and often broke through the crust, floundering in deep snow. Mincing strides seemed to give us a few more yards without smashing through the crust. Sometimes we crawled, which was slow, but this prevented us from wallowing. On the final Heartbreak Hill Mike snowshoed ahead to dig out our landing-strip snowcave and fix hot drinks. Roger collapsed several times, and I went back to cajole and coax him onward. He murmured the name of Sir Robert Scott, who had died crawling back from the South Pole in 1912.

Recovering in the snowcave, I couldn't believe we had climbed the Cassin in winter. Roger came alive too, so we dug out a Walkman and listened to Judy Collins while sipping steaming cocoa. The music stirred me deeply. When I realized the extent of our sensory deprivation, how much we had suffered, how far the cold and the dark and the altitude had twisted us, I ducked into my sleeping bag and let the briny tears wash my face.

When I came out, Roger was grinning contagiously, holding his breath. Smoke filled the cave and Mike was coughing, trying to wave the cloud away. Mike said the climb hadn't really been difficult and he had never felt extended; I half-believed him. Roger's lungs were close to bursting and his eyes were narrow slits. He offered me the joint, but I waved it off, because I could scarcely control my emotions.

By our second day of waiting, our various irritations with one another and our tardy bush pilot would no longer permit normal conversation. The cave turned into a soot-blackened repository for all of our frostbitten misery. We ached to leave this frozen hell and endlessly fantasized of the pleasures we would own once we escaped.

Unbeknownst to us, our pilot flew in three Spanish climbers on our third afternoon of waiting. Although he saw our ice axes and crampons lining the cave entrance, we could not hear his shouts, so he flew back out.

At dawn I hobbled out into the arctic gloom and discovered the Spanish tent. At this point I no longer knew what was real, so I shuffled over, yanked off my mittens, then rubbed the tent fabric between my fingers. The Spaniards woke up, unzipped their door, and jumped back when they saw my terrified face.

From then on the only subject Mike and Roger and I talked about with any mutual accord was our pilot's rationale in leaving us stranded in sub-zero anguish. Although Roger had been the only uninjured one among us, on the fifth day of waiting he fell into a crevasse and destroyed his knee cartilage so badly he could not stand. Thereafter, three derelicts grunted monosyllabically at one another, limping out of the cave only for matters of the toilet. Food rationing began.

Fortunately, the Spaniards swore they would not begin climbing Mount Hunter until we were successfully evacuated. On the eighth day, after our *compadres* dug the word *HELP* in forty-foot-high letters, a passing bush pilot came to our rescue.

The depressive ennui that followed our unsuccessful high adventure totaled me. Next to climbing Denali in winter, everything—relationships, work, exercise—seemed worthless. It took me months to re-adapt to normal living. While I recovered from my frostbite (and inertia) in Colorado, a friend loaned me a room and a car, which I promptly crashed into the garage. Because I had squandered all on Denali, I had neither a cent nor a job.

Other climbers heard of our "success" and invited me on the big Himalayan trips I had always dreamed of. I told them that Denali had defeated me; I told them that I had quit climbing and I told them that summits had lost all meaning.

My inability to quit the climb, even with the red flags of injury and sickness waving in my face, can be written off as the shining brashness of youth. But I am still haunted by a partnership that never happened, by a cold with claws, and by a wind so corrupt I could smell its breath as it knocked me onto the glacier, my pants fouled with shit. I did not lose my innocence in 1964 when I saw my grandfather's corpse, nor with my first lover in 1973. I lost my innocence on the Cassin Ridge in the winter of 1982.

In the ensuing years my back stiffened as I heard about other winter climbers on Denali. In February 1983, Charlie Sassara was knocked off by his partner, Robert Frank. Sassara self-arrested on the fifty-degree ice, then watched Frank plummet thousands of feet, spraying flecks of bone and skin and blood on the way down the west rib.

In January 1984, the Japanese soloist Naomi Uemura disappeared after trudging down alone from the storm-washed summit on his birthday. That April I helped twenty Japanese search for his body, but we never found it.

And in the winter of 1986, Vern Tejas soloed the west buttress. Tejas, who had been inspired by Uemura, not only showed the world that the mountain could be soloed in winter, but he climbed it during a stormy February, sans frostbite or epics.

The following winter, Dave Staeli walked in to solo the Cassin. He took one look and wisely proceeded up the west rib.

Meanwhile, three Japanese alpinists, who had climbed several 8,000-meter peaks, were blown off the west buttress and killed. Staeli abjectly snuck up to the summit a day later. Although the Japanese autopsies read "hypothermia," anyone who has withstood the breath of Denali in winter knows that the wind murdered them.

During these climbs, I envied the climbers not a whit; I worried about them a lot. Now I see Art and Dave and Charlie and Vern and Dave infrequently. But when we greet one another in Anchorage, we stop and look into each other's eyes and beam at one another with little talk. We know full well what we got away with.

Climbing changed for me because of the Cassin. Now I like to revel in the mountain's virility rather than my own. I like to say that in ten trips, I have gone to the summit only once, via the west rib in 1981— which is true and feels quite fair.

I like to say that we climb because mountains are sacred places and climbing is a form of worship. We climb because the mountains are our church. Indeed, It—the Creator, Allah, God, the Great Fly Swatter, or Buddha—can't be any greater than the sight of the aurora borealis at fifty below, where the wind hums over a fin of ice and the light cuts right through to your soul.

Roger wrote and expressed the "hollow feelings" the Cassin had left him with. After surgeons overhauled his knee, he returned to Alaska and limped up an unclimbed, saber-edged ridge on coveted Mount Deborah. Afterward, he was nearly arrested in Cantwell for counting his own change out of the cash register, and when he got to Talkeetna his smile lit my afternoon.

Several years later, still gimpy, Roger pulled a sled to the South Pole, retracing the footsteps of Scott. He refused to carry a radio, his support ship sank with their plane, and he went into six-figure debt.

Meanwhile, Mike bagged a new route on Annapurna IV, got married, splintered his leg as a result of a long fall in the Alps, and fathered a daughter. In 1989, just before the sap ran in northern Vermont, we met again. He was thirty-six, I was thirty-two. Encountering Mike that day was extraordinary and unplanned. He lived in California and I lived in Colorado. Our spontaneous rendezvous at the house of some mutual friends could only be explained as one of the inescapable circles that connect climbers' lives. His arrival at the remote place I was staying was announced by four whitetail deer charging out of the clearing and into the forest. When he came through the doorway, surprise painted our faces because it had been a long time.

My skin prickled with terrible and textured remembrances: the acrid smell of falling rocks, Mike's anger when I dropped his water bottle into a crevasse, and the mountain trembling as an avalanche crashed down beside us.

The timbre of Mike's voice was as familiar as an old rock-and-roll tune from high school, and he telegraphed his thoughts before he spoke. Undoubtedly I did the same for him. I could scarcely imagine him playing the respectable faculty member at a Palo Alto hospital. His stately eyebrows jitterbugged above an unlined face, and he had the same untended chocolate mop of curls. I said that he looked no different than before.

"What did you expect," he asked, "an old man?"

Still, the climb would not go away, and we were held apart as if Denali sat between us on the table. We exchanged stilted formalities for a long hour. Finally I asked him if he wanted to go for a walk. He pulled on his boots.

We strolled side by side up the trail and sank into the snow rather than walk behind one another. Neither one of us knew exactly how or where to begin, although our intended destination was clear.

As a preamble, I called it providential that we had met again. Without knowing what my next words would bring, I told him I had been trying to forget what happened to us on Denali. I told him that nothing would make me happier than to go climbing or skiing together. In turn, Mike told me that he had recently climbed an ice gully on Mount Washington, our old stomping grounds. He had stopped midway and remembered our having climbed all of the gullies twice in five hours. Mike said that he treasured these memories, and I instantly recognized the kinder and higher-pitched burr to his voice. We both laughed. Too soon we were standing at the trailhead exchanging addresses.

A year and a half later, at the American Alpine Club meeting in San Diego, we met again. I was surprised to see him because he used to declare that formal climber gatherings—with all their attendant glad-handing and self-congratulation—were a waste of time. But he let it slip that he had come to be with friends. I knew that family dilemmas and city life offered him much more difficult mountains to climb, yet he never breathed a complaint.

Through all of the lectures about other climbers and different mountains, we hung close to one another and endured the weekend. It felt as if we were still relying upon one another, but uncomfortably so, as if still jailed in that putrid, soot-smeared cave during the winter of our discontent. Because of our competitiveness and our numbed toes and our mutual betrayals, we know one another better than I know any other climber, or any climber knows me. As those around us basked in their own deeds on warmer and higher peaks, Denali preyed on both of us. Finally, when no one could overhear, he said it: "You know, we really pulled off a coup up there, didn't we?"

1993

8

IN DEFIANCE OF
REALITY

Editors' Introduction

As we mentioned in our introduction to Chapter 5, in 1974 we offered readers our first lengthy piece of fiction, Jeff Long's "The Soloist's Diary." In the next issue we snuck in two long pieces. Then in 1980, confident that readers appreciated our new emphasis on fiction, we went whole hog, offering three long pieces plus a 35,000-word novella, *Like Water and Like Wind,* by David Roberts. A distinguished mountaineer as well as an exceptional writer, Roberts was the first author ever to craft a long work of authentic climbing fiction.

Simultaneously, we encountered a problem common to many business endeavors: we had competitors. Several good magazines on mountaineering had appeared, and all were vying for articles of topical interest. But mainstream climbing periodicals couldn't stress fiction, that we knew. Advertisers, going for glamor, wanted famous people struggling up famous climbs. Real climbs, not make-believe ones. We relaxed: the way was clear for us to stress fiction even more than before.

The 1984 volume featured seven pieces of fiction, including a retelling of the Faust legend, a Himalayan expedition epic with an Ahab-like character, and another story by our old friend Jeff Long, "Angels of Light."

By the mid-1980s we were publishing occasional "fantasy fiction," stories that approached that vague classification known as science fiction. As realists, we had a slight aversion to the sci-fi gambit, at least as it applied to mountaineering. Climbing on Mars among aliens with puny green heads? No thanks. But when sci-fi is done in a thoughtful fashion, it can tell us volumes about human behavior under stress. Implicit in the genre are the views that humans adapt quickly when faced with adversity and that good will always conquer evil.

At the end of the decade we overcame our reluctance to present real sci-fi and brought out two bona fide voyages into the future: Stanislaw Lem's "Aniel's Accident" and Robert Walton's "El Peligroso."

This final chapter features six previously unpublished pieces of fiction. A few are unabashed science fiction; a few hover on the edge of sci-fi, impossible to pigeonhole. And a few are much more traditional, categorized as fiction only because their authors embellish actual events or create composites of true stories.

Climbers from Great Britain and Ireland have long been among our favorite authors, and we have published many of their works. In this issue we present three more of these eloquent islanders, all new to *Ascent*. Dermot Somers, the first Irishman to have climbed all the six great north faces of the Alps, checks in with "A Tale of Spendthrift Innocence," which tells of one of these routes, the sweeping face of the Petit Dru. Memories of youth mingle with difficult climbing, confrontations with a French group, and a light show for the ages.

Terry Gifford, an English cragsman and poet, spins a mysterious tale of climbing amid the legendary hills of far western Ireland in "The Book of the Burren."

Rounding out our British/Irish crew, Dave Gregory lets his imagination run wild in "The Latter-Day Saint," a tale involving a visitor from Above who links up with a typical group of cragsmen on the gritstone edges of the Midlands.

Robert Walton uses a familiar locale for the setting of his fantasy, "Spiderman." Since the Eiger is the most written-about peak in Europe, it's natural that storytellers would also write about it. Two Americans predict a romp up the sinister face. But even climbers with space-age equipment can get into trouble. Our heroes indeed have a crisis, but high on the wall they meet their savior.

A planet with diabolic storms is the locale of "The More Things Change . . . " Ian McRae tells of two adventurers who defy authority in a sterile world. But what caused these genetically engineered youths to rebel?

Finally, Steven Jervis brings us back to Earth with "Taking Off," a story inspired by a tragic event that happened twenty years ago.

Mountaineering fiction is obviously here to stay. But we sense a problem ahead, one that could bring us back full circle to the criticisms earlier expressed about the authors of yesteryear. When writers not intimately familiar with the nuances of mountaineering attempt this type of literature, they usually fail. Our plea, then, is simple: we ask the active, literate climbers of the world to try their hand at this stimulating new genre.

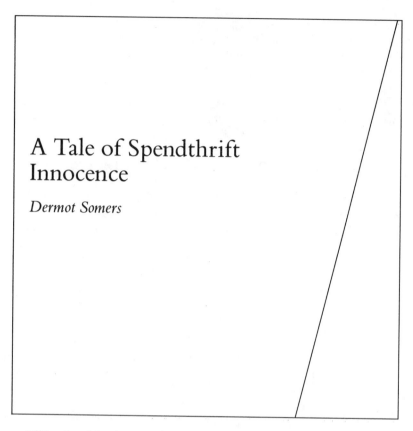

A Tale of Spendthrift Innocence

Dermot Somers

I'll begin with a bang and save the whimpering for later. We cowered near the violent summit of the Dru, Tom Curtis and I, trying to bury ourselves alive on a high mountain ledge. The midnight wind was acrid with the sulfur of a storm. Hail pelleted against the anoraks wrapped around our sleeping bags. Lightning flailed and the slender mountain jolted like a whipping post.

Shall I introduce Tom first, or the Dru? Tom, I think. The Dru has been there forty million years and knows how to wait. Tom was twenty-one then and not expecting to get much older. With five alpine seasons, including climbs like the Walker Spur, the Frêney Pillar, and the north face of the Eiger, he was probably the best of the young British alpinists. Stocky and bespectacled, with a tangle of fine, fair curls, he had plenty of other ambitions. He wanted to find and liberate the joke trapped in everything; he wanted to expose the exploitation of the Third World; and he wanted a permanent suntan for his social image. Earlier in the week, relaxing in Grindelwald, Tom surveyed himself with a happy gush of satisfaction: "Brown legs, north face of the Eiger . . . I've had a bloody good holiday!"

The ledge was agonizingly inadequate. Two bodies in a single grave. Before the storm struck we spread the sodden ropes under us. We slid our feet into the rucksacks and pulled them up—up to the knees in my case. I insulted Tom's stature by insinuating that he could pull his up as far as the shoulders. Our axes hummed like Chinese fiddles in the electric air. Wet hail built up in mounds upon our huddled forms, then slid down between us and melted into our bags. Cold encircled us, bringing with it the insidious certitude of disease. The intense wait for incineration was a slow death in itself. We couldn't challenge the lightning, but we had to defeat the horror.

"It's not enough, you know," Tom pronounced, hiccups of effort in his voice, "to boycott Nestlé because they supply baby formula to Third World maternity wards. Do you know how much tea-pickers earn so that you can drink tea for next to nothing in Ireland?"

The wind stalled. A sense of violent revelation. The air chilled and tightened. The axes hummed their unearthly requiem. "It's coming again!" I warned. "Keep talking, Tom. How much do they earn?"

"The tin industry is even worse." Tom's voice vibrated with conviction and electricity. "In Bolivia—"

A roaring hiss. A flash hit the summit. The explosion blocked our ears with pain. Electricity seared down the cracks. A hundred fifty feet below the summit the charge hit our niche, the gap in the sparkplug. It picked us up like puppets: heads, legs, arms jerking and twitching. Fuses buzzed in the nerve circuit. "Next time," I thought, dazed at having survived. "It must be next time. We can't get away with this."

Tom was on the outside of the ledge and getting the worst of everything. He was still kicking and twitching well after my strings had been dropped. I thought he was overdoing it to get more space.

"Jesus Christ," I swore and prayed simultaneously. My voice wobbled as if worked by elastic bands. "Are you okay, Tom?"

"I think so," he quavered. "Do people survive this kind of thing?"

"Electric shocks are good for you," I assured him bracingly. "They tone up the nervous system."

The Executioner peered down at his two victims strapped to the electric chair in the death chamber of the Dru. He ground his teeth with chagrin and looked surreptitiously around. There were no constitutional lawyers at 10,000 feet to demand a technical reprieve. "Go again!" he thundered. The air was a cold, dead skin. Nerves stretched in my body like barbed wire, my scurrying mind caged in its skull, trying to bail out through the window slits. As the tension tightened again toward crescendo, my hair stood entirely on end.

Tom was cursing out of a mixture of hysteria and hilarity. Some of the Alpine peaks have a little storm-scarred Virgin statue on the summit to irritate the pagan elements. He blamed the statue for the inferno, swearing that the thing was attracting the lightning and conducting it to us. His language crackled with blasphemy in the tense air. I felt the primitive pull of old superstitions in my blood. "Not now, Tom! Not now! Don't talk like that just now," I advised.

Long years of Irish indoctrination had left scars on me that reappeared when extremity pinched the skin. Nothing too embarrassing, no rosaries or anything like that, just . . . a Catholic sense of voodoo. I cast around for a way to explain my unease to Tom, who was actually brought up with the same sorcery, though nothing in England approaches the claustrophobia of the Irish version.

"It's . . . ah . . . it's bad magic," I offered lamely.

The Dru itself is a gigantic lightning rod anyway—a massive statue in its own right.

Hundreds of miles from the Alps there is a particular little town in the south of France: clay-red roofs, medieval walls and tiled towers, olive trees on the stony hillsides, cicadas in the dry light. Overlooking that town is an ancient statue of a saint. Neither cast nor sculpted, it was built of bricks and stones and then plastered over crudely to create a column of a body with a rudimentary head on top. It was weathered to reveal the textures of its rough components—broken bricks gaping out of the belly, fleshy strips of plaster stuck to the shoulders and sides, the face entirely eaten away. It is a terrifying statue for its cruel depiction of corruption and decay.

The Dru has that kind of shape and compulsive presence but its meaning is radically different. Overlooking Chamonix, it is the archetypal column, comprising all the symbols that characterize the history of human aspiration: a monolith, an obelisk, a round tower, or a cathedral spire, depending on the angle of view. Whether it is its phallicism or its sense of architecture that attracts climbers, the great column of the Dru has been a seminal source of mountaineering progress.

The rock is granite, but the color and texture vary with the aspect.

The north face is cold and austere, ribbed, cracked, and grooved. The rock contrasts darkly with the eye of the Niche, a hooded icefield in the center of the face. The west face, with its southerly pillar named for Walter Bonatti, who spent six days and nights alone on its first ascent, is a sheer, smooth wall from base to summit, made all the more elegant by the rougher rock on both sides.

The first time I saw the Dru from the squalor of a climbers' campsite I thought it achieved an impossible perfection of form, something like the magic of myth: the Sword in the Stone. Only a king could rip the saber out of the rock. Hadn't Bonatti done it? He proved that like every jutting handle in history it was not a sword at all, but a challenge to the imagination.

I was impressionable that year, and determined to be impressed. Alighting from the train at dawn, I had been transfixed by the serration of granite peaks sawing the sky above the town. That high horizon, I learned eventually, could act like the jawbone of some insatiable carnivore, but for the time being I was all elation and spendthrift innocence. I watched the Aiguille du Midi engrave its precision on the sky with the point of a needle. Later that day I discovered from a cheap postcard that the exquisite peak of the Midi was a concrete pillar built on top as part of the *téléphérique* station. I felt embarrassed, caught out in a Three-Card-Trick on the first visit to town.

But the Dru didn't deal in illusions.

If an imaginary architect had to design the ideal mountain, the result would be some kind of Dru: inspiring in appearance; accessible, though not without effort, with classic climbs on a number of faces and the potential to challenge new generations; and escapable in bad weather, though not so easily as to diminish the commitment required.

Few mountains qualify under all these conditions, though they may be none the worse for that. Some boast an excess of one quality, which can be a virtue in itself. The Eiger, for example, offers a poor exchange rate between life and death, but pays a higher dividend on success. The Matterhorn—to stick with the public mountains—is all aesthetics from afar, and whoever makes the mistake of probing its instability will only succeed in kicking holes in that perfection. Mont Blanc, I suspect, is more than one mountain. The great faces of its Frêney, Brouillard, and Brenva aspects simply happen to share a broad summit. I calculate with a little geometry that if Mont Blanc were twenty thousand feet high instead of fifteen, all the good routes could finish directly on a pinpoint. There'd be problems of course: those easy routes via the Grands Mulets and the Dôme du Goûter might overhang in their upper sections.

It must be obvious by now that I'm reluctant to rescue those twitching wretches from the summit of the Dru. Tom will be all right, of course: he was born to survive. But shouldn't I do the decent thing by my alter ego, zoom in on the Dru, typewriter clattering like a chopper, and pluck that lanky insomniac off the ledge, in *deus ex machina* style?

But this is an irresistible chance to conduct an experiment, an advance on those infamous cruelty tests when people were instructed to give massive electric shocks to other individuals, with medical assurance that it was for the victims' own good. The torturers were the *real* subjects of the experiment, since the patients were only miming pain: there was no current. The object was to see how much pain people would inflict, under instruction, against all evidence of agony.

Now, can I bring myself to extend the storm, step up the voltage, intensify the whip-flash, and make a true hell of that bivouac halfway between earth and heaven?

Back at the experiment the wires are heating up nicely and the sparks are spitting. I must admit there is a strange temptation to step up the pressure on those unfortunate characters on the ledge, an obscure desire to *make something happen*. It is, of course, a futile urge to shock one of them into a glorious statement, a timeless speech from the dock, a fist brandished in the face of fate. Something, in short, I didn't have the courage to shout when I had my chance up there to challenge death. After all, survival is more important than heroics, and after two hours of torture I had yielded up no secrets other than a feeble sense of irreligion and of the politics of the Left. The storm had appointments with other souls; it packed its black bag of truncheons, wires, and batteries and moved on to the next cell.

The climbers will sleep till dawn, exhausted by trauma and by the second bivouac. And so there is time to abseil down the dangling puppet strings, back to the real beginning.

The weather was perfect for the north face. A cynic would have smelled an ambush. The mountain sweated under the strident cosmetics of the sun like a thawed-out film star back in fashion. Long days of heat treatment caressed the rock, massaging the ice out of the deep wrinkles. Scores of people came courting. Half of Belfast was up there: Eddie Cooper, Dawson Stelfox, Ian Rea—all found the face in a carefree mood, autographing guidebooks, having its grapes peeled.

A clean translucent dawn—that suggestion of a polished glass sky—

greeted us when we left Snell's Field, stumbling heavy-loaded toward Argentière. The sulky statue brooding on the skyline didn't look in the least like a mountain anyone was about to climb. Along the road I fought that trudging lethargy, as if trapped on a milk train passing sleeping villas, dewy orchards, and shuttered bars. The real morning streamed past me in its urgent air—light, color, excitement sped by on another track. I felt the illusion of sliding into reverse. Tom was leaving me behind too, with the reproachful air of one who has never quite learned to be angry. I tilted forward on my toes and kicked a gaping hole in my lassitude.

The climb began at the base of a broad gully, three hundred feet high. A long stripe of fresh snow bedded the groove, rock-ribs showing through. A lip of ice fading out on a brief rock bulge barred entry. Tom hacked a few moves upward, dispensed with the axe, and pulled up on rock, crampons scraping and hooking. Water flowed as the fresh snow melted. The moves were unexpectedly hard. I locked my hand between ice and rock and groped uneasily for a hold.

Scrabbling overhead, a flurry of small stones introduced company. Three bedraggled climbers had bivouacked overnight on a ledge system to make an early start and were outraged by nocturnal snow. They were going down, they informed us in shivering French, and formed a low opinion of our judgment when we continued. But we, after all, had spent both a dry night and a cable-car fare. As other groups of refugees plunged down past us, it was obvious that a general exodus was underway. We were pleased with the thinning out of the queue.

There was no longer any impression of the inaccessible magnificence of the Dru. It was simply another mountain-shaped cliff. After partnership on the Walker Spur, the Frêney Pillar, and the Eiger, our procedures were automatic: brief immersion in a lead, then while Tom climbed I contemplated savagery and civilization as proposed by the wild aiguilles and the teeming valley below.

The roofs of Chamonix glowed with miniaturized perfection in the depths of the daily world. The sinuous river and the gleaming motorway flowed together through the long, tight valley. I swung a size eleven boot out over the void and casually obscured a vast area of civilization. I experimented thoughtfully, stamping out the town of Chamonix, and then, with a quick jab of the heel, I stubbed out Snell's Field.

Paying out the rope to Tom, who was involved with a steep and intimate crack, I wished I was down there, sitting in a warm bar with *un grand café au lait* in hand and a flaky croissant to dunk, with the climb wrapped up in a neat cassette of memory playing away quietly behind the eyes and ears.

Half an hour later, I was balanced in a steep, wet groove, the minutes leaping off the face like rats, wishing I had an extension ladder. I was supported by one boot braced with an air of strained credibility against a rib of wet rock. The flared groove contained a malevolent core of old ice that left just enough space for a fist and a boot. I scrounged and grudged painfully up the groove, my back lodged against one gurgling wall and a sodden knee genuflecting piously against the other. At the top I hauled onto a flooded ledge, soaked, scraped, and enraged.

Ladders were on my mind because the situation recalled a filthy day spent painting the gutters of a Dublin school. Water and dirt had turned the paint to greasy sludge. You can save time on a long ladder by bouncing it at the top so that it jerks along the wall and gives a wider reach, while the bottom remains in the same position. Tilt too far and the ladder will slip, of course, but if there is a gutter or a windowsill to hang on to, you can lean to a ridiculous extent. I had reached the angle of absurdity, clinging to the gutter and painting away, when the wind whipped the ladder out from under me. As it went, I grabbed the lip of the gutter and hand-traversed along it until I got my knees on a windowsill. Water poured down my sleeves and trickled inquisitively into my armpits, while the window was opened out against me from within by an entertained audience.

I stood dripping on the stance above the icicle and the wind skinned me like a knife-thrower's model. The weather was going downhill. Chamonix exuded a desperate nostalgia as mist erased it like a lapse of fond memory.

I shouldn't shift focus again, since mountain and story are already littered with stranded *doppelgängers,* spitting images awaiting deliverance from ledges, windowsills, and waterfalls. As I write this in an old cottage in County Wicklow, however, I'm no better off than any of them. It's pouring rain outside, and the roof is sieving it mournfully into buckets in the kitchen. The vast, cranky fireplace has its priorities obstinately reversed: the heat goes up the chimney and the smoke comes into the livingroom. At intervals I have to stand at the back door for air and relief, sprayed by rain and wreathed in smoke. There is no comfort here at all for the man on the mountain, shrouded in mist and spat upon by the elements.

There was an airlock in the plumbing too and earwigs were living in the taps. I coupled an aqualung to the sink and gave the system a blast at two thousand pounds per square inch. It cleared the blockage and the earwigs, but now there's an inch of rusty water on the bathroom floor. Yes, and the rent is due. I wish I were back on the mountain; it might take my mind off things. Meanwhile, the fellow shivering on the ledge wishes he were back here! People are never satisfied.

Mont Blanc and the higher aiguilles were still clear of the weather and Tom was fully in favor of going on. That, I pointed out severely, was suitable sentiment for an effervescent youth who had climbed the icicle with a rope from above. But I was less optimistic. The effects of last night's storm would be worse the higher we climbed. And how could we trust a forecast that had already betrayed us once? With all the hard climbing still above, there was no guarantee of the summit that day. Still, I too wanted to go on—Tom's great ability and enthusiasm, and the deviousness I had developed with age, fitted us for this route in almost any condition.

Onward then! We turned heroic eyes toward the heights once more and blinked blindly into the mist.

We were not alone.

A pair of voices—one faint, the other frantic—had been yodeling above us for some time. Burrowing vertically between fog and rock, I arrived below a blocky wall just as a large rump and rucksack disappeared overhead. French climbers dress to a high standard of elegance, but this rump was clad in a rough boiler suit. The rucksack bulged prodigiously and was saddled like a hiker's backpack with a roll of canary-yellow Karrimat. The scene had the mock-serious quality of a cartoon: hapless hitchhiker takes a wrong turn in the fog, the road gets steeper and steeper, until he is dangling by a finger from an overhang, still thumbing hopefully. I pursued him and he lurched upward, blunt boots scrabbling, the voice hissing desperately for a tight rope.

"*Avale! Avale!—Merde!—AVAAALE!*"

The slack rope jerked suddenly—a lasso coming tight on a bullock—and he was hauled bucking and kicking over the horizon. I was intrigued, as by a circus act when a bucket-footed clown wobbles on a tight rope, but the steep pitch ahead demanded full concentration. Its massive ice-bedded flakes stuck out at eccentric angles. Some of the bigger blocks made minor overhangs. A hundred feet higher I reached a flat ledge, hooked my fingers over the rim of the cartoon frame, and squeezed into the picture beside the portly boiler suit. I saw his slimline partner silhouetted above us, entirely unburdened by any sack at all. The mystery cleared. The dungaree-man was carrying the lot: two sets of bivy-gear, double raingear, all the food. And since the leader was wearing a light pair of rock shoes, his heavy boots, crampons, and ice axe must also be in the bag.

The man in the boiler suit welcomed company with a broad, red-faced beam.

"*Est-ce que vous avez fait bivouac sur les terrasses la-bas?*" I inquired amiably.

A flash of teeth. "We haf bifouack on ze terrass las' night," he informed me.

My sympathy hardened instantly to resentment. If there is one linguistic conceit I cannot stand, it is that continental habit of speaking English to foreigners no matter what the foreigner wants to speak. In resorts like Chamonix and Zermatt the shops employ staff who can speak Anglo-American, and they are so anxious to prove their competence in threadbare slang that they will speak nothing else no matter how earnest your French or German may be. The hitchhiker was one of these.

"Where you are from?" he articulated proudly.

"*Irlande,*" I gritted. "*Je suis Irlandais!*" with a pronounced accent on the *Irl* since nine people out of ten hear *Hollande* instead. If they grasp the Irish angle they differentiate between North and South, Catholic or Protestant, often accompanied by gunfire mime. We are characterized internationally by the twin terrors of violence and religion.

"Ah! I haf' been many time in Amstairdame."

"*Est-ce qu'il y avait beaucoup de neige pendant la nuit?*" I interrupted the autobiography.

"Zere was much snow," he assured me with satisfaction, as if the place wouldn't have been the same without it.

I busied myself bringing Tom up, and soon the Anglo-garrulous Jacques was winched creaking and panting off the ledge like a fat pantomime-fairy with yellow rubber wings.

"We'll have to pass them," I warned Tom as he prepared to lead through. "I'll be damned if I'm going to listen to pidgin English from here to the top." A lot of British climbers would have taken this as a reflection on their own conversation, but Tom let it go.

The rock was continuously sheer and difficult now, a grainy gray-green granite with clean corners and cracks, and there was no chance of passing the pair ahead. Jacques and I worked out a stubborn compromise: he practiced his foul English, and I responded in what I hope was slightly less atrocious French. Tom led our rope with panache up the severely exposed Lambert Crack, a thin slit in a solid wall, hounding Jacques' heels, and I stepped up the pressure on the next pitch. Unfortunately, Jacques' partner wasn't always responsive to Jacques' panted needs—"*Avale, imbecile! AVALE!*"—and at times a dribble of slack rope gathered on his paunch while he hung by his fingertips and hissed for tension.

Finally, we seized our chance to pass when the route branched in the uncertain mist. I jumped into one of those evil grooves that appear to have been built upside down, and emerged somewhere along the lower edge of the Niche. Visibility was down to twenty feet and the thick snow cover blended with the mist to rob the eye of focus. Progress in the haunted half-light was arrested by huge warts and carbuncles of rock, rheumy with ice.

We were lost. A voice mewed piteously out in the mist. He wasn't speaking English now, I thought spitefully. Tom was brilliant on this kind of terrain. Being lost suited him: he could pick the hardest way ahead and pretend it was the only way to go. The guidebook had nothing to offer; I shoved it down my jumper and sent Tom out into the unknown with the air of Columbus throwing pigeons at the New World. He ducked beneath an overhanging bulge and was gone. I was left with the frail rope, the sling that bound me to a flake, and the shapes that came and went in the pale fog. The mountain was no more substantial than a pillar of cloud and snow scoured by the wind. Hunched within myself, I brooded. The human body has reflexes common to all creatures, and a mountaineer on a windswept stance bears a marked resemblance to a hen on a windy day: clucking disconsolately, the head withdrawn, elbows clamped against the ribs like scrawny wings, alternate legs doubled up under the body. Every now and then the querulous head extends a squawking inquiry into the outside world.

Eventually Tom called and I thawed into movement. I'd love to have left an egg on the foothold in a salute to the surreal. Instead, I lost the guidebook. Ducking under the bulge, I saw it swoop into obscurity, covers spread like wings. It was lucky we had maintained diplomatic relations with the French! Guidebooks, I realized, were above language barriers. I listened ardently for Jacques' voice in the mist. Beyond the ice, at the base of the pillar, lay a sloping terrace, broad enough for a few uncomfortable bodies. The wind screeched into a higher register and a spatter of hail raked the ledge. The weather was hardening, breaking up into pellets of its own solidity. The day's climbing was over, and we settled into an amicable ambush for the French.

"Allo! Can you 'elp me, please?"

Thus, as we had been warned in Catholic myth, the voices of damned souls cry for release from Hell, and must be kicked in the teeth by the righteous.

"Ici," we yelled, "Ici! A droite!"

Jacques stumped out of the mist like a refugee from purgatory and cramponed across the ice.

"Où est le sac, Jacques?" I quipped, wondering if the pack had joined our guidebook at the foot of the Dru, and if it had, if their book was in it.

"'Enri 'as ze sac now." Jacques beamed with the satisfaction of justice done. He squatted on the tiny portion of ledge we had allowed for their occupation and anchored himself with extraordinary thoroughness. No danger of him being pulled off his perch.

"'Enri 'as no—" He pointed at his feet in explanation.

"No crampons?" We were surprised at such an oversight.

"No boots," Jacques corrected calmly.

"No boots!" We gaped at each other in amazement. No boots on the north face of the Dru, on a second bivouac, before a second storm?

"'E 'ave only 'ees—"

"Rock boots," we filled in automatically, still stunned. No crampons, no boots. How was he going to tackle the icy cracks and chimneys above? Worse still, how would he descend the crevasse-ridden Charpoua Glacier on the other side? Were we being cast as guardian angels when we were looking for guides ourselves? The blind leading the blind—we were going to need a description in Braille.

As Jacques began to take in the rope, bawling instructions at Henri, an impossible suspicion struck me. Jacques was advising Henri to climb *down* first and traverse lower across the rock. That could only mean. . . .

"Est-ce qu'il a un piolet?" I asked faintly.

"'E 'ave no axe," Jacques sighed, as if he too were beginning to find Henri's nakedness a little trying. Invisible offstage, Henri swore that he'd be damned if he would descend any of the frightful rubbish he had just climbed. He insisted he could traverse the ice in his rock boots. Jacques was adamant that he couldn't do anything of the sort without ice tools. He promised Henri that when he fell off his body would swoop in a great bruising arc across the Niche and smash at high speed into the side of the pillar a hundred feet below us.

I knew this scene from somewhere else. The dialogue and the characters were absurdly familiar: any moment now the mist would sweep aside like a cinema curtain and something wildly incongruous would come trundling up the ice—not a hen or a hitchhiker but . . . a *grand piano!* That was it—Laurel and Hardy mullocking the piano up the thousand steps all over again.

There was something simultaneously disastrous and invincible about this pair—the rubberbones of roughhouse comedy. I felt that if Henri took his hundred-foot swing and pancaked onto a rock he would simply raise his little bowler hat of a helmet, measure the lump on his head, stalk up the rope, and punch Jacques on the nose, who would promptly somersault a hundred feet down the north face only to spring back like a Jacques-in-the-box, and . . .

I settled down to enjoy myself, and then Tom spoiled it all. He put on his crampons, took both our axes, and disappeared into the mist to rescue Henri.

Henri and Jacques, it happened, had embarked on the north face of the Dru under the impression that it was a straightforward rock climb. They knew nothing of the complex descent. Henri was a good rock-climber and Jacques wasn't bad on ice, so here they were. They had light sleeping bags, already soaked from the previous night. They had no stove and little food, but they gave off a fine sense of tolerance for their shortcomings. The final touch of distinction came with a pair of old-fashioned cycling capes that buttoned around the neck and covered the sleeping bags in condensation. We gave them tea and studied their route description. It was a French pamphlet notable for the number of synonyms it offered for the word *fissure.* Everyone knows the north face of the Dru is composed of slits, slots, fissures, cracks, grooves, chimneys, and off-widths, but this pamphlet was a full page from a thesaurus.

It snowed intermittently through the long night, but the weather cleared before dawn. Shining snow amplified the lucid brilliance. The Vallot Hut, a gleaming trinket, winked on the shoulder of Mont Blanc. Chamonix had sunk to an immeasurable depth below the huge headland of the mountain. Lightly hazed in blue mist, the tiny, clustered town—pale pebbles and mica flashes of light—was no more than stony shingle at the bottom of a deep pool. It had sunk beneath us while we tunneled up into the cloud, and now it was submerged in a slow, fluid light. The current of the hours flowed into the high end of the valley, meandered through towns and tents, and washed wasted time and silted light down and out into the lowlands.

The first *téléphérique* cabin spidered down from the Midi: alpinists descending from the Vallée Blanche. If they considered the iced confection of the Dru, they quietly congratulated themselves on gliding down to hot coffees, warm tents, and dry clothes.

I felt the resentment of the bound against the free. There was an ice pitch ahead to avoid a snow-plastered pillar. We must bring Laurel and Hardy with us, not only for humanitarian reasons but also to share their guidebook. I chopped and kicked up the ice, warming the blood with a flurry of action when suddenly, in that vast purity of shining altitude, the resentment burst into a flare of exultation. Breakfast sugar in the bloodstream, of course, but it had a spiritual thrust far above biochemistry. I could have rung hosannas and echoes from the great belfry of the Niche. Belayed, I hauled in the innocent climbing rope, summoning the faithful to a celebration. As a small altar boy, it was my job to ring an old church bell with a rope that hung down the gable into the Gothic porch. A few brazen clangs were sufficient, but one splendid morning I got carried away by the mighty clamor I was arousing and the way the rope hauled me high into the echoing air with every ring and then hurled me back to earth again. I could no more stop than I could resist the temptation to pull a fairground swing-boat high enough to flip full circle over the bar, human contents stuck to the upended seats like that mystery of upside-down water in a whirling, arms-length bucket.

The valve for a fit of jubilation is a song at full volume, and I cracked the crystal air with Ewan McColl's great anthem of hard labor, "Kilroy Was Here."

> Who was here when they handed out the heavy jobs? Jobs with the hammer, the pick and shovel.

I substituted *crampons* for *shovel* under the circumstances. Tom came groping up the rough, easy-angled ice.

> Who was here in the furrowed field stooped over? Pain shapes a question in bone and muscle.

Tom had the French rope in tow, and I brought them up while he jumped into the golden cracks overhead. Crafty Jacques held onto the route description for an exercise in translation. Every time I asked, he translated laboriously with the hangdog hesitancy of a pupil who hasn't learned his vocabulary but is determined to bluff it out.

"Take ze fissure . . . ze craque? on ze right . . . no, ze left, I tink . . ."

"*%£@! Donnez *£% moi!" I snarled at last, and grabbed the page.

Snow, ice, and error slowed progress to a crawl. There was a tedium to the terrain now, best left undescribed, or catalogued in weary syllables: long, dull, slow, wet, cold, steep.

A hole, often exaggerated as a tunnel, led through a thin ridge a couple of hundred feet below the summit. Crawling through the little hatch, I emerged on the Quartz Ledges on the other side of the mountain. Tom's shoulders and rucksack jammed. For a moment his curly, grinning head protruded, outlined in the northern light, and he seemed to wear the rim of the hole like the frame of a baroque portrait.

In a little niche on the Quartz Ledges lay a couple of characters sound asleep, smoldering with sulfurous dreams. We kicked them back to the start of the story and settled down in their places under a sky pregnant with apocalypse.

Les Hautes Alpes: Spectacle en Son et Lumière. The performance began at dark, with muted pyrotechnics in the distance and spotlights warming up and flickering across the walls and ramparts of this Acropolis among mountain ranges. Tympanic voices rumbled the ritual responses among the ruined temples of the aiguilles. Lightning outlined quivering horizons. The storm drew in its acolytes toward the great central altar, and the focus concentrated on Mont Blanc, the very Parthenon itself, the ice-marbled temple of the Alps. A subtle crown of lightning glowed behind the peak.

The scene was prepared for some unearthly set-piece now, a *tableau vivant* to invoke the temple goddess Athena, who sprang by parthenogenesis from the cleft skull of Zeus. But within the burning chamber of the storm an infernal metamorphosis occurred: the spotlight, arclights, footlights, and floodlights forked around the laboratory; instead of Athena, the mountain gave birth to a fire-and-ice Medusa, with lightning snake-locks to turn observers if not to stone, at least to ash.

"By the way, congratulations!" interrupted Tom.

"Congratulations? For what?"

He broke into an excited sports commentary: "Mr. Dermot O'Murphy, first 'Oirishman' to climb the six north faces!"

Ah, yes, I thought, shivering in my bag: *This is your Life!* And isn't it wonderful?

The magnificent menace of the *Son et Lumière* spilled over the edge of the stage—the occupying Turks stored ammunition on the Acropolis, and in 1645 lightning struck the powder. Then they placed their guns in the shattered walls. Massive eruptions ripped through the orchestra pit, drums and cellos burst like balloons. Flash-fires raged in the front seats. The audience fled up the aisles, out the exits, into the *téléphériques*. Modern theater is okay, but who wants audience participation in a Greek tragedy? Who wants to go home with their eyes poked out? The flames were racing through the balconies now and licking up into the gods.

The sports commentator came on again: "The award was conferred posthumously on O'Murphy."

At daylight we began the descent. Jacques and Henri, further along the ledges, were having a lie-in, so we left them there in their cycling capes and bowler helmets. Another fine mess. The abseils went smoothly, stitches of rope unraveling, and soon we were on the knife-edge of the Flammes de Pierre. The blazing sun stripped the sheets of snow off the rocks like an angry host whisks the bed-linen off of an unwelcome guest. We left the hungry ice behind, shuffled down weary paths, and scrabbled across the endless gravel to the Mer de Glace. I loathed the mountains and every atom in them. After every hundred yards of jarring descent I collapsed on a rock, cursing the gratuitous idiocy of mountaineering and the pangs of hunger, thirst, and pain.

Tom pinned down a mirage and filled a mug. Life held nothing more exquisite than the icy treble of water in the throat against the pounding bass of the blood.

And still the Mer de Glace to ford, threading a path across the ice in a maddening labyrinth of crevasses. Then up and up, up the far side to Montenvers, boots dragging, sweat dripping, and the last train missed.

Hunger drove us at a run toward the empty station. On the platform, above the sweeping ice, in spite of the disapproving Dru and the outraged Jorasses, we plunged headfirst into the garbage bins. Buried to the waist, Tom rooted out six tins of pâté, four cartons of yogurt, and a hard-boiled egg. The egg was unshelled and delicately dusted with Gauloise ash. Thoughtfully picking orange peel out of a salvaged cheese roll, I gazed around me at the savage splendor.

Satisfaction resurged as pain subsided. I savored again the old pieties: on top of the world . . . purity and peace . . . at one with nature . . . bird's-eye view . . . lords of creation . . . because it is there . . . trackless wastes . . . untrodden summits.

I wiped the cigarette ash off the finest egg that was ever laid and bit into it pensively. That humpy hulk of a mountain over there behind the Dru, the huge Aiguille Verte, we hadn't climbed that yet. What about the Nant Blanc face, then over the top, and down that huge snow-gully—see it there raking down from the summit: the Whymper Couloir—to finish the season with a bang?

1993

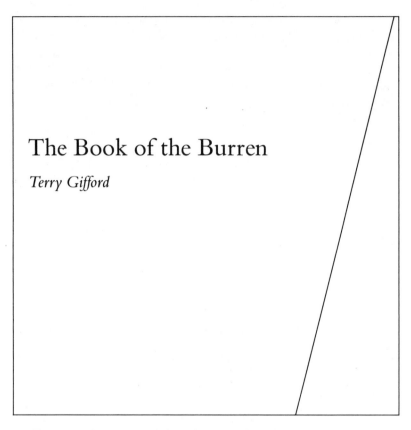

The Book of the Burren

Terry Gifford

The two pilgrims paused at the top of the hill. They had come a long way. Now, below them, where the road wound down to the sea, where the Aran Islands could almost be touched offshore—there at last lay the Burren, the fabled limestone land on the western edge of Ireland.

They had come in search of a book. Many by now had been moved and uplifted by the Book of Kells, but few had actually seen the Book of the Burren. It was rumored that the illuminations of the Book of the Burren were even more vibrant and more varied, skillfully linking the natural and the unnatural in images woven even more intricately around the text. Each spring, during the season of pilgrimages, travelers came from afar seeking the book.

The two pilgrims rested by the Labyrinth Stone at the top of the hill. Carved into the sparkling granite of the strange waymarker stone was a Celtic maze of concentric circles. It might have been a map of the landscape of lanes in the Burren below. It might have been a warning of the water-worn labyrinth that lay under the Burren. Or was it a sign to pilgrims nearing the end of their journey that showed them the meaning of the pilgrimage itself, a stone-carved symbol of their inner journey, one which could not simply end upon reaching the West? None knew the lost message of the Labyrinth Stone; it had come to be accepted as part of the mystery of the place. But, where within this limestone maze would Ronan and Kevin find the Book of the Burren?

Long after their return, Ronan had asked of other pilgrims they had met on those western cliffs, "And what do you remember best of the Burren?"

"The Dolphins," said Stella.

"The Guinness," said Johnny.

"And the rock," said Stella, remembering that she spoke to a scribe of their stone-climbing sect. "Quite technical but sharp-edged, with friction and fossils. Did you climb Pis Fliuch after we left? The only rightly recorded route we followed all week."

"But someone should record," insisted Johnny to Ronan, "that those boulders at the bottom of the Mirror Wall have been shifted back by the storm tides. Few of those routes have been reclimbed by their new starts."

The pilgrims had heard tales of the ferocity of the winter storms from Calvin Torrans as he sat in his tent between clifftop and road. "You know," he had said with his Northern accent and perpetual smile, "sometimes you can arrive on a winter weekend and find seaweed being thrown up over the cliff and onto the road."

Well, that Whitsuntide the sun shone at Ailladie, the main cliff of the Burren, where everything is less than a rope's length above the Atlantic. The way down the fluted limestone cliff is through grass studded with upthrust fists of purple and pink orchids, delicately spotted and ignorant of paths. In the micro-climate of crevices rare ferns shelter and tentatively finger the air. At the sea's edge of this green world, a short steep descent leads to a wide nontidal platform. From here, when the weather is wild, pilgrims can at least do "Gogo at Hard Severe," as their language has it, or if penance is due, follow the undercut traverse and razor jams of Mad Mackerel. But many travelers to the Burren seem to prefer to tune into the steepness of Ailladie by way of the awkward ramp of Bonnain Bui or the thin diagonal crack of Ground Control. It was below this crack that Ronan made a discovery he was later to honor in his chapbook:

> The fiddler of Doolin was sleeping
> But the pub window advertised
> "Music Food Drink Crack"

Out there, in the bright early light,
The Aran Islands slept, shifting a little,
Uneasy in a chill Atlantic sea.

Through the green patchwork of cut
And uncut meadows, lanes tacked toward
The stepped white sheets of the hill
Where club-foot ferns crouched in folds and clints
And orchids bristled up through cliff-top tracks.

We were approaching a new crag again,
Sniffing out, as usual, signs of the descent,
Then balanced across cliff-bottom boulders
Reading cracks and corners from a thin book.

Following a ledge leading under a wall
That reared sheer and seductive,

Suddenly we stepped on flowers,
Sweating under cellophane. "For Simon"
Said the faded card pinned down
By stones from the crag that killed him
And that we had come to climb.

Reverence, mixed with a little unease, delayed the ascent of Ground
Control until late in their stay. Then Kevin led it nervously, tiring himself
by placing too many small wires and twice having to descend for a rest.
They knew that the boy from the North had been killed on the harder
crack to the right of their line, and anyway, their order demanded that life
must go on. Rock must be engaged by the limbs of the living if they are
to learn the awe and elation offered by the diligent reading of texts.

Ronan and Kevin marveled at the memorable lines of the walls and
corners of Ailladie. They watched Keefe Murphy at his oblations on
Brother Gibson's inspired line up the center of Mirror Wall, making
regular offerings of nuts to the thin crack called The Cutter. It was a
lesson in steadiness on steep, unrelenting rock from the local maker of
lines. To the left, a young acolyte had rushed halfway up Wall of Fossils
and hand-traversed out onto the hanging arête called Fall of Wossils. He
quickly clipped the peg and was girding himself for the long, unprotected ascent of the arête. At last he moved up, hanging first left and
then right, off the straight edge. His cry at the top left no doubt that a
pilgrim had found ecstasy.

Ronan found that his faith was tested by the bold step across a wide
crack at the top of Moon Rill, one of the easier corners. But he transferred his weight and his trust across the void, finding unseen holds

coming to hand as he did so. Then, preparations complete, the two pilgrims approached the final stations of their devotional journey. Afterward, they remembered this as the day of the trinity of visions, as much for the revelations of the sea as of the rock. This was the day they read three uplifting lines on Boulder Wall, each prefaced by a small epiphany during the abseiling ritual.

The first abseil brought them to a ledge just above a dark velvet sea, which appeared to be carpeted with diamonds that sparkled with the brilliance of a miracle. They turned their backs on this wonder to look up the arête at the left end of the ledge. Here lay the dazzling charms (they were now looking into the sun) of Doolin Rouge. A delicate slab led to a bulge where a dubious but necessary nut could also get in the way of a clumsy high step. If this nut rattled back down to the ledge, the piety of a pilgrim would be severely tested by the steep (and now totally unprotected) traverse across the top wall. Ronan was glad he'd agreed that they top-rope Doolin Rouge when his foot slipped from a small edge as he climbed badly over the bulge. He was ready to accept that the climb was better than this particular climber.

A glance down before the second abseil produced the vision of the jellyfish. Now the sea was translucent with floating pink ghosts, which had strangely vanished when the pilgrims stood again on the ledge. Kevin led off up a wide, black crack as sharp-edged as though cut by lightning only yesterday. This was Great Balls of Fire. An arm-bar and knee-bracing struggle suddenly turned into a fingertip traverse left to a steep crack leading up to the sunlight.

The third abseil was remembered for their discovery of the auks. They had probably been there all the time—this, the pilgrims were coming to realize, was the mystery of the Burren. Guillemots and razorbills, bobbing black and white on the water, had surely been watching them all the time, out on the margins of their rock-focused vision. Then they remembered passing above the chattering birdcliffs of Moher on their way to the Labyrinth Stone. But now they were confronting what was to be the most rewarding test of all: Black Magic. The key to deciphering this text was to escape each dark groove by moving up right into the next. High on the wall a horizontal break offered Ronan a rest to gather inner resources for the final soaring fingerlocks up a vertical crack to the top. These were magic moves out of the black wall and into the clear light of the Burren, with the doors of perception cleansed.

It is in the nature of a pilgrimage such as this that the opening of one door is the closing of another. Now that the climbers' eyes were opened, the sky darkened with rain. Still, they ascended the mountain, crossing the massive white pavements to worship at Murroughkilly. Their first climb, An Mhear Fhada, revealed a new texture to the rock, which seemed like white, fragile charcoal, until a falling stone drew blood from Kevin's unhelmeted head. An audience with The Cardinal over at Eagle's Rock had also been planned until Calvin had warned them of the dense, overgrown approach: "You know, that is probably the very wood where Sweeney lost an army. In any case, the name is more impressive than the route." Useful advice from Ireland's sage of the stone.

So, as the rain fell the pilgrims pulled up their hoods and made for the Ailwee Caves to receive instruction in their formation. Then they pressed on up the road to the bleak plateau above where they prostrated themselves before the Poulnabrone dolmen, vying for the best vision in their lenses as it loomed stark against the dark sky. It was an unnatural rock form, but this neolithic burial chamber was as much a part of the mysterious power of the Burren as were its famous sunsets or its music.

It is the custom in the Burren that each evening pilgrims and pagans alike make their way to the inns to Doolin, where the Guinness is always already settling in pint glasses on the bar. The musicians of Doolin exert a westward pull felt throughout Europe. Their fiddles, guitars, pipes, and bodhran make music as intricate as a Celtic design and as clear as the light of County Clare. So, long after the colors have left the evening sky behind the Aran Islands the inns of Doolin retain the colors and tastes of Ireland.

Halfway up the road out of the Burren, Ronan and Kevin sat down to look back. They had long ago forgotten their hopes of finding the Book of the Burren, that long-lost manuscript of fabled illuminations. And they knew they would not have the luck to find it now, buried beneath this field wall, these strange upright slabs against which they leaned. Kevin marveled at the squirls of the serpents fossilized in the famous Doolin Stone. To Ronan these relief shapes seemed to echo the carved spirals of the Labyrinth Stone, that mysterious waymarker on the bend above the Burren.

Before leaving on this pilgrimage, they had received a letter from Dermot Somers, the Wicklow hermit and teller of tales. "An extraordinary area," he had said, "quite apart from the climbing, which you would lose in Pembroke, except for its rich cultural, archeological, and geological context." Slowly the pilgrims began to decipher the meaning of the fossil hieroglyphics on the Doolin Stone. They were reading a page of the Book of the Burren, bordered here by interwoven grasses and the delicate yellow heads of buttercups. The stone pages they'd read in the Burren had each been illuminated in the margins of their vision by dolphins and dolmen, the birds and the beer, the music of County Clare and the caves of Ailwee, the rare flowers among the rocks and the flotilla of jellyfish in the sea.

Indeed, this book may still be found by alert pilgrims who venture to the west of Ireland. For, better than the Book of Kells, the Book of the Burren is alive, its illuminations constantly renewed, its stone pages open to different readings every day.

1993

The Latter-Day Saint

Dave Gregory

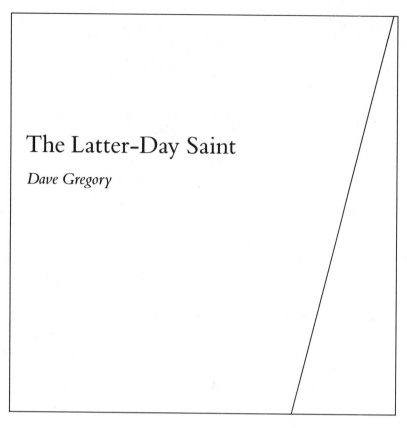

I suppose I was getting typecast. I've been down three times altogether, and each time I've had a connection with climbing, which is
something of a miracle because the bureaucracy up here couldn't orga-
nize a piss-up in a brewery, to use a phrase I heard on my last visit. The
first time wasn't too bad an experience, but it could have been nasty. I
spent a spell as a camel driver working for a merchant based in Baghdad. Many of his caravans went south toward Mecca, where Mo-
hammed was starting to run riot. Events down there were getting
fervid and militant.

But I was comparatively lucky. The merchant sent me north on a
caravan going through Turkey to Tbilisi. He had gotten it into his head
to find out if Noah's ark had really come to rest on Mount Ararat. He
wasn't actually going to go himself, fat capitalist, but I was a likely
looking young fellow whom he had come to trust. I would get a guide
and some guards for the approach journey and could choose my own

companions for the actual ascent. Quite an uneventful expedition it was: some brigands, a bear or two, pretty cold at night but pleasant in the daytime. Hard work, that mountain. Shattered rock. Rotten gullies, some packed with snow. We found something—nothing you'd want to go to sea in, but it would be a few thousand years old by then, wouldn't it? A pile of timbers lay spread over about a hundred yards. We brought him back some bits of wood and a few brass nails, and he paid us well.

Afterward, I closed my eyes in a caravansary after a particularly pleasant evening with a young dancer and found myself up here. It could have been worse. They could have whisked me back after I'd paid my money but before I got the worth of it.

The organization up here hasn't got the omnipotent control over events down there that the Judaic Bible literalists imagine. Births and deaths are pretty much at the whim of chance, mischance, human agency, and scientific laws—much more *Que será, será* than divine ordering. Earth's scientists have established many of the microscopic and macroscopic laws, but if a heavy loss of life occurs because of some seismic or atmospheric incident the general population blames someone or something beyond its understanding—and its puzzlement leads to the concept of some omnipotent, arbitrary, and ill-tempered hyperpower.

It is precisely because "up here" has no control over "down there" that observers are sent down at intervals, sometimes two at a time, although they don't realize it. The ones who are sent are fairly retiring types who fit in fairly well when they get down there, except for the occasional mismatch.

All the observers, of course, have to be debriefed when they are recalled and consequently have to be able to remember what they saw and to analyze the state of the disunion of personkind. (You see how we pick up the current jargon.) It's from them that we get to know about the slip-ups.

The second time I went down I began as a ragged youngster, guiding people around Petra and spending my spare time finding ways up cliffs. Treasure was supposedly hidden in the caves of the cliffs, but although I became skilled at reaching ledges the others thought unattainable I found nothing but scraps of useless parchment.

The senior guide grew angry with me. I was guiding more customers than he because I could take the nimbler ones on hair-raising ways around the higher ruins, and the tourists would fill a turban when I swung across the rock face between one cave and the next, hanging from a rope. It didn't improve matters when he found out I was meeting his granddaughter after dark. My father thought it best to send me to Damascus to work for his cousin, so I turned out to be a camel driver again.

I hoped that if there were a third time it would be no more eventful than the earlier times, and would allow more stability in my relationships. And this is how it proved to be at first. All the observers comment, on their return, that no one seems surprised at their presence. They all think they have just arrived on the scene, yet the person they are seems to have been there all the time. So it was with me. I was given the usual warnings: just observe, follow the lifestyle of the person you find yourself to be, and don't behave in any unusual or noticeable ways. Lastly and most important: never invoke supernatural aid, even in extremis.

I had drawn across the black velvet (the sun is bright up here and sleeping is impossible without opaque curtains), slipped gently into sleep and, as on the earlier occasions, found myself transported.

I was sitting on a leather-covered bench, leaning back against the wall of a noisy, crowded room, drinking from a curious glass vessel. It had indentations all over its surface, and I was holding it round its considerable girth with my fingers in the dents, despite its having a perfectly functional handle. The liquid it contained was brown and bitter, of repelling taste. The others in the room found drinking it no penance, replenishing their glasses a great deal faster than I wished to refill mine.

The young man beside me was the life and soul of our group, holding its attention, calling forth great guffaws. Eventually, Mike, as he was called, called over a fellow named Joe, who had just come in, and explained that I was looking for a room. Was the one next to his still empty? It was, and matters were soon settled. I could make my first payment when I cashed my Giro check (what was a Giro, for Earth's sake?).

The next morning the two of us piled into Mike's van, picked up a fellow named Dave, and drove to one of the local hedges. Hedgers? Edges? A fin of rock, I discovered. This trip was the first of many, though I had taken to rockclimbing at the wrong time of year. The days were getting shorter and the weather colder and wetter, but Mike, Dave, and Joe persevered with me. I was given some tattered, smelly, toe-compressing footwear. The local market, quite unlike those in Baghdad, provided nether garments well within the scope that my Giro provided.

Although I had settled in nicely, I soon realized I would hardly be able to report on society in general. My group was in no way representative, but I fit into it and looked forward to visiting the edges.

These outcrops were chosen with some care by my mentors, who sought out particular ascents. The first visits were agony. One of my new friends would climb up first, safeguarding his ascent with small pieces of metal on special clips. Another would follow him, taking out the small pieces of metal. The third would rapidly ascend, and then one or two, or all three of them would cajole, bully, push, or haul me up.

Gritstone these edges were made of. They called it God's Own Rock, but to me it was the invention of the Devil. The backs of my hands showed a mass of scratches, and my body was a solid ache from waist to head-top, but gradually I improved. For a couple of quid (how my vocabulary was widening) I became the puzzled but grateful owner of a modern-day chastity belt. I was given any stray gear we found, and on one red-letter day I bought a rope at a sale of recovered stolen stock.

Came the day when they tied me on to what they called the sharp end of the rope and pointed at a route within my capabilities. I reveled in it, and as spring came and the weather warmed I led more and more. Joe, of course, was far more experienced than I, but I was learning quickly, and we were developing into a compatible team. The four of us began to range farther afield in the van, and the routes we did became harder, longer, and more enjoyable.

The habits of my previous visits of inspection were, to some extent, still with me. Unguardedly, I once commented on the degree of display common among young women, for, after all, mini-skirts and tank-tops hadn't been common in Baghdad. I also never grew to like the bitter brown liquid, preferring a variety of fruit juices.

They called me The Saint on account of these puritanical traits, even after the barmaid at the local pub, who had a room near ours, took a fancy to me and kept coming around to borrow sugar and further our acquaintance. This involved my getting some early and unexpected experience in debriefing. This activity was familiar to me, the sort of thing I had come across as a camel driver.

Helen lived in a room not far away from mine, one with a large double bed. It seemed foolish to be paying for two sets of rooms, so I moved myself and my expanding collection of belongings in with her. Though the others were envious, they didn't stop calling me The Saint. I had a few twinges of conscience as to what would happen to Helen and any offspring when I was recalled, but I accepted my good fortune and pushed to the back of my mind the fact that not many people could avoid their responsibilities as easily as I was going to.

The team capitalized on my not drinking. I was taught to drive and pressured into applying for a license. Mike would drive to the crag, from the crag to the pub, and I would drive back from there until he awoke from his slumbers in the back of the van and judged that he had sunk below the limit.

Sometimes, during a spell of good weather, Mike would take a few days off, and on such occasions and on major feast days (Bank Holidays they called them) we would manage longer trips to the south of the country. We visited the seacliffs, which were still being developed then, and managed a few minor new routes. Mike sent an account of one of these ventures to a climbing magazine and a jumbled version duly appeared in print. The others were obviously gratified, but I wondered: when I was recalled, would the mention of my name disappear? And would the person I now am still be here when I was recalled? The physical presence and all its trappings, the National Health Service number, Giros, and acquaintances were obviously all here before I used them and presumably would be here when I had gone. Where, however, was the person who had been me before I came? Would he come back with the same physique or did the system work on a multiple shuffling of souls? Would the returned, permanent inhabitant be a rock-climber or would he, in some horrific leading situation, discover that he had lost his nerve and, if he got away with his life, switch to disco dancing or salmon fishing.

Mike, Dave, Joe, and I traveled far south on one of the major holidays to a great black cliff that took our breath away. It swept up smoothly, unbroken by any obvious features after the initial barring overhang above the flat platform over which the high seas rushed. A couple of routes had been established on the cliff already, taking breaches through the overhang. We each chose one route.

Our line followed a shallow groove, an almost invisible feature. The protection wasn't too sparse and, although in its upper reaches the rock became less sound, the climbing became much easier.

We had time enough to return to sea level and look for other lines with eyes now more accustomed to the crag. Possibilities existed, but only one could we see ourselves trying. That evening was spent in the pub, and since no other groups of climbers were about, we let our imaginations and conversation run riot on that possible line. One thing we knew: the team would need all the small wires we'd got. Narrow cracks seemed to be the order of the day. We'd have a good look at the possible route the next morning.

The following day, however, it rained, and we spent our time in cafés, bookshops, and a museum. Three of us were for a trip to the flicks in the evening, but Joe wanted an early night. He wanted an early night so that his mind would tell him he'd had a day off and a good night's sleep and was in good form. Joe and I, just the two of us, were for the new line; I knew it for certain.

Joe agreed to tackle the top pitch, where the rock might be totty, but I was to get us established on the wall. The major feature of this line, too, was a shallow groove with a faint crack in its back. Although there was no direct entry to it, a narrow, steep rib lay off to the right. Steep and polished shiny-black by the sea wash, the rock would be solid. It would be higher up that the manky stuff began.

The rib was still wet from the surf, and the sun was not yet round to dry it off, when I teetered up the rib in fear until I could reach over the gap between its top and the overhang of the main face. I had hoped to get a piece in the break, but there was no crack in the back of it and its angle was too obtuse for the cams to hold. At least the crack offered a handjam of sorts while I reached over the lip and fixed a chock into an oval pocket. With two right-hand fingers in the pocket alongside the chock, and my feet on the very top of the rib, I could barely reach a small, flat hold with my left hand. A finger-straining pull-up and a scrabble of the feet and I was established on the face.

Two faint cracks led leftward, broken by pockets at intervals, some-times undercut but occasionally with a bottom lip jutting out—not a Mick Jagger special, but as pretty to me as any Damascus houri's. Swarms of what looked like lice came pouring out of the top crack as I thrust my fingers into it. I was careful to blow the creatures gently out of my way: being on the verge of parting with life gives you a respect for someone else's right to existence. The two cracks offered sufficient holds to allow me to balance precariously leftward and reach the crack in the faint groove.

The crack was narrow and pinched, but it took fingers and small wires when it opened, and the horizontal bedding of the rock gave minute finger corners in the crack and small ripples on the right wall of the groove, barely adequate for the feet. I was thankful for the nest of RPs and Little Rocks bristling from my bandolier. They were the only gear the crack would take, and I was whanging them in like they were going out of fashion.

The day had warmed by the time I reached a ledge in the groove big enough to get two half-feet on. This meant the belay was not quite a hanger, and I could bring Joe up in relative comfort, warm and able to keep changing my weight on my legs and feet. I put his rope through a couple of wires above me, and he yelled that he was starting up the rib. It was quite dry now and he made good time, soon hanging beside me from the wires. We sorted the gear he had collected, and he carefully racked it after his usual pattern. I could see him shrugging his shoulders under the weight, debating whether he dared leave some of it behind. He squinted up at the wall, which was black, not shiny now, seamed with narrow cracks. He left the Big Rocks and hexes hanging on the belay and made his move. "Hanging here looking at each other won't get our names in the books," he said.

He struggled over me in a most ungainly fashion, hitting me in the eye with the swinging skirt of hexes. Neither of us had mentioned it, but we both knew where the Rubicon was to be. Well above us, the groove we were following seemed to fade out just as the face tilted back: that was where the Rubicon was. If he could get out of the groove and onto the wall above, he was going to have to decide which way to go. We knew that not far above, the rock at least had holds of a sort on it.

Although Joe was stopped for a time at the top of the groove, he placed a runner at its apex. "That," he yelled "is a belter." Some of the tension vanished. He worked his way higher up the groove for a look at his likely line and shouted down his decision to go right. He rearranged his ropes so that the left-hand one ran through the belter; the other would be available to be clipped into whatever was coming.

Two or three tries saw him move out of the groove and onto the wall round the blunt arête to its right. He disappeared from view and the rope ran out slowly. Scraping noises came faintly down above the swish of the waves and the sough of the wind. Fragments of rock clattered down the upper wall and bounced free, whirling in the wind, onto the rock platform below us. He must be scratching out a gear placement. The cracks must have begun.

The ropes played out slowly, slowly. Twice they came slack again, and I could take several feet back on one of them. So, yo-yoing was going on. Life must be getting hard in the upper stories. Once the wind-blown information floated down that he was having a rest. This could only mean he'd given up the battle for an ethical ascent, had placed a good nut, and had leaned back on it.

It must have been five minutes later that he shouted down that he was climbing again. One rope started to move out while I took the other in. They started to move out together, quickly at first, then more slowly, and then they stopped just before a strangled cry of "Watch it!" whipped into a scream as Joe spun into view and came to a jolting stop. I let out the ropes and lowered him to my level. He half-climbed, half-pendulumed sideways into the groove and clipped into the belay.

He'd shot his bolt and it would have to be me. He had been in the middle of a sequence of thin moves when he had fallen. Standing on a pair of small holds, he had been reaching up for the bottom of a small rib when his feet had slipped. There might be, he said, a crack left of the rib where it joined the face. Might be. Might not.

We swapped places and I went for my try. Beneath us I could see the rock platform starting to wet over as the tide reached higher. Getting up was certainly going to be hard, but it might be easier than getting down. After all, not many camel drivers can swim.

The groove wasn't too bad, and the runner at the top was a real comfort. I found the moves out of the groove very hard, and doubted I could have done them without the ropes from above.

There are days when you feel euphoric. You never notice cruxes, you're not bothered if it's going to be hard, and you just float past stuff. Wet rock, loose rock, they're hardly noticed as you sail past, glorying in the ease of it all. This is your day and there's no gainsaying you. But this was obviously not one of those days. This was one of those days when the mind dwells long and deeply on the problems ahead. Doubt looms large and failure seems more likely than success, but you have to have your go and give it your best shot. So it was now, but I felt physically less and less capable as I approached Joe's high point.

The nut that had held him was now well seated in its niche. Ten feet above it I could see his two small footholds, one with a smear of squashed leaf upon it. I moved up sufficiently to be able to brush it clean with my fingers and blow any remaining dirt away. I dithered on the moves and made the last high step to stand on the holds with a hesitant series of shuffling pushes of my trailing left foot. There was a fingerhold in a minute V-niche at head height for the right hand, near a rib. But nothing for the left foot. Absolutely bloody nothing. There was nothing for it except to smear my foot flat on the face and go for that rib.

My right arm was shaking with the strain when I finally grasped the bottom of the rib. I tried to lean leftward to see if there was a crack nearby. Nothing, bloody nothing. I jerked up on the rib, and, as my body moved slightly up, I let go and lunged for a slightly higher pinch. Thank God, my fingertips reached the comfort of a crease. But still no crack!

I swung my right hand blindly up the rib, my right foot flailing, and grabbed the rib above my left hand. I had to get some push to the left from somewhere. I threw my right foot up into the tiny V-niche and pushed myself left to look up the groove beside the rib. Bloody nothing. A small foothold appeared way out to the left, so I switched feet on that smooth, smooth slab, then threw my left foot onto that trivial hold. God, if only I could get my shoulder to the left of the rib and lean on it to take the strain off my hands!

Inch by inch I moved my hands up that flimsy rib, coming nearer and nearer into balance. But gravity was winning. My arms were pumping; they felt as rigid as wood, but their strength was going. I was going to go. My left leg started to sewing machine, almost shaking my foot off the hold. I pulled wildly on the rib crest with my right hand, like a man trying to open a jammed sliding cupboard door, to free my left hand to feel wildly up the corner beside the rib. I found a hairline crack but it was no good, no good. I was going to go. I let my right foot slip off its useless smear and put my knee to the left of the rib, pushing rightward against the rib.

The fire in my right arm was beyond bearing as I unhooked my nut tool and tried to scratch some of the flaky contents out of the hairline crack, hoping to place one of my smallest RPs. My arm started to go, and I slashed at my bandolier with the crab on the tool, slapping my hand back on the rib. The crab had not caught, and the tool clattered down the wall and out of sight, to put the fear of God into Joe. I saw some of the slight slack in the ropes below me taken in as he readied himself for the peel.

"A crack, a crack, please, God, give me a crack!"

And suddenly, there it was. The hairline crack had miraculously opened to a width that let in all four finger ends. By using only two of them I could squeeze a nut into the bottom of the crack.

I finished the remainder of the pitch easily, only to sit at the top in a state bordering on remorse, an emotion I certainly could not explain to Joe. He was elated, on a real high, full of congratulations, and could not understand my gloom. He started to talk about a name and insisted on my having the choice because, according to him, I'd led it all.

I decided on a name while we were driving home. It wasn't one Joe particularly liked, but he accepted it, and we wrote the route up from memory, using a torch to light up the paper in the back of the van.

The ride home was uneventful and we were dropped off at our respective flats well after midnight. Helen was glad to see me but couldn't understand why I was so despondent. She did her excellent best to make me forget my gloom and, utterly spent and snuggled up against her with my hand on her growing belly, I went blank-minded to sleep.

I never saw the morning. I was recalled up here and shall never get sent down again because of my transgression. I think a lot about my time down there. There isn't much else to occupy the mind up here, some psalm singing or mantra chanting, depending on your allegiance before you came up. Plenty of time to think.

How is my replacement on the rope making out? Where was he while I was Joe's ropemate? Is that fingerhold in the crack still there? If it's not the grade we gave it, it's going to be a real sandbagger. What grade did the guidebook give "Exit The Saint"? It would be nice to know.

And Helen. And the child. How have they got on?

1993

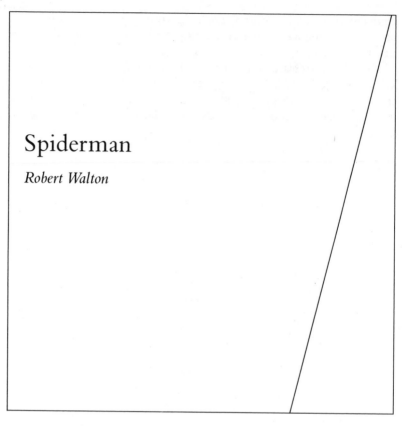

Spiderman

Robert Walton

Obsidian-black, lava-hot: my first coffee in more than a month. The first sip is an electric-caffeine shock; the second, I savor.

I breathe deeply of the morning air, neither fresh nor cool. Holding it in, I taste its cargo of smoke, its tang of ozone. I experience some of the self-destructive pleasure a smoker must feel: this is awful for my body, but oh, so pleasing to my soul. And the body passes; the soul is eternal, is it not?

Sultry, heavy with the coming heat of the last day of August, the air teases my lungs, makes me think of ancient cities: the white spires of Venice, rotting but full of sensual promise, shine in my mind. I raise my eyes and see, not a *campanile,* but the Lost Arrow poking hazily through the Valley's murk.

A barbed pain stumbles about within me like a hermit crab trapped in a drying pool. Its desperate claws grip my heart. Yosemite, you are my Venice; your holy spires are sinking beneath brown tides of smog. I come here and keep my eyes down. I come here and wrap myself in blankets of people. Sooner or later, though, some abused piece of you shines through and makes me sad. I know I should be somewhere else. Why did I come?

I look down at my hands. They're covered with small scabs, rock kisses. One hand holds a mug of cooling coffee. The other holds a check for ten thousand dollars. I guess that's reason enough to be here. It should get me through Christmas and then over to Australia for the Qantas Sport Climbing Championship.

I look up to where Upper Yosemite Fall used to be. Someone told me that water dribbled down its dark-streaked face back in April. Amazing. We're in the twenty-first year of what is called the Great California Drought. Everybody but the government knows it isn't a drought anymore; it's a permanent climatic change. No more rain or snow. We're part of the Great Basin desert now.

I suddenly feel as dry as the little pain-crab in my heart. I sip the lukewarm coffee. I need water, snow, ice. Why am I hanging around? The contest is over.

Yes, the contest. The pain of preparation is still too great for the result to rest easily in my mind. I finished fifth overall. All that work for fifth place.

Mixed doubles went about as expected. Speed is all that counts. You swing leads as fast as you can for eight pitches up the Glacier Point Apron. My partner, Max, is a big guy, and he can climb like Superman—or like an elephant seal. For three of his pitches he was Superman. We finished fourth.

Free-climbing disappointed me the most. The hundred-meter course was top-roped, naturally. It's tough enough to find an unbolted stretch of cliff in the Valley any more, let alone anything resembling a route. The contest officials didn't want to add another thirty bolts to the thousands already present. The course was adorned with pressure-sensitive red adhesive patches simulating protection points. You snake upward between these and slap them when you get close enough; then they turn green and a signal sounds at the judging platform. Your belayer is only then allowed to pull in an appropriate amount of slack. This keeps the thrill-factor in the climb. The higher you get, the higher you finish. Just as I stretched for a red patch, my left foot popped off a crystal, and I took a six-meter fall. I finished ninth.

Getting old? Maybe. But the Olympics are only a year away, and it'll be the first time rockclimbing has been included.

I *did* finish second in computer-enhanced firsts. This is the newest sport-climbing event. Only three places in this country—Snowbird,

Yosemite, Boulder—possess the expensive simulator complexes. You compete while enclosed within a windowless room and are connected electronically to a robot three centimeters tall. This figure, clinging to a nearby boulder, cheered on by crowds, actually does the route—or falls. The idea is creative, I guess. For something three centimeters tall there are thousands of El Caps in the world, millions of unclimbed walls.

I glance idly at the boulders in front of the nearby restrooms. They were the site of last year's computer-enhanced firsts. That was the first time I'd tried to make the tiny metal-and-fiberglass climber move up virgin rock. The visual simulation was better this year, but I could still tell I was hooked up to the computer's framework of sensors and screens. It's difficult, too, to maintain one's concentration while being attached by hands and feet to a device that resembles nothing as much as a giant cross.

I look at the boulders more closely. The delicate lace of light, shadow, and crystal enfolds my mind for a moment. Infinite climbing possibilities exist here—with the computer. This thought, somehow, is not as reassuring as it should be.

"Hey, Lara."

He's come back. Mr. First Place is approaching, thirty-five thousand dollars richer and bathed in the soft glow of glory from his improbable victory in the free-climbing competition. His crux move—a one-meter horizontal leap out from the wall, flowing into a dyno mantle off a pinch-grip hold, and ending on a microflake foothold—stirred even that jaded Valley audience.

"Lara, glad to see you're still around. Any plans?"

No. And I'm still around because I'm waiting to see if he'll ask me to do something with him. I understand this now but was too ashamed to admit it at the time.

"No, Trav, no plans. I just want to quit training for a while. I can afford a couple of weeks off, I think."

"Yeah, I could use a change, too. Have you done any ice?"

I look at him. He's much taller than I am. His hair is soft, blond, fine as a baby's. His eyes are gray, a strangely flat and faded gray, and his lashes are long. His slender body is taut; he is full almost to bursting with vitality, an energy nearly too potent for flesh and bone to contain.

I say, "A few routes in the Sierra, some stuff above Lee Vining. Why?"

"Just wondered. Hey, let's get out of here. The Valley's the pits in September."

Most other times, too, now. This was an invitation, I guess. He saw assent in my eyes before he ever needed to ask. Perhaps he only assumed it, out of habit.

"Let's do some real climbing. Together. Switzerland?"

His fingers find my shoulder and rest there as gently as moths. This sweeps me away. I know what explosions of power those fingers are capable of, yet they rest so lightly on my skin. I'm a soft touch, I admit it. Many women have had this problem since time began. It's mine now. That touch, that hint of gentleness, brushes away all the evidence my mind has assembled that this man cannot understand me, cannot possibly care for me in any meaningful way.

"Sure," I say.

"Thinking about the climb?" Trav's hard arms slide smoothly around my waist from behind.

He is beautiful, almost perfect, the shining diamond-heart of a star, blue-white and burning. I can almost love his beauty. I do in a way. But he is hard and cold, and so very alone. When he sees me he sees only what he expects, only a reflection of his few needs. I sense this will always be so. I understand, too, that I have known this since I met him; my hope and loneliness deluded me. Soon I must leave him. Soon.

"No," I answer at last. I glance up at the Wand, the Nordwand, the Mordwand. I've seen many pictures of the Eiger. Who hasn't? But pictures give no sense of its reality. It's a pit, not a face—a great cave spiraling down through endless falls of ice and black rock, a bottomless cave. Looking down, looking up, I feel a touch of dizziness.

I shake my head again and say, "Just thinking about all that's happened up there. The Germans. The Italians. The Direct."

"Hey," he presses my waist, "don't worry."

I do worry. I worry, but not in the way he supposes. The shuttle plane took us from L.A. to London in an hour. A few hours later we were in Kleine Scheidegg, blowing his money and mine on an expensive room. Then came dinner, a real dinner with warm bread and soft, sweet butter, and many glasses of wine. Thick as blood, red as a garnet, that wine was my first in six months—a drastic break in training. Then came bed.

He was a fierce and competent lover. What else could I have expected? Our motions were lustful, but our passion was more distant to me than the flames of stars. I watched his grace and animal beauty. I waited. I waited for him to finally come to me, see me, touch me. But he looked only inward, and his pleasure carried him only deeper into himself.

I worry that this climb will be like our lovemaking: an exercise, a route checked off in the guidebook.

Mists crawl like feeding caterpillars across the slopes of the Second Icefield. I shiver and he presses more tightly against my back. "Hey, don't worry," he murmurs. "It's cake, pure cake. Used to be tough, but it's a weekend climb now. Chouinard soloed it on his sixty-fifth birthday."

Cake? No—spiders. Frost-spiders on my eyelashes, on the backs of my overmitts. And the great Mother-Spider, silver and silent, poised and waiting beneath the points of my crampons. We started yesterday, climbed to the bivouac cave near the Shattered Pillar. We set out from there at midnight, using headlamps. All went well. We roped up only for the Hinterstoisser, the Ice Hose, and parts of the Ramp. It's just before noon now and we're nearly up the White Spider.

Trav is ten meters above me and a bit to my left. We're climbing unroped again. He's slowed down for some reason, so I'm taking a break. I've placed my deep anchor; its microwave heat tip went in at least half a meter. My tools are planted, and I'm leaning back on the main anchor's cable. One arm at a time, I stretch. The muscles in my shoulders and forearms are tight and heavy. I'm going to be sore tomorrow.

Trav is climbing again. He plants one tool, then the other. My thoughts drift restlessly. I'm aware of a vague sadness. We have climbed well but, as I had feared, separately. The headlamp climbing on the First Icefield was especially eerie: two glowing island-universes moving swiftly into deep, cold infinities. This is not what I hoped the climbing would be. In fact, most of my adult life—the obsessive training, the competition, the commercials, the videos, the contests, the rivals—is not what I hoped climbing would be.

Ice chips skitter past me in a futile dance with gravity. I hear a deeper, sharper sound. I look up to see stones falling. They sail down lighter than snowflakes, but in the last instant they acquire terrible voices. I huddle against the ice as the stones rip the air. There is a thud above me, then a cry, a strangled whimper. My mind moves so slowly; several seconds pass before I realize Trav has been hit.

I look up. He is hanging from his tools, his feet dangling loosely, crampons scratching aimless designs in the ice. I engage the heat release on my deep anchor, pull it out, and begin to move toward him, concentrating utterly on each movement, each tool placement.

I have been hit by rockfall once in my life. It was the most terrifying thing I've ever experienced: the humming blade of sound that was the stone's approach, the shocking explosion of pain when it hit my leg, the deep pain that nauseated me for hours and turned my muscles into limp rags. And the fear. The fear—humbling, belittling, making all that is human insignificant—its shadow is with me yet.

Trav is moving, thrashing against the pain of the hit. Good and bad. He's alive, but his tools might soon work loose.

I am four meters below him when he suddenly slumps. His left tool, the short axe, has pulled. Now he's hanging from just his Lowe hammer. Some instinct penetrates his agony. Eyes gaping, he freezes in place.

The cable on my deep anchor is three meters long. I make two more moves toward him and then stop. Hurrying, hurrying, but not rushing, I engage the microwave unit, plant the anchor. I pull on it. It's in. I check the cablelock on my harness and then look up.

Trav is now hanging motionless from the hammer. His eyes are glassy, unmoving. I move up to him, plant both tools, and reach for a sling. I clip it to my harness, then to his. Just as I do this, his hammer breaks loose.

He falls. I have time to curse myself for using such a long sling. His weight hits me, yanks me sideways. Both my tools jerk free. I'm twisting, turning, falling, coupled to this man who could not climb out of himself to know me. The cable on my deep anchor has never been fully extended under stress. Design limits. I have time to wonder if it will hold.

It does. Alpiglen swings below me. Trav is slicing me in half; the sling is too long. Can't reach him, can't move up, can't move. We're pinned on a vast window of frosted ice.

"Hallooo!" A call floats down from above. "You have trouble?"

"Yes," I yell, "yes."

"I come."

Climbing sounds, the brutal crunch of steel against ice, move closer.

A man's voice, a cheerful, accented tenor, speaks from just above Trav. "I hear the stones. I see you fall. There is hurt to your friend?"

"Yes," I answer. "Please, get the deep anchor off his harness and plant it just above him."

"Deep anchor? *Was ist los?*"

His query puzzles me. I take a long, slow breath and speak calmly. "The yellow metal stake on his right side. Take it off him."

He fumbles with the locking biner on the stake.

I wait impatiently. "Good. Now set the dial on three—*drei*. Place the tip against the ice. Right. Now press the green button. Now the red one—*rot*. Okay. Push and it will go in automatically."

Following my instructions clumsily, he finally clips himself in, then Trav, who sinks wordlessly onto the taut cable. A giant claw lets go of my waist.

"*Unmöglich,*" he mutters, inspecting the anchor. "But it goes in and it grips."

I look closely at him for the first time. Surprise suddenly mutes my fear reaction. He's old, very old. His beard is as white as Spider ice, though it's clipped too short to belong to Santa Claus. His cheeks are broad and red, his nose is sharp and long. He is broad himself and as sturdy-looking as a stump. His eyes are a penetrating blue.

His attire is bizarre. He's wearing a wide-brimmed hat of soft felt. His anorak is made of closely woven cloth, not synthetic. Beneath it I can make out a thick wool guide's sweater. His pack is one of those ancient awkward rucksacks found only in black-and-white photos.

He asks, "You have rope?"

"Yes, in Trav's pack."

"Good." He fumbles with the pack's fastenings, finally gets them open. He pulls out the neon chartreuse end of our ultra-lite. "This . . . your rope?"

I am baffled by his puzzlement. Ultra-lite technology has been around for ten years at least. Our rope is six millimeters thick and a hundred twenty meters long, and it will hold nine UIAA falls. He stares at it as if it were a piece of rotten string.

"It's a good rope," I say, "new this summer."

"Well." He ties the rope to his waist with a strange-looking knot. "I will progress over to the rocks. Then we will look to your friend. There is much blood and the arm is hurt. Also the head. You belay me?"

"Of course, but first let's tie these anchors together."

"Ha," he laughs. "*Verzeihung.* Two, that is best."

We arrange the anchors and I engage my belay device. "Fix the rope to a good anchor and I'll bring Trav up."

He seems about to ask a question, but then nods, smiles, and sets off diagonally up the ice. He has only one tool, an axe. Its shaft is at least eighty centimeters long and is made of wood. He moves swiftly and soon disappears around a bulge. The rope slithers steadily across the ice while thoughts of more rockfall nibble like mice at my composure.

"*Stand,*" his shout drifts down at last. "Come now."

I sigh and begin my work.

The rescue winch on my Petzl ascender makes the job easier, but two hours pass before I get Trav up to the old man's stance. He was semiconscious throughout the ordeal and not much help. His left arm, though I stabilized it as best I could, was causing him great pain.

The old man helps me pull Trav onto a meter-wide ledge. We then drag him back into a deep scoop in the cliff. It is roomy and sheltered, with space enough for all of us to lie down. We stretch Trav between us. He moans.

The old man says, "Look to him. I make a tea."

I check Trav's eyes, his pulse. No concussion. He has deep contusions on his left shoulder and on his chest. The collarbone is probably gone. No one-armed chin-ups for a while. Shock is the main enemy now.

I get Trav's crampons off, loosen his boots, then break out his sleeping bag and work it around his legs. The old man turns away from the cooker to help me. We get Trav into the bag without too much trouble.

"Water ready?"

"Yes, tea."

"See if you can get him to take these." I hand the old man two capsules, a painkiller, and an anti-shock tab. He cups them in a broad palm and turns to Trav.

I look out to see the face shrouded in mist. It is cold, colder even than the morning's darkness. Flakes of snow sift silently down. I realize I have no idea where we are. The Exit Cracks? I don't think so.

"He sleeps now."

I nod. Sleeping—not dead, not screaming in unendurable pain, not slowly turning into a mound of crystallized cells. Sleeping. My eyelids slide down, not because I myself am slipping into sleep, but because the need for sight is gone. The stones of responsibility have fallen away and they can close now, those eyelids.

"You are tired, my dear."

I open my eyes. The old man has lit a stubby candle. His bearded face is gold and silver in its angel-halo glow. "Yes," I reply. "But I don't think I can sleep."

"We will speak now? This *Jüngling*"—he nods toward Trav—"is good, no?" His cornflower-blue eyes regard me steadily.

"Yes, very."

"Of course, so. Only the best go to the Nordwand: Kurz, Heckmair, Habeler, Terray, Buhl, Haston, and so many more. I was once good, also. Do you believe it?"

I smile. Is it the first time in years, or does it just seem so? "Yes, I believe you were good. You must still be not too bad."

"Ha! You speak kindness! I am old. Old is not good, but it is better than the other." He rummages in his rucksack and finally pulls something out. "*Schokolade?*"

"Please." I take the oxidized bar but cannot eat it. I realize my mouth is stone dry.

"We drink again the tea?" He hands me a steaming cup. "Some snow, my dear, or you'll burn yourself."

"Thanks." I sip, sigh. The liquid is life itself.

"It is nothing." He pauses. Snow-burdened wind swirls around the entrance to our cave. "This *Jüngling,* he looks like Harlin. You love him?"

What can I say? I do. I don't. The tangle of feelings is beyond unraveling, beyond being cut by a sharp question.

He reads the shadows in my eyes and nods. "So. An old man asks too much. Your name, it is?"

"Lara."

"I am Heini."

"Heini—" I pause. "Just what are you doing up here?"

"*Bergsteigen,*" he chuckles.

"Where are we, anyway? There's nothing like this cave in any route description I've ever seen."

The old man looks at me for a moment, eyes sparkling in the candlelight. "This," he gestures, "I find it myself. I spend much time on this wall."

I consider this.

He continues, "And you, my dear, why come you here? You are great alpinist also?"

I sigh. And then, for God knows what reason, I tell him everything. I tell him I'm sick to death of targeted muscle groups; preprogrammed, calorie-specific meals; petty rivalries; endless traveling; vulture-eyed audiences. I tell him how I puke before each competition, how I stiff the other climbers to establish a psych-edge, how I can't find the mountains I used to love.

He is silent when I finish. At last he looks up. "How happens this to you, Lara?"

I shake my head. "I'm good. On some days I'm almost the best."

"Ah, *verständlich,* but the mountains do not know 'good.' They are better than us. Only people know 'good.' Good made fame and politics in my day. It is money now?"

"Yes. I was so happy at first. I could do what I wanted most to do, what I'm good at, and they paid me for it. Then . . . somehow, it changed."

"People use you. A powerful man once used me so. He gave my *Kamaraden* and me medals for a good climb. I lost the mountains then. But I found them again. You can also. Climbing is sport. It is play. So it is worth doing. We are alpinists. It is our duty to enjoy life, to climb. And," he rubs the side of his nose slyly, "not to die on the wall."

I look out into snow-filled air. Night has crept down upon us.

"Your Yosemite, I have never seen it. I'm sure it is hurt, as you say. Here also is great hurt. Vandals dirty the mountains. But know this, my dear: the mountains live long. We are with them only a short time. We learn to live—how do you say? Gentle? Gently? We learn to live gently, learn to take care for the mountains, the forests, the waters. I believe this."

I look up at him again. His eyes rest steadily upon me. I say, "I hope you're right."

"Oh, I am. And we alpinists must go first down the path, the path of kindness, of respect, of modesty."

I shake my head. "This path of yours is nearly impossible."

"No, no, it is simple. Alpinists who climb only to find the ego-mountain inside are lost. Such alpinists will go from the world. Isolation defeats us. Maybe now we start to see this."

I glance over at the sleeping Trav. "I'm not so sure."

"Ah," he smiled. "But you are tired. You are more tired from listening to an old man than you are from the Nordwand. Sleep now?"

I mutter agreement, though I feel certain there is no sleep in me. I watch the old man shove his feet deep into his battered rucksack and cushion his head incongruously on our rope.

I turn and again look into the darkness. I murmur soft words to myself. A night prayer? Perhaps. I suddenly realize that I am more relaxed than I have been for years. I lean back and fall instantly to sleep.

The summit is ours. It wasn't easy, that final push, but Trav was able to help some. In fact, he is even now resting nearby, woozy but recovering.

I turn to the old man. "Are you coming?"

"No. You will be able to get down the west flank with him." He looks up. "Besides, the weather is improving. I think I'll climb a little more."

I breathe deeply, slowly. "Heini, who are . . . what are you?"

He smiles. "A ghost? Here, take my hand."

I do. It is solid, warm, strong. I squeeze his big, calloused fingers hard. Suddenly, uncontrollably, tears fill my eyes.

"A ghost. Well, perhaps I am. Probably I am. I cannot explain what happened to us. I only know that I can go no more with you."

I blurt, "But I want you to come down. I want us to sit by a fire and drink wine."

He gently presses my fingers and then releases them. "Thank you, my dear. Yours are good words for an old man's ears . . . and heart."

He rises, takes a few steps back down the slope. My tears flow shamelessly now. He turns and looks back.

"Lara, I believe time is not as we suppose. Think on this. And remember me. I send the little angels to be with you on the way down. *Wiedersehen,* my dear."

And he is gone.

The west flank was a slog. Trav stumbled and was buried by small avalanches several times, but I hauled him out. The gods were kind and the angels were on duty: we got down safely.

Trav? He has recovered and is now correctly polite. And more distant than ever. He acknowledges that I saved his life, but he doesn't really believe it. He will believe it less as time passes. It doesn't fit in with his understanding of the universe, his understanding of himself. The Eiger will become vague to him, especially the accident. It may disappear from his memory entirely, except for (I hope) a sharp pain in the left shoulder when the weather turns damp. What's interesting is that he doesn't remember a thing about Heini. Shock, I guess.

Me? To hell with my diet. To hell with my muscle groups. To hell with the Olympics. I'm going to work at something else now. Then I shall play. I shall play in the mountains; I shall climb.

1993

The More Things Change . . .

Ian McRae

As the two humans struggled with the steepest part of the climb, an unknown life form jumped out of a cave above them.

"Eeeeck!" shrilled the human named Spleechdorf, who, trailing a silicon rope from his waist, balanced precariously ten meters above his partner. "What is it?"

"Simian, apparently," yelled up Ordspleef, holding the rope rather inexpertly, not being familiar with the ancient technique. "Perhaps a relative of the riparian slime-monkey."

The creature above them resembled an improbable blend of baboon and gibbon. Thick gray fur covered most of its body, which had an enormous torso and curiously attenuated legs. The creature dangled from an overhang by one arm—and that arm was the most awesome piece of rockclimbing phenotype ever seen on a primate-like being. Structurally, it was similar to a human arm except that the proportions were elongated, the musculature was more flexible and powerful, and the fingers were more strongly tapered. And then there was the crea-ture's tail: prehensile, twitching nervously in the air with a set of fin-gerlike appendages on the end, it was obviously a long anterior third arm. And it seemed to be communicating the creature's anger through a series of flailing gestures.

With the slightest twitch of its mighty arm the creature catapulted its body through the air, sailed for five meters with nothing below but the void, and landed noiselessly in a crouch onto some knobs in the middle of a steep slab only seven meters from Spleechdorf. Its open jaws revealed curved fangs; its eyes were narrowed and murderous.

"Eeeeck!" yelped Spleechdorf for the second time. "Hit it with the ray, hit it with the ray!"

Ordspleef, ten meters below, had already drawn the ray-gun and sighted it on the creature, yet he did not fire immediately.

"What are you waiting for? Skrooch 'im!"

But young Ordspleef had been programmed as a scientist and pos-sessed a reflexive awareness of the importance of their biological dis-covery; he did not want to damage the new life form unless absolutely necessary. He held the red point of the ray-gun on the ape's neck and took the opportunity to study the creature.

"Note the unusual size," commented Ordspleef in a loud, bass voice, his tone unconsciously imitating Spock, his favorite twentieth-century television hero. "Probably omnivorous. A cave dweller. Most likely it subsists on the rock-rodents we observed earlier. Marvelously adapted to its environment."

Spleechdorf, close enough to the actual creature to smell it, fidgeted on his perch. "Skrooch 'im," he moaned. "Just skrooch 'im, please. I think he intends to eat me!"

"Not necessarily; perhaps it is merely defending its territory. I would suggest that you remain motionless and watch how it reacts."

"What?" yelled Spleechdorf.

At that moment the ape threw its head back and released a high-pitched shriek that echoed across the cliffside for a good ten seconds. The creature then scuttled upward over difficult terrain with an ease of motion that made the little humans gasp.

"Oh, shee!" shouted Spleechdorf, huddling on his tenuous stance. "He's going to throw rocks at us!"

"No, no!" responded Ordspleef excitedly, pointing his finger up-ward. "He is a *she*. Of course!"

High above, on a rounded horizontal ledge, a pair of baby apes peered over the edge with curious eyes. The two infants had white fur and long, prematurely developed arms. The hairy rock-ape (and "ape" is what the creature would come to be named under the haphazard, derivative taxonomy of the planet) was a mother protecting her young.

This knowledge did not benefit the hapless Spleechdorf, busy ducking his unhelmeted head under a barrage of stones thrown by the mother. "Skrooch 'im, skrooch 'im!" came his muffled shouts.

Ordspleef, at the belay, was about ready to fire the ray when he heard a familiar sound at the edge of his awareness. He froze to listen. A low rumble vibrated the air, barely detectable. Above, both human and creature had also heard the sound and frozen. All three of them recognized the sound for what it was; no inhabitant of the planet could have failed to identify it.

For a moment ape and human locked in silent communication and held their breaths to listen, to make sure. Then the instant ended as Spleechdorf voiced the thought each was thinking: "Cyclone!"

A great whirlwind was approaching, far in the distance now, but spinning closer. Spleechdorf and Ordspleef, who had feared the possibility of a cyclone from the start, were already acquainted with its physical characteristics: the wind would bring a self-contained vortex of swirling air and rain, similar to a tornado except that it traveled with a slower rotational velocity. And, unlike a tornado, it propagated itself independently of other meteorological phenomena, propelled by the gravitational effect of the planet's moons rather than by convection. Cyclones occurred commonly on the planet; the first human settlers had quickly learned to contend with them by remaining indoors. No one had ever been caught out in the open by one and survived.

The rock-ape had momentarily vanished but reappeared seconds later, already hundreds of meters above the humans, ascending vertical rock with astonishing alacrity. The babies wrapped their tiny arms around their mother's shoulders like a pair of tight-fitting rucksacks as she liebacked up a smooth dihedral. She traveled with considerable haste, taking an uncompromisingly direct line with no regard for relative difficulty.

The rock itself consisted of vertical stacks of brown volcanic slabs textured with crumbly pebbles, and the ape flowed over this terrain with perfect distribution of weight. Ordspleef was mesmerized by the sight: she looked more like some form of mammalian spider than a simian. The dihedral opened into a wide, flared crack, and without pausing she jammed one side of her body into it and proceeded upward with a rhythmic, undulating motion. She made good use of her tail, pulling on the outer edge of the crack with it. Then, through a series of dynamic arm-pendulums from invisible holds, she traversed a sheer face to reach an icy couloir leading to the lee side of the ridgecrest.

Such grace and swiftness, Ordspleef thought, rendered paltry most of the gymnastic feats he had seen documented by humans in the Library Computer Archive. But he had no further time to observe the ape, for the cyclone approached the peak with the surety of a bathtub whirlpool being sucked toward an open drain.

The vulnerable humans, stuck on the wall because of their inferior climbing abilities, yelled to one another in anxious tones through the expectant air.

"It's coming this way!"

"Ninety-one percent probability!"

"I'm climbing down to you!"

"Insufficient time!"

Ordspleef began fumbling with the protection devices, trying to insert more of them into the pocket-sized holes in the igneous rock. The pair had manufactured these climbing gadgets using the Matter Transformer. To their surprise, precise specifications for such tools had been easy to locate in the archive; the practice of climbing mountains, it seemed, had endured such popularity among Earth populations of the late twentieth century that it had become industrialized—many patents and manuals had been filed.

Spleechdorf had discovered for himself the difficulties of climbing down what one has already climbed up, and he soon found himself stuck in a desperate posture, flat against the wall with arms and legs splayed. His rope hung directly down to Ordspleef with no intervening protection. Without needing to look, he knew the storm was close, for it emitted an all-too-familiar oscillation that Doppler-shifted hideously in his ears.

The cyclone followed the path of least resistance as it raced up a river valley and howled up a drainage through rising foothills. Encountering the mass of the rock peak, it soared and screamed toward the luckless climbers clinging like insects to the cliff face, joined by a silver strand. As the first gusts hit, their nylon clothing whipped rapidly against their bodies.

They stared with horror directly down into the heart of the cyclone, funnel-shaped and with a curious lack of exterior disturbance. It rose directly toward them, its rhythmic oscillation growing in intensity and frequency until the nodes coalesced into a great, rumbling roar. The pair could do nothing but curl into semifetal positions and hope for the best.

They screamed as the force hit them.

Ordspleef felt he would be torn in half by the straps of his harness. Or worse: the very cells of his body would be ripped apart from within. Breathing was impossible. The rope ran through his hands at great speed, but he was powerless to stop it. His lungs seized; he was losing consciousness.

Later, they would not remember how long it lasted. Not long, probably, for no animal could long survive a cyclone. The gale did not feel particularly cold, nor was it laden with debris; it was simply a steady, forceful, rotational pressure. A ghastly pressure.

A lull. Momentarily, Ordspleef looked up through the surreal tunnel of rain formed by the vortex. What he saw struck him as both comic and dreadful: Spleechdorf had been blown into the air and was twirling in tight circles at the end of the rope like a ribbon flailing on a hot-air vent. Ordspleef feared the worst: if his partner were to strike the rock, he would be converted instantly into a bloody, spinning sack of flesh.

The cyclone continued upward, straining to crest the peak. The wind slackened, and as suddenly as the storm had hit, it passed.

Ordspleef hung at his belay station, gasping, shivering, dripping. The rope led upward, but he could not see his partner. The great wind receded in the distance on the lee side of the peak.

"Spleechdorf?" shouted Ordspleef.

No reply.

"Spleechdorf? Spleechdorf!"

Silence.

What to do now? thought Ordspleef. Should he try to climb unprotected in what looked like a futile effort to rescue his friend? Should he tug on the rope and risk dislodging the body? The rope could have broken, and he might be pulling on nothing.

Ordspleef could not identify the noise at first; it sounded like the grunting of a dangerous creature. The rock-ape? He looked down for his ray-gun. Gone, ripped away by the cyclone.

The grunts began to be recognizable as individual phonemes of English. Spleechdorf was still alive! The lingering turbulence distorted his words, chopping and mixing them. Like a radio transceiver suddenly being tuned to the correct frequency, Spleechdorf's voice materialized in mid-gibber as the ether returned to its porridgelike consistency.

"Wait . . . wait, stand by. Over. I've lost my backpack. Whoa! What's this? I'm near the top. Stand by. The wind must have carried . . . I'm dizzy. Ordspleef! My chromo—"

"Say again?" yelled Ordspleef.

"Hello?" yelled Spleechdorf.

"Are you damaged?"

"What?"

"Are you *damaged?*"

"Neg . . . a . . . tive. But I'm all wound up in the rope."

Spleechdorf had been blown past the steep section of the climb and had been carried, bruised but alive, to the ridgecrest by the cyclone. After a long interlude, he yelled down for his partner to climb.

Shaken but able to proceed, the two humans finally emerged onto the summit of the peak. The air grew colder, as if the tip of the tower were embedded in the jet stream. Runnels of ice glowed in the nearby crevices. The humans huddled on the pointed summit and gazed out at the full panorama, a view nearly as extensive as that afforded by a trip in a Jingyplane. Yet, as Spleechdorf remarked, the sensation of sitting on this soaring tower was entirely different than being in one of those noisy flying contraptions. The planet was theirs alone—and silent. Time had taken on a frozen quality.

The atmosphere on the planet (the third planet in the Epsilon Eridani system, referred to by its human inhabitants simply as Eridanus) differed from that of Earth's. The oxygen-carbon dioxide ratio was approximately the same, as was the effective gravity. An improbable interaction of gravitational and barometric forces, however, resulted in making the air on Eridanus somewhat fluid, with a higher aqueous component than on Earth. As a consequence, the view from the summit was filtered through a gauzy, slate-colored haze, transparent and semirefractive as well, so that the contours of the land were visible as if seen from the bottom of a semiliquid sea. This haze, acting as a solar filtering mechanism, was the key reason that Homo sapiens could live on Eridanus; the physical similarities between it and Earth were little short of miraculous.

Tundra-covered uplands stretched dimly away in every direction, and an extensive network of lakes and rivers showed darkly on the face of the land like a cortex. The humans could see no real horizon, only a zone of diminishing shade within the haze. Epsilon Eridani, the primary sun, was similarly invisible, although its presence was made known by a region glaring in the haze.

Spleechdorf and Ordspleef felt euphoric and immensely satisfied. Theirs was an ancient feeling, a link back to a remote time and place, but poised up on the summit they did not know about this link, nor would they have cared even if they had known. Nor did they understand why they had come up there in the first place. Both of them had learned long ago not to question the strange impulses they carried in their genes like some virus. This lack of introspection had a root cause: they had been educated on Eridanus by automated computers since birth.

They lingered atop the rock tower. Spleechdorf managed to doze; Ordspleef collected data. Among other observations, he spied another rock formation in the distant haze. Was that tower also home to rock-apes? And, come to think of it, where were the rock-apes who lived on this tower? What if they had territorial fixations on the summit and were even now powering their way upward?

Ordspleef stood abruptly and shook his partner's leg. "The night tides are breezing! We must go down at once!"

Night was a serious proposition on Eridanus. When a hemisphere passed into shadow, the thick haze that regulated the thermodynamics within the biosphere would lift, and the temperature would plummet far below the freezing point of water. The planet had no seasonal cycle to speak of, but each night was a winter unto itself. Each morning the land would be covered with snow, the lakes and waterways frozen solid. No human had ever survived a night in the open.

Since a bivouac was unthinkable, Spleechdorf and Ordspleef had not bothered to pack a cumbersome sleeping pod. They had estimated they could make their climb in a single day, but the journey to the mountain had been more arduous than they had anticipated. But since each rotation of the planet lasted the equivalent of seventy-two hours on a Terran scale, the pair had ample time to descend and cover the twenty kilometers back to their building complex.

"Do you recall the techniques for rappelling that we studied?" asked Ordspleef.

"Uh, approximately," replied Spleechdorf. "First we need to locate—what did they call it—anchor?"

"Correct," said Ordspleef.

They had done their research quite thoroughly. Four rappels with some downclimbing brought them to the base of the tower with only a few problems, one of which came when Ordspleef insisted they make a detour to collect rock-ape scat and Spleechdorf could not be persuaded.

Once at the bottom they paused to drink water and eat the last of their green slime-cakes. Fortified, they began the long, wet slog through the twilight toward home.

They reached their complex just as the first snowflakes fell. As they crossed the outer fence of the colony perimeter, the mist was already

lifting with the onset of nightfall. They turned in time to see the mountain etched prominently against a purplish sky.

"Explain," demanded the subcommander.

"We desired to climb the mountain," replied Ordspleef.

"You used the Matter Transformer without authorization, you traveled beyond the perimeter without authorization, and you needlessly
endangered valuable genetic resources—and by this I am referring to
yourselves, although at this point I am unsure whether you belong in
that category. Do you consider your actions justified?"

Neither climber thought it prudent to answer; they were unsure of
themselves and still weary from their effort of the previous day. But
just wait until their report was filed, thought Ordspleef. It would contain an impressive amount of data. The rock-ape alone constituted the
most significant biological find since Grepnib's discovery of the Giant
Carnivorous Newt frozen into a glacier. Perhaps, hypothesized Ordspleef, the newt, a remnant of the planet's Arboreal Age, was the original biological agent that forced the ape's evolution to take place in the
sanctuary of the heights.

"Well," cut in the stern voice of the subcommander, "the Old Lady
wants to see you both."

At this piece of information, Spleechdorf and Ordspleef exchanged
concerned glances. The term "Old Lady" was a sobriquet for Dr. Wayomo, the sole remaining Earth-born on the planet, a member of the
original eight-person crew of Space Colonization Project 83828, and
the oldest human on Eridanus. It was necessary for her to live in a
hermetically sealed chamber that simulated the exact physical conditions of her original Terran environment. Since she rarely involved
herself anymore with the day-to-day affairs of the community, she had
assumed mythical status in the eyes of the laboratory-bred progeny
whom she had helped create.

Ordspleef and Spleechdorf were led through an unfamiliar part of
the complex. Then, after lengthy rituals in sterile chambers, they were
announced by intercom and ushered into the Old Lady's room.

She was the most ancient woman either of them had ever seen. Her
wrinkled skin covered with brown spots, the hairless, stooped woman
approached them haltingly, a metal-alloy cane in her hand.

"Would you like some tea?" she asked.

The two heroes looked at her blankly.

"I see . . . you don't know about tea. I'll prepare it anyway."

Her voice was remarkably forceful despite her withered condition. She had been born in Asia, lived a quarter-century on Earth, traveled ten light-years in cryogenic suspension, and lived many additional revolutions around Epsilon Eridani. Her age was incalculable.

When the tea had been served (a blend of cured slime-molds from an ancient dried-up pond), she made her way to a chair opposite the youths, sat down, and silently scrutinized them for several minutes. Both exhibited medium-length black hair, gaps in their teeth, and sunburned faces. They seemed taller and thinner than she remembered humans as being. But lots of tall, skinny kids were running around here lately. Could it signify some sort of accelerated response to the heavy atmosphere? Natural selection arising from the milk plague of the first year? Lack of genetic diversity after all their efforts to promote it? The variables were all muddled in her head; she had grown too old to formulate a hypothesis out of the welter of her thoughts.

Instead, she prodded Ordspleef in the gut with her cane. "How old are you?"

"Approximately four point eight years," he replied instantly.

"What is that on a Terran scale?" she demanded.

"Unsure without the conversion factor."

"How were you born?"

"Natural."

"Your friend here?"

"Natural."

"What generation are you?"

"Second. Or third. I . . . I am not sure."

"Well," said Dr. Wayomo, raising her teacup, "you look like you're about seventeen. That would be about right, anyway." She sat quietly for a minute, contemplating her next question.

"So you climbed Shiprock, did you?"

"Shiprock? The mountain is called Shiprock?" asked an intent Spleechdorf.

"Because it is shaped like the bow-shield of a spaceship."

The climbers looked disappointed.

"How was the climb?"

But neither of them knew exactly what she meant by that question, and they glanced at each other, confused.

"You know," she continued, "I always meant to slip away and give that rock a try."

"You?" exclaimed Spleechdorf with disbelief.

"I was younger once," smiled the old woman. "The peak is similar in appearance to its namesake on Earth. Wiesack, especially, wanted to climb it very badly, but we were always too busy. Project objectives. . . . " She heaved a sigh and began to mumble almost inaudibly. "We were, well, *lonely* in those days. Sort of . . . desperate to get on with it, you know. Just so there'd be people around." She began to cough violently, her frail body racked with spasms.

Feeling awkward, Ordspleef snapped to attention in the manner of a trained soldier-scientist and began to report.

"Shiprock, as it is so named, consists of a large volcanic plug of composite mineral content. A cyclone was survived on the ascent. The mountain is home to a Type-C anthropoid that I strongly suspect is yet another example of Terranalogous sexual dimorphism and which displayed aggressive behavior on the part of the female toward—"

"All I wish to know," cut in Dr. Wayomo, ever so gently, "is this: *Why?*"

"Why?" repeated Ordspleef.

"Why did you feel the need to climb the mountain?"

A strained silence followed. Spleechdorf, whose computerized education had been engineered with the intention of producing a type of hybrid priest/psychologist to function as a counselor in the community, was about to blurt something passionate and illogical when Ordspleef, the scientist, interjected his own half-formed hypothesis.

"We acted according to an inner compulsion," he said.

"Where," said Dr. Wayomo, now sitting erect and narrowing her brow, "where in the psyche would you say this 'inner compulsion' lies?"

Ordspleef paused thoughtfully. "I would say that it lies *outside* the psyche, primarily."

"Well, then, where in the *brain* does it originate?"

"The compulsion undoubtedly originates in the lower brain."

"And therefore cannot be described using words," chimed in Spleechdorf. Seeing that he now had the floor, he felt obliged to continue. "However, what is known for sure is that the experience of climbing the mountain is one I wish to repeat."

"Where did you learn the techniques?" asked the doctor.

"The Library Computer Archive contained numerous references," replied Ordspleef.

"But you consulted the Archive only *after* you had felt this 'compulsion from within'?"

"Affirmative."

"Then the impulse came from within you, was not placed there by an exterior source?"

"Presumably. Or, rather, not determinable. The shape of the mountain in the clearness of the night seemed to suggest the idea of climbing it."

Dr. Wayomo cradled her empty teacup and silently regarded the two boys. She tried to remember why it was that people climbed mountains. Perhaps it was the same urge that had brought Earthlings here—to spread their toxic matrix across the surface of a new host. Thinking about it brought a deep, familiar melancholy.

"So this is how it's going to be after all," she muttered, sagging back in her chair.

"Antecedent?" queried Ordspleef.

She sighed. *"Plus ça change, plus c'est la même chose."*

Another awkward silence followed. Ordspleef and Spleechdorf sensed they had offended the Old Lady. They had each been educated on the subject of twenty-first-century Earth and its systemic problems, but neither had ever really thought about the subject in any relevant way. (It was a moot history lesson, anyway, since Alpha-wave transmissions from Earth had ceased for unknown reasons many years earlier.)

There remained much the two climbers wanted to ask the doctor, but something kept them from it.

"Leave me now, please. I am tired." Her eyes had gone hollow.

As the climbers were heading through the door, Spleechdorf turned and said, "Thank you for the tea."

"Your knowledge of ancient Terran customs is to be commended," Dr. Wayomo said wistfully. Or was it something other than knowledge? Then they were gone from the room.

1993

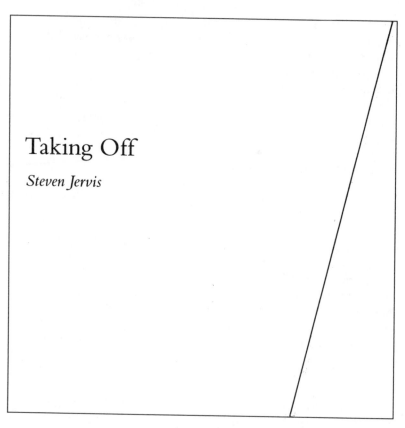

Taking Off

Steven Jervis

Aaron shouldered his rope and gave me a pleading glance. "Come on and climb with us, Martin. Angela's just a beginner. She could use a little support." He added, "I did some dental work on her once," as if that explained her sudden appearance at the cliffs. The girl grinned. Her patched, faded jeans looked ready for the landfill, and her socks poked through her flimsy tennis shoes. Although Aaron told me she was twenty-four—which still made her a good fifteen years younger than either of us—she looked like a teenager: very slight, too much lipstick, and a ridiculous punk haircut. Her hair was purple, with a swath of orange.

"We're heading for North Pillar, if nobody's on it yet," Aaron said. "Come on, Mart. We could use a warm-up."

Though "pillar" sounded imposing, the route was one of the easiest on the cliffs. Its two-hundred-feet of quartz conglomerate were steep, but good holds abounded, as though they had been put there for neophyte climbers.

When we reached the pillar Angela said, "This looks like scary shit."

"It's only 5.2," Aaron said, with a comforting smile. "The ratings go all the way up to 5.11 these days."

I found Angela's presence unfunny and interfering. Aaron had become the perfect climbing partner for me, a vivid and happy contrast with his predecessor, R.J., who, like me, was a physicist at Bell Labs. In the year and a half since my break with R.J., Aaron and I had been jointly sharpening our climbing skills. Almost every weekend, while our wives managed home and children, we attempted successively tougher routes. During the week, Aaron was a temperate, hard-working dentist: a large, gentle man, almost as tall as I was and a good bit heavier. His soft, pale flesh overlay rigorously trained muscle—persistence had compensated for a lack of physical gifts.

Aaron could have flown up the first pitch of the Pillar—he and I were solid 5.7 climbers by then. But he took it slow, issuing instructions and explanations: "Only one person climbs at a time, and only the leader takes any risks. Those metal things sticking out of the rock are called pitons." And so on. He stepped up to a ledge. "See this little pine tree? You'll want to pull up on it, but don't. Move left like this and there's a bucket hold for both hands." He was always methodical, but I'd never seen him take such care with a beginner.

When Aaron called "on belay," I helped Angela tie her waistloop, inhaling sweetish perfume in the process. She paused for a few puffs of what was obviously not tobacco. "Off you go," I said. She moved faster than I had expected, but with great clamor and protest: "Pull that rope up! Oh God I'm gonna fall. Where do I put my foot now? Aaron, goddamnit, help me!"

North Pillar turned out to be Angela's only climb of the day—and I hoped of her career. But she hadn't done badly: she made a lot of noise but she got up. "That's what counts," I told Aaron later, halfway up a climb of our own.

"I guess so." His voice cracked with embarrassment, and he kept taking off his glasses and adjusting their rubber tie-cord.

"Look, you've fulfilled your obligations. She won't want to try again."

"Oh my, I hope not. She just phoned me out of nowhere and said she was coming up. I haven't seen her in three years. I hardly remembered her name. I guess I did invite her once, but I do that with lots of patients, just to make conversation before I start to drill. This is the first one who ever took me seriously."

It was late April, and the cliffs were crowded—every year brought more climbers. But if you walked half a mile down the carriage road or simply looked for less popular routes, you could have almost any climb to yourself. Aaron had much of R.J.'s muscle without (thank God) his overbearing energy. He, like me, was a devoted family man. His dental office, where I occasionally picked him up on my way to the cliffs, was decorated with pictures of his wife and four children. The older two were in high school, and Aaron was struggling to save for their college tuition. Other photos showed him on the cliffs in a red Gore-Tex jacket, inching up a thin face and leading a spectacular overhang, his rope bellying out behind him. I wondered what his patients thought of those photos, and of the set of weights that he trained on between appointments.

I was in high gear the following weekend. "Next stop, 5.9," I shouted down to Aaron after I'd pulled past an overhang. The air was fresh with pine and laurel. We quickly finished the route, clambered down the trail, and started up another 5.8. It was Aaron's turn to lead. His finesse did not match his strength; halfway up, his legs started to shake. I braced myself for a fall, but it never came. "Didn't know you had it in you," I said when I joined him at the belay ledge.

He grinned. "It's amazing how these tiny holds can support a big, clumsy guy like me." Some climbers were passing along the carriage road below, their hardware slings jangling. At the base of the cliff (and right in the line of any rocks we might dislodge) a girl was waving and calling up to us. "Oh, Mart," Aaron said in a stricken voice. "I didn't know she was coming up this time. I swear." As I discovered back at the Staging Area, Angela was transformed: the awful punk hair had turned a rational light brown, the lips an unadorned pink. She smelled of pine trees, not of Shalimar or whatever it had been. The patched jeans remained, but a couple of bright new Salewa carabiners were clipped to her belt loops. With a surge of resentment, I realized she was going to be around for a long time.

Aaron stared at her as he would at a patient with an untimely toothache. I got away as soon as decency allowed—maybe sooner. I sat on my good-luck boulder and ate my cheese and jelly sandwiches. Then I dipped a cup of water from the stream while talking to Maury Hopkins and Rod Ross, a pair of young hotshots. Their hands were white with chalk, an innovation I thought superfluous at best. Maury and Rod were college dropouts—Dartmouth and New Paltz, respectively—on their way to becoming climbing bums. "We're out to Yosemite next week," Rod told me, "before it really heats up. We want to do a big-wall climb, maybe the Nose. Then up to the Wind Rivers and Canada."

I felt a stab of envy. Since the birth of Laurie, our second child, I hadn't been anywhere near the big mountains.

"We'll be back," Maury said. "Everybody comes back to the cliffs eventually." They swigged their water and set off for some ferocious 5.11 or other.

I wanted to try a hard route called Moonbeam, but when I saw Angela shouldering a climbing rope I knew my ambitions would have to wait. Aaron looked sheepish as hell; I think he even blushed. "She drove that VW all the way up from White Plains. We can't just let her sit around." *We?* I would have tried to lead Moonbeam if I could have found a decent belayer. But no one was free; the cliffs had grown more anonymous in the ten years I had been coming there. I ended up on Cantata, another beginner's climb, with Aaron and Angela.

This must have been at least my twentieth ascent of the route, but it was unlike any other. Angela had lost all her fear. She charged up the rock with foul-mouthed bravado, faster than Aaron could take in the rope. The wind blew her shirttails around her waist, revealing smooth, youthful flesh. She was wearing a tight new pair of climbing shoes, instead of discolored sneakers, and she darted over a 5.4 variation that Aaron had pointedly omitted. Only a high reach made her pause. I scrambled up after her, unroped—there was something in the girl's boldness that I needed to match.

Mother's Day claimed my next climbing weekend. When I returned, everything had changed. Angela was there, as I had feared she would be, standing by her old VW, coolly gearing up. She sported a red and black Chouinard waist harness, a hardware sling with a selection of wired stoppers, and a half-dozen carabiners. They had clearly seen some use: I was sure she had been climbing with Aaron the previous weekend. For an awkward moment we stood on the carriage road—the three of us, or the two of them—poised for an uncertain destination. Finally Aaron declared, "Let's go." Driven by outrage and curiosity, I followed.

I was shocked to see how thoroughly Angela had absorbed the codes and routines of rockclimbing. The minute we had scrambled up the boulderfield to the base of the climb (an intermediate route this time) she carefully uncoiled Aaron's rope, hitched up her harness, and looped a tie-in around a tree. "Want some extra biners?" she asked Aaron, who was preparing to lead the first pitch. I stood slack, a spectator. Aaron had new gear himself, including some multi-colored sewn slings, and was absurdly overequipped for a 5.5. He started off like a freight train, all bells and whistles. Angela was stretched tight against her belay loop as though a major fall were imminent. She seemed too frail for her job, but she paid out the rope and flexed her thin arms like the climbing pro she obviously intended to be. I didn't trust her technique, however, and when it came my turn to lead, I insisted that Aaron do the belaying. "I can hold you all right," Angela claimed. "Just try me."

"Thanks, but I'll let you practice on somebody else." But she insisted and I kept quiet. The going was only about 5.3 now, and my arms and feet moved automatically. I wasn't thinking about my next handhold, but about my next climb. My plans to lift Aaron and me into the realm of 5.9 rock—modest for many others, real stratosphere for us—seemed like dreams. If I were to get there, it would have to be with some other partner.

"You got twenty-five feet of rope left!" Angela howled up.

"*Off belay*, goddamnit! Take it easy." I had never felt so happy to reach the top. All I wanted was to hurry down the descent trail and find somebody else—*any*body else—to climb with.

But the Staging Area was almost empty when I reached it, well ahead of Aaron and Angela. There were a couple of bikers, a few wives or girlfriends sunning themselves, and a golden retriever tethered to my boulder. Then I saw Rod Ross; he had postponed his departure for California because of poverty and a fight with Maury: "He was getting stoned all the time. It was like he was in a goddamn trance the minute he woke up in the morning. Not the best way to climb, if you ask me."

We looked poorly matched, Rod and I—he was much stronger and younger—but we had the same immediate aspirations. I told Aaron I would be busy the rest of the afternoon. He looked not at all sorry to hear it.

Rod and I did three routes, hardly exchanging a word—no pep talks, such as I often had with Aaron, no pauses to steady our nerves. We just kept moving, with Rod taking the toughest leads, and me doing a gratifyingly confident job with the rest. I felt fresher than I had in years.

Halfway up our last climb, as though it had just occurred to him, Rod said, "Hey, man, how come you aren't with the dentist today?"

"He's picked up a camp follower."

"Yeah, I noticed. Robbing the cradle."

"She's not as young as you think." Older than Rod, come to think of it. Was I a cradle robber too, seizing the chance to climb beyond my middle-aged abilities? These three routes were the hardest I had ever done. After a good day there is always one move you remember, with the clarity of a perfect dive or a tennis ball smacked just right. This one came on my next lead, where a twelve-foot roof forced a move around a smooth, blocky corner to the left. I would have to swing around it on a single small handhold, while smearing my feet on whatever I could find. Then quickly, before I would tire, switch hands on the hold and stretch left to a vertical crack. Ordinarily, I would have rehearsed the sequence half a dozen times before embarking upon it. Not today. I didn't even tell Rod to "watch me"; I just set off. My hands fell into place with a gymnast's precision, and my shoes pulled their own way up the rock. In that moment I felt that I could climb anything, that I could *be* anything. When I reached a breathing place I glanced down at Rod. He was staring out over the green checkered expanse of the valley, oblivious of my achievement, but I must have replayed it a hundred times in my tent that night. I was tired but not sleepy. I could feel every muscle, which reminded me both of my age and of my strength. Then came the first tappings of rain on the tent fly, promising a wet Sunday and a welcome rest.

In the morning I saw Angela emerge from Aaron's tent, her head poking through a large raincoatlike trash bag. Later he told me, at unnecessary length, that she had moved in only when the rain started— and he could hardly have turned her away, could he? She had only a light Dacron sleeping bag in all this lousy weather.

"Just don't carry the hospitality too far," I said.

"You're being ridiculous, Mart." He wiped his glasses, replaced them, wiped them again. Whatever might have happened in that tent, he looked like a guilty man. I hardly felt like climbing with him and Angela the next Saturday, even after I learned that Rod had gone to California after all. But for me, that Saturday never came anyway: two days before, taking my morning wind sprints with extra determination, I tripped and tumbled into a ditch. Though I didn't realize it till midday, my left ankle was badly sprained. My climbing boots would stay untouched in the basement for a long time.

Aaron stopped by to commiserate, along with his wife and their two youngest children. Miriam, who occasionally filled in as a receptionist at the dental office, was a pretty, slightly overweight young woman with a pinkish-white complexion and dark, abundant hair. She greeted me as "my husband's accomplice."

"Temporarily out of commission," I said. "This sort of thing makes you feel pretty vulnerable." My swollen ankle, encased in an old cotton sock, was propped on a footstool.

"Well, you'd better heal up soon. Aaron's spirits sink like a stone if he can't go climbing. I don't know what he's going to do without you on Memorial Day."

I thought I knew, as I told Ellen after our visitors had left. "I don't believe it," she said. "He's the most domesticated man I've ever met. Can't you see how Miriam has him tamed? And he dotes on those kids. They were jumping all over him."

"I'm concerned."

"How can this girl be so tempting? She sounds like an outdated hippie to me. Why are you so concerned about her, anyway?"

"I'm not concerned about *her*—and I don't find her tempting. I don't want to lose my partner, that's all."

My ankle stayed stubbornly swollen and tender. I was able to drive myself to the lab, borrowing Ellen's automatic so I wouldn't have to depress the clutch, but I was still hobbling along the corridors and grabbing the banisters whenever I tried the stairs. It was midsummer before I could walk without limping, just in time for the family vacation in Nova Scotia. I didn't return to the cliffs until Labor Day.

Aaron had not mentioned Angela, and I wondered whether she had vanished as abruptly as she had arrived. But no: she was more elaborately outfitted than ever, with a bright selection of sewn slings, a full hardware rack, and even a half-empty chalkbag. She and Aaron wore blue "Go Climb a Rock" tee-shirts. Her gear must have weighed half what she did, but she seemed right at home with it. When I asked Aaron what he wanted to climb, it was Angela who answered: "Moonbeam."

"Wait a minute. I haven't been on the rocks for over three months."

"You don't have to lead," she said. "Don't worry. Shit, man, you're safe with us. Right, Ari?"

They headed down the carriage road hand in hand, elbows swinging. I snatched my rope and followed them like a client trailing after his guides. At the start of the route, Angela led off without a word and Aaron tied in to belay. I couldn't believe it: she had started climbing less than six months ago, a scared little girl, and here she was leading a hard 5.8. Aaron clearly sensed my shock. "Take it easy, Mart. You'll see."

I would, and soon: the toughest part was twenty-five feet off the ground—a sharp overhang, with a thin, nearly vertical face above. The guidebook said that "delicacy and strength" were needed to gain a flaring crack ten feet higher. Moreover, the protection was very poor. I stationed myself beneath the fall line, just in case.

It's more nervewracking watching hard moves than doing them yourself. Angela would either float up the rock or thrash around and peel off. Aaron looked completely relaxed, as though she could not fall, or the laws of gravity would be suspended for her if she did. She was up the easy first few feet in a flash, her feet racing after her hands. She paused to clip an ancient piton, then moved up on smaller holds—more slowly, but apparently still in total control. Then she was beneath the overhang, near enough to touch it if she were as tall as most of us. The only protection was a piton that looked even older than the first. Its eye was broken and it was beyond Angela's reach anyway. "Don't wear yourself out," I said. "Come down for a rest."

"I'm all right."

"Try a stopper next to the pin," Aaron advised. But she would have to make the move first and place the protection afterward. Already the first piton was too far down to break a fall—she would land right on top of me. She couldn't weigh a hundred pounds, but I was not looking forward to the impact. I braced myself as Angela started up. One smooth motion and a grunt—she grabbed the stopper, which she had clamped between her teeth, and thrust it into the crack.

"Attagirl, Angie!" Aaron shouted. But as she tried to clip a biner, the stopper tumbled right out and landed by my feet. Aaron's eyes bulged, as though he had just dropped a gold inlay down a patient's throat. He froze on the belay, nearly pulling Angela off. But she got her hands above the overhang, flashed the vertical face, and jammed a chock into the flaring crack above. "Piece of goddamn cake," she said.

She had made quite a lead. But later, when Aaron was out of earshot, I said, "You damn near came off down there, didn't you?"

"It was kinda desperate," she admitted, with a wide, shaky grin.

"You don't have to prove anything. That isn't what climbing is about." We were sitting on Broadway, the tree-filled ledge that runs the entire length of the cliff; Angela was sorting her hardware while I belayed Aaron up the last pitch. Her hair was laced with twigs and pine needles. I felt like brushing them off. Instead, I asked her what she did.

"What do I *do*?"

"You know, for a living. Like Aaron's a dentist, I'm a physicist."

"Yeah, and I'm a waitress and a grad student and a dealer."

"A what?"

"You're so straight, Martin, you could fucking break in half. You should try something new in your life, you know that? A *dealer*. Just pot, nothing hard. I get seventy-five dollars an ounce, if the stuff is good. A girl's gotta live. I want to go to med school some day, you know. I had a 3.7 average at Stony Brook." She turned her head, displacing a few twigs. "Shit, you look shocked out of your skin."

"Why are you climbing with Aaron?"

"Because I *like* him. He's a terrific guy."

"I know that."

"I wonder if you really do. You don't know him as well as you think. We're a team, you know—we climbed in New Hampshire together last month."

News to me. I wondered when I would have the chance for a few private words with Aaron. Finally, all I managed was a hurried, almost furtive exchange outside the Brauhaus that evening, while Angela lingered briefly, talking to some college climbers. I took him by the arm. "Aaron, what's going on with you and Angela?"

"What do you mean? Angie's a natural talent. You saw her on Moonbeam."

"I saw her. Climbing ability wasn't what I meant, Aaron. We've been friends a while. Our families are friends."

"Yeah, all right. Listen, Mart, I didn't invite her up here. Well, not really. Look, there are things you can't control. She's fifteen years younger than me, and it's all very temporary. There's never been anything like it before, and there won't be anything again. Miriam doesn't know, so nobody's getting hurt."

As the days grew shorter, I struggled to squeeze in three or four routes by dark, climbing with whomever I could find. Rod and Maury were back, stronger than ever, and several old friends often drove all the way from Pittsburgh. For a while Angela and Aaron seemed just two of the many hundreds of visitors to the cliffs. She was gaining a little fame, however: substituting guile for muscle, she could find her way up almost anything.

One bright, crisp morning, the coolest of the season, I found Aaron at the Staging Area, arranging his hardware sling. He would unclip a biner full of wired nuts, sort them, then get to work on his formidable collection of chocks and stoppers. He must have gone through everything twice, while I pulled on my harness and stowed my day pack. "Want to climb, Mart?" he said in a strange, pleading voice.

"Sure. Why not? Your choice."

"Anything, Mart. Anything you want is fine with me."

"Okay: Intemperance, then. I've never led the second pitch."

I got up it: a series of inside corners topped by a committing overhang that damn near defeated me. Even after I had brought Aaron up to my belay, I felt the adrenalin surge that had propelled me past the final obstacle. "By the way," I said, "where's Angela?"

"Oh, she's around." His tone was as studiously casual as mine. "With Maury, I think. He promised to take her on a 5.9."

Wherever she was the rest of that day, it wasn't with Aaron and me. We kept moving, but once he forgot to remove one of my chocks after unclipping and had to descend fifty feet to retrieve it. He nearly left his tie-in sling on top of a climb, and his rope handling was distracted, to say the least.

We had supper in the Brauhaus, at one of the tables around the bar—the only section permitted to climbers, whom Franz, the owner, carefully segregated from his respectable patrons. Aaron turned voluble. "David's getting braces, you know. He's almost eleven. It's incredible how fast they grow up, Mart." I learned more about Aaron's children, and their dental health, in that half-hour than I had in all the years I had known him. But halfway through a description of little Sarah's gums, Aaron flicked his eyes to the door behind me. The biggest table in the place had been filled by a bunch of young climbers, including Rod, Maury, and Angela. They were starting a pitcher of beer. Aaron's talk accelerated like a record playing at the wrong speed; he hardly picked at his sauerbraten. On the drive back to the campground I asked no questions. They were all answered for me the next morning, when I saw Angela crawl out of Maury's tent, yawn, and fire up his small propane stove. Her sleeping bag was draped over her shoulders.

Aaron looked red-eyed but was full of energy. "I want to do Triple Overhang," he announced.

"Get serious, Aaron—that's 5.10."

"I know what it's rated. I can do it."

"Then it's your funeral. Who do you want for pallbearers?"

The venture seemed pretty crazy, but if there was any 5.10 Aaron could handle, this was it: three consecutive roofs, increasingly difficult. Aaron chinned himself fifty times a day on a doorsill. But I had seen Rod Ross nearly peel off that third overhang, and I was sure it would be too much for Aaron.

I'll say this for him: he got up the first two 'hangs not just quickly but well. He was as smooth as I'd seen him, placing his feet carefully, saving his muscles for last. There were lots of holds, but the angle was fantastic: I had to tip my head way back to check his progress. The protection was fine; resting places were not. Aaron was poised beneath the final overhang, feet high, arms out. He hoisted himself up a couple of tentative times; then he shouted "Okay!," seized a hold above the overhang, cranked himself up, and fell. It was a dramatic little tumble, but harmless. The rock was too steep for him to hit anything, and I stopped him easily after less than ten feet. Letting loose a volley of curses, he pulled himself back up to his piton. "Mart, that hold was goddamn slippery!" He chalked up his hands and repeated the maneuver, including the fall.

"Take it easy," I told him. He was breathing like a steam engine.

"I was two inches away," he said. *"Two fucking inches!"* Without pausing, he launched himself up once more. Every muscle seemed ready to burst as his left hand sought that key hold. Two inches, one . . . with a cry of fury he was off again, plummeting those now-familiar ten feet. "I almost had it!" he roared.

He made four more ferocious lunges, with successively earlier falls. The spectacle attracted a small crowd on the carriage road below. Finally I had to lower him like an exhausted whale and, with difficulty, retrieve the hardware myself. I took a quick, harrowing look at that final overhang, amazed that Aaron had come so close.

Chastened and silent, he followed me up an easy escape route a hundred feet to the right. Along the trail he started muttering, but said nothing to me until after lunch. "I never should have tried it," he admitted miserably.

"Come on. It was very gutsy of you. You got a lot higher than I ever thought you could."

Now on our way to an easier climb at the remote, uncrowded end of the cliffs, we kicked aside the brittle leaves that blew across the road. "What really gets me," Aaron said, "is that I *had* it that second time. I should have jumped my foot up—that's all it would have taken."

"It's a 5.10, Aaron, for God's sake. We had no business being on it. We're not a couple of kids anymore."

"I wish we were," he said bitterly. "I wish I'd started when I was fourteen. I wish I weren't a middle-aged dentist."

"Don't be ridiculous, Aaron. You never talk like this."

"Maury could have made that move," he said. "Angela, too," he added in a voice full of pain.

Aaron's phone call jolted Ellen and me out of our sleep. I stumbled up to the extension phone in my attic study, half tripping over a computer cable. "What's the matter?" I said. "It's the middle of the night."

"I know, Mart. I'm sorry. This has never happened to me before. I can't sleep. I don't know what to do."

"Okay, calm down. Have you talked to Miriam?"

"Miriam is a wonderful woman."

"You haven't been drinking, Aaron?"

"No, no, of course not. I did smoke a little of Angie's marijuana. Just to help me sleep, Mart—been doing that a bit lately. I thought I would be all right, that it wouldn't make any difference, but I can't bear it."

"For God's sake, she's just a child. You knew it had to end—you said so yourself. She's with Maury now, right?"

"Yes, yes, but I don't blame her. He's a stronger climber than I am. She told me about it very nicely. But it feels so strange—like we were just getting started, and now it's over. It's so terribly incomplete. Haven't you ever felt this way?"

"Aaron, she treated you badly, all right? Get *angry*, for God's sake. Blow off some steam and get on with your life. You have Miriam, the kids, your practice. You're climbing better than ever."

"Don't say anything against her, Mart. Please. She was never nasty or anything. We're still friends. She just had to move on."

By the time we finished talking, it was after three, and I was the one who couldn't sleep. I slid in beside Ellen and slipped an arm beneath her nightgown. She responded with something between a sigh and a grunt. We shared everything except climbing, but I felt only relief that she didn't ask me what had been on Aaron's mind at so strange an hour.

Aaron had ended our phone conversation by saying how much better he felt, but his voice still sounded cracked and miserable. So I was relieved to find him at the cliffs the next Saturday, looking almost cheerful. His face had something like its familiar gentle grin. I was reminded of how smoothly he moved for a man of his bulk, and of how far he had progressed, over the years, through sheer determination. It was early November now. We had to pause every twenty feet or so to breathe the circulation back into our hands. He didn't say a word about Angela until dinner at an Italian restaurant in town, where we had gone to escape the Brauhaus crowd. After several glasses of wine he told me that he had started seeing a psychologist. "Just once a week. Nothing major. He's helped me get this Angela thing in perspective. He says it was something I had to do. I shouldn't feel bad about it, but I should put it behind me."

"Sounds good to me." I meant the last part. I wondered whether Aaron had been observing Angela's progress. She had started climbing with a group of women who called themselves the Rock Bitches. "Well, I'm glad to have you back," I said. "For a time there, you seemed to be off in some other country."

"I guess I did." His glance slid upward. "I'm getting better now. It's like recuperating from surgery. The pain fades, and you come out stronger than you were before. My life is finally taking off." He tilted his head a little, as though monitoring his own explanation.

Aaron was getting so much better that we kept climbing past the first snowfalls. He continued his "recuperation"; he still talked about Angela, but always in the past tense, which is where I thought she belonged. She was out of sight now, as if in hibernation. Each weekend Aaron and I had to add a layer of clothing. We finally called a halt in early December—the holidays were coming up, and the temperatures on the cliffs were more than my fingers could take.

To my surprise, Aaron and his entire family attended our Christmas Day party. We had routinely invited them for years, but just as a formality, since they observed only Hanukkah. Miriam looked bewildered by the tinsel and the poinsettia, but Aaron and the children threw themselves into the frolic. Aaron was like an outsized boy, especially after he had been at the eggnog a while. His cheeks were almost as red as his bright turtleneck. He spun around the dining room like a 180-pound top. Later he danced, clumsily but energetically, with Miriam and Ellen. He was the last to leave, with Miriam tugging at the sleeve of his down coat.

Aaron phoned me two days later, from the office. "I hope we didn't overstay our welcome."

"Don't apologize for having a good time."

"I won't. The party really cheered me up. It gave me an idea, too: I don't want to just sit around the house New Year's Day. How about a quick trip to the cliffs? We'll have the place to ourselves."

"With good reason."

"Just think about it, Mart. Just think about it. The days have been warming up. This could be our last chance till spring."

"Aaron, you're getting crazier every day. But it would be an exciting way to start the year—let me talk to Ellen about it. And do make some sensible resolutions, okay?"

Aaron was not at the Staging Area when I arrived that brisk New Year's morning. Nobody was. I did a few wind sprints to warm up, then looked at the bulletin board: the usual offers to sell hardware, the pleas for climbing partners (sometimes explicitly female), reports of lost equipment. I saw a fresh scrap of paper tacked right in the middle: "Martin—am soloing Brimstone. Ari."

Brimstone! That was hard enough in warm weather. It culminated in a huge roof, which I assumed Aaron would have the sense to avoid by the simple alternate to the right; but even easy soloing seemed foolhardy in such conditions. I set off down the road, anxious about where his exuberance had led him. "Aaron," I shouted, "what the hell are you doing up there, you crazy man?" There was no response, and no sign of him on the rock. With the leaves off the trees, the whole route was visible. He must have completed it already. I shouted a few more times, then started back toward the Staging Area. I'm not sure what made me stop—perhaps some notion that Aaron was playing a trick on me, lurking like a mischievous child in the tumbled boulders leading up to the cliff. I started up to look, calling his name, waiting for him to jump out, grinning.

Then I saw him lying beneath the climb. "Cut it out, Aaron," I shouted. "You're too old for these games." He was in an impossible position. One leg was tucked under him, the other thrust out in a weird V. Blood was still flowing from an enormous head wound. Amazingly, his glasses were still attached.

I rolled him over and for ten terrible, exhausting minutes tried my CPR. When I had no breath left, I gave up. After climbing for ten years, I had never seen anything worse than my own sprained ankle. I couldn't believe how unanswerable Aaron's injuries were.

I had to rouse the ranger from his home outside town and notify the state police. It was noon before a dark blue pick-up truck, with a lumpy, blanketed shape in back, could make its way slowly down the carriage road and onto the highway. When I phoned Miriam, she cried for what felt like hours, and I could find nothing to console her.

There was a service, with a rabbi and a box of spare yarmulkes. I took one, but it only made me feel more exposed and vulnerable. Angela, I learned later, had left for California with another young woman. She sent some flowers to Aaron's home. The chamber was full of his friends and patients. Several spoke of his weekend recreation in reverent, mystified tones. "It is hard to see the hand of God in so terrible an accident," one man said falteringly. "Yet we know it is there." I did nothing to disturb this comfortable interpretation of Aaron's catastrophe. But it had been obvious to me, from the distance of his body from the cliff, that he must have taken a running leap from the top. I wondered whether this was what he had in mind the day he phoned me from the office, or whether it had occurred to him only as he gazed over the valley and saw his life spread out before him. I like to think that he had completed the climb, the hard way over the brim, before he took off.

1993

Appendix 1

The following is an annotated table of contents of every issue of *Ascent* except this one.

1967 (VOLUME I, NO. 1)

Front cover photograph by Allen Steck of Mt. Logan's Hummingbird Ridge, Yukon Territory.

"Found in a Storm." Poem by William Stafford.

"Ascent of Hummingbird Ridge." By Allen Steck. Account of a thirty-seven-day ascent of a major ridge on Mt. Logan, in the Yukon Territory.

"Pens Over Everest." By Bernard Hollowood (first name misspelled as "Bernhard"). Short satirical piece reprinted from a 1952 issue of *Punch*.

"American Antarctic Mountaineering Expedition." By William Long. Account of the expedition that made the first ascent of Antarctica's highest peak, the Vinson Massif.

"A Visitor to Yosemite." By Ian Howell. An English climber is impressed with the Valley's notorious cracks.

"Yosemite Valley." Eight black-and-white photographs by Glen Denny.

"Games Climbers Play." By Lito Tejada-Flores. Essay on hierarchical "rules" of mountaineering.

"Yerupajá." By Lief-Norman Patterson. Account of the second ascent of Peru's most beautiful peak.

"A Climber's Guide to Lover's Leap." By Steve Roper. First-ever guide to area near California's Lake Tahoe.

"A Moment of Suspense." By Giusto Gervasutti. (First name misspelled throughout issue.) Introspective account of a solo climb in the Dolomites in the 1930s. Reprinted from *Gervasutti's Climbs*.

"L'enfer des montagnards." By Samivel. Witty drawing and letter by well-known French artist.

"The Icefall." By Hans Morgenthaler. Short prose poem about an afternoon in the life of an icefall. Translated by Allen Steck from the 1920 book *Ihr Berge*.

"Yosemite Mountaineering Notes." Edited by Chuck Pratt. Descriptions of selected Yosemite climbs done between 1964 and 1966.

"Sierra Nevada Mountaineering Notes." Edited by Steve Roper. Several routes described.

"Editorial." By the editors. Explanation of the need for yet another mountaineering journal.

"Contributors." By the editors. Short biographical sketches.

Back cover photograph by Dave Bohn of Mt. Fairweather, Alaska.

1968 (VOLUME I, NO. 2)

Front cover photograph by Steve Roper of climber on the southwest face of Yosemite's Liberty Cap.

"The Rock Is." Poem by Joe Fitschen.

"The West Face." By Royal Robbins. Account of first ascent of El Capitan's "hidden" face.

"Behold Now Behemoth." By Pete Sinclair (misspelled as "Sinclaire"). Essay on regulations concerning climbing in U.S. national parks. With extensive comments by the editors.

"Tuesday Morning on the Lyell Fork with Eliot's Shadow." By Doug Robinson. Reflective account of a day's outing in Yosemite National Park.

"Canada." Four black-and-white photographs by Ed Cooper.

"Mt. McKinley: The Direct South Face." By Dave Seidman. Account of first ascent.

"Climbing in Britain." Five black-and-white photographs by Ken Wilson.

"The Bat and the Wicked." By Robin Smith. First ascent of a difficult route in Scotland. Reprinted from the May 1960 issue of the *Scottish Mountaineering Journal*.

"Climbing on Ice." By Yvon Chouinard. Description of modern techniques. Photographs by Tom Frost.

"Accidents in 1968." By Joe Kelsey. Parody of American Alpine Club's Accident Report.

"Climber's Guide to Mt. Shasta." By Steve Roper. Guide to Northern California's glacier-clad peak. Photographs by Ernest Carter.

"Mountaineering Notes." Edited by Dave Dornan. Descriptions of new climbs in Yosemite, Sierra Nevada, the Southwest, Shawangunks, and Canada.

"Book Reviews." Five reviews by Joe Fitschen.

"Editorial." By the editors. Announcement of a price increase from $1.00 to $2.50 per issue!

"Obituary of Larry Williams." By the editors.

"Contributors." By the editors. Short biographical sketches.

Back cover photograph by Barry Hagen of sunset on Peru's Jirishanca.

1969 (VOLUME I, NO. 3)

Front cover photograph by Barry Hagen of Mt. Waddington.

"Yerupajá." By Dean Caldwell. Account of new route on Peruvian peak.

"The Climber as Visionary." By Doug Robinson. Essay on the alteration of consciousness while climbing.

"The Jewel in the Lotus." By James McCarthy. First ascent of the sweeping face of Lotus Flower Tower, in the Northwest Territories.

"The Fiend." By Tom Higgins. Short story of "world's best climber."

"Interview with Fritz Wiessner." Edited by Dave Dornan. A talk with one of the world's most noted climbers. Emphasis on his role in 1939 K2 expedition.

"Mt. Waddington." By Barry Hagen. Short history of British Columbia's remote and challenging peak. With extensive bibliography.

"Photo Essay." By Barry Hagen. Black-and-white photographs of Mt. Waddington and environs.

"White Elephant, White Whale." By Ed Ward-Drummond. Short account of attempt on El Capitan.

"Matterhorn." By Dennis Eberl. Account of a climb up the north face.

"The Conquest of Tillie's Lookout." By Ira Wallach. Parody of expedition climb. Reprinted from *Mad* magazine.

"Eleven Domes." By Steve Roper. Climber's guide to Tuolumne Meadows.

"Mountaineering Notes." By the editors. Descriptions of new climbs in Yosemite, Sierra Nevada, and Idaho.

Five books reviewed by various people.

"Editorial." By the editors. Climbing restrictions in national parks.

"Contributors." By the editors. Short biographical sketches.

Back cover photograph by Alex Bertulis of the south ridge of Alaska's Mt. Foraker.

1970 (VOLUME I, NO. 4)

Front cover photograph by William (Dolt) Feuerer of climber on Totem Pole, Arizona.

"Fromage to Patagonia, or the Sorry of Fats Ray." By Lito Tejada-Flores. Avant-garde fiction full of word plays.

"Up Against the Walls." By Joe Fitschen. Account of California expedition to the remote Kichatna Spires of Alaska.

"Dhaulagiri: A Mind Odyssey." By James Janney. Introspective reflections on 1969 tragedy.

"Tis-sa-ack." By Royal Robbins. Ultra-personal account of first ascent of a multi-day route up Yosemite's Half Dome.

Untitled. Five black-and-white photographs by various photographers of snow textures.

"Four Corners." By Steve Roper. Illustrated history and guide to desert climbs in the American Southwest.

"The View from Deadhorse Point." By Chuck Pratt. Humorous reflections on climbing trips to the Southwest from 1960 to 1969.

"Upper Crust." By Howard Bussey. Short take on the future of climbing.

"Mountaineering Notes." Edited by Steve Roper. Descriptions of routes in Yosemite and Sierra Nevada.

"Editorial." By the editors. Plug for *Mountain* magazine.

"Contributors." By the editors. Short biographical sketches.

Back cover by David Singer. Photomontage from a Fillmore West poster showing a giant hand hovering above El Capitan.

1971 (VOLUME I, NO. 5)

Front cover photograph by Yvon Chouinard of Doug Tompkins soloing on Hell's Lum, Cairngorms, Scotland.

"Waiting: Maroon Bells Campsite." Poem by Millie Marchand.

"Climbing Down Under." By Rob Taylor. Illustrated history and guide to Australian climbing areas.

"Little Mother up the Mörderberg." By H. G. Wells. Humorous fiction about climbing a small Alpine peak. Reprinted from the April 1910 *Strand* magazine.

"Yosemite's Other Valley." By Galen Rowell. Account of climbing in Hetch Hetchy Valley.

"Rojo's Peón." By Lito Tejada-Flores. Fictional account of adventures in Patagonia.

"The Lay of the Luckless Mountaineers." Poem by René Daumal. Reprinted from *Mount Analogue*.

"The Incubus Hills." By Ed Ward Drummond. Account of first ascent in the Orkney Islands.

"Reflections of a Broken-Down Climber." By Warren Harding. Humorous autobiographical ravings by legendary Yosemite climber.

"The Slippery Game." By Doug Robinson. Photographs and reflections on the then-obscure sport of pure ice climbing.

"A Pocket Guide to the Slippery Game." By Yvon Chouinard. Descriptions of places to climb ice in U.S. and Canada.

"Who Needs the AAC?" By Chris Jones. Opinion piece about American Alpine Club.

"Second Thoughts on Cerro Torre." By Douglas Tompkins. Short rumination on Caesar Maestri/Cerro Torre controversy.

"The Nine Deadly Sins." By David Roberts. Critique of "how-to-climb" books.

Five books reviewed by various people.

"Notes." Edited by Steve Roper. Descriptions of new climbs in Sierra Nevada and Trinity Alps.

Back cover photograph by Galen Rowell. Telephoto of the Nose of El Capitan.

1972 (VOLUME I, NO. 6)

Front cover photograph by Galen Rowell of climber on ledge, east face of Keeler Needle, Sierra Nevada.

"The Edge of the Sea." By John Cleare. Illustrated history of sea-cliff climbing in Great Britain.

"An Early Ascent of Half Dome." By A. Phimister Proctor. Account of an 1883 ascent of Yosemite's landmark. Reprinted from the 1946 *Sierra Club Bulletin*.

"The Moose's Tooth." By Tom Frost and Bradford Washburn. Five black-and-white photographs of the imposing Alaskan peak. With text.

"In Due Time." By Tom Higgins. A three-act satirical play about well-known Yosemite climbers and traditions.

"A Zion Story." By Jeff Lowe. Account of the first ascent of Jacob, Zion National Park, Utah.

"The Zion Guide." By Jeff Lowe. Descriptions of climbs in untouched Zion National Park, Utah.

"Rock." Four black-and-white photographs by Ed Cooper of rock textures.

"Icarus." By Ian Rowe. Short fiction about the best climber in the world.

"Alone on the Cima Grande." By Emilio Comici. Account of a 1937 solo ascent of a great Alpine north wall. With extensive introduction by Hans Kraus.

"Snow." Four black-and-white photographs by Ed Cooper of snow textures and glaciers.

"The Seventh Rifle." By Galen Rowell. Reflections on first ascent of west face of Canada's North Howser Tower.

"Climbers' Camp, Chamonix." By John Svenson. Prose poem about life below the aiguilles.

"Coonyard Mouths Off." By Yvon Chouinard. Opinion piece about bolts, responsibility, overpopulation of routes.

"Overpopulation and the Alpine Ego Trip." By Lito Tejada-Flores. Essay on potential destruction of the alpine experience.

"Reviews." By David Roberts. A look at the climbing magazines of the day.

Reviews of five books by various people.

"Notes." Edited by Steve Roper. Descriptions of new climbs in Yosemite and the Sierra Nevada.

"Contributors." By the editors. Short biographical sketches.

Back cover photograph by Galen Rowell of the moon over a Sierra ridge.

1973 (VOLUME II, NO. 1)

Front cover photograph by Leo Dickinson of Cerro Torre in storm.

"Mirror, Mirror." By Ed Drummond. Epic first ascent of Norway's Trolltind Wall.

"West Side Story." By Greg Donaldson. Accounts of new routes on western flank of Sierra Nevada.

"First on Alberta." By Jean Weber. Short account of first ascent of difficult Canadian peak. With extensive comments by Chris Jones.

"Canada in Winter." By Jim Stuart. Five aerial black-and-white photographs of significant peaks in the Canadian Rockies.

"The North Face of Alberta." By George Lowe. Account of the first ascent.

"The Taurus." By Harold Elwood. History of mountaineering in central Turkey's major range. With map and extensive bibliography.

"White Out." Poem by Ray Hadley.

"Moses: A Desert Phenomenon." By Fred Beckey. Account of first ascent of sandstone tower in American Southwest.

"Direktas." By Dennis Mehmet. Account of first ascent of remote Turkish spire.

"The Innocent, the Ignorant, and the Insecure." By Jim Bridwell. Essay on the Yosemite Decimal System. With a special section on the rating of difficult Yosemite free climbs.

Reviews of three books by various people.

"Excerpt from *Dhaulagirideon*." By Michael Charles Tobias. Experimental philosophical ramblings.

"Notes." By the editors. Descriptions of new routes in Yosemite and the Sierra Nevada.

"Contributors." By the editors. Short biographical sketches.

Back cover photograph by Jim Stuart. Telephoto of climbers near the Great Roof on the Nose of El Capitan.

1974 (VOLUME II, NO. 2)

"Magic Mountain." Front cover microphotograph by Edward Gelus.

"Rappelling." Poem by Gary McClellan.

"Freakers' Ball." By Jeff Salz. Account of climb and tragedy in Patagonia.

"Bouldering." Seven black-and-white photographs taken by Jim Stuart at Indian Rock, Berkeley, California.

"The Soloist's Diary." By Jeff Long. Surreal fictional story of an infinite climb. Lithographs by Jesse Allen.

"Yosemite." Six black-and-white photographs by Ed Cooper.

"The Rock Gods." By Joe Kelsey. Fiction involving Yosemite climbers after the "Great Mist."

"Epilog." Six-panel cartoon by Sheridan Anderson.

"La Derive." Poem by Carol Macgee.

"Fashion, Climbing & Dhaulagiri." By Todd Thompson. Expedition politics on world's ninth-highest peak.

"The Ridge." By Andy Harvard and Todd Thompson. Storms and worries on Dhaulagiri.

"Druggs in Himalaya." By Drummond Rennie. Humorous look at Kathmandu pharmacopeia.

"Dresden." By Steve Roper. Account of trip to East Germany's magnificent climbing area, the *Elbsandsteingebirge*.

"Swiftly & Surely." By Yvon Chouinard and Doug Robinson. Short account of ice-climbing techniques.

"Ice Is Nice and Will Suffice." By Bill Sumner. Account of trip to the Alaska Range.

"Sweet Potatoes." By Dick Isherwood. Account of early ascent of Australasia's highest point, the Carstensz Pyramid on New Guinea.

"Meditation VII." Poem by M. W. Borghoff.

"Dedo de Deus." By Malcolm Slesser and E. J. Henley. Differing accounts by participants of a climb on a spire near Rio de Janeiro.

"Climbing as Art." By Harold Drasdo. Essay on artistry in climbing.

"The Guidebook Problem." By Lito Tejada-Flores. Discussion of whether guidebooks help or hurt an area.

"Patey Agonistes: Or, a Look at Climbing Autobiographies." By David Roberts. In-depth look at a fascinating genre.

Reviews of eight books by various people.

"Contributors." By the editors. Short biographical sketches.

"An Editorial." By the editors. Discussion of money and the future.

Back cover photograph by Jeff Salz of climber traversing a ledge in a snowstorm, Patagonia.

1975/76 (VOLUME II, NO. 3)

Front cover photograph by George Lowe of climber on the north face of North Twin, Canadian Rockies.

"Preface." By the editors.

"North Twin, North Face." By Chris Jones. Account of first ascent in Canadian Rockies.

"Dream Ascents." Six drawings by Carol Ingram.

"In Thanks." By Tom Higgins. Reflections on a difficult Tuolumne Meadows rock climb.

"Southeast Alaska." By Fred Beckey. Geography and history of mountaineering in the Panhandle.

"Poontanga." By Geoffrey Childs. Fictional spoof of Himalayan expedition.

"Songs of the Vertical Desert." Six black-and-white photographs by Gordon Wiltsie.

"Leadership." By Harvey Manning. Humorous reflections on being in charge.

"Mount Dickey." By Galen Rowell. Account of a fearful climb in the Alaska Range.

"Resurrection." By Jeff Long. Fiction.

"Spring Weekend Love Affair." By Eric Sanford. Witty rendition of life in the climbers' camp in Yosemite.

"Baltoro." Six black-and-white photographs by Jack Turner of the Karakoram. Includes prose poem by Lito Tejada-Flores.

"Smiley's Initiation." By Dan Burgette. Noephytes in the Tetons.

"Lo que el alpinista tendrá presente." Author unknown. In Spanish. Features numerous old-time illustrations.

"Janus." By Bob Godfrey. Free climbing in Colorado. Photographs by Dudley Chelton.

"The Aeolian Wall." By Larry Hamilton. Account of an early climb at Red Rocks, near Las Vegas.

"Brooks Range: Inukshuk." By Kenneth Andrasko. Adventures in the Far North.

"Brooks Range: Summer & Winter Ascents." By Dennis Schmitt. Climbs in Alaska's remote range.

"A Climb." By Chris Kopczynski. An ascent of the Eigerwand.

"A Film." By Chic Scott. Problems of filming a climb of the Eigerwand for the 1974 Clint Eastwood film, *The Eiger Sanction*.

"Illusion and Reality." Eight black-and-white photographs by John Cleare concerned with the filming of *The Eiger Sanction*.

Reviews of nineteen books by various people.

Back cover photograph by Galen Rowell of unnamed peak near Chogolisa, Karakoram.

1980 (VOLUME III)

Front cover photograph by Ed Webster. Climber on first ascent of Supercrack, near Canyonlands National Park, Utah.

"Introduction." By the editors.

"Man Meets Myth: A True Fantasy." By Ron Matous. Ascent of the Eiger's famed north wall.

"Eighteen Years After the Riesenstein Hoax: A History of the Cathedral Spires." By Mike Graber. Overview of Alaska's noted range.

"The Cathedral Spires." By various photographers. Ten color photographs of Alaska's great range. First interior color in *Ascent*.

"The Way of the White Serpent." By John Daniel. Fiction involving rites of native culture.

"The Ribbon Option." By Jim Balog. Ascent of the Black Ice Couloir in the Tetons.

"Climbing Aconcagua." Poem by Frances Mayes.

"The Great Match." By Etienne Bruhl. Witty fictional look at the future of climbing. Illustrations by Samivel. Reprinted from *Appalachia*, 1932/33.

"Drawings." Six drawings by M. K. Berrier-Petranoff.

"Like Water and Like Wind." By David Roberts. Novella with lots of action on remote Alaskan peak.

"Slouching Toward Everest: A Critique of Expedition Narratives." By David Roberts. Essay revealing numbing dullness of this genre. Includes list of the author's favorites.

"Drawings." Four drawings by John Svenson.

"Anti-Climbing at Pinnacles." By Tom Higgins. Reflections on climbing at a small California area.

"Images of the Southwest." Ten color photographs by Ed Webster and others.

"The Conquest of the Riffelberg." By Mark Twain. Tongue-in-cheek account of a "climb" in the Alps. Reprinted from *A Tramp Abroad*.

"Cruising Up the Salathé Wall." By Dick Shockley. An ascent of El Capitan.

"In the Constellation of Roosters and Lunatics." By Jeff Long. History of building climbing and a personal story of an adventure in downtown San Francisco.

"About the Contributors." By the editors. Short biographical sketches.

Back cover photograph by Mike Graber of sunset on Tatina Glacier, Cathedral Spires, Alaska.

1984 (VOLUME IV)

Front jacket photograph by Alan Kearney of climber on the Central Tower of Paine, Patagonia.

"Introduction." By the editors.

"The Man Who Climbed Too Well." By Joe Kelsey. Fictional retelling of the Faust legend. Illustrations by Debra Smith.

"Masherbrum, and Back Again." By Ron Matous. Journey to and from the Karakoram.

"On and Around Denali." Ten color photographs of North America's highest peak by various photographers.

"The Mountain Beyond the Cabin." By David Grimes. Reflections on North America's highest peak.

"The Kahiltna Open." By Paul Willis. An epic trip up Denali.

"Roughing It on Denali." By Eric Sanford. Humorous look at some strange events on Big Mac.

"The Ascent of Typewriter Face." By David Gancher. Humor.

"Angels of Light." By Jeff Long. First chapters of a novel-in-progress about Yosemite climbing, drug intrigues, love. Complete book, with same title, published in 1987 by William Morrow & Co.

"The Public Climber: A Reactionary Rumination." By David Roberts. Implications of climbing "publicly." Illustrations by JL Benoit.

"A Bouldering Gallery." Twelve color photographs by Hank Levine.

"Cold Shadows and Rushing Water: Rockclimbing in the Black Canyon of the Gunnison." By Ed Webster. Illustrated history of climbing in Colorado's sinister gorge.

"Slater's Tale." By Chris Noble. Fiction. Illustrations by Debra Smith.

"Confessions of a Guidebook Writer." By Joe Kelsey. Trials and tribulations involved in this genre.

"Portraits of Patagonia." Seven black-and-white photographs by Olaf Sööt.

"Dreams and Doubts: Six Weeks in the Paine Cordillera." By Bobby Knight. Climbing hard and biding time in windswept Patagonia.

"Mrs. Robertson Is Climbing Again." By Rick Slone. Story of a remarkable Scottish climber.

"Twelve Scenes from the Life of Crow." By Charles Hood. Avant-garde fiction.

"Tricksters and Traditionalists: A Look at Conflicting Climbing Styles." By Tom Higgins. Discussion of rap-bolting controversy.

"A Matter of Character." By Talbot Bielefeldt. Fiction involving a strange climber who talks to himself. Illustrations by Margaret Berrier-Petranoff.

"Leviathan," By Geoff Childs. Fiction about Himalayan climb and Ahab-like character. Illustrations by Jamichael Henterly.

"About the Contributors." By the editors. Short biographical sketches.

Back jacket photograph by Olaf Sööt. Los Cuernos del Paine, Patagonia.

1989 (VOLUME V)

Front cover photograph by Ed Webster of a Sherpa on Mt. Everest's west ridge.

"Introduction." By the editors.

"Stone." By Edwin Drummond. Account of wet solo adventure on El Capitan. Excerpted from *A Dream of White Horses*.

"To Become a Mountain." Poem by Elizabeth Stone O'Neill.

"El Peligroso." By Robert Walton. Fictional account of climbing in the future.

"The Best of Times, the Worst of Times." By Joe Kelsey. Recollections of the Golden Age of Yosemite climbing while on a trip to Joshua Tree with old buddies.

"The Faller." Poem by John Hart.

"Headwall." By Tim Ahern. Fiction about a gay climber's encounter with the climbing scene.

"Mount Everest and Environs." Nine color photographs by Ed Webster showing many facets of the world's highest peak.

"The Eyes of Buddha." By Gary Ruggera. Soulful account of tragic climb in the Himalaya.

"Tse-n-t'ytl." By Brian Povolny. Account of hidden desert climb.

"Neighbors." Poem by William Stafford.

"The Collector." By Anne Sauvy. Fiction about an obsessed and secretive climber of the 1930s.

"Karass and Granfalloons." By Alison Osius. Reminiscences about climbing friends.

"The Climbers (Yosemite Valley)." Poem by Edwin Drummond.

"For the Record." By Steven Jervis. Fiction involving two climbers and their differing stories of an accident.

"Retreat." Poem by John Hart.

"Pilgrimage to the Sacred Mountain." By Daniel McCool. Reflections atop Arizona peak.

"Aniel's Accident." By Stanislaw Lem. Science fiction about a robot missing on an otherworldly crag. Reprinted from *Tales of Pirx the Pilot*.

"Fifty Crowded Classics." By George Bell, Jr. Reflections on the popularization of certain noted climbs in North America.

"Notes from a Rescue." Poem by John Hart.

"On the Mountain." By Ben Groff. Fictional account of a near-death experience on Mt. Rainier.

"Terra Incognita of the Mind." By Reinhard Karl. Stream-of-consciousness account of climb of El Capitan.

"The Climbing Wars." By Charles Hood. Avant-garde spy thriller set in the Alps.

"The Climb." Poem by William Stafford.

"Backtracks." By David Stevenson. Adventures in Peru, both on the peak and in the lowlands.

"On Shoulders of Giants." By Dennis Higgins. Old friends climb and bicker in the Pacific Northwest.

"About the Contributors." By the editors. Short biographical sketches.

Back cover photograph by Charlie Fowler of climber on frozen Cornet Falls, near Telluride, Colorado.

Appendix 2

The following alphabetical list shows major *Ascent* contributors from all issues including this one. Individual book reviewers, most photographers, and many illustrators are not shown. Titles of works (where relevant) and years of publication are given.

Ahern, Tim. "Headwall" (1989)
Anderson, Sheridan. Numerous cartoons (1967–1974)
Andrasko, Kenneth. "Brooks Range: Inukshuk" (1975/76)
Balog, Jim. "The Ribbon Option" (1980)
Beckey, Fred. "Moses: A Desert Phenomenon" (1973); "Southeast Alaska" (1975/76)
Bell, George, Jr. "Fifty Crowded Classics" (1989)
Berrier-Petranoff, M. K. "Drawings" (1980)
Bertulis, Alex. Back cover photograph (1969)
Bielefeldt, Talbot. "A Matter of Character" (1984)
Bohn, Dave. Back cover photograph (1967)
Borghoff, M. W. "Meditation VII" (1974)
Bridwell, Jim. "The Innocent, the Ignorant, and the Insecure" (1973)
Bruhl, Etienne. "The Great Match" (1980)
Burgette, Dan. "Smiley's Initiation" (1975/76)
Bussey, Howard. "Upper Crust" (1970)
Caldwell, Dean. "Yerupajá" (1969)
Childs, Geoffrey. "Poontanga" (1975/76); "Leviathan" (1984)
Chouinard, Yvon. "Climbing on Ice" (1968); front cover photograph (1971); "A Pocket Guide to the Slippery Game" (1971); "Coonyard Mouths Off" (1972); "Swiftly & Surely" (coauthor) (1974)
Cleare, John. "The Edge of the Sea" (1972); "Illusion and Reality" (1975/76); various photographs (1972–1984)
Comici, Emilio. "Alone on the Cima Grande" (1972)
Cooper, Ed. "Canada" (1968); "Rock" (1972); "Snow" (1972); "Yosemite" (1974); numerous photographs (1968–1989)

Hollowood, Bernard. "Pens Over Everest" (1967)

Hood, Charles. "Twelve Scenes from the Life of Crow" (1984); "The Climbing Wars" (1989)

Howell, Ian. "A Visitor to Yosemite" (1967)

Ingram, Carol. "Dream Ascents" (1975/76)

Isherwood, Dick. "Sweet Potatoes" (1974)

Janney, James. "Dhaulagiri: A Mind Odyssey" (1970, 1993)

Jervis, Steven. "For the Record" (1989); "Taking Off" (1993)

Jones, Chris. "Who Needs the AAC?" (1971, 1993); "North Twin, North Face" (1975/76)

Karl, Reinhard. "Terra Incognita of the Mind" (1989)

Kearney, Alan. Front jacket photograph (1984)

Kelsey, Joe. "Accidents in 1968" (1968); "The Rock Gods" (1974, 1993); "Confessions of a Guidebook Writer" (1984); "The Man Who Climbed Too Well" (1984); "The Best of Times, the Worst of Times" (1989)

Knight, Bobby. "Dreams and Doubts: Six Weeks in the Paine Cordillera" (1984)

Kopczynski, Chris. "A Climb" (1975/76)

Lem, Stanislaw. "Aniel's Accident" (1989)

Levine, Hank. "A Bouldering Gallery" (1984)

Long, Jeff. "The Soloist's Diary" (1974, 1993); "Resurrection" (1975/76); "In the Constellation of Roosters and Lunatics" (1980); "Angels of Light" (1984)

Long, William. "American Antarctic Mountaineering Expedition" (1967)

Lowe, George. "The North Face of Alberta" (1973); cover photograph (1975/76)

Lowe, Jeff. "A Zion Story" (1972); "The Zion Guide" (1972)

McCarthy, James. "The Jewel in the Lotus" (1969)

McClellan, Gary. "Rappelling" (1974)

McCool, Daniel. "Pilgrimage to the Sacred Mountain" (1989)

Macgee, Carol. "La Derive" (1974)

McRae, Ian. "The More Things Change . . . " (1993)

Manning, Harvey. "Leadership" (1975/76, 1993)

Marchand, Millie. "Waiting: Maroon Bells Campsite" (1971)

Matous, Ron. "Man Meets Myth: A True Fantasy" (1980, 1993); "Masherbrum, and Back Again" (1984)

Mayes, Frances. "Climbing Aconcagua" (1980)

Mehmet, Dennis. "Direktas" (1973)

Morgenthaler, Hans. "The Icefall" (1967)

Noble, Chris. "Slater's Tale" (1984)

O'Neill, Elizabeth Stone. "To Become a Mountain" (1989)

Ortenburger, Leigh. Numerous photographs (1967–1989)

Osius, Alison. "Karass and Granfalloons" (1989)

Patterson, Leif-Norman. "Yerupajá" (1967)

Povolny, Brian. "Tse-n-t'ytl" (1989)

Pratt, Chuck. "Yosemite Mountaineering Notes" (1967); "The View from Deadhorse Point" (1970, 1993)

Proctor, A. Phimister. "An Early Ascent of Half Dome" (1972)

Rennie, Drummond. "Druggs in Himalaya" (1974, 1993)

Robbins, Royal. "The West Face" (1968, 1993); "Tis-sa-ack" (1970, 1993)

Roberts, David. "The Nine Deadly Sins" (1971); "Reviews" (1972); "Patey Agonistes: Or, a Look at Climbing Autobiographies" (1974, 1993); "Like Water and Like Wind" (1980); "Slouching Toward Everest: A Critique of Expedition Narratives" (1980); "The Public Climber: A Reactionary Rumination" (1984)

Robinson, Doug. "Tuesday Morning on the Lyell Fork with Eliot's Shadow" (1968); "The Climber as Visionary" (1969, 1993); "The Slippery Game" (1971); "Swiftly & Surely" (coauthor) (1974)

Roper, Steve. "A Climber's Guide to Lover's Leap" (1967); "Sierra Nevada Mountaineering Notes" (1967); front cover photograph (1968); "Climber's Guide to Mt. Shasta" (1968); "Eleven Domes" (1969); "Four Corners" (1970); "Mountaineering Notes" (1970); "Notes" (1971); "Notes" (1972); "Dresden" (1974, 1993)

Rowe, Ian. "Icarus" (1972, 1993)

Rowell, Galen. "Yosemite's Other Valley" (1971); back cover photograph (1971); front cover photograph (1972); "The Seventh Rifle" (1972); back cover photograph (1972); "Mount Dickey" (1975/76, 1993); back cover photograph (1975/76)

Ruggera, Gary. "The Eyes of Buddha" (1989)

Salz, Jeff. "Freakers' Ball" (1974); back cover photograph (1974)

Samivel. "L'enfer des montagnards" (1967)

Sanford, Eric. "Spring Weekend Love Affair" (1975/76, 1993); "Roughing It on Denali" (1984, 1993)

Sauvy, Anne. "The Collector" (1989)

Schmitt, Dennis. "Brooks Range: Summer & Winter Ascents" (1975/76)

Scott, Chic. "A Film" (1975/76)

Seidman, Dave. "Mt. McKinley: The Direct South Face" (1968)

Shockley, Dick. "Cruising up the Salathé Wall" (1980, 1993)

Sinclair, Pete. "Behold Now Behemoth" (1968)

Singer, David. Back cover photomontage (1970)

Slesser, Malcolm. "Dedo de Deus" (coauthor) (1974, 1993)

Slone, Rick. "Mrs. Robertson Is Climbing Again" (1984)

Smith, Debra. Eight drawings (1984)

Smith, Robin. "The Bat and the Wicked" (1968)

Somers, Dermot. "A Tale of Spendthrift Innocence" (1993)

Sööt, Olaf. "Portraits of Patagonia" (1984); back jacket photograph (1984)

Stafford, William. "Found in a Storm" (1967); "The Climb" (1989); "Neighbors" (1989)

Steck, Allen. Front cover photograph (1967); "Ascent of Hummingbird Ridge" (1967, 1993)

Stevenson, David. "Backtracks" (1989)

Stuart, Jim. "Canada in Winter" (1973); back cover photograph (1973); "Bouldering" (1974)

Sumner, Bill. "Ice Is Nice and Will Suffice" (1974)

Svenson, John. "Climbers Camp, Chamonix" (1972); "Drawings" (1980); various drawings (1972 to 1984)

Taylor, Rob. "Climbing Down Under" (1971)

Tejada-Flores, Lito. "Games Climbers Play" (1967); "Fromage to Patagonia, or The Sorry of Fats Ray" (1970); "Rojo's Peón" (1971, 1993); "Overpopulation and the Alpine Ego Trip" (1972); "The Guidebook Problem" (1974); untitled prose poem on page 71 (1975/76)

Thompson, Todd. "Fashion, Climbing & Dhaulagiri" (1974); "The Ridge" (coauthor) (1974, 1993)

Tobias, Michael Charles. "Excerpt from *Dhaulagirideon*" (1973)

Tompkins, Douglas. "Second Thoughts on Cerro Torre" (1971)

Turner, Jack. "Baltoro" (1975/76)

Twain, Mark. "The Conquest of the Riffelberg" (1980)

Wallach, Ira. "The Conquest of Tillie's Lookout" (1969)

Walton, Robert. "El Peligroso" (1989); "Spiderman" (1993)

Ward-Drummond, Ed. *See* Drummond, Edwin

Washburn, Bradford. Numerous photographs (1968–1984)

Waterman, Jonathan. "Aurora" (1993)

Weber, Jean. "First on Alberta" (1973)

Webster, Ed. Front cover photograph (1980); "Images of the Southwest" (1980); "Cold Shadows and Rushing Water: Rockclimbing in the Black Canyon of the Gunnison" (1984); front cover photograph (1989); "Mount Everest and Environs" (1989)

Welch, Tad. Six drawings (1989)

Wells, H. G. "Little Mother up the Mörderberg" (1971)

Willis, Paul. "The Kahiltna Open" (1984)

Wilson, Ken. "Climbing in Britain" (1968)

Wiltsie, Gordon. "Songs of the Vertical Desert" (1975/76)

About the Contributors

HAROLD DRASDO helped establish the extreme grade in British rockclimbing in the early 1950s—he was a contemporary of Joe Brown—and is still leading climbs at a fairly high standard. He has written two climbing guidebooks and a pamphlet on outdoor education, from which "Climbing as Art" was reprinted. He was coeditor (with Michael Charles Tobias) of *The Mountain Spirit* and has recently written several essays for *High,* including "The View from Plato's Cave" and "A Trespasser's Guide to the Conwy Valley." Drasdo, who admits to being a slow but unrelenting essayist, is working on a book of reminiscences and reflections tentatively titled *Sermons in Stones.* He lives in North Wales.

EDWIN DRUMMOND is an English climber whose individualistic and image-intensive prose is familiar to *Ascent* readers. His style as a climber has always seemed off-beat and out of the mainstream of British climbing. In a country of fierce little crags, he has become a "big wall man," and though his climbs, like his prose, have aroused controversy, several are recognized as masterpieces. "Since (almost) soloing the North America Wall," he says today, "I've spent far more time writing and talking about climbing than actually perambulating vertically—all due to becoming a father three times over and because of my work for 'Climb for the World,' a project I direct on behalf of the United Nations." *A Dream of White Horses,* a collection of his poetry and writings, was published in 1989.

GIUSTO GERVASUTTI was an Italian climber of the first rank. His close friend and climbing partner Lucien Devies called him "one of those rare, outstanding figures who emerge from time to time in every sport." The brilliance of his achievements was matched only by the zest of the man himself, as readers will learn from his short piece, "A Moment of Suspense." Gervasutti began climbing in the early 1930s and quickly made a name for himself. His best-known first ascent was the Gervasutti Pillar on the Frêney face of Mont Blanc, in 1940. He was killed in 1946, at the age of thirty-seven, in a rappelling accident on Mont Blanc du Tacul. "A Moment of Suspense" is one of the most philosophical passages in *Gervasutti's Climbs,* his posthumously published book.

TERRY GIFFORD is director of the International Festival of Mountaineering Literature, held annually at Bretton Hall College in Wakefield, England, where he is senior lecturer in English. From his home in Sheffield he is able to climb year round on the famed gritstone edges of Derbyshire; in his words he is "a connoisseur of the classic easier climbs." His recent collection of poems, *Ten Letters to John Muir*, stems from a visit to the Sierra Nevada, where he discovered a soulful kinship with the memory of John Muir. Gifford's other collections of poetry include *The Stone Spiral* and *Outcrops*. He is currently poetry editor for the British climbing magazine *High*.

DAVE GREGORY has been climbing so long that he no longer recalls when he started, though he has vague memories of struggling up the gritstone edges of England's midlands in the late 1940s. Nowadays, his main interest in climbing revolves around England's Peak District, where he has done a few new routes of what he terms "significant unimportance." Gregory strongly disapproves of the spread of bolted climbing onto British rock. "In my opinion," he says, "this will kill the technique of using 'chock' protection and ruin 'risk climbing,' the traditional British style." He lives in Sheffield and is currently chair of the British Mountaineering Council's guidebook committee, which publishes rockclimbing guides to the Peak District. He has taught for many years at a state comprehensive school and is dreaming these days about what to climb after retirement.

KITTY CALHOUN GRISSOM began climbing at the age of eighteen on the crags of her native South Carolina. While attending college in Vermont she took up ice climbing to round out her skills. Grissom's rise to prominence began on a trip to the Cordillera Blanca in 1984. Shortly afterward she turned her attention to the Himalaya. After an epic failure on Thalay Sagar, she made an alpine-style ascent of Dhaulagiri, the adventure related in this volume. In the spring of 1990 Grissom led a six-person expedition to Makalu, climbing it via the classic west pillar; she was the first woman to climb the peak. Grissom, who has been a guide for the American Alpine Institute since 1985, is currently working on her MBA at the University of Washington.

WARREN HARDING is one of the most enigmatic characters ever to climb in Yosemite Valley. Early on he shunned free climbing and instead became a legendary "iron man," able to bolt his way up overhangs for long stretches. His ascent of the Nose of El Capitan in 1958 was mocked by many, yet the climb soon became the most sought-after big-wall climb on Earth. His other bolting escapades on Yosemite's great cliffs were frowned upon by the resident climbers, yet within a few years the same climbers were repeating and enjoying these very routes. His literary ravings outraged people, yet made them think about their values. In short, Harding questioned the traditional way of doing things. He lives now in Moab, Utah.

ANDY HARVARD began climbing in the late 1960s while he was attending Dartmouth College. By 1970 he was accomplishing new routes in Bolivia; later he climbed on Dhaulagiri, Nanda Devi, and Minya Konka. In the early 1980s he visited the enormous Kangshung Face of Mount Everest several times, climbing to 25,000 feet in 1983. In addition to his mountaineering interests, Harvard has kayaked and rafted rivers throughout the world, produced numerous films, and written extensively. He has been deeply involved with the American Alpine Club for nearly fifteen years, serving on numerous committees and the board of directors. He currently lives in northeast Indiana, serving as general counsel to the Central Soya Company.

E. J. HENLEY was innocently teaching physics at the University of Brazil when he made the mistake of accompanying a Scottish climber-friend, Malcolm Slesser, on a day's outing to a pinnacle near Rio de Janeiro. Henley was, in his own words, "a feeble, middle-aged, New York City cliff dweller." He had never tied a rope around his waist, never climbed anything higher than the Empire State Building—and that by elevator. And, as far as *Ascent* can ascertain, he never climbed again. His rebuttal to Slesser's account of their climb, reprinted here in "Dedo de Deus," is written with tongue firmly in cheek, yet it shows that two sides exist to every story. Henley presently teaches chemical engineering at the University of Houston.

TOM HIGGINS is pessimistic about the outcome of the dilemmas expressed in "Tricksters and Traditionalists," the essay included in this volume. "The bolting madness," he says, "has brought us into conflict with other users of the mountains, not to mention government policymakers. And the 'solution,' I fear, won't come from climbers themselves, through the voluntary agreements I urged in my article. There are too many climbers—and no organization capable of imposing self-regulation locally or nationally." Higgins, who still waltzes with ease up the domes of Tuolumne Meadows, says he no longer cares how hard a route is: "Climbing is still vital for me, but at age forty-eight, I'm now free to climb purely for joy." He lives in Oakland, California, with his wife and daughter, and is co-manager of a transportation consulting company.

JAMES JANNEY returned from the 1969 Dhaulagiri tragedy with the aim of providing basic care to people in need. He went to medical school and is now a small-town doctor in the relatively poor county of Klickitat, in Washington State. His climbing career has languished during the years, though he climbed in Peru and Bolivia with Todd Thompson and Andy Harvard, two Dartmouth friends who climbed on Dhaulagiri in 1973. In 1983 Janney hiked to the base of the mountain that held so many memories and came across a stone chorten dedicated to the seven men who died. "It struck us," he says, "as being a simple and powerful—though inadequate—tribute to the lives of our friends." When not doctoring, Janney visits the nearby Columbia River Gorge to go windsurfing, his latest passion.

STEVEN JERVIS learned to climb in the Tetons under the tutelage of such luminaries as Leigh Ortenburger and Willi Unsoeld. As a teenager he made, with Unsoeld and Mary Sylvaner, the first complete ascent of the Jensen Ridge on Symmetry Spire in 1953. After obtaining degrees from Harvard and Stanford, he visited the Peruvian Andes, the Hindu Kush, and the Ruwenzori. His stories have been published in a number of journals, including the *Florida Review* and the *North Dakota Quarterly*. His Rashomon-like story "For the Record" appeared in the 1989 *Ascent*. Jervis's book reviews appear regularly in the *American Alpine Journal*. Although he usually teaches English and computer programming at Brooklyn College, he recently completed a semester as a Fulbright Lecturer in English at Tribhuvan University, just outside Kathmandu.

CHRIS JONES immigrated to the United States from England in 1965. By that time, at age twenty-five, he was already an accomplished mountaineer, having climbed the Walker Spur on the Grandes Jorasses and the Bonatti Pillar on the Petit Dru. Later climbs with his American friends were equally impressive: a new route on Patagonia's FitzRoy and many climbs in Canada, including the remarkable first ascent of the north face of North Twin with George Lowe. In 1976 he wrote *Climbing in North America,* a carefully researched and comprehensive history of mountaineering that he assembled while recuperating from a skiing accident. He presently works for a computer firm developing software for the wine industry and lives with his wife, Sharon, high on a hillside above the town of Glen Ellen, California.

JOE KELSEY holds the longevity record for *Ascent* authors: his total of five articles span more than two decades, from the second issue to the present. Though he climbed extensively in Yosemite Valley during the Golden Age, he now prefers less crowded areas. Reflecting on "The Rock Gods," Kelsey says that "civilization slogs on, requiring the one-time Rock Gods to remain earthbound and share with us the inevitability of aging. They, and we, have discovered that we are all made of the same easily damaged flesh, and now we climb together, a mythless community of old farts, climbing simply to touch rock." Kelsey guides in the Wind River Range and the Tetons during the summer, then gravitates in the autumn to the San Francisco area to work on computer software manuals.

JEFF LONG credits *Ascent* for helping launch his writing career with the publication of "The Soloist's Diary." During his youth, the tall, soft-spoken climber from Boulder, Colorado, worked as a stonemason, security guard, and climbing instructor. At the same time he was writing numerous stories for *Mountain Gazette, Climbing, Mountain,* and, of course, *Ascent*. His first book, *Outlaw: The Story of Claude Dallas,* the tale of a mountain man who killed two game wardens, was followed by *Angels of Light* in 1987. Long's third book, *Duel of Eagles: The Mexican and U.S. Fight for the Alamo,* is a revisionist history that attempts to refute the myth of the Alamo. *The Ascent: A Novel,* the story of an American expedition to the north side of Everest, was published in 1991.

IAN McRAE climbed all over the American west during the 1980s, but he now is making an effort to "de-climberize" himself in hopes of becoming a functioning member of society—or, in his words, "a conquistador of something other than the useless." An expatriate Californian, McRae works as an itinerant laborer and schoolteacher while taking a full course load at the University of Alaska in Fairbanks. He is uncertain whether he is a climber who writes or a writer who climbs. Although he has been creating imaginative stories for most of his life, "The More Things Change . . . " is his first published piece.

HARVEY MANNING claims to have a hard time remembering why he ever took up the strange sport of mountaineering. It was in Washington in the late 1930s—that much he recalls. And he thinks he decided to give up climbing with human partners because of all the disasters he was associated with as a leader for the Seattle Mountaineers. But, heedful of that group's iron-clad rule—"A party of three is the minimum"—he does not travel solo. His two Shelties accompany him, do the routefinding, and bark from the summits. Manning has had a long and illustrious history as a writer and editor. In 1960 he was instrumental in assembling *Freedom of the Hills,* a classic mountaineering instruction manual. He has since written extensively on the parklands, trails, and wilderness areas of the Pacific Northwest.

RON MATOUS cannot stay put in the Tetons, where in theory he lives. During the 1980s, for instance, he visited the Himalaya five times and Peru twice. He is unconcerned about not yet reaching the top of an 8,000-meter peak: "The primary objective may remain unfilled, but my dreams do not." In his spare time, Matous guides in the Tetons, hangs out with his family, and goes hang-gliding. He has twice held the chess championship of Wyoming, a feat he modestly likens to being "rodeo champion of Brooklyn." Of his 1976 Eiger-wand climb Matous says, "It is difficult to recapture that sense of commitment and abandonment to fate. It was perhaps the most emotionally powerful three days of my life." When he finds the time, he writes for various magazines.

CHUCK PRATT first put hand to rock in 1956 and within a few years had left an indelible mark on the history of Yosemite climbing. Among his many first ascents are the Salathé Wall and the North American Wall, both on El Capitan. He was equally talented as a writer, but this aspect of his career was over almost before it began, a situation that disappointed his admirers. His explanation of this phenomenon is typically forthright: "I don't want to talk about climbing; I don't want to take pictures of climbing; I don't want to write about climbing. I just want to climb." Pratt has done exactly that for all his adult life, guiding in the summers in the Tetons and visiting Devil's Tower and the Southwest regularly. A recent concession: he spends his winters lounging on the shores of Thailand's Andaman Sea.

DRUMMOND RENNIE's quest for high-altitude urine finally got the better of him. For years, as director of the Nephrology Department at a medical center in Chicago, he tramped over snowfields in the Yukon, the Andes, and the Himalaya collecting this dreary substance for his research in high-altitude medicine. He finally decided to seek other work. "I switched from clinical nephrology," he says, "to editing medical manuscripts. After a few years with the *New England Journal of Medicine,* I became deputy editor of the *Journal of the American Medical Association* and professor of medicine at the University of California, San Francisco. The decline in all my abilities has been nicely reflected and rewarded by promotion." Rennie has been forced to restrict his research into the physiological effects of high altitude owing to hip-joint surgery, but he still manages to write widely on medical topics.

ROYAL ROBBINS was the best-known American rockclimber during the 1960s. His name is so intertwined with Yosemite's El Capitan—the scene of his greatest adventures—that it is easy to overlook his other accomplishments, such as his three new routes up the face of Half Dome and his bold ascents in Alaska and the Alps. His list of first ascents is enormous and impressive. He wrote about these routes with the same intensity that distinguished his climbing, and one can only regret that he doesn't write more. Robbins put his talent and energy into kayaking in the early 1970s and soon made first descents of numerous wild rivers in the Sierra Nevada and in Chile. During the same time, he and his wife, Liz, founded a successful clothing company. They live in Modesto, California.

DAVID ROBERTS, like many of our contributors, began climbing in the early 1960s. The Far North fascinated him and he soon made some truly memorable first ascents: the Wickersham Wall of Denali, the south face of Mount Huntington, and the southeast face of Mount Dickey. His writing career zoomed after the 1968 publication of the classic *Mountain of My Fear,* the story of the Huntington expedition. Other books followed, as did dozens of well-regarded articles and essays. A decade after he published his novella *Like Water and Like Wind* in the 1980 *Ascent,* one reviewer called it "one of the most inspired pieces of mountain fiction yet written." Roberts, once a professor of English, lives in Cambridge, Massachusetts and writes full time on a variety of subjects.

DOUG ROBINSON came to *Ascent's* editors one afternoon in 1968 with a dog-eared manuscript in hand. An hour later, entranced with "Tuesday Morning on the Lyell Fork with Eliot's Shadow," the editors said yes, in what was surely a record time for acceptance. "If *Ascent* hadn't printed that piece," Robinson said later, "I probably would have thrown away my pencil." He gave us another article the following year, the one printed in this volume, and his writing career blossomed. He later lived for many years under the east flank of the Sierra Nevada, pursuing his favorite activity: ski mountaineering. He also found time to write, to establish new routes on the local crags, and to serve as the first president of the American Mountain Guides Association. Robinson now resides near Santa Cruz, California, working for MontBell, a clothing and equipment manufacturer.

STEVE ROPER has been coeditor of *Ascent* since its inception. He began climbing in the mid-1950s, a mere stripling who stood in awe as local legends Willi Unsoeld and Allen Steck thrashed up overhangs on the minuscule rocks of Berkeley, California. "After a few seasons in Yosemite," Roper says, "I submitted a sheaf of rambling climbing notes to the Sierra Club, and to my great surprise and pleasure they published my Yosemite guidebook in 1964. This single event gave me the confidence to work with words as a profession." Since then Roper has written many articles and several more books. On a recent visit to Dresden he was pleased to see that a regional museum prominently featured Berndt Arnold, Herbert Richter, and Fritz Wiessner—his companions from the East German adventure described in this volume.

IAN ROWE climbed extensively in the 1960s in his native Scotland. Farther afield, he made the first winter ascent of the central spur of the north face of Les Courtes. But a job and a family interceded, and in 1972 we at *Ascent* received this droll comment: "I now have a collar and a tie, a house, a telly, and a life insurance if I die." Nevertheless, he visited Dhaulagiri IV in 1973, an expedition replete with "carnage, failure, cynicism." He moved to Canada shortly thereafter with his family and claims this event marked the end of his serious mountaineering. "Once-valued climbing periodicals," he recently wrote us, "known to make me turn off my chain-saw, served merely as reminders to pay dues." He now regards "Icarus" as "appallingly misogynistic. The person who wrote that article was not happy."

GALEN ROWELL, once the proprietor of a greasy auto-repair shop, decided one day in 1972 to become a photojournalist. *Ascent's* editors applauded this bold career move and were pleased to be a part of Rowell's new vision, one that to us was never in doubt. Brimming with talent and self-confidence, he slowly rose to what now can only be called international acclaim. His first book, *The Vertical World of Yosemite*, appeared in 1974. Soon thereafter, his high-quality color photographs appeared in numerous of his books, including *In the Throne Room of the Mountain Gods* (dealing with the Karakoram) and *Mountains of the Middle Kingdom* (dealing with Tibet). When Rowell is not traveling the world in search of the perfect photo, he lives in Berkeley, California, with his wife and collaborator, Barbara.

ERIC SANFORD'S rise to fortune and fame is a study in textbook American capitalistic enterprise. For years he operated Liberty Bell Alpine Tours in Mazama, Washington; in the off-season he increased his fiefdom by acquiring such additional entities as a campground, restaurant and lodge, store, post office, gas station, and a heli-ski operation. He bailed out in 1987 with a reasonable amount of capital and moved to Hood River, Oregon, where he continues his life as a local land baron. Windsurfing changed his life; the kinesthetic pleasure, he feels, is much the same as climbing, although the danger is not as great. "Basically, I windsurf much of the time," he writes. "I also travel all over the world racing and doing photo and writing assignments for a dozen publications and companies."

DICK SHOCKLEY has seen up years and down years since his ascent of the Salathé Wall, the climb described in this volume. He did a few other major Yosemite routes, including the intimidating south face of Mount Watkins. But soon a period of self-examination set in. "The drive to the cliffs," he says, "the familiarity with the old routes, the sight of new faces at the stone, the absence of old faces—all these made me uncomfortable and even a little bored. I would get to the top of a boulder problem and realize I hadn't proved anything." Yet the lure of clean, white granite is irresistible and errant souls usually return. Shockley, reconsidering, climbs again at Joshua Tree. He lives in San Diego, where he is employed as a civil-service scientist.

MALCOLM SLESSER was one of the first to describe, in English, the Pamir Range, that huge and isolated group of peaks in the far-western Himalaya. In 1962 he was the deputy leader (under Sir John Hunt) of what turned out to be a minor but interesting breakthrough in East-West relations—the first British-Soviet expedition to the range. Tragically, Wilfrid Noyce and Robin Smith, two British mountaineers noted for their brilliant writing skills, died in an inexplicable fall. Slesser later wrote *Red Peak*, a moving account of the expedition and a classic in its genre. Born and raised in Scotland, he has taken part in six expeditions to Greenland and several to other parts of the world. Among his many books is *The Andes Are Prickly*, an account of a trip to remote sections of Peru.

DERMOT SOMERS took up climbing at age twenty-seven in his native Ireland. His early ambitions led him to make ascents of the six notorious north faces of the Alps. He has also climbed in the Andes, the Himalaya, and California, where he completed ascents of many Yosemite classics, including the Nose of El Capitan. His short stories have appeared in *High, Climber and Hillwalker*, and *The Irish Climber*. An astute observer, Somers creates his fiction by using his climbing experience as a framework for close observations of character under tension. A collection of his stories, *Mountains and Other Ghosts*, was published in 1990. Now at age forty-five, he lives in the Wicklow Mountains south of Dublin, in a house built entirely by himself and his wife, Maeve.

ALLEN STECK recalls with the utmost clarity his very first climb, in 1942. Before he ever knew of ropes and pitons, he climbed a virgin ridge on Mount Maclure in California's High Sierra. Later he learned about technical climbing with the Sierra Club's Rock Climbing Section and went on to make some notable first ascents in Yosemite Valley and elsewhere in the world. Of the Hummingbird Ridge, he says, "If I were ten years younger, I'd be preparing now to try for the second ascent. That climb was my most intense mountaineering experience, a triumph of will, a total commitment of mind, body, and spirit." Though he has other interests, Steck is grateful that he is still able to climb at age sixty-seven, in spite of two stiff and scarred ankles, badly broken in a climbing accident in 1989.

LITO TEJADA-FLORES labored at *Ascent* for several years shortly after its inception and was influential in turning a provincial magazine into a polished and acclaimed international publication. Born at 13,000 feet in the Bolivian Andes, he has spent the greater part of his life since then far above sea level. Tejada-Flores is a noted climber, skier, and kayaker, and has written about all three. Among his publications are *Wilderness Skiing, Wildwater, High Color: Spectacular Wildflowers of the Rockies,* and *Red Rock, Blue Sky: Mysterious Landscapes of the Southwest.* The last two books are illustrated by his wife and collaborator, photographer Linde Waidhofer. The couple run Western Eye Press, an independent book-publishing firm in Telluride, Colorado. The town's elevation is 8,700 feet—does oxygen deprivation have anything to do with creativity?

TODD THOMPSON began climbing in the mid-1960s and well remembers one of his earliest experiences. Doug Tompkins and Steve Roper invited a bewildered kid along on a big-wall climb in the Bugaboos. Their motive was clear: they wanted a porter. And Thompson looked strong and naive. At the base of the wall he was handed a pair of Jumar ascenders. "What are these?" he asked. But he soon learned the ropes, hauling a monster duffel bag up slanting crack systems. And that night he enjoyed his first big-wall bivouac—standing in slings. It's no wonder Thompson later preferred mountaineering to rockclimbing. Referring to his Dhaulagiri article, he says, "Andy Harvard and I wanted to put human texture, humor, ambivalence into a mountaineering book, avoiding the we-went-up, we-went-down genre." Thompson lives in San Francisco.

ROBERT WALTON has been a schoolteacher for twenty-three years, a writer for seventeen. Before he thought of writing stories about climbing, he concentrated on children's books, of which he has published three. His short fiction has won several prizes, of which the John Steinbeck Award in 1981 is his most treasured. Although he visits the Tetons when he can, his bailiwick is California. "Despite my advanced age," Walton says, "I still climb at a consistent 5.10 level. And at Pinnacles National Monument I have participated in sixteen ground-up first ascents. I climb in the Sierra and Yosemite as often as I can—

but not enough." Walton lives in King City—less than an hour from Pinnacles—with his wife and two sons, both of whom often troop to the cliffs with their dad.

JONATHAN WATERMAN has enjoyed a long and fruitful association with Alaska's greatest mountain. Experiences gained from a decade of guiding and rangering in Denali National Park led to his book *Surviving Denali,* an overview of the known casualties on the mountain, published in 1983 (and republished, with new material, in 1991.) *High Alaska: A Historical Guide to Denali, Mount Foraker & Mount Hunter* followed in 1988 and contains, as the title suggests, information on the early mountaineers who toiled on these three major peaks of the Alaska Range. Waterman's latest work, *In the Shadow of Denali,* to be published by Dell Expedition Series, is a comprehensive look at the many facets of the mountain. A freelance writer living in Colorado, Waterman was recently appointed chair of the American Alpine Club's publication committee.